Everything in Its Place

Virgilio Piñera, 1949. Photo courtesy of Princeton University Library, Department of Rare Books and Special Collections.

Everything in Its Place

The Life and Works of Virgilio Piñera

Thomas F. Anderson

Lewisburg
Bucknell University Press

© 2006 by Rosemont Publishing & Printing Corp.

All rights reserved. Authorization to photocopy items for internal or personal use, or the internal or personal use of specific clients, is granted by the copyright owner, provided that a base fee of $10.00, plus eight cents per page, per copy is paid directly to the Copyright Clearance Center, 222 Rosewood Drive, Danvers, Massachusetts 01923. [0-8387-5635-2/06 $10.00 + 8¢ pp, pc.]

Associated University Presses
2010 Eastpark Boulevard
Cranbury, NJ 08512

The paper used in this publication meets the requirements of the American National Standard for Permanence of Paper for Printed Library Materials Z39.48-1984.

The author is grateful to the following for permission to reprint previously published works by Virgilio Piñera: Grupo Santillana de Ediciones, S.A., Madrid, for excerpts from *La carné de René*, © 1985, *Pequeñas maniobras*, © 1986, and *Cuentos conpletos*, © 1999; Tusquets Editores, S.A., Barcelona, for excerpts from "Testamento," "Final," and "El hechizado" in *La isla en peso: Obra poética*, © 2000; Mark Shafer, for excerpts from his translations of *Cold Tales*, © 1987, and *Rene's Flesh*, © 1989. All photographs as well as excerpts from Virgilio Piñera's papers are reproduced with permission of the Princeton University Library.

Library of Congress Cataloging-in-Publication Data

Anderson, Thomas F., 1970–
    Everything in its place : the life and works of Virgilio Piñera / Thomas F. Anderson.
      p.   cm.
    Includes bibliographical references and index.
    ISBN 0-8387-5635-2 (alk. paper)
    1. Piäera, Virgilio, 1912–   I. Title.
PQ7389.P49Z54   2006
868'.6409–dc22
                                                                               2005053602

Contents

Introduction ... 7

Part I: Virgilio's Damned Circumstances: A Literary Life
1. Living on the Margins (1912–46) ... 19
2. From the Outside Looking In: Exile in Argentina (1946–58) ... 45
3. Disillusion to Revolution and Back Again (1958–79) ... 86

Part II: Writing from the Margin
4. Tales of Absurd Hope and Senseless Logic ... 121
5. Religion, Philosophy, and Sexuality in *La carne de René* ... 154
6. The Signs of Sebastián: Guilt and Sexual Frustration in *Pequeñas maniobras* ... 198
7. Odd Couples: Frustrated Love and Imperfect Unions in Three Plays ... 224

Epilogue: The Death and Resurrection of an Iconoclast ... 257

Notes ... 265
Bibliography ... 290
Index ... 310

For Marisel—beloved wife, best friend, intellectual collaborator

*Borinquen, nido de flores
donde comencé a soñar*

Lola Rodríguez de Tió, "A Puerto Rico"

Introduction

Ahora bien, cuando algo se trata de poner en su sitio, es preciso, si no se quiere que lo pongan a uno en su sitio, que las cosas quedan firmemente demostradas.

[Now then, when trying to put something in its place, it is necessary, if one doesn't want to be put in his place, that things are firmly proven.]

—Virgilio Piñera, "Cada cosa en su lugar"[1]

Virgilio Piñera tal vez sea entre nosotros el autor más ignorado, célebre y olvidado.

[Virgilio Piñera is, perhaps, the most obscure, celebrated, and forgotten author among us.][2]

A SHORT BLURB ON THE COVER OF A RECENT SPANISH EDITION OF Virgilio Piñera's collected short stories hails this Cuban author and his works as nothing less than an "extraordinary revelation" for the modern reader.[3] If we understand the term "revelation" in this context as the disclosure of something not before recognized or appreciated, this remark is emblematic of what many have referred to as a contemporary rediscovery of one of the great masters of modern Cuban letters. Indeed, though he was underappreciated throughout most of his lifetime and virtually forgotten during the last decade of his life and for nearly as many years after his death in 1979, Virgilio Piñera is now one of the most widely read and studied Cuban literary figures of the twentieth century. Scores of scholarly articles have been published on Piñera in recent years, and his name has finally begun to appear in anthologies, encyclopedias, and histories of Latin American literature.

This surge in academic and popular interest in Piñera and his works has been fueled by several factors. Most important among these is, perhaps, the publication by major Spanish, Cuban, and other Latin American presses of over a dozen new editions of his novels, stories, poetry, and plays in the last several years. It is important to point out that many of these books had been out of print for decades and are just now being read for the first time by a large and diverse Spanish-speaking audience. Moreover, the publication of numerous translations of his works into English, French, German, Portuguese, and several other languages in the last several years has sparked general and critical interest outside of Cuban and Latin American literary circles. In short, it seems that with the dawn of the new millennium Virgilio Piñera has finally begun to receive the respect and recognition that eluded him during his lifetime.

Despite Virgilio Piñera's now widely recognized standing as a major Latin American intellectual and author, however, only a handful of books about him—most of which focus on just one of the many genres that he cultivated—have been published to date. And except for a relatively small number of scholarly articles and book reviews, very little has been published on Piñera in English. It is interesting to note that while significant, book-length academic studies in English have appeared recently on many of the other major Cuban authors of the twentieth century—Carpentier, Guillén, Lezama Lima, Cabrera Infante, Arenas, Sarduy—until now a comprehensive examination of Virgilio Piñera's life and works was not available to a non-Spanish-speaking audience.

The present study responds to a growing need for serious scholarly evaluations of Virgilio Piñera's legendary personality and his diverse writings, and with it I aim to fill a major gap in Cuban and Latin American literary criticism. I should point out that though this book is by no means an exhaustive study, I have made a sincere effort to elucidate what I consider to be some of the most salient aspects of Piñera's life and work and to make this noteworthy figure of world literature more accessible to a broader range of readers and scholars.

Since no biography has been published on Virgilio Piñera in either Spanish or English, I have conceived the first part of this study as a literary biography of sorts, which combines a detailed outline of Piñera's life as an author and critic with an in-depth discussion of a wide variety of his writings and intellectual pursuits. It is not the central aim of my book to underscore concrete links between Piñera's works and his life experiences, but I should clarify in this brief introduction that I do not subscribe to the theory that a work of literature or art cannot be interpreted in light of its relationship to its creator or to the society in which it was conceived. Indeed, I am of the opinion that in order to fully appreciate Virgilio Piñera's diverse and culturally heterogeneous oeuvre, the reader must acquaint him/herself with the biographic details—the author's provincial origins, his economic hardships, his aesthetic sensibilities, and his homosexuality, for example—that not only served as the precarious foundation of Piñera's marginalized existence in Havana and Buenos Aires, but also bore a profound influence on his personality and his writings.

Piñera's life circumstances in many ways served to enhance his reputation as a polemicist and nonconformist. Many scholarly articles on Piñera and his works make reference to the author's subversive tendencies and to his affinity for provocative social and cultural criticism. However, few of these studies delve into Piñera's critical articles and editorials, which are largely responsible for such a reputation. Likewise, few scholars of Piñera's work have contextualized the cultural scandals and so-called literary battles—which were often provoked by both aesthetic differences and personal issues—in which Piñera became embroiled both in Cuba and in exile in Buenos Aires.

In his illuminating article "Carne y papel: El fantasma de Virgilio" (Flesh and Paper: The Ghost of Virgilio), Enrico Mario Santí correctly observes that far too often contemporary critics of Piñera base their evaluations of the Cuban author on readings of his canonical texts—*Cuentos fríos* (1956), *La carne de René* (1952), *Teatro completo* (1960)—while ignoring the polemical context in which they were created.[4] Throughout my book I argue, as Santí does, that Piñera's little-read and thematically diverse critical writings, which number nearly two hundred, are important keys to understanding his lifelong estrangement from both Cuban and Argentine literary and cultural circles.

The title of my book reflects two of its central objectives. On the one hand, I aim to present an accurate portrait of Virgilio Piñera the polemicist, provocateur, and master of counterdiscourse. Piñera was well known for his concerted efforts to settle scores and to put individuals—especially writers, artists, and literary critics—in their proper place, so to speak. As part of his self-proclaimed role as a disrespectful author, Piñera went to great lengths to expose hypocrisies and to deflate egos among cultural and intellectual circles, and to knock art from the pedestal upon which, in his opinion, many of his contemporaries had placed it. In numerous articles—"El País del Arte" (The Country of Art), "Ballagas en persona" (Ballagas in Person), "Las plumas respetuosas" (The Respectful Pens), "Aviso a los conformistas" (A Warning to Conformists), and "Cada cosa en su lugar" (Everything in Its Place), just to name a few—Piñera underscored his steadfast adherence to personal convictions, his rejection of blind imitation, and his defiance of the bourgeois values of the cultural and political mainstream.

To a certain extent Piñera viewed the hardships and the marginality of his own existence as noble consequences of his assumed role as an "eterno insumiso" (eternal rebel).[5] Piñera summed up this idea as follows in an article written in 1959:

> Me siento bien con mi falta de respeto. . . . El sacrificio de la vida radica en sufrir mil y una privaciones desde el hambre hasta el exilio voluntario—a fin de defender las ideas, de mantener una línea de conducta inquebrantable.[6]

[I feel good about my lack of respect. . . . Life's sacrifice lies in suffering one thousand and one deprivations, from hunger to voluntary exile, in order to defend one's ideas, to maintain an unbreakable line of conduct.]

The second principal objective of my book is to delineate Virgilio Piñera's intellectual development and to situate his creative and critical writings within the contemporary ideological and cultural climate of Cuba and Argentina, the two countries where he wrote his works and endured his life on the margins. As I suggested above, Virgilio Piñera has just begun to garner the international recognition that he deserves, and in this respect the title of this study also suggests my conviction that the Cuban writer and his works deserve to be placed among the ranks of the literary masters of his homeland and the rest of Latin America.

This book is divided into two parts. The first part, as I have already indicated, approximates a literary biography, and it is broken down into three chapters that at once present a coherent chronology of Piñera's life, and explore various aspects of his writings and intellectual endeavors from his early days in Camagüey, to his prolonged exile in Buenos Aires, to the period of official silence that cloaked his final decade in Havana.

Chapter 1 opens with general information about Piñera's childhood and his formative years, but it is dedicated primarily to Piñera's early literary career and the various circumstances that led to his self-imposed exile to Argentina in 1946. I explain the role of the Spanish bard Juan Ramón Jiménez in the formation of the so-called poetic generation of 1936, and chronicle the emergence of José Lezama Lima as the leading figure of a new literary and intellectual circle, many of whose members would eventually become the core figures of the legendary *Orígenes* group. Special attention is given to Piñera's assiduous collaboration in *Espuela de Plata* and to his polemical split from the group, which was fueled largely by Lezama's decision to appoint a Catholic priest as the journal's codirector. Citing correspondence with Lezama Lima and articles from *Poeta*, the ephemeral journal that Piñera founded shortly after severing his ties with *Espuela de Plata*, I demonstrate how Virgilio's self-proclaimed role as a nonconformist and provocateur can be traced back to this incident from 1941. In my discussion of Piñera's increasingly temperamental relationship with Lezama Lima and other members of his intellectual circle, I point out that many of his early critical writings and poems—especially *La isla en peso* (1942)—manifest his desire to disaffiliate himself from a generation of poets whose literary tendencies he often claimed to disdain. The final section of chapter 1 considers the birth of *Orígenes* in 1944 and Piñera's precarious relationship with the journal, to which he contributed several important texts, and the group associated with it. I also call attention to the fact that despite its eventual evolution into one of the most influential literary reviews of its day, *Orígenes* had many detractors among the Cuban literary establishment and government-sponsored cultural organizations. Finally, I explain how Piñera's criticism of *Orígenes* resulted in his marginalization from the group and may have been a motivating factor in his decision to depart for Buenos Aires in 1946.

Chapter 2 concentrates on the twelve years (1946–58) that comprised Piñera's three periods of exile in Buenos Aires. During the first stay in the Argentine capital, which lasted from February 1946 to December 1947, Piñera was involved in a number of intellectual activities. He collaborated in the translation of *Ferdydurke*, the first novel by the Polish author Witold Gombrowicz, he contributed stories to *Anales de Buenos Aires*, which was at the time under the direction of Jorge Luis Borges, and made important contacts with other major Argentine intellectuals and literary figures of the day. In the first part of this chapter, I discuss at length Piñera's dealings with Borges, Victoria Ocampo, and other members of the *Sur* group, and I examine his provocative assessments of the Argentine intelligentsia's views on art and literature in critical articles, newspaper editorials, and radio interviews. It is my opinion that Piñera's important association with Borges has been greatly downplayed and underestimated by contemporary critics, a point that I corroborate with a detailed chronicle of their various interactions in Buenos Aires. Much attention is also given in this chapter to the profound influence of Gombrowicz on both Piñera's polemical personality and his writings.

In the second half of chapter 2, I explicate the complicated chain of events that brought about the demise of *Orígenes*, and I discuss Piñera's subsequent collaboration in *Ciclón*, the innovative literary journal that replaced it. I examine Piñera's most significant contributions to *Ciclón*, and show how they reveal important clues about how to read and interpret much of his literary production from the same period. In this section I draw on Piñera's correspondence with José Rodríguez Feo in order to elucidate the most important aspects of this pivotal period in his literary career.

The following chapter opens with a brief account of Piñera's disillusioned homecoming in September 1958, and his subsequent penning of the dramatic work *Aire frío* (1959), which he based on the misery and frustration of his own family during the Batista years. Like the majority of Cubans, Piñera embraced the Revolution as a cause for enthusiasm on many fronts. Within days of Castro's triumphant march into Havana in January 1959, Piñera published the first of the scores of articles and editorials that he eventually contributed to the Havana newspaper *Revolución* and its literary supplement, *Lunes*. Piñera's position as a frequent collaborator in the official newspaper of the new Cuba, which had a circulation of more than half a million, represented a major boost in his career and it placed him on the cutting edge of the Cuban cultural scene. In this chapter I underscore Piñera's growing role as a polemical social critic by delving into a representative sample of his articles and editorials, which range from promotion of literary and cultural reform, to praise of the achievements of the Revolution, to testy criticism of Cuban authors, cultural institutions, and their figureheads. I emphasize that it is difficult to appreciate Piñera's reputation as a polemicist and nonconformist or to understand his eventual fall from glory without first reading this key body of texts.

Given that academic studies on Piñera have tended to ignore his contributions to *Revolución* and *Lunes*, this chapter is an especially valuable contribution to the growing body of Piñera criticism. Throughout this chapter I also draw on dozens of unpublished letters from Piñera to his friend Humberto Rodríguez Tomeu, with whom he had lived during his exile in Argentina. This correspondence offers illuminating insights into both Piñera's unprecedented success during the early years of the Revolution and his rapid decline into oblivion that began in the mid-1960s. In this chapter I also make use of speeches by Fidel Castro and various other cultural documents to elucidate how the ever-increasing cultural repression in Cuba brought about Piñera's untimely downfall.

The second part of my book comprises four chapters of a more analytical nature in which I explore Piñera's short stories, novels, and plays from a wide range of critical and theoretical perspectives. My approach is best described as multidisciplinary, given that I draw on theoretical, philosophical, anthropological, historical, and political documents in my analysis of Piñera's diverse writings.

In chapter 4 I examine a representative sample of the short stories that Piñera wrote during the early years of his literary career. I open with a brief explanation of the diverse connotations of the terms "grotesque" and "absurd," both of which are used frequently, though not always defined or contextualized, in discussions of Piñera's writings. I explain how in stories such as "La carne," "La cena," and "El álbum," the grotesque manifests itself largely through the paradoxical nature of the texts themselves, but also through the range of emotions and responses that they provoke. I also explain how these tales from the 1940s attest to the fact that from an early stage in his career, Piñera's worldview echoed signature attitudes of the aesthetic of the absurd. Several of the texts discussed in this chapter embody the senselessness of modern man's attempts to make something of his irrational or tormented existence. Moreover, the air of nonsense, the masterful mix of pathos and comedy, and the fundamental incongruity between bizarre circumstances and the protagonists' responses to them are also signature elements of literature of the absurd that permeate these seminal texts. Throughout the chapter I make an effort to point out the subtle sociopolitical undertones of these early stories by demonstrating how their recurring motifs—poverty, hunger, frustration, mixed-up priorities, miscommunication—while clearly anchored in the aesthetic of the absurd, also echo certain aspects of Cuba's sociopolitical reality in the 1940s.

Chapter 5 is an ambitious and groundbreaking study of what I consider to be Piñera's masterwork, his first novel *La carne de René*. My analysis of this singular work of fiction demonstrates how Piñera's constant references to Christian icons and biblical concepts and his daring treatment of human corporeality call attention to his parody of traditional Christian concepts of body and the soul. One of this chapter's main objectives is to show how Piñera masterfully manipulates sacred images and Catholic doctrine in order to express some of his own radical views on religion and sexuality. I discuss at length the influence of the writings of Søren Kierkegaard and the Marquis de Sade on Piñera's worldview, especially in terms of his defiance of Christian morality and his daring treatment of sexuality, sadomasochism, and seduction. I also maintain that the carnal cult lead by René's father, the erotically charged atmosphere of the all-male Escuela del Dolor, and René's painful journey of sexual discovery underscore not just the novel's strong homoerotic subtext, but also Piñera's desire to debunk the myth of the aggressive, sexually domineering Latin American macho.

Chapter 6 focuses on Piñera's second novel, *Pequeñas maniobras* (1963), which has been the subject of surprisingly few serious scholarly studies. In my discussion of the novel I show how despite obvious differences in tone and style *Pequeñas maniobras* shares certain common ground with *La carne de René*. Much like René, for example, Sebastián, the novel's thirty-year-old protagonist, is an eccentric outcast who is beleaguered by the constant efforts of others to impose their beliefs on him. Both protagonists stand out for their supposed effeminate qualities, their aversion to physical contact and intimate relationships, and their desire to be left alone. In my study of one of Piñera's most compelling characters I make the case that Sebastián's overwhelming anxiety, his tendency toward self-deprecation, his marked distaste for Catholics, and his fear of the sacrament of confession are all manifestations of his closeted homosexuality. In this chapter I again call attention to the influence of the works of Kierkegaard and the Marquis de Sade, which can be seen in Piñera's bold mockery of Christianity and traditional attitudes about sexuality. I also bring to light the many parallels that exist between *Pequeñas maniobras* and Witold Gombrowicz's novel, *Ferdydurke*, which Piñera helped to translate into Spanish in 1946.

The final chapter comprises a reading of three dramatic works—*La boda* (1957), *El no* (1965), and *Dos viejos pánicos* (1968)—in which problematic or unconventional heterosexual relationships call attention to the author's implicit repudiation of traditional Cuban views on sexuality, engagement, and matrimony. I establish an important link between these plays and Piñera's oft-cited article "Ballagas en persona," in which he fiercely criticizes the cultural and social pressures that he felt pushed many Cubans to repudiate behavior or personality traits that were unpalatable to the so-called moral mainstream. In his article and in the three plays, Piñera implicitly ridicules the idea that matrimony is a measuring stick of normalcy that resolves emotional insecurities or dilemmas of sexual identity. In my analysis of *El no* and *Dos viejos pánicos*, I discuss the polemical themes of both plays in light of the increasingly repressive atmosphere of postrevolutionary Cuba, where moralistic rigidity and idealistic visions of a "New Man" led the government to send homosexuals, nonconformists, and other so-called social deviants to camps to be "rehabilitated" before being reintroduced into "normal society." I also demonstrate how metaphors of asphyxiation are used in both plays to underscore the protagonists' overwhelming fear in the face of the concerted efforts of the government and fellow citizens to make them change their eccentric lifestyles by conforming to ideologies that they do not espouse.

I conclude my book with some general comments about Piñera's final years, and I discuss the recent boom in scholarly and popular interest in his life and works. I feel that it is important to reiterate at this point that while I consider this book to be comprehensive in the sense that it delves into a wide range of texts, it is not an exhaustive study of Virgilio Piñera's life or his diverse oeuvre. The reader must keep in mind that Piñera wrote hundreds of poems, scores of stories, four novels (of which one remains unpublished), dozens of dramatic works, and well over one hundred and fifty critical articles and editorials. Furthermore, he left behind an impressive array of hundreds of unpublished and unfinished texts, including poems, essays, stories, dramatic works, and his novel *El banalizador*. In short, Virgilio Piñera's collected works would fill several large volumes, and it would be far beyond the scope of a single book to explore all of his writings. I have tried to focus on what I consider to be a representative selection of his work, and it is my sincere hope that for my readers, the value of this study will far outweigh whatever shortcomings it may have.

Everything in Its Place

I
Virgilio's Damned Circumstances: A Literary Life

Virgilio Piñera, Havana, 1948. Photo courtesy of Princeton University Library, Department of Rare Books and Special Collections.

1
Living on the Margins (1912–46)

La historia de mi familia es la historia de cualquier familia cubana de clase media. ¡Clase media! Decirlo es casi una irrisión . . . Somos clase media pero también clase cuarta o décima.

[The story of my family is the story of any Cuban family of the middle class. Middle class! To say that is almost a mockery . . . We are middle class but also fourth or tenth class.]

—Virgilio Piñera, "Piñera teatral"[1]

No bien tuve la edad exigida para que el pensamiento se traduzca en algo más que soltar la baba y agitar los bracitos, me enteré de tres cosas lo bastante sucias como para no poderme lavar jamás de las mismas. Aprendí que era pobre, que era homosexual y que me gustaba el arte.

[I was barely of the requisite age when thought is translated into something more than drooling and shaking one's arms, when I became aware of three things that were dirty enough that I would never be able to wash myself of them. I learned that I was poor, that I was homosexual, and that I liked art.]

—Virgilio Piñera, "La vida, tal cual"[2]

T<small>HE THIRD OF SIX CHILDREN, VIRGILIO DOMINGO PIÑERA LLERA WAS</small> born in Cárdenas in the province of Matanzas on August 4, 1912. His family, like so many others in provincial Cuban towns in the early years of the republic, was beleaguered by poverty and hunger. Piñera's father, Juan Manuel, who was trained as a land surveyor and a railroad engineer, struggled constantly to secure steady employment, but more often than not he was without work. When he lost his job as a land surveyor in 1917, the Piñera family was forced to subsist on the meager earnings of Virgilio's mother, who worked as a public school teacher.

Persistent economic hardships lead Juan Manuel Piñera on a desperate search for a means to provide for his wife and six children, which occasioned several moves during Virgilio's formative years. In 1921 the Piñera family relocated to Guanabacoa, a small town on the outskirts of Havana. There Virgilio's father opened a small candle shop, which, as Piñera noted in his unfinished memoirs, was one of several unsuccessful business ventures that failed to remedy the family's precarious economic situation.[3] In 1925, convinced that he would never make ends meet as a candle maker, Juan Manuel Piñera decided to pack the family's bags once again, and they headed for the provincial town of Camagüey where they would endure similar economic constraints until moving to Havana in 1939.

Shortly after the move to the provincial capital, Virgilio enrolled in classes at El Instituto de Segunda Enseñanza de Camagüey, where he studied intermittently until receiving his *bachillerato* in 1934. An annotation on his student record made by an instructor of military education, a required course for all students during the Machado era, suggests that in his formative school years Piñera had already begun to develop the nonconformist bent that would later become the trademark of his literary personality: "Muy poco cuidadoso de su uniforme y apariencia personal. Poco respetuoso y nada puntual."[4] (Very careless with his uniform and personal appearance. Disrespectful and not at all punctual.) Piñera's nascent spirit of rebelliousness was also evidenced by his involvement in a student political group that opposed the increasingly corrupt and repressive tactics of Gerardo Machado, who in 1930 closed a number of Cuban universities and high schools in order to silence the students, professors, and intellectuals who had become his most outspoken opponents. Machado's drastic measures ended up provoking the formation of secret terrorist cells, whose members answered government oppression with various forms of reprisal. Though Virgilio was not involved in the violence, he was arrested twice under suspicion of conspiring against the government. When a bomb exploded in the Escuela Normal de Maestros de Camagüey in 1931, for example, Virgilio, his brothers, and a number of other students who had not participated in the crime were arrested, questioned, and briefly jailed. A few years later, Virgilio, along with his brother Humberto and sister Luisa, was detained again, this time for distributing *Indio bravo*, a clandestine anti-Machado newspaper, to students in Camagüey.

By the time Piñera completed his secondary education in Camagüey in 1934 Machado had fled the country and was replaced by Fulgencio Batista, a new political strongman who governed Cuba either directly or through puppet presidents for the next several years. Though the situation of Cuban intellectuals and the outlook for cultural reform remained bleak in the mid-1930s, Piñera made his first true incursions into a literary vocation during this period. In 1935, for example, with his friends Luis Martínez and Aníbal Vega, he cofounded Camagüey's chapter of La Hermandad de Jóvenes Cubanos, an organization that aimed to invigorate Cuba's stagnant cultural scene by promoting literary and intellectual endeavors throughout the island. With fellow members of La Hermandad Piñera, who was named director of the new chapter, organized literary and artistic events in the provincial capital including poetry readings and a visit in December 1936 of a group of actors from La Cueva, an experimental Havana theater directed by Luis A. Baralt.

Virgilio's interactions with the Havana theater troupe in 1936 ended up having a profound influence on his burgeoning literary career. Indeed, his association with the actors at once afforded him an invaluable early contact with the theater and inspired him to write his first dramatic work, *Clamor en el penal* (Clamor in the Prison). The first act of the play was published in the short-lived Havana journal *Baraguá* in September 1937. It was accompanied by a brief but favorable review by the magazine's director, José Antonio Portuondo, who spoke of Virgilio's great promise as a dramatist and noted that the play was outstanding among the country's limited contemporary dramatic production. The following year the play received an honorable mention in a national drama competition, but Piñera considered *Clamor* to be an experimental work with little literary merit. Found among Piñera's papers after his death, *Clamor* was never performed or published. The play represents, nonetheless, a significant first step in his illustrious career as a dramatist.[5]

Around the time that he became involved with La Hermandad de Jóvenes Cubanos, Virgilio befriended the Camagüeyan poet Emilio Ballagas, who by that time was an up-and-coming Cuban intellectual and poet. Inspired by his friendship with Ballagas, to be sure, Piñera began to compose verse and to give public lectures on poetry during his final years in the provincial capital. Despite his best efforts to pursue his artistic and intellectual interests in Camagüey, Piñera was well aware that the town had little to offer an aspiring artist like himself. By the final months of 1936, therefore, he began making arrangements to move to the Cuban capital, where he planned to live with an aunt and to attend classes at the University of Havana. Piñera hoped that in Havana he would find an environment that was more suitable to both his artistic and sexual sensibilities. To a certain extent he found what he was looking for, but he was quick to realize that his provincial origins, his economic hardships, and his homosexuality would become defining elements of his marginalized existence in Havana.

In March 1937 Piñera applied for free enrollment to the school of philosophy and letters at the University of Havana. According to his statement on the application, he and both of his parents were unemployed at the time, and the only regular source of income for his family of eight was the meager $58, monthly salary that his sister Luisa earned as a kindergarten teacher in Camagüey.[6] Piñera's application was approved, and in October 1937 he moved to Havana to begin his studies. In Havana Piñera's economic situation remained grave, and he constantly moved from one guesthouse to another in search of more affordable living quarters. More often than not he barely had enough to pay his rent or to eat a decent meal. But Piñera, who would later declare that he was willing to suffer 1,001 hardships in order to pursue a literary career, was not one to give up easily.[7]

The Dawn of a New Artistic Generation

In 1930s Cuba, intellectuals were largely viewed as eccentrics, and writing was not recognized by the mainstream as a valuable profession. In an editorial written after the triumph of the Revolution Piñera noted with characteristic humor that "los sinónimos de escritores en Cuba eran: loco, idiota, delirante, irresponsable, raro y, por supuesto, muerto de hambre"[8] (The synonyms for writers in Cuba were: crazy, idiotic, delirious, irresponsible, strange and, of course, dying of hunger). Despite his indigence, his recognition that his chosen career was not a highly respected one, and his acute awareness of his provincial origins and his cultural underdevelopment, Virgilio was determined to pursue a literary career and to leave his mark on the intellectual history of his country.

Shortly after beginning course work at the University of Havana in October 1937, the aspiring author became an active participant in the Havana intellectual scene. It is important to point out that despite his growing interest in theater and his eventual mastery of multiple literary genres, Piñera wrote mostly poetry during his early years in Havana. His first publication in Havana was a poem entitled "El grito mudo" (The Mute Scream). This brief composition was included in *La poesía cubana en 1936* (Cuban Poetry in 1936), an important anthology edited and introduced by the Spanish poet and future Nobel laureate Juan Ramón Jiménez. Jiménez had been invited to Cuba in 1936 to give a series of academic conferences at the Institución Hispanocubana in Havana. While in Cuba he took a great interest in the country's young poets, and it was his idea to invite them to submit unpublished, original works to a poetry competition in January 1937. After sifting through the hundreds of submissions, Jiménez compiled an anthology of poems by sixty-three Cuban authors ranging from established poets such as Emilio Ballagas, Euginio Florit, and Nicolás Guillén, to relative newcomers like Piñera and José Lezama Lima.

This significant publication gave birth to what Piñera later referred to as the exceptional generation of 1936, whose most important member was Lezama Lima.[9] At the time of Jiménez's arrival to Cuba, Lezama, as his friends called him, was working toward a degree in law at the University of Havana, but he was also quickly becoming a central figure in the Cuban literary and intellectual scene. As Lezama and other members of his generation would later acknowledge, the visit of Juan Ramón Jiménez to Havana, which lasted from November 1936 through January 1939, had a pronounced impact on the history of Cuban poetry. In a survey about the impact of Jiménez's stay in Cuba, which was published in *La Gaceta de Cuba* in 1969, for example, Lezama suggested that the Spanish bard's visit was important not so much in terms of direct poetic influence, but because his presence in Havana served as a catalyst to the formation of a new generation of poets in Cuba.[10] Likewise, in a 1979 interview, Cintio Vitier similarly called attention to the great significance of Juan Ramón's visit. Vitier noted, for example, that while he, Fina García Marruz, and to a certain extent Eliseo Diego, saw Jiménez as a mentor and teacher who helped to rouse their poetic careers, Lezama viewed him more as a fellow poet and intellectual with whom he could converse about matters of high culture. More importantly, however, Vitier underscored the fact that Jiménez served to bring together the poets of the future *Espuela de Plata* and *Orígenes* groups, who at the time of his arrival in 1936 had yet to become acquainted with one another: "Yo creo que Juan Ramón empieza a ser como un vínculo unitivo entre nosotros . . . Nosotros en ese momento no nos conocíamos, pero empezamos a conocernos y a reconocernos *en* Juan Ramón"[11] (I think that Juan Ramón began to be something of a unifying vehicle among us . . . At that moment we did not know each other, but we began to get to know and recognize each other *in* Juan Ramón).

In 1937 Lezama cofounded the journal *Verbum* with a fellow student of law, René Villarnovo. As one critic has aptly put it, *Verbum* was a review that had little to do with law and much to do with poetry.[12] Though only three issues of the journal were published between June and November 1937, it was a significant prologue to Lezama's illustrious editorial career and it signaled the birth of a new artistic generation in Cuba. *Verbum*, whose first two numbers opened with essays by Juan Ramón Jiménez, was the first of a series of important journals in which a group of poets and artists headed by Lezama published their original works and expressed their literary and aesthetic preoccupations.[13]

It was around the time of *Verbum*'s demise that Piñera first met Lezama. Though neither of the young poets could have suspected it at the time, their friendship, which was largely based on mutual literary and intellectual interests, would quickly turn into one of the most polemical and legendary relationships in the history of Cuban letters. After a year-long hiatus, Lezama, along with the art critic Guy Pérez Cisneros and the painter Mariano Rodríguez, founded a new journal: *Espuela de Plata*. Though *Espuela de Plata* was also a short-lived journal—only six numbers were published between August 1939 and August 1941—it was important for a number of reasons. First and foremost, it represented a major step toward the definitive formation of the *Orígenes* group. Many of those listed as consultants on the first number of *Espuela*—Jorge Arche, José Ardévol, Gastón Baquero, Alfredo Lozano, René Portocarrero, Justo Rodríguez Santos, and Cintio Vitier—as well as the authors whose names were later added to the list, Ángel Gaztelu and Virgilio Piñera among others, would later make up the core of one of Latin America's most important literary circles.

But *Espuela de Plata* was also noteworthy in terms of the originality, variety, and the academic seriousness of its publications. It was conceived mainly as a journal of poetry, but essays on music and art, short stories, and works of literary criticism also appeared among its pages. Original drawings and tipped-in reproductions of paintings by some of Cuba's leading artists added to the quality and the attractiveness of the journal.

Lezama, *Espuela de Plata*, and the Birth of a Polemicist

By the time of the founding of *Espuela de Plata*, Lezama and Virgilio had become close friends. From the outset, Virgilio Piñera was one of the magazine's most assiduous contributors, and his numerous publications in it—which included nearly a dozen poems and three essays—earned him an important place among Cuba's newest literary generation. While most of the poems that Piñera published in *Espuela de Plata* reveal the influence of Lezama's verse, Piñera's early recognition of his deference to his friend and fellow poet motivated him to develop his own highly unique poetic voice. Piñera claimed some twenty years later in the pages of *Lunes de Revolución*, for example, that his lack of erudition and his ignorance of the works of important poets, such as Guillaume Apollinaire (1880–1918) and André Breton (1896–1966), during his formative years compelled him to imitate the verse of the only poet he really knew:

> Como Lezama era lo único que tenía a mano, pues le eché mano. Por es época yo era joven (¡que diablos, alguna vez se ha sido joven!) y todo cua-

nto hacía por el momento era lo que podría resumirse en la frase de Gautier sobre Baudelaire: "Un joven que se preparaba lentamente en la sombra..." ... Pues yo me preparaba... Y cuando lo juzgué oportuno me quité la piel de cordero para asumir mi papel de lobo feroz. Mi primer mordisco me valió la salida de *Espuela de Plata*.[14]

[Since Lezama was the only poet available to me, I resorted to him. At that time I was young (what the hell, one can't be blamed for being young!) and all I was doing at the moment was what could be summarized by Gautier's phrase about Baudelaire: "A youth who was slowly getting ready in the shadows..." ... Well, I was getting ready ... And when I considered the moment opportune I took off my sheep's clothing to assume my role as the big, bad wolf. My first bite afforded me a way out of *Espuela de Plata*.]

As Piñera's comments suggest, the origins of his notorious role as a polemicist can be traced back to his rather dramatic rupture with Lezama and *Espuela de Plata* in 1941. Early that year Lezama had decided to invite his longtime friend Ángel Gaztelu, a Spanish-born priest and poet, to codirect the journal with him. Despite the fact that Gaztelu had been affiliated with Lezama since before the foundation of *Verbum*, Lezama's selection of him for a directorial position represented something of an affront to Piñera for two distinct reasons. First, it seems that Piñera felt slighted by his friend who he felt should have chosen him for the position but opted instead to follow a more conservative course of action. In a lengthy letter to Lezama, dated May 29, 1941, Piñera clearly alluded to this issue.

Ante un problema de "mano derecha o mano izquierda" optaste por el procedimiento de la mano izquierda.... Quien debía ser negado era confirmado; quien por propio reconocimiento tuyo significaba una integridad entre defecciones era arrojado, ignorado, desoído. Yo siempre temí que llegase el tiempo de las grandes decisiones, porque habiéndote movido tú en un círculo de familia conservadora te habías nutrido de bastantes indecisiones [que] te impidieron ponerte de mi lado (que era el tuyo) obligándote a aceptar la amañada fórmula del personaje condenado la víspera.[15]

[Faced with a problem of "right hand or left hand" you opted for the left-handed procedure.... The one who should have been rejected was confirmed; the one who by your own recognition signified integrity amidst defections was cast aside, ignored, disregarded. I always feared that the moment of big decisions would arrive, because having moved about in a conservative family circle you had nourished yourself with plenty of indecisiveness that kept you from taking my side (which was yours) obligating you to accept the clever formula of the person that you had condemned the night before.]

Ben Heller has correctly pointed out that Piñera was especially upset because Lezama had opted to stick to his conservative past and to forge an alliance "with a traditional center of power in Cuban society."[16] Lezama's capitulation to tradition and conservatism was something that a rebellious spirit like Piñera would never have considered. Piñera's letter also clearly suggests that he was profoundly disillusioned because he felt that Lezama had betrayed their friendship and their rare intellectual bond by implicitly disavowing the subversive tendencies that the two poets ostensibly shared.

Furthermore, Piñera, who was an atheist, was understandably concerned that Gaztelu's role as codirector of *Espuela* would enhance the magazine's religious tone and thus serve to devalue Piñera's position in the group. Piñera emphasized in his letter that he was especially irked with a particular member of the literary circle—who he refers to as "la serpiente de última hora" (the eleventh-hour serpent) and "el maniqueo a la moda" (the fashionable Manichaean)—for shamelessly suggesting that *Espuela de Plata* was an exclusively Catholic journal. Heller has suggested that the Manichaean was "possibly Cintio Vitier, who had converted to Catholicism."[17] Vitier did not convert to Catholicism until April 1953, however, and it is thus unlikely that he was the target of Piñera's remarks.[18] Other critics have posited that the individual in question was Guy Pérez Cisneros.[19] Though such a theory is indeed possible, it seems most likely to me that the "maniqueo," the " buen presbítero" (good priest), and the anonymous "él" to whom Piñera referred in the letter were actually the same individual, that is, Gaztelu himself.[20]

> He tenido que soportar que este mismo maniqueo, con un impudor e insinceridad que eran de esperarse por su misma condición de maniqueísta, me comunicase que *Espuela de Plata* era una revista católica y se había tomado el acuerdo de elegir al buen presbítero porque todos ustedes (ustedes son el poeta, el pintor, y él)[21] eran católicos, no ya sólo en sentido universal del término, sino como cuestión dogmática, de grupo religioso, que se inspira en las enseñanzas se la Santa Madre Iglesia. Así expresado creo más en una cuestión de catoliquería que catolicidad y esto por que catoliquería significa lo mismo que alcahuetería o sanguinolenta disentería de unas pobres palabras.[22]

> [I have had to put up with the fact that this same Manichaean, with shamelessness and insincerity that were to be expected from his very nature as a Manichaean, informed me that *Espuela de Plata* was a Catholic magazine and that the decision had been made to elect the good priest because all of you (you are the poet, the painter, and him) were Catholic, not only in the universal sense of the term, but in terms of dogma, as a religious group, that

draws inspiration from the Holy Mother Church. Expressed in such a way I believe more in a question of catholicking than catholicity and this because catholicking means the same thing as pimping or blood-stained dysentery of wretched words.]

Heller is probably accurate in his assertion that Piñera's problem with *Espuela de Plata* was not so much spiritual as it was worldly, that is, that Piñera was more opposed to Lezama's "catering to tradition and authority" than he was to the actual religious beliefs of the journal's directors.[23] But we must not overlook the fact that Piñera was an atheist who greatly distrusted Catholic doctrine. Consequently, the selection of a Catholic priest as codirector of *Espuela* and the subsequent claims that the journal to which Piñera had contributed so much time and energy was expressly affiliated with a religious cult upset him deeply.[24]

Moreover, it has been suggested that Lezama's selection of Gaztelu to codirect *Espuela* was a mere formality that should not have upset Piñera.[25] However, the latter made it clear in his letter that he did not see it that way by underscoring the fact that he felt offended by the man he had so recently considered to be a dear friend and kindred spirit: "yo creía en ti . . . y por ello acudía a tus convivios por considerarte entre los poquísimos con derecho al elegante diálogo. . . . Yo sentía que respiraba gracias a tu anhélito"[26] (I believed in you . . . and for that reason I came to your banquets considering you among the very few with the right to elegant dialogue. . . . I felt that I breathed thanks to your labored breathing.)

Piñera closed his contentious letter by stating that though he had lost trust in Lezama, he would continue his allegiance to the journal. But the polemic that he had stirred up eventually led to the demise of *Espuela de Plata* and to the subsequent formation of three new literary journals, each of which was directed by former members of the group.[27] Lezama and the Gaztelu founded *Nadie Parecía: Cuaderno de lo Bello con Dios* (No One Appeared to be: Notebook of Beauty with God), the longest running of the three journals. Its ten numbers ran from 1942 to 1944. Marcelo Uribe has pointed out that the coeditors of *Nadie Parecía* attempted to distance themselves from the scandal that Piñera had provoked by turning away from the Cuban members of the *Espuela* group and focusing instead on classical poets and established foreign writers.[28] However, Piñera must have seen the journal's overtly pious subtitle as both an allusion to the recent polemic and a symbolic blow from Lezama and Gaztelu.

A group headed by Gastón Baquero and Cintio Vitier founded another short-lived journal, *Clavileño: Cuaderno Mensual de Poesía* (Clavileño: Monthly Poetry Notebook), in the summer of 1942. The five issues of this attractive publication were illustrated by Cuban artists René Portocarrero and Felipe Orlando, and texts by most of the former contributors to *Espuela de Plata*, with the notable exception of Lezama, were printed among its pages.[29] Riccio has observed that Lezama's absence from *Clavileño* had little to do with the tensions caused by the breakup—indeed, several texts by Gaztelu and Piñera were printed in the ephemeral journal—but rather owed to the fact that he was relatively inaccessible to the younger members of the group.[30] Piñera contributed four poems and a bookish piece of art criticism "De la contemplación" (On Contemplation) to *Clavileño*, but he was left with the urge to further provoke Lezama and to criticize the magazine's directors, who he felt were trying too hard to promote camaraderie and reconciliation. In 1942 Piñera decided, therefore, to start his own magazine.

The first issue of *Poeta: Cuaderno Trimestral de la Poesía* (Poet: Trimestral Poetry Notebook), appeared in November of that year. The second, and last, was published in May 1943. Each of the two issues of *Poeta* is just eight pages in length, but they include an interesting variety of texts that range from original poems and essays by Piñera and other writers of his generation, to his own translations of poems by the Martinican poet Aimé Césaire (1913–) and the French poet and critic Paul Valéry (1871–1945), to a critical article by the important Spanish scholar and philosopher María Zambrano (1904–91). Despite his differences with the members of *Espuela de Plata* group, Piñera published brief essays by Cintio Vitier and Gastón Baquero and also French translations of poems by Lezama, Gaztelu, Baquero, and Vitier, which were written in honor of the 100th anniversary of the birth of the French poet Stéphane Mallarmé (1842–98). The translations, which were signed "Charles S," were done by Piñera himself.

Notwithstanding the brevity of its existence, *Poeta* was a landmark publication for Piñera. It represented a vehicle through which the budding provocateur could channel the critical punch that was fast becoming the trademark of his public and literary personality. It is worth adding here that in addition to having developed contentious relationships with Lezama and other members of the *Espuela de Plata* group, Piñera had managed to provoke many other members of the Cuban intellectual community by the time he began to publish *Poeta* in 1942. In early 1941, for example, José María Chacón y Calvo (1892–1969), director of Cuban culture and founder of *La Revista Cubana*, had invited Piñera to give a talk on the poetry of Gertrudis Gómez de Avellaneda (1814–73) at the Lyceum in Havana. According to Piñera's own account in his article "Las plumas respetuosas" (The Respectful Pens), the prominent Cuban intellectual was scandalized when the young poet turned the darling of nineteenth-century Cuban letters into a butt of criticism. In the same article Piñera claimed that from then on he was considered to be a "disrespectful" author in Havana.[31] Later in the same year Piñera reinforced his growing reputation as a nonconformist by refusing to defend his thesis on Avellaneda's poetry, allegedly because he felt that a discussion of his work with a jury of professors would be a farce. Even when he was offered a respectable job as a secondary school teacher if he received his diploma, Piñera declined to take part in the academic exercise.

From his early days as a writer Piñera took great pride in his consistent refusal to take the easy road by catering to tradition or currying favor of the literary establishment. As he put it in an article written some twenty years later, "Había otros caminos más fáciles . . . Sólo con decir 'Sí' mi vida material cambiaría de la noche a la mañana. Pero yo siempre dije 'No,' y proseguí, en Cuba, siendo un 'loco,' un 'idiota,' un 'irresponsable' . . . , es decir, seguí siendo un escritor."[32] (There were other easier roads . . . By simply saying "Yes" my material existence would have changed from night to day. But I always said "No," and I continued, in Cuba, being a "fool," an "idiot," an "irresponsible man" . . . , that is, I continued being a writer.) *Poeta* certainly served to bolster Piñera's growing reputation as a nonconformist among members of his own generation, and it even provoked a feisty exchange of letters with Jorge Mañach, cofounder of the avant-garde journal *Revista de Avance* (1927–30). Among his countless literary disputes, Piñera's 1942 confrontation with Mañach, which predates Lezama's much-discussed feud with the author of *Indagación al choteo* by some seven years, stands out as one of the most significant since it serves as an early indication that Piñera and other members of the future *Orígenes* group felt marginalized and "abandoned" by members of Cuba's literary establishment and state-run cultural organizations.

After receiving a copy of *Poeta*, which Piñera had sent him along with a request for financial support, Mañach took advantage of the opportunity to point out in a letter to the young author that despite the journal's merits, its polemical bent seemed somewhat petty and irresponsible. Mañach further noted, in a rather patronizing tone to be sure, that Piñera had inherited his apparent "impatience" and desire to go against the grain from Mañach's generation: "[Eso] lo trajimos nosotros, no lo olviden."[33] (We brought that, don't you forget it.)

Notwithstanding his bittersweet appraisal of *Poeta*, Mañach included with his letter a modest sum to help fund the journal. But Piñera was taken aback by Mañach's reaction to it, and was loath to accept a donation from someone who he felt did not share in the spirit of his publication. The following week, therefore, he returned Mañach's check with an antagonistic letter in which he expressed, in no uncertain terms, his utter disillusionment with Mañach and other members of his generation.

> Y sabe Usted que no hay cosa más difícil para una nueva generación que toparse con que la precedente ha capitulado. Y a nosotros—de quienes se dice que somos erizados puercoespines, supercríticos de todo—ha tocado representar ese difícil papel de rebeldía . . . en un medio, que después de la pseudo revolución machadista, solo quería . . . el conformismo en todos los órdenes y en todas las esferas.[34]

> [And you know that the most difficult thing for a new generation is to come up against the fact that the previous one has capitulated. And we—who are said to be prickly porcupines, hypercritical of everything—have been called on to play that difficult role of rebellion . . . in a society, which after the Machadista pseudo-revolution, only wanted . . . conformism in all orders and all spheres.]

Piñera also rebuked Mañach for his implicit censure of "Terribilia Meditans," the brief editorial that introduced *Poeta*, arguing that the Mañach of *Revista de Avance* must have passed away, since he would never have been scandalized by such an article.

Piñera's editorials in *Poeta* and his letter to Mañach epitomize his provocative and somewhat insolent approach to literary and cultural criticism. In "Terribilia Meditans" Piñera insisted that his journal should not be seen as an attack on the members of the defunct *Espuela de Plata* group—"Poeta no está o va contra nadie" (Poeta doesn't stand or go against anybody)—but in the opening editorial he overtly criticized them and their new journals and emphasized his assumed role as provocateur.

> Clavileño se resume en "revista de amistad." Nadie parecía en "revista de catolicidad." . . . En el caso de Clavileño . . . el "está bien" o el "es discreto" puede ser prueba de amistad pero no de cultura. En el caso de Nadie parecía la insistencia de lo católico descubre claramente un modo de hacer literatura (la mejor literatura) como otro cualquiera.
> . . . Poeta es parte de la herencia de Espuela; familiar de Clavileño y Nadie Parecía. Sólo que en este consejo poético la salvación vendrá por el disentimiento, por la enemistad, por las contradicciones, por la patada de elefante. Por eso Poeta disiente, se enemista, contradice, da la patada.

> [Clavileño boils down to a "magazine of friendship." Nadie parecía to a "magazine of Catholicity." . . . In the case of Clavileño . . . "it's fine" or "it's prudent" might be proof of friendship but not of culture. In the case of

Nadie parecía the insistence on things Catholic clearly reveals a mode of creating literature (the best literature) like any other.

. . . Poeta is part of the legacy of Espuela de Plata; relative of Clavileño and Nadie Parecía. Except that on this poetic board salvation will come from dissention, enmity, contradictions, the kick of the elephant. For that reason Poeta dissents, makes enemies, contradicts, and delivers the kick.]

Piñera's allegation that concord, discretion, and religiosity were neither proof of one's high level of culture nor appropriate tools for the promotion of cultural reform represents something of a literary manifesto that would guide him throughout his career. Piñera was always more inclined to rock the boat than to encourage harmony, and he firmly believed that his assumed role as a "disrespectful" author would be of great value to the future of Cuban letters.

In "Terribilia Meditans . . . (II)," which appeared in the second number of *Poeta*, Piñera was more direct in his criticism of Lezama. Though he credited Lezama with initiating change in a poetic tradition that had been stagnant for many years, he also accused him of becoming stuck in a poetic rut and failing to try to get out of it. Revealing a sense of disillusionment with the poet who he had so recently viewed as something of a master, Piñera derided Lezama for his supposed reluctance to expand his poetic horizons:

Lezama, tras haber obtenido un instrumento de decir se instala cómodamente en el mismo y comienza a devorar su propia conquista. Después de Enemigo Rumor—testimonio rotundo de la liberación—era preciso, ineludible haber dejado muy atrás ciertas cosas que él no ha dejado. Era absolutamente preciso no proseguir en la utilización de su técnica usual.

[Lezama after having obtained an instrument of expression installs himself comfortably in it and begins to devour his own conquest. After Enemigo Rumor—convincing testament of liberation—it was necessary, essential to leave way behind certain things that he has not left behind. It was absolutely necessary not to continue utilizing his usual technique.]

It should not be overlooked that Piñera clearly alludes here to his great admiration of Lezama's poetry. Indeed, the heterodox bent of some of Lezama's early poems such as "La muerte de Narciso" (Death of Narcissus) (1937) and certain texts from *Enemigo rumor* (1941) — with their exploration of a pagan legends and their treatment of themes related to sex and transgression—appealed to Piñera's subversive sensibilities. However, Piñera was decidedly opposed to other aspects of Lezama's writings, such as his celebration of Christian traditions and his allegedly willful use of hermetic metaphors, *cultismos*, and Latinized syntax. While Lezama advocated the notion that only difficult things could be stimulating, Piñera often claimed, as many of Lezama's detractors did, that such a mentality simply made his writings inaccessible to most readers.

Even before composing the scathing editorials of *Poeta*, Piñera had implicitly addressed the importance of finding new modes of poetic expression in a letter to Lezama, in which he discussed *Las Furias* (*The Furies*) (1941), his first collection of poems. The title poem, "Las Furias," clearly reveals affinities with Lezama's "Muerte de Narciso"—especially in terms of its rich metaphors and its original treatment of motives from Greek legends—but Piñera saw this and the other three poems in the slim volume as examples of his concerted attempt to break away from his earlier verse, from Lezama, and from the other members of their generation. As Piñera put it in the closing lines of his lengthy letter, "estas Furias . . . sí van contra todo lo que se puede ir y contra todo lo que no se deba ir. Bajo este aspecto van contra tu poesía, van contra la mía; contra el yo de mi persona y contra el tú de la tuya y el de todos . . ."[35] (These Furies . . . indeed go against everything they can and shouldn't go against. From this point of view they go against your poetry, against mine; against the I of my persona and the you of yours and of everybody's . . .)

While the poems in *Las Furias* were perhaps Piñera's first conscientious attempts at poetic renovation, his long poem *La isla en peso* (The Island Fully Burdened), published the same month as the second number of *Poeta*, marked a dramatic change of focus and a definitive departure from the poets of the future *Orígenes* group.[36] *La isla en peso* is an unsung masterpiece of Caribbean verse that shares certain points of contact with the celebrated elegies of other Caribbean authors such as fellow Cuban poet Nicolás Guillén, Aimé Césaire of Martinique, and the Dominican Manuel del Cabral. It is important to point out, though, that the common ground between Piñera's poem and Guillén's *West Indies, Ltd.* (1934), Césaire's *Cahier d'un retour au pays natal* (*Return to My Native Land*) (1939), or Cabral's *Por las tierras de Compadre Mon* (*Through the Land of Comrade Mon*) (1940) is not so much a matter of literary influence, but more of thematic similarities. Like the above-mentioned poems, *La isla en peso* stands out for its negative tone, its implicit condemnation of imperialism, and its unmasking of the rampant problems of contemporary island life. Furthermore the poem's disconcerting images of misery, frustration, and racism similarly serve to demystify the stereotypical image of the Antilles as a tropical paradise.

The poem's powerful first stanza is illustrative of Piñera's drastic change in direction, and of his desire to expose the absurdity and harshness of contemporary island life through the type of shocking images and coarse rhetoric that would soon become trademarks of his unique voice:

> La maldita circunstancia del agua por todas partes
> me obliga a sentarme en la mesa del café.
> Si no pensara que el agua me rodea como un cáncer
> hubiera podido dormir a pierna suelta.
> Mientras los muchachos se despojaban de sus ropas para nadar
> doce personas morían en un cuarto por compresión.
> Cuando a la madrugada la pordiosera resbala en el agua
> en el preciso momento en que se lava uno de sus pezones,
> me acostumbro al hedor del puerto,
> me acostumbro a la misma mujer que invariablemente masturba,
> noche a noche, al soldado de guardia en medio del sueño de los peces.
> Una taza de café no puede alejar me idea fija,
> en otro tiempo yo vivía adánicamente.
> ¿Qué trajo la metamorfosis?[37]

[The damned circumstance of water everywhere / compels me to sit down at the café table. / If I hadn't thought that the water surrounds me like a cancer / I would have been able to sleep without a problem. / While the boys stripped off their clothes to go swimming / twelve people were dying in a compression chamber. / When in the early morning the beggar woman slips in the water / at the precise moment she washes one of her nipples, / I become accustomed to the stench of the harbor / I become accustomed to the same woman who inevitably masturbates, / night after night, the soldier on call in the midst of the dream of the fish. / A cup of coffee cannot remove my firm idea, / in another time I lived like Adam. / What brought about the metamorphosis?]

Throughout the poem Piñera skillfully juxtaposes traditional Caribbean images—the seemingly endless sea, rainstorms, cane fields, tropical fruits, and sandy beaches—with images of death, destruction, and anguish. His presentation of Cuba as a sad, sick, and lonely place turns the very notion of insularity into a wellspring of distress. The disturbing vision of the island surrounded by a boundless, malignant sea suggests isolation from the rest of the world at the same time that it imbues the poem with a tangible atmosphere of hopelessness.

Mangrove swamps and beaches, traditional icons of the island's natural splendor, become symbolic barriers that make escape seem impossible. According to Piñera's uncannily prophetic vision, the people of the inhospitable island are like prisoners in a place from which flight is impossible:

los siniestros manglares, como un cinturón canceroso,
dan vuelta a la isla,
los manglares y la fétida arena
aprietan los riñones de los moradores de la isla.
Sólo se eleva un flamenco absolutamente.

¡Nadie puede salir, nadie puede salir!
La vida del embudo y encima la nata de la rabia.
Nadie puede salir:
El tiburón más diminuto rehusaría transportar un cuerpo intacto.
Nadie puede salir:[38]

[the sinister mangrove swamps, like a cancerous belt, / encircle the island, / the mangrove swamps and the fetid sand / squeeze the kidneys of the island's inhabitants. / Only a flamingo soars absolutely. / No one can escape, no one can escape! / Unjust life and on top of that the scum of rage. / No one can escape: / The most minute shark would refuse to carry an intact body. / No one can escape:]

The feeling of entrapment expressed by the poetic voice who longs to flee the island is, in fact, portentous in two ways. On the one hand it suggests Piñera's own desire to escape the asphyxiating atmosphere of prerevolutionary Cuba. By the time Piñera penned the poem, he had already begun to entertain seriously the idea of a voluntary exile in Argentina.[39] Just over two years after the publication of *La isla en peso*, Piñera left for Buenos Aires, where he would live on and off for over a decade. On the other hand, with the benefit of hindsight Piñera's poem seems like an eerie divination of his own situation in the years after the triumph of the Revolution. For him and many other authors and intellectuals who fell out of favor with the Castro regime, leaving the island became impossible by virtue of a revolutionary law that made exile illegal.

La isla en peso is also unique among Cuban poetry of the period in terms of its intentionally shocking and aggressive language.[40] The grotesque images, taboo subjects, and copious vulgarisms indeed offer a stark contrast to the neoromantic poems of Ballagas, the so-called pure poetry of Brull, the social poems of Guillén, or the luscious, erudite verse of Lezama. In terms of its air of absurdity, its scandalous vocabulary, and its scatological imagery *La isla en peso* can be seen as a significant precursor to many of Piñera's poems, stories, novels, and plays.

More than fifteen years after the publication of *La isla en peso*, Piñera, from the pages of *Lunes de Revolución*, made an enlightening observation about how the language of his poem underscored his assumed role as a literary rebel, and he recalled how several of the poets of his generation expressed their dissatisfaction with it:

Como la poesía lujosa y verbalista me daba náuseas . . . escribí *La isla en peso*. Recuerdo que antes de su publicación ofrecí una lectura en casa de Vitier. Hubo consternación general. "Hay sífilis en tu poema, y esto no me gusta"—me dijo Cintio. Por su parte Baquero, en el Anuario Cultural del Ministerio de Estado, me enfiló los cañones. En cuanto a Lezama . . . Pues no salía de su asombro: ¡alguien se atrevía en Cuba a escribir un poema empleando un lenguaje que no era el suyo! . . . Este poema será mejor o peor, pero nadie negará que es el antilezamismo en persona.[41]

[Since lavish, verbalist poetry made me nauseous . . . I wrote *La isla en peso*. I remember that before its publication I offered a reading at Vitier's house. There was general consternation. "There is syphilis in your poem, and I don't like that"—Cintio told me. For his part Baquero, in the Anuario Cultural del Ministerio de Estado, enfiladed the cannons at me. As far as Lezama was concerned . . . He couldn't escape his astonishment: someone in Cuba dared to write a poem using language that was not his? . . . This poem may be good or bad, but nobody will deny that it is antilezamism in the flesh.]

Piñera's allusion to Vitier, Baquero, and Lezama's reactions to his poem is especially significant since it calls attention to the ever-increasing tension in the 1940s between Piñera and other members of his generation. It is important to point out, though, that Vitier and Baquero's much-discussed critical appraisals of *La isla en peso* were motivated by more than exclusively literary concerns. Indeed, personal tensions were brewing even before the publication of *La isla en peso*. For example, Piñera had deliberately antagonized both poets through his harsh criticism of their journal, *Clavileño*, and their alleged attempts to promote harmony and concord among the members of the disbanded *Espuela de Plata* group. Likewise, soon after Vitier published his second book of poetry, *Sedienta cita* (Eager Engagement) (1943), Piñera sent him a rather feisty letter. In it he reproached the twenty-two-year-old poet for his supposed failure to improve on the poetry of his teenage years, and he implied that Vitier's poems underscored his fear of taking risks: "*Sedienta cita*, en oposición a *La isla en peso*, aparece como un libro muy seguro. Su poeta sabe perfectamente qué terreno pisar y qué terreno no pisar."[42] (*Sedienta cita*, in opposition to *La isla en peso*, seems like a very safe book. Its author knows perfectly what terrain to tread and what terrain not to tread.)

In August 1943 and February 1944 Piñera had also sent Gastón Baquero two confrontational letters, in which he chastised the young poet for accepting a position as columnist for the Havana newspaper, *Información*.[43] In both letters Piñera insisted that his friend's new profession signified not only his spineless acceptance of the easy path in life, but also his death as the poet. Baquero responded to Piñera's personal attacks with a rather severe review of *La isla en peso*, which was published in *El Anuario Cultural de Cuba*. In his article, "Tendencias actuales de nuestra literatura" (Current Tendencies of Our Literature), Baquero insisted that Piñera's poem was totally disconnected from Cuban modes of expression and that the island that he portrayed was calculatingly inauthentic: "es una isla de plástica extra-cubana, ajena por completo de la realidad cubana ... De aquí que este poema ... viene a aportarnos una de las tendencias extremistas, negativistas, deformadoras intencionadas de nuestra realidad."[44] (It is an island of extra-Cuban sculpture, completely foreign to Cuban reality ... Hence this poem ... serves as an example of the extremist, negativist, intentionally deforming trends of our reality.) Baquero's criticism of *La isla en peso* clearly represented more than a mere literary difference of opinion. It was also a retaliatory strike, an attempt to get even with the feisty provocateur who had delivered the first blows. As was the case with Cintio Vitier, Piñera's relationship with Baquero continued to deteriorate as the years passed. Many years later Piñera alluded to his tensions with Baquero from the pages of *Revolución* when he coined the phrase "el baquerismo literario" to denote the confusing, conformist, and dishonest approach to literature and culture that he felt Baquero, who was by then editor of *Diario de la Marina*, exemplified.

Piñera's notoriously polemical relationship with Vitier is a much more complicated matter. It seems fair to say, though, that Vitier's numerous polemical appraisals of *La isla en peso* played a key role in the ever-mounting hostility between the two poets. Vitier's negative reaction to Piñera's poem in 1943 was followed two years later by a passing reference to *La isla en peso* in a reactionary review of Piñera's *Poesía y prosa*. In his essay, which was published in the second issue of *Orígenes*, Vitier noted that the poem's occasional moments of tenderness were misleading since Piñera's antipoetic vision had little to do with intimacy, compassion, or intelligence. In his important anthology of the poets of the *Orígenes* group, *Diez poetas cubanos* (1948), Vitier further devalued *La isla en peso* not only by excluding it from the collection, but also by referring to the poem as a "falsa experiencia pseudo-nativista"[45] (false, pseudo-nativistic experience).[46]

The ever-mounting hostilities between Vitier and Piñera will be discussed further throughout this study, but for now we should return to the year that witnessed the birth of *Orígenes*, Lezama's most ambitious and longest lasting journal.

From *Orígenes* to Exile

The year 1944 was, in many ways, a momentous year in the history of Cuban letters. By then the polemic that had triggered the breakup of the *Espuela de Plata* group had calmed down considerably, Piñera and Lezama were on speaking terms—at least for the time being—and the three ephemeral journals that had resulted from their confrontation in 1941 had all ceased to exist. The atmosphere was ripe for the creation of a new literary journal, and Lezama was once again the driving force behind the movement to get one under way. With the financial backing of José "Pepe" Rodríguez Feo—a wealthy, Harvard-educated Cuban who had numerous contacts with foreign authors and who had just returned to Havana—Lezama's new venture became a reality.

Orígenes was largely an extension of a group of poets headed by Lezama, many of whom had already collaborated in the three other journals that the great Cuban man of letters had directed since 1937. But *Orígenes* was much more than a Cuban poetry review. Among its pages were published original poems, short fiction, drama, and essays on literature, plastic arts, music, and philosophy by Cuban and foreign authors. Rodríguez Feo's admirable talent as a translator made possible the inclusion of works by a number of major American and European authors and intellectuals such as Anaïs Nin (1903–77), T. S. Eliot (1888–1965), Wallace Stevens (1879–1955), Dylan Thomas (1914–53), and Albert Camus (1913–60). *Orígenes* was a very aesthetically pleasing publication thanks in large part to four important Cuban artists—René Portocarrero, Wilfredo Lam, Amalia Peláez, and Mariano Rodríguez—whose illustrations graced the magazine's covers and many of its pages.

From its foundation in 1944 until its definitive demise in 1956, *Orígenes* was among the most influential Latin American literary journals. According to Nobel laureate Octavio Paz, *Orígenes* was the most important Spanish-language literary review of its day. Likewise, Spanish poet and Nobel Prize-winner Vicente Aleixandre hailed *Orígenes* as one of the finest magazines of the Hispanic world, comparing it to Spain's *Revista de Occidente* and Argentina's *Sur*.

It is crucial to point out, however, that for most of its twelve-year run, *Orígenes* had many detractors among the Cuban literary establishment, the press, and government-run cultural organizations. Certain members of the Minorista generation, such as Jorge Mañach, Francisco Ichaso, Félix Lizaso, and Juan Marinello, for example, were among those who consistently aimed to alienate *Orígenes*. As Rafael Rojas has noted, these intellectuals saw themselves as "spiritual guides of the political regime that took power in 1940 [and] they behaved, at times, like the guardians of its cultural continuity."[47] They were taken aback, therefore, when members of the new generation failed to acknowledge their links to the cultural legacy of *Revista de Avance*.

The marginalization of the *Orígenes* group was set into motion long before the advent of the journal itself. In the first issue of *Verbum*, Guy Pérez Cisneros had published "Presencia de 8 pintores" (Presence of 8

Painters), in which he reprimanded Cuban intellectuals for abandoning the country when it most needed them.[48] He specifically mentioned Marinello and Mañach, who were living in Mexico and the United States respectively, and accused them of being mercenaries who sold Cuban culture to foreign countries.[49] With obvious sarcasm he added that "El arte cubano es Mañach y Marinello que han tenido que huir de Cuba para salvar sus inteligencias."[50] (Cuban art is Mañach and Marinello who have had to flee Cuba to save their minds.) As Rojas has noted, Pérez Cisneros's criticism apparently "aimed at cutting the lines of poetic and political continuity between the two generations."[51] In a letter to Lezama dated April 18, 1938, Mañach, who was determined to set the record straight, rejected Pérez Cisnero's "cruel allusions" and insisted that the contributors to *Verbum* were following in the footsteps of *Avance*: "Por sus actitudes y sus logros, por su querer de finura y altura, Uds. están continuando la labor que nuestra *Revista de Avance* dejó iniciada."[52] (Through your attitudes and your achievements, through your desire for excellence and loftiness, you are continuing the labor that our *Revista de Avance* initiated.)

Virgilio Piñera's 1942 clash with Jorge Mañach similarly demonstrates that before the birth of *Orígenes* tensions were brewing and that the stage was being set for future conflicts. We must recall that Piñera had accused Mañach and his cohorts of capitulation and conformism, and he implicitly denied the existence of a link between the two groups.

In 1948 Cintio Vitier defended *Orígenes* from unnamed detractors in his article "El PEN Club y *Los diez poetas cubanos*" (The Pen Club and Ten Cuban Poets), which was published in the nineteenth issue of the journal. Vitier argued vehemently that the group's supposed "clandestine isolation" and their conscious disaffiliation from the public sphere were necessary measures that allowed them to work more earnestly and to dedicate themselves wholly to their intellectual pursuits. In an apparent reference to Mañach and his cohorts, Vitier warned the magazine's detractors that by seeking comforts and concessions in government-run cultural agencies, they were headed for an irremediable downfall. Later in his essay Vitier rejected two of the accusations to which the *origenistas* had often been subjected: "Estamos . . . los poetas de mi reciente *Antología*, muy lejos de constituir esa exquisita especie de evadidos que algunos imaginen. Tan lejos . . . como estamos de ser los desarraigados seguidores de las últimas escuelas europeas."[53] (The poets of my recent *Anthology* are very far from being that exquisite species of deserters as some imagine. As far . . . as we are from being the uprooted followers of the latest Eurpoean schools.)

The mounting tensions between the intellectual establishment and the *Orígenes* poets came to a head in September 1949, when Mañach published in *Bohemia* "El arcano de cierta poesía nueva: Carta abierta a José Lezama Lima" (The Arcanum of Certain New Poetry: Open Letter to José Lezama Lima). In his editorial Mañach took advantage of the recent publication of Lezama's *La fijeza* (Fixity) to pass judgment on the latter's poetry and that of his cohorts, which he claimed was unintelligible and completely foreign to the aesthetic sensibilities of all but those associated with *Orígenes*. Mañach further expressed his disapproval with *Orígenes*' ongoing claims that no filial link existed between them and Mañach's generation.

Lezama responded promptly from the pages of the same magazine with "Respuesta y nuevas interrogaciones: carta abierta a Jorge Mañach" (Response and New Interrogations: Open Letter to Jorge Mañach). In the first part of his elegant letter Lezama derided Mañach's declaration that the poems in *La fijeza* were incomprehensible, stressing that "el no entendimiento surge . . . de indolencia e indiferencia"[54] (lack of understanding is a product of . . . insolence and indifference). Lezama went on to offer a rather harsh appraisal of *Revista de Avance*, which he referred to as a disorganized collection of miscellaneous articles and aesthetic sensibilities. Lezama dedicated the final part of the letter to what could be termed a definitive rejection of *Orígenes*' hereditary ties with Mañach and *Revista de Avance*:

> Esa falta de filiación es la que según usted levanta cierto resentimiento. No podíamos mostrar filiación, mi querido Mañach, con hombres . . . que ya no tenían para las siguientes generaciones la fascinación de la entrega decisiva a una obra y que sobrenadaban en las vastas demostraciones del periodismo o en la ganga mundana de la política positiva.[55]
>
> [That lack of filiation is what, according to you, has brought about certain resentment. We could not show filiation, my dear Mañach, with men . . . who no longer preserved for future generations the fascination of a decisive commitment to their work and who floated around in the vast demonstrations of journalism or in the worldly windfall of positive politics.]

While *Orígenes* was the target of numerous attacks from the outside, a great deal of conflict also arose from within the group itself. Even though Piñera has traditionally been considered an important figure of *Orígenes*, for example, he was also one of its most outspoken detractors. Moreover, his radically subversive literary tendencies, his open homosexuality, and his professed atheism created much tension and resulted in his own marginality within the group. Piñera's comments in a March 1945 letter to Lezama, for example, indicate that even a year after *Orí-*

genes' foundation he still did not consider himself to be a member of the group:

> entre lo que forma y se llama *Orígenes*, todo viene a ser juego de palabras . . . Por dos veces, Ustedes (*Orígenes*) se han molestado para molestarme pidiéndome colaboración. . . . Las dos veces—y parece un juego de locos—han postergado mi envío porque sí; sin razón suficiente."[56]
>
> [between what *Orígenes* is and what it is called, everything becomes a play on words . . . Twice now, you (*Orígenes*) have taken the trouble to bother me, asking for my collaboration. . . . Both times—and it seems like a game of fools—you have disregarded my submissions just for kicks; without sufficient reason.]

In the same letter Piñera ridiculed assertions that *Orígenes* was the best arts review in Cuba. With typical sarcasm, he noted that such claims were of little value since no real competition existed.

It is important to stress that the exclusion of Piñera's articles from the first four issues of *Orígenes* was largely his own fault, since he insisted on criticizing the journal and provoking its contributors. After receiving a copy of the inaugural issue of *Orígenes* in May 1944, for instance, Piñera, who apparently had not been invited to collaborate, immediately responded with a derisive letter to its editors in which he ridiculed the journal's supposed lack of innovation and its detachment from Cuban reality.[57] With characteristic effrontery Piñera summarized his opinion of the new publication with the following remarks: "[*Orígenes* es] un impotente estatismo que nada sostiene. . . . *Orígenes* tiene arte pero carece de fuerza." (*Orígenes* is an impotent stillness that sustains nothing. . . . *Orígenes* has artistry but it lacks force.)

From the very birth of *Orígenes*, then, Piñera was something of a vacillating provocateur who insisted that he was not interested in being a part of the group—"no publicaré jamás en *Orígenes*" (I'll never publish in *Orígenes*), he wrote in a letter to Lezama[58]—at the same time that he decried the apparent efforts to exclude him from it.

Over the magazine's twelve-year life span texts by Piñera appeared in just five issues of *Orígenes*. His contributions were, nonetheless, significant, especially in terms of their diversity. The eight texts (three poems, three essays, a book review, and one play) attest to Piñera's numerous literary and cultural interests and to his mastery of multiple literary genres. However, when compared to the number of times that other figures of the group published in the journal (Lezama 39, Vitier, 19, Lorenzo García Vega, 17), Piñera's reduced number of publications in *Orígenes* seems especially small, and has served to justify claims (by

Piñera himself as well as many critics) that he was never a principal member of the group.

Whether or not we consider Piñera a true *origenista*, his sparse contributions to the journal can be explained by three major factors. First, Piñera himself often went to great length to deny his affiliation with *Orígenes*. Second, certain members of the group resisted embracing an individual who had proved to be a tireless agitator. And, perhaps most importantly, during most of the magazine's tenure Piñera was in Buenos Aires, where he resided off and on from 1946–58, and his contact with the group was therefore quite limited.

Marcelo Uribe has erroneously observed that Piñera had already left for Argentina by the time Lezama and Rodríguez Feo founded *Orígenes*.[59] This is a major oversight indeed, since by the time he left for Buenos Aires, Piñera had already provoked several literary skirmishes with the editors and had contributed three poems, a book review, and a very important essay — "El secreto de Kafka" (Kafka's Secret) — to the magazine.

Piñera's essay on Kafka is especially significant among his critical writings for two reasons. First and foremost, his assessment of the writings of the great Czech writer confirmed at an early date a notable influence on Piñera's own works. The existential anguish that permeates Piñera's early stories, plays, and novels and his manifest fascination with absurdity and the grotesque reveal his debt to Franz Kafka.[60] Furthermore in "El secreto de Kafka" Piñera also speaks of the ingenious inventiveness of the English satirist Jonathan Swift, whose masterful mix of derision and humor resonates in much of Piñera's work.[61]

"El secreto de Kafka" is also important because, as Barreto has astutely noted, through it Piñera responded indirectly to Cintio Vitier's reactionary review of his recently published collection of poems and short fiction, *Poesía y prosa* (Poetry and Prose) (1944).[62] In this sense, Piñera's essay is much more than a critical appreciation of Kafka's work. In fact, "El secreto de Kafka" can be seen as something of a literary manifesto in which Piñera underscores his conviction — which he would repeat in later articles such as "El País del Arte" (The Country of Art) (1947) and "Aviso a los conformistas" (Warning to Conformists) (1959) — that the essence of good literature is innovation and originality as opposed to imitation.

In his review of *Poesía y prosa*, Vitier had recognized Piñera's radical departure from the works of his Cuban contemporaries, but he asserted that the eight poems and fourteen stories in the collection exemplified Piñera's inherent rebelliousness more than his literary innovation. Vitier was quick to point out that Piñera's debt to certain authors — he specifically mentioned Kafka — was so obvious as to border on ingenuousness.[63] Furthermore, Vitier argued that Piñera's overwhelming pessimism, and his implicit rejection of religion and tradition were rendered ineffective by his caustic irony and aggressive language, which Vitier found to be in bad taste. Vitier backed his assertion by calling attention to "la profunda frecuencia de lo cursi"[64] (the overwhelming frequency of bad taste) in both *Poesía y prosa* and *La isla en peso*. Vitier closed his somewhat retrogressive critique with an observation about Piñera's poems that was at once incisive and deliberately mordant:

> aparte de su altísima calidad literaria y el puesto inconmovible que le corresponde en el empeño expresivo de la actual generación, este libro de Virgilio Piñera podrá ostentar en todo caso el honor de haberse enfrentado, para delatarlo y ceñirlo insuperablemente, con el vacío inasible y férreo que representa para nosotros . . . el demonio de la más absoluta antipoesía.[65]

> [aside from its very high literary quality and the unshakable position that corresponds to it in the expressive enterprise of the present generation, this book by Virgilio Piñera will in any case hold the honor of having confronted, in order to reveal it and hem it in insuperably, the unobtainable, ferrous void that represents for us . . . the demon of the most absolute antipoetry.]

In "El secreto de Kafka," then, Piñera implicitly derided what he interpreted as Vitier's resistance to literary innovation by stressing his conviction that successful writing was impossible without risk taking and invention. From his eternally polemical standpoint Piñera viewed Vitier and other so-called followers of Lezama as conformists who, as he later put it, had become "as indistinguishable from one another as drops of water."[66] Piñera saw himself, on the other hand, as an innovative author who, like Kafka, was willing to break molds and to rebel against tradition in order to forge truly unique modes of expression.

Vitier's use of the term "antipoesía" to describe Piñera's poems is especially significant when considered in light of Piñera's frequent insistence that he embodied "el antilezamismo," a term that he coined to denote his deliberate rejection of the poetic discourse of Lezama and other *Orígenes* poets. One of the poems in *Poesía y prosa*, "Vida de Flora" (Life of Flora) is particularly illustrative of Piñera's so-called antipoetic tendencies. As its title intimates, "Vida de Flora" can be read as a sort of caricature of Lezama's "Muerte de Narciso." Though certain heterodox aspects of Lezama's early masterpiece appealed to Piñera's poetic sensibilities, Piñera parodied various dimensions of Lezama's poetic vision that he found less agreeable. Against the complex metaphors, voluptuous vocabulary, and lofty tenor of Lezama's poem, for example, Piñera pitted crude language, unrefined imagery, and a conversational tone. Moreover, while Lezama's Narciso recalls the universally recognized symbol of youthful beauty, Piñera's Flora is an anonymous "everywoman" who stands out only because of her enormous feet.

Much like *La isla en peso*, "Vida de Flora" exudes an overwhelming air of sadness, anguish, and frustration. And while it could be argued that Flora's monstrous feet serve as a comic device, the poetic voice makes clear that they are also a source of shame and dejection. Flora's physical imperfection not only stands in stark contrast to the beautiful, highly idealized Narciso in Lezama's poem, but it is also illustrative of Piñera's tendency to oppose the aestheticism of the poets of his generation by means of grotesque and distorted images that often portray corporeal deformity. The vulgar language and disturbing images in "Carga" (Burden) and "Muchas alabanzas" (Many Praises) also clearly reflect this notion. In those two poems from *Poesía y prosa*, the poetic voice speaks of showers of urine, a pile of feces, storehouses filled with rotting corpses, a woman with a lacerated breast, a mutilated artist, syphilitic prostitutes, decapitated chickens, and men deformed with cancer. Likewise, in many of the highly original stories from the same collection—"La caída" (The Fall), "La carne" (Meat), "La cena" (Supper), "Las partes" (The Parts), "El álbum" (The Album)—Piñera made use of deliberately unrefined language and shocking imagery to underscore his quest to fashion a distinctive, innovative literary voice.

By mid-1945 Piñera was well aware of his ever-increasing incompatibility—on both personal and artistic grounds—with many of the writers of his generation. Though his hard-nosed opposition to *Orígenes* had softened somewhat (we should recall that in March 1945 he had sworn to Lezama that he would never publish in the journal), his relationship with Lezama was precarious at best, his feelings toward Vitier had become quite hostile, and his distaste for the religious views of several members of the largely Catholic group had become a constant source of tension.[67] In short, Piñera surely felt something like a fish out of water, and the prospect of finding a climate more suitable to his eccentric personality and tastes became increasingly attractive. Though it would be disingenuous to suggest that Piñera would have preferred being accepted to being seen as a polemical and rebellious intellectual, it seems fair to say that the more he realized that he didn't fit in, the more he felt the need to leave Cuba and to escape the inherent tensions of being a writer there.

Moreover, Piñera suffered from the typical economic woes that plagued many Cuban writers. He rarely made any money from his publications, and felt that staying in his homeland would ruin his chances for both literary success and financial solvency. His increasing desire to leave for Argentina, then, was not simply a product of personal tensions and literary incompatibilities, but also of economic necessity. Finally, in February 1946, after securing a scholarship with the help of a professor from the University of Havana, Virgilio Piñera departed for Buenos Aires where he would reside, excluding several lengthy visits to Cuba, until 1958.

2
From the Outside Looking In: Exile in Argentina (1946–58)

> El escritor respetuoso nunca arriesga nada.
>
> [The respectful author never risks anything.]
> —Virgilio Piñera, "Las plumas respetuosas"[1]

> Yo por Dios, *no me achico*, ni aconsejo achicarse a usted . . . ya sabe que la batalla será dura, así que hay que conocer la actitud del enemigo
>
> [I, for God's sake, *will not belittle myself*, and I don't suggest that you belittle yourself either . . . you know that the battle will be difficult, so you have to know the enemy's attitude.]
> —Witold Gombrowicz[2]

WHEN REFERRING TO HIS YEARS IN ARGENTINA IN HIS AUTObiography, Virgilio Piñera stressed that this important period of his life should be divided into three distinct periods: "Mi primera permanencia en Buenos Aires duró de Febrero de 1946 a Diciembre de 1947; la segunda de abril de 1950 a mayo de 1954; la tercera de enero de 1955 a noviembre de 1958."[3] (My first stay in Buenos Aires lasted from February 1946 to December 1947; the second from April 1950 to May 1954; the third from January 1955 to November 1958.) Except for his error concerning the month of his definitive return to Cuba, which was actually September 1958, and his failure to mention that he returned to Havana for several lengthy visits, the dates that Piñera gives are accurate. I make this point because certain inexact statements about Piñera's exile in Argentina have led to misunderstandings about his experiences there. Many critical articles, for instance, simply indicate that Piñera lived in Buenos Aires for twelve years without clarifying that he returned to Cuba many times and that he spent more than three of those years in his homeland. Moreover, numerous critics have incorrectly observed that Piñera, like many Cuban intellectuals who were living abroad in the 1950s, returned to the island after the triumph of the Revolution, when he was actually back in Cuba several months before the momentous events of January 1959.

Piñera's first trip to Argentina was arranged by one of his professors who secured him a prestigious scholarship from the Comisión Nacional de Cultura de Buenos Aires. Piñera's arrival in Argentina represented a notable change in both economic and literary terms. The funds from the one-year research grant were designated for the young author's study of Latin American poetry, and they allowed him to pursue his intellectual interests while living in relative comfort. It is interesting to note that Virgilio arrived in Buenos Aires on February 24, 1946, the day Juan Domingo Perón was elected president of Argentina. In his unfinished autobiography he commented that his first notable experience in the Argentine capital was his taxi trip from the airport during which he observed crowds of people casting their votes for their new leader.

Piñera's arrival at the dawn of a period of remarkable political and social transformation in Argentina certainly added to his initial enthusiasm with his new surroundings. Buenos Aires immediately impressed him on several levels, especially in terms of its sophisticated, cosmopolitan atmosphere when compared to Havana. Whereas he considered the Cuban capital to be little more than a stifling provincial town—"La Habana . . . es una ciudad grande pero nunca una gran ciudad"[4] (Havana . . . is a large city but not a great city)—Buenos Aires seemed like a stimulating and lively urban center with everything he would need to engage in his intellectual endeavors.

From the outset Piñera made a concerted effort to establish connections with Argentine and foreign authors, from whom he often solicited articles for *Orígenes*. Adolfo de Obieta, editor of *Papeles de Buenos Aires* and the son of the Argentine author Macedonio Fernández, was one of Piñera's first important contacts in Buenos Aires. Piñera had corresponded intermittently with Obieta from Cuba since submitting a poem to *Papeles de Buenos Aires* in 1943,[5] and it was through him that Piñera was introduced, just weeks after settling in Buenos Aires, to the Polish novelist and playwright Witold Gombrowicz (1904–69).

Gombrowicz had come to Argentina in August 1939 on the inaugural voyage of a Polish ocean liner. He had been invited to give a series of lectures in Buenos Aires, and intended to return to his homeland after a brief visit. But the German invasion and occupation of Poland in September of the same year changed his plans and his fate. Gombrowicz ended up spending the next twenty-four years in Argentina. Despite his current status as a major figure in world literature, Gombrowicz was something of a nobody who lived a makeshift existence during his exile in Buenos Aires. In this regard, Piñera shared much in common with the Polish author, with whom he felt united from the start by a common struggle to make names for themselves in the midst of a rather inaccessible intellectual community. Piñera's early association with Gombrowicz was especially important since it led to numerous collaborations and to a relationship that would forever leave its mark on his personality and his work.

Early Encounters: Gombrowicz and Borges

Piñera's collaboration in the Spanish-language translation of Gombrowicz's first novel, *Ferdydurke* (1937), was among his most significant experiences in Argentina. In many ways the project of translating this surrealist tragicomedy about a man who regresses to his teenage years left an indelible impression on the young Cuban writer. The relatively complicated undertaking was carried out by a group of young authors, which included, among others, Adolfo de Obieta, Carlos Coldaroli, Piñera, and his Cuban friend Humberto Rodríguez Tomeu, who had also recently moved to Buenos Aires.

By the time Piñera met the Polish author, three chapters of his novel had already been translated, but soon after joining the translation committee Piñera, who allegedly had the most time on his hands, was named its president. The group met frequently in the Café Rex on the Calle Querandí, where Gombrowicz would arrive with pages he had translated into what Piñera referred to as a "faltering Spanish."[6] The committee members would then refine and rework Gombrowicz's version as needed. According to Humberto Rodríguez Tomeu's account, working at the Café Rex became too distracting, so once he and Piñera assumed control of the translation, they completed it with Gombrowicz in the apartment that the two Cubans shared at Calle Corrientes 758.[7]

After nearly a year of work, *Ferdydurke* was published in April 1947 by Editorial Argos, an Argentine publishing house for whom Piñera had worked briefly as a translator of French literature. According to Piñera's fascinating testimony in his essay "Gombrowicz por él mismo" (Gombrowicz on Himself), the Polish author was obsessed with the release of the novel, which he envisioned as a momentous literary event. Months before the publication of *Ferdydurke* in Argentina, Gombrowicz launched an impressive propagandistic campaign. Determined to communicate his moral and aesthetic doctrines to as large an audience as possible, he urged Piñera and other members of the translation committee to praise *Ferdydurke* in public and to speak of the novel's many supposed admirers. To promote the novel Gombrowicz also composed a series of laudatory prospectuses that he hoped to publish in various Argentine literary journals, and with the same intention he wrote the script of a so-called interview that he and Piñera read over Radio del Mundo in April 1947. In this self-serving dialogue, the Polish author underscored the novel's great importance and communicated one of his principal literary tenets: "Nosotros, las naciones menores, debemos dejar la tutela de París y tratar de comprendernos directamente. . . . *Ferdydurke* nos abre el camino para conseguir la independencia, la soberanía espiritual, frente a las culturas mayores que nos convierten en eternos alumnos."[8] (We, the lesser nations, should forget the tutelage of Paris and try to understand each other directly. . . . *Ferdydurke* opens the way for us to achieve independence, spiritual sovereignty, in the face of higher cultures that turn us into eternal students.)

Despite feeling that Gombrowicz went overboard in his promotion of *Ferdydurke* in Argentina, Piñera believed passionately in the novel's literary and cultural importance. To be sure, both authors saw *Ferdydurke* as something of a standard-bearer of change that would have a drastic impact on Latin American letters. Though their frequently conflicting views made for a rather antagonistic relationship at times, the two authors were united by a common desire to wage literary battles against the intellectual establishment, and they hoped that *Ferdydurke* would serve as a call to combat.

A brief critical appreciation of the novel, signed by Piñera and printed on the front flap of the first edition, attests to Piñera's symbolic enlistment in Gombrowicz's literary war. In it Piñera praises *Ferdydurke*'s literary merits and insists that the intentionally provocative novel will at once serve to scandalize the intellectual community and to promote cultural reform. He concludes by declaring—with the admixture of humor and seriousness so typical of both authors—that the "battle of the ferdeydurkistas" in Latin America had begun.

A few days after the publication of *Ferdydurke*, Gombrowicz dedicated a copy of the novel to his Cuban friend. In the inscription the Polish author named Piñera the official leader of a new literary movement: "A tu inteligencia e intransigencia se debe este nacimiento de *Ferdydurke*. Te otorgo, pues, la dignidad de Jefe del Ferdydurkismo Sudamericano y ordeno que todos los ferdydurkistas te veneren como a mí mismo. ¡Sonó la hora! ¡Al combate!"[9] (To your intelligence and intransigence *Ferdydurke* owes its birth. I grant you, therefore, the rank of Chief of South American Ferdydurkism and I command that all Ferdydurkists venerate you as they do me. The time has come! To combat!)

The translation of *Ferdydurke* was relatively well received by certain members of Argentina's intellectual community, but it was by no means the resounding success that Gombrowicz and Piñera had envisioned.

As Piñera pointed out years later, while the novel did serve to increase Gombrowicz's literary stature in Argentina, the so-called battle of *Ferdydurke* was not won until it was published in Paris more than a decade after its release in Argentina.[10] In the meantime Gombrowicz, often with Piñera at his side, continued to provoke and scandalize the Argentine intelligentsia.

During his first period of exile in Argentina, Piñera met and associated with many members of the Argentine intelligentsia, including Borges, Eduardo Mallea, Macedonio Fernández, Ezequiel Martínez Estrada, Oliverio Girondo, Adolfo Bioy Casares, and Ernesto Sábato. Among these intellectuals it seems that Jorge Luis Borges first captivated Piñera's attention. Luckily for Piñera, Borges was likewise one of the first in Argentina to take notice of him.

Piñera met Borges in March 1946 through Adolfo de Obieta, whose father, Macedonio Fernández, was a close friend of the author of *Ficciones*. It has been suggested that the importance of Piñera's acquaintance with Borges and his connections with the *Sur* group have been exaggerated.[11] However, it is my opinion that this important aspect of Piñera's life in Buenos Aires has actually been downplayed and greatly underestimated. Piñera's relationship with Borges was by no means intimate, but it was one of mutual respect, and it lasted for many years. Most of Piñera's dealings with Borges were related to intellectual and literary pursuits—collaborations in *Los Anales de Buenos Aires* and *Cuentos breves y extraordinarios*, lectures on Cuban literature at the Biblioteca Nacional, solicitation of original Borges texts for *Ciclón*—but the two authors also took part in activities of a more personal nature. In his correspondence with José Rodríguez Feo, for example, Piñera mentioned afternoon teas with Borges and his mother, Leonor Acevedo, dinner parties, and tours of the Biblioteca Nacional.

Enrico Mario Santí is certainly correct to point out that Piñera could not have felt completely at ease in what he refers to as the rarified air of Buenos Aires' literary circles. Piñera's daring criticism of Argentine literature and culture in articles such as "Notas sobre la literatura argentina de hoy" [Notes on Argentine Literature of Today] and "El País del Arte" clearly supports this opinion. However, it is important to point out that Borges himself often felt somewhat out of place among other Argentine intellectuals and even among some members of the *Sur* group. Borges's relationship with Victoria Ocampo is a case in point, as Rodríguez Monegal has pointed out. Though Borges respected Ocampo greatly and remained faithful to *Sur*, the two approached matters of life, culture, and literature from radically different angles.[12]

It is not surprising, therefore, that when Borges was offered a position as editor of the recently founded *Los Anales de Buenos Aires* in 1946, he gladly accepted. Borges's eclectic tastes and his vivid imagination were clearly represented in the issues of *Los Anales* that he edited. Unlike the editors of *Sur*, who mainly sought out texts by famous, well-established authors, Borges went to great lengths to publish works by young writers who shared his literary sensibilities.[13] Among the young authors that Borges discovered were three of Latin America's greatest short story writers: the Uruguayan Felisberto Hernández, Julio Cortázar, whose classic story "Casa tomada" (House Taken Over) first appeared in *Los Anales*,[14] and Piñera himself, who contributed several texts to the journal while Borges was its editor.

Piñera's first significant contact with Borges took place at a perfect moment, that is, shortly after Piñera submitted his story "El muñeco" (The Dummy) to a literary contest organized by *Sur*. The members of *Sur*, who correctly interpreted the story as a mockery of Juan Perón and Peronism, were understandably not willing to take the risk of publishing it.[15] Borges, who was an anti-Peronist to the core, must have been impressed and delighted by the originality of Piñera's story, given that shortly after reading it, he extended two important invitations to the young Cuban author. First, he urged Piñera to submit an original short story to *Los Anales*, and second, he invited him to present a conference on Cuban literature at the Sociedad Argentina de Escritores, of which Borges was president. Piñera accepted both offers.

Piñera's "En el insomnio" (Insomnia), a masterful single-paragraph story about a man who resorts to suicide as an escape from insomnia, appeared in the October 1946 issue of the journal. The story, which Piñera wrote specifically for *Los Anales*, is especially interesting when read in light of Borges's own fascination with sleeping and sleeplessness, and its relationship to Borges's poem "Insomnio" (1936) is notable. In this text the poetic voice speaks of insomnia as horrible immortality, dreadful wakefulness, and permanent death. In much the same way, the desperate protagonist of Piñera's story finds that insomnia is an eternal punishment since even after blowing his brains out he cannot get to sleep.

We should note that "En el insomnio" might have been inspired by Borges's own drawn-out battle with insomnia, but it also evoked a more immediate personal crisis that Borges was undergoing when the two authors met in 1946.[16] In that year Borges was rejected by Estela Canto, a sprightly Uruguayan woman to whom he had proposed marriage in late 1945. According to James Woodall, tension and arguments with Estela—largely provoked by her expressed dislike for Borges's mother—eventually led the author to consider suicide. "On the fifth-floor balcony at a friend's," Woodall writes, "[Borges] had contemplated throwing himself into the void."[17] Though I have not been able to determine if Piñera was aware of this detail, it seems fair to say that his story about a man whose suicide fails to free him from his existential anguish must have made quite an impression on Borges in his time of personal crisis.

Agitating the Argentine Intelligentsia

Given Piñera's marked tendency to stir up literary scandals at home, it is hardly surprising that he was quick to turn Borges and other members of the Argentine intelligentsia into targets of feisty critical appraisals. Piñera's great respect for Borges did not deter him from reading a captious commentary on Argentine literature over state radio in Buenos Aires. Piñera's eagerness to express publicly his polemical opinions harked back to his provocative run-ins with Mañach, Lezama, Vitier, and other Cuban intellectuals. He was positively proud of his growing reputation as a polemicist in Cuba—"Me dicen que la Habana quedó exorcizada con mi partida"[18] (They tell me that Havana was exorcized by my departure), he wrote to Lezama in 1946—and he apparently saw no reason why he should not stir things up a bit in Buenos Aires.

It is worth noting that Witold Gombrowicz clearly had a profound influence on Piñera when it came to agitating the Argentine literary community. It follows, then, that the latter's brash decision to read his unfavorable assessment of Argentine letters over Radio del Estado in the summer of 1946, while working on a daily basis with Gombrowicz on the translation of *Ferdydurke*, was most certainly encouraged by the Polish author. The dull title of the talk—"Notas sobre la literatura argentina de hoy" (Notes on Argentine Literature of Today)—contrasted sharply with Piñera's unique and contentious appraisal of the literature of one of Latin America's most distinguished intellectual circles.

In his talk Piñera used the Greek myth of Tantalus as a point of departure. Tantalus was the son of Zeus, whose audacious arrogance and betrayal of the gods—he tried to turn them into cannibals by serving them a stew made from his cooked son—led to a brutal punishment. He was sent to Hades where he was condemned to remain eternally submerged in a pool of water that disappeared when he tried to drink it. Above him, branches laden with fruits were eternally just out of his reach.

Piñera commenced by comparing the practitioners of Argentine letters to this doomed figure of Greek mythology:

> Si quisiéramos definir por medio de una imagen o metáfora lo más representativo de la literatura argentina de hoy diríamos que es tantálica, que sus escritores son tantálicos ellos mismos y que segregan esa sustancia—lógicamente nueva—que se llama tantalismo.[19]

> [If we wanted to define by way of an image or metaphor the most representative aspect of Argentine Literature of today we would say that it is tantalic, that its authors themselves are tantalic and that they secrete that substance—logically new—called tantalism.]

Later in the same essay Piñera added that "el escritor [argentino] persiste atado a una segunda naturaleza—ornamentación, fórmula formal—y el verdadero mundo de la realidad se le escapa, o al menos, desdibuja.[20] (The [Argentine] writer remains tied to a second nature—ornamentation, formal formulas—, and the true world of reality escapes him, or at the very least, it becomes blurry.) Piñera's critique of the supposed Argentine predisposition to bookishness and their predilection for formal modes of expression is especially interesting when considered in light of his outspoken criticism of certain Cuban authors, whose writings he had frequently, and often unjustly, ridiculed for similar "shortcomings."

Piñera claimed to be especially bothered by Borges's "tantalismo" since he believed that despite possessing all of the necessary tools to become a world-class writer, Borges had failed to achieve such prominence because of his alleged obsession with bookishness, complex language, lavish imagery, and Byzantine topics. He wrapped up his assessment of Borges with a rather flippant remark that underscored his increasing comfort with his role as provocateur: "En este caso se encuentra Borges. Por eso mismo es hoy el logógrafo redivivo 'par excellence' de las letras americanas."[21] (Borges finds himself in such a situation. For that reason he is the new logographer "par excellence" of American letters.)

Impudent as it is, Piñera's appraisal of the writings of his Argentine counterparts is nonetheless quite insightful, and judging from a comment that Piñera made in a letter to Lezama the following week—"Este breve ensayo mío es polémico y no se anda por las ramas. Me parece (y aquí me lo han agradecido muchos escritores) que planteo el caso argentino con bastante claridad"[22] (This brief article of mine is polemical and it doesn't go off track. It seems to me [and here many writers have thanked me for it] that I present the Argentine case quite clearly)—the young author clearly saw his commentary as an important critique of a group of authors whose influence had begun to spread throughout Latin America and Europe.

2: FROM THE OUTSIDE LOOKING IN: EXILE IN ARGENTINA

It may come as a surprise that Borges was not upset by Piñera's frank and somewhat unfavorable judgment of his writing, but we should recall that the two authors had much in common when it came to their unorthodox approaches to literature and culture. Shortly after hearing Piñera's presentation of the essay on state radio, Borges called him to request permission to publish it in *Los Anales de Buenos Aires*. In a rather amusing passage in his memoirs Piñera referred to Borges's unexpected reaction with the following comments:

> Borges reaccionó rogándome le cediera el ensayo para publicarlo en *Anales de Buenos Aires*...; al mismo tiempo, me hizo saber que aceptaba lo del tantalismo en lo que a él se refería, y por último, a manera de confirmación y soberanía insertaba en dicho mismo número de *Anales*, y junto a mi Nota, uno de sus relatos más tantálicos—"Los inmortales."[23]

> [Borges reacted by begging me to hand over my essay so he could publish it in *Anales de Buenos Aires*...; at the same time, he let me know that he accepted all that about tantalism as far as his own case was concerned, and lastly, as a means of confirmation and sovereignty he inserted in the same number of *Anales*, next to my article, one of his most tantalic stories—"The Immortal."]

The article was eventually published in both *Anales* and *Orígenes*, and Piñera's reputation as a polemicist was thus further solidified among the members of the two literary communities that had become frequent victims of his critical bite.

※

In Buenos Aires Piñera did not limit himself to critiquing the literature of that country. He also spoke and wrote about the past and present state of Cuban letters for an audience that for the most part knew little about the Caribbean island. In his article "Los valores más jóvenes de la literatura cubana" (The Youngest Figures of Cuban Literature), published in December 1946 in the Argentine newspaper *La Nación*, Piñera started out by summarizing his country's literary history for his Argentine audience. Echoing his previous polemical critiques of Cuban culture, Piñera compared his country's underdeveloped literary history to an undercooked pot of soup. "La literatura cubana está haciéndose. Tenemos la esperanza de que en breve podremos llamar a todas las puertas para decir '¡La sopa está a punto!'[24] . . . Algunas veces hemos creído que—¡por fin, al fin, qué alegría! . . . —pero pronto se reparaba en que el fuego no había vencido aun la dureza de los alimentos." (Cuban literature is being prepared. We hope that soon we can knock on every door and say "The soup's ready!" . . . A few times we have believed that—finally!, at last!, what joy! ... —but quickly noticed that the flame had not overcome the toughness of the food.)

Piñera was careful not to suggest that Argentine literature was somehow superior to that of Cuba or other countries in Latin America. Throughout his exile in Buenos Aires the Cuban author consistently avoided bolstering the image of a literary circle that he felt had a tendency toward self-aggrandizement. By pointing out in the article that the literary traditions of the rest of Latin America also showed signs of backwardness, for instance, Piñera insinuated that Argentine letters were not so far ahead of the rest of the continent as some of the country's intellectuals seemed to believe.

In his candid assessment of Cuban literature Piñera refrained from direct criticism of Lezama and the *Orígenes* poets, but he implicitly downplayed the importance of their intellectual enterprise by noting that his country had still not managed to produce representative writers and texts or to excel in any particular literary genre. Later in the article, Piñera conceded that since 1936 Cuban poets had written many texts worth reading—he specifically mentioned Lezama's *Enemigo rumor* (1941)—but he also observed (with a hint of sarcasm to be sure) that Cuban poetry of the 1940s was among the most refined, extravagant, and hermetic verse in Latin America. It was surely not a coincidence that these same qualities were the focus of his criticism in "Notas sobre la literatura argentina de hoy."

By the end of 1946 Piñera had begun to feel at ease with his role as provocateur in Buenos Aires, and his frequent meetings with Witold Gombrowicz only served to enhance his polemical bent. The tepid reception of *Ferdydurke* by the Argentine literary community moved Gombrowicz to wage a critical campaign against the members of the *Sur* group, and especially its leader, Victoria Ocampo. In the summer of 1947 the Polish writer invited Piñera and Humberto Rodríguez Tomeu to help him put together an anonymous pamphlet that he envisioned as a mockery of Argentina's most exclusive literary circle. According to Rodríguez Tomeu, Piñera and Gombrowicz argued, as they often did, about the format and content of the proposed publication, and after failing to reconcile their differences each decided to compose his own pamphlet.[25]

It is important to note, though, that Piñera often corrected and collaborated in Gombrowicz's texts in Spanish, and the style of the writing indicates that he clearly had a hand in the final version of Gombrowicz's "Aurora: Revista de la Resistencia" (Aurora: Review of the Resistance),[26] a four-page pamphlet with several brief articles and commentaries. In "Aurora" Gombrowicz, with Piñera's complicity, took aim at various members of the *Sur* group, who he ridiculed for their penchant for seriousness, lofty erudition, and formality. The brief opening article starts with a series of rhetorical questions that aimed to rile up the members of the intellectual circle:

> ¿Por qué la gente no es metafísicamente asirio-babilónica como Borges, monumentalmente castiza como Larreta, y orientalmente árabe como Capdevila?[27] ¿Por qué al tonto pueblo le gusta la palabra directa y ágil mientras su Literatura a menudo se deleita con un Verbo ornamental, retórico, rebuscado y un tanto estéril? ¿Por qué será que un inculto vendedor de diarios se permite expresarse con más soberanía, originalidad y belleza que todas las revistas que vende junto con todas las personas cultas que las compran?[28]

> [Why aren't people metaphysically Assyrio-Babylonic like Borges, monumentally authentic like Larreta, and orientally Arabic like Capdevila? Why does the simple public like direct and agile words while their Literature often delights in ornamental, rhetorical, contrived and somewhat sterile Language? Why is it that the uncultured newspaper vendor is allowed to express himself with more sovereignty, originality, and beauty than all of the magazines that he sells and all of the cultured people who buy them?]

The spiteful tone of the pamphlet is in keeping with Gombrowicz's frustration with certain members of the Argentine literary community who he felt had given *Ferdydurke* a lukewarm reception. Even before the novel's publication Gombrowicz was deeply bothered that important Argentine intellectuals such as Raimundo Lida, Arturo Capdevila, and Ernesto Sábato had criticized the so-called uncultured language used in the translation. In fact, Gombrowicz had urged Piñera to have the translation read and corrected by a respected stylist like Ezequiel Martínez Estrada or Borges, but this never happened. The result was a translation full of colloquial language that certain Argentine readers found inappropriate. In a letter to Piñera, Gombrowicz expressed his dismay that Raimundo Lida—who was secretary of *Sur* at the time—considered the translation to be "absolutely awful." The Polish author was equally disappointed that Ernesto Sábato objected to the use of certain *cubanismos* such as "carro" instead of "coche."[29]

Though Gombrowicz was frustrated by not having won the recognition that he desired from his writing, he adamantly refused to curry favor of the *Sur* group, as he explained with characteristic sarcasm in a 1968 interview: "Si algún renombre pude alcanzar en Argentina, no fue como autor, sino como el solo y único escritor extranjero que no hizo el peregrinaje al salón de la señora Ocampo."[30] (If I was able to achieve any fame in Argentina, it was not as an author, but as the only foreign writer who never made the pilgrimage to Victoria Ocampo's waiting room.)

Despite the fact that he admitted frequently that Latin America and Eastern Europe were underdeveloped and therefore less "mature" than Western European countries, Gombrowicz was especially irked by the Argentine obsession with French literature and culture. In "Aurora" Gombrowicz implicitly evoked this theme when he ridiculed members of the *Sur* group for placing too much importance on European artistic and literary trends:

> Ese asunto de la inmadurez americana y de la madurez europea está ya muy gastado. Ni América es tan inmadura, ni Europa es tan madura. El que quiere conseguir la soberanía espiritual frente a las personas o culturas mayores debe comprender *primero*: que los mayores también son inmaduros, aunque en distinto plano; *segundo*: que nos conviene apoyarnos firmemente sobre *nuestra propia realidad*.[31]

> [That subject of American immaturity and European maturity is already very overused. America is neither so immature, nor is Europe so mature. He who wishes to achieve spiritual sovereignty in the face of older peoples or cultures should understand *first*: that the elders are also immature, although on a different level; *second*: that it behooves us to ground ourselves firmly in *our own reality*.]

Though Gombrowicz was ostensibly mocking the vogue of things French among many of the members of the *Sur* group, Victoria Ocampo was eventually singled out in critiques of a more personal nature. In a short piece dedicated to Argentina's leading woman of letters Gombrowicz opened with sarcastic praise for the "Suma Sacerdotista del culto inmaduro de la Madurez"[32] (High Priestess of the immature cult of Maturity) and went on to deride Ocampo's unapologetic devotion to French literature and culture, which had long been a bone of contention for her detractors. According to Doris Meyer, many intellectuals felt that Victoria Ocampo was a "foreignizer" who essentially neglected her Argentine roots in her writing.[33] Indeed, for years Victoria Ocampo wrote almost exclusively in French and also discussed literature in that language. Meyer notes, however, that though Ocampo was at times "unjustly biased against the language of her own country," this was largely due to the fact that her education tended to favor French and English cultures over those of Spain and Latin America.[34]

The author(s) of "Aurora" capitalized on these details by exaggerating Ocampo's predilection for things French. Gombrowicz suggested, for example, that Ocampo regressed into an adolescent state—much like the protagonist of *Ferdydurke*—by the mere thought of the French poet and critic Paul Valéry (1871–1945): "Se convierte en una niña temblorosa cuando se enfrenta con lo que ella misma llama 'Valéry y

Francia.' ¡Muera Victoria Ocampo! Vedla cómo se esquiva, se aniquila, se inmaduriza ante Valéry."[35] (She becomes a tremulous little girl when she comes face-to-face with what she herself calls "Valéry and France." Down with Victoria Ocampo! Look how she withdraws, she deteriorates, she becomes immature in the presence of Valéry.)

Although "Aurora" stands out for its hostile, cynical, and overly critical tone, Gombrowicz and Piñera were certainly not alone in their harsh criticism of *Sur* and the literary circle that surrounded it. The magazine had detractors throughout Latin America, and despite being one of the most significant Hispanic literary journals of its day, it was at times the object of scorn. Even Borges, a highly unorthodox writer and intellectual when compared to some of the other members of *Sur*— and especially Victoria Ocampo—had certain reservations about *Sur* and its members. According to Emir Rodríguez Monegal, for instance, Borges and Ocampo "had vastly different views about literature and life, about culture, and mainly about what a journal should look like."[36] As Borges himself put it, "The magazine was run in a very strange way. . . . Besides, Victoria had strange ideas about what a literary journal was: she wanted to publish only pieces by famous writers . . . a collection of pieces by famous people does not make a journal."[37]

It is important to note that even if their flippant criticism of the journal did ruffle some feathers among the members of *Sur*, they were for the most part either not taken seriously or ignored altogether. But these two "disrespectful" authors were not dissuaded by the relative ineffectiveness of their attacks, since they enjoyed delivering blows, ineffective as they were, to the intellectual upper crust. While both authors were united by their common tastes for literary scandal, they also took pride in their self-sufficiency when it came to waging intellectual battles. Since the two authors allegedly disagreed on a number of issues concerning "Aurora," Piñera decided to work on the sly on his own attack on the *Sur* group.[38] In terms of format and content, "Victrola: Revista de la Insistencia" (Victrola: Review of Insistence) is very similar to "Aurora," and like its predecessor, which hit the press one day earlier, only about one hundred copies were printed and distributed among the Argentine literary community.

The title of the four-page pamphlet, besides its obvious evocation of the name "Victoria," implicitly poked fun at what Piñera saw as the tendency of Argentine writers to copy the literary trends of other countries. Like the gramophones that produced sounds mechanically, Piñera suggested in a series of highly sarcastic sketches that many contemporary writers were more concerned with reproducing old literary trends than with creating new ones.

In his sarcastic commentaries, which perfectly reflect his tendency to lace literary criticism with ridicule and wit, Piñera parodied "Aurora" and its condemnation of elevated, ornamental rhetoric. As if to take the side of the group he had so often derided, Piñera offered an ironic defense of loftiness in the humorous opening section of the pamphlet, entitled "Pasaje sobre las alturas" (Passage on Loftiness):

> Señoras y señores. Entro enseguida en materia. Mi tema es la altura. Sin altura me sofoco. Lo de abajo me repugna, el sótano me da mareos, el subterráneo me apaga, la catacumba me simplifica. Yo quiero ser complicado, difícil, yo quiero elevarme.... Hay que elevarse ... encaramarse sobre los hombros de Valéry y aspirar desde allí el tonificante oxígeno de sus alturas.[39]

> [Ladies and gentlemen. I shall get to the point right away. My theme is loftiness. Without loftiness I suffocate. Lowliness disgusts me, the basement makes me nauseous, the subterranean turns me off, the catacomb simplifies me. I want to be complicated and difficult, I want to lift myself up.... One must lift oneself up ... climb onto the shoulders of Valéry and breathe in from there the invigorating oxygen of his loftiness.]

In the section entitled "Defensa Francesa" (French Defense) Piñera humorously declared his opposition to "Aurora," while pretending to defend Victoria Ocampo: "AURORA ataca a Victoria Ocampo. La intocable. Amurallada en Sur.... Y todo porque Victoria adora a Valéry. Desaparece ante Valéry. No respira en presencia de Valéry.... Defendemos a Victoria contra AURORA."[40] (AURORA attacks Victoria Ocampo. The untouchable. Walled in at *Sur*.... And all because Victoria adores Valéry. She vanishes in the presence of Valéry. She does not breathe in the presence of Valéry.... We defend Victoria against AURORA.) In "Victrola" Piñera predictably cited France and England as sources of his intellectual enlightenment, but he added that *Sur* was also a major fountain of inspiration in his quest for refined expression.[41]

In 1947, shortly after composing "Victrola," Piñera penned one of his most significant critical essays, "El País del Arte." In the article, which was published in *Orígenes* in the winter of that year, Piñera ridiculed contemporary writers, artists, and intellectuals for their falseness and their lack of originality, among other things. One of the most interesting aspects of the article, which is something of an anomaly among Piñera's critical writings, is the lack of references to specific places or individuals. Piñera's "País del Arte" is at once Cuba and Argentina, but it is also any place where artistic form is given more importance than content, and where attitudes about art are governed by false standards or preconceived concepts.

Despite the fact that Piñera mentioned no names, certain passages of the essay pointed to specific individuals or groups. His criticism of those who mixed art and religion, for example, was clearly aimed at Lezama Lima and members of his literary circle, whose writings Piñera often ridiculed for their Catholic bookishness. In "El País del Arte," Piñera contended that introducing religion into art was especially problematic since the artist given to adoration of any kind usually ended up sacrificing his sovereignty as a creator: "Allí donde se le erige un altar, donde se le rinde culto se presenta como todo menos como arte. . . . Pierde soberanía el que adora."[42] (The place where an altar is erected, where homage is paid, reveals itself to be anything but art. . . . He who adores loses sovereignty.)

Piñera's mockery of attitudes about art in "El País del Arte" is infused with the voice of Gombrowicz. In fact, Piñera directly referred to the Polish author in order to give emphasis to a major point of his article, that is, that too many contemporary artists and intellectuals praised, imitated, and paid homage to works of the so-called masters without really understanding them: "¿Es qué nadie percibe que el arte no resiste la simulación? ¿Es qué—como dice Gombrowicz—alguien puede conmoverse sin conmoverse y decir que comprende sin comprender?"[43] (Is it that no one realizes that art doesn't tolerate pretense? Is it that—as Gombrowicz says—someone can be moved without being moved and say he understands without understanding?) Piñera explained that such a phenomenon was especially evident in the frequent exhibitions held at the homes of painters. According to Piñera, such gatherings, which had become increasingly popular, were farcical in nature since the so-called art enthusiasts in attendance "interpreted" the paintings according to convention rather than personal conviction.

To a certain extent Piñera's essay echoes Gombrowicz's conviction that the adoration of art and literature had led many contemporary artists to shun creativity and originality in favor of impersonation and imitation. Gombrowicz was convinced that such a disposition among artists simply bred mediocrity, a notion that he expressed in many of his writings. In the fourth chapter of *Ferdydurke*, "Prefacio de Filifor forrado de niño" (Introduction to Philifor Honeycombed with Childness), for example, Pimko chastises his students for their obsession with Shakespeare, Goethe, and Chopin, and insists that their veneration of the masters has turned them into eternal servants of Art with a capital "A."

> Mas vosotros, en vez de procuraros concepciones y opiniones según vuestra propia medida y concordantes con vuestra realidad, os adornáis con plumas ajenas—y he aquí por qué os transformáis en eternos candidatos y aspirantes a la grandeza y la perfección. Eternamente indolentes y siempre mediocres, os volvéis sirvientes, alumnos y admiradores del Arte. . . . Porque todo

eso es sólo imitación, es aprendido de los maestros—y vosotros no hacéis otra cosa que agarraros al faldón de los genios.[44]

[But you, instead of equipping yourselves with ideas and opinions suited to your measure and in harmony with your situation, adorn yourselves with borrowed plumage—and that is why you transform yourselves into eternal candidates, eternal aspirants to greatness and perfection. Eternally impotent and always mediocre, you become servants, pupils and admirers of Art. . . . Because it is all only imitation, repetition of what you learned from the masters—and all you do is cling to the coattails of genius.][45]

Like Gombrowicz, Piñera believed that far too often writers and artists aspired to reproduce the style of their predecessors at the expense of losing their own voice, as the following remark from "El País de Arte" suggests:

La aspiración—muchas veces secreta, otras, expresa—de cien de estos artistas del país del arte es llegar a escribir o a pintar como un Kafka o un Picasso. . . ; la obra de estos grandes artistas se les ha convertido en una meta, pero meta trágica puesto que el demonio de la imitación se hace pagar nada menos que con el alma del quien imita.[46]

[The aspiration oftentimes secret, other times explicit—of a hundred of these artists from the country of art is to be able to write or paint like a Kafka or a Picasso. . . ; the work of these great artists has become their goal, but a tragic goal given that the devil of imitation makes he who imitates pay with nothing less than his soul.]

The two authors' aggressive criticism of their literary counterparts often served to underscore their bitterness and frustration over their own lack of success. Moreover, while Piñera and Gombrowicz both went to great lengths to denounce the elitism and snobbery that they claimed had taken control of contemporary intellectual circles, their own views and attitudes often came across as snobbish, arrogant, and self-serving. To be sure, through their mockery and faultfinding they implicitly suggested that their own approaches to art and literature were more genuine and original than those of the so-called literary establishment.

It seems fair to say that had the two toned down their criticism and shown more respect for their fellow artists, they might have in turn garnered the esteem and admiration of more of their colleagues. Like true polemicists, however, Piñera and Gombrowicz were not interested in giving up their assumed roles as disrespectful authors and agitators of the intelligentsia.

The Disrespectful Author Comes Home

Shortly after "El País del Arte" appeared in *Orígenes* in winter 1947, Piñera returned to Cuba. Within days of his arrival in January 1948 he managed to aggravate the Cuban intellectual community through a series of bold comments in an interview with Ernesto Ardura of the Havana newspaper *El Mundo*. The article's headline — "El Tono de la Vida Cubana de Hoy es el Disparate, Afirma Virgilio Piñera" (The Tone of Cuban Life Today is Foolishness, Virgilio Piñera Affirms) — was an appropriate announcement of the return of Cuba's self-proclaimed disrespectful author. In his conversation with Ardura, Piñera made a number of sweeping allegations against Cuba's stifling social, economic, and cultural climate.

One of Piñera's typically categorical statements, part of which was printed in the article's subtitle, epitomized his affinity for stirring up scandal: "En lo político, lo económico, aun en la simple relación de personas domina el absurdo. . . . Tal parece que todos [los cubanos] se hubieran propuesto este esquema enrevesado de razonar: pregunta, ¿se levanta usted temprano?; respuesta, mi tía se llama Chacha."[47] (In things political, things economic, even in simple relations between people the absurd dominates. . . . It seems as if all [Cubans] had proposed this complicated scheme of reasoning: question, do you get up early?: response, my aunt's name is Chacha.) Given that he had just arrived from two years in exile in Argentina, and had been back in Cuba for only a few days, Piñera's comments must have seemed especially audacious to many readers. To those who knew him best, however, Piñera's criticism of Cuban life and culture served as a reminder that he was back in town and that more polemics would likely follow.

Indeed, later that year Piñera became embroiled in a nasty literary scandal, which erupted shortly after the October 23 debut of his play *Electra Garrigó*. Apparently unprepared for this radically original work, but also eager to beat the provocateur at his own game, many critics such as Mirta Aguirre — codirector of *La Gaceta del Caribe* and longtime detractor of the *Orígenes* poets — and the Spanish-born theater director Luis Amado Blanco, responded to the Piñera's Heleno-Cuban tragicomedy with harsh critiques. Ironically, much of the unfavorable criticism was aimed at what would later be considered the play's most original aspects: its colloquial language, local color, and its atmosphere of absurdity, irreverence, and humor.

According to Lezama, who commented on the play's debut in a letter to José Rodríguez Feo, the local theater critics were not only unimpressed by the play, but were especially blunt in their articulation of their distaste for it. "La crítica idiota y burguesa, le ha sido tremendamente hostil" (The idiotic, bourgeois critics have been tremendously hostile with him), he wrote to Pepe.[48] Lezama added, however, that given Piñera's constant desire to stir up a "sabroso escandalito"[49] (a tasty little scandal), the harsh appraisals of so many Cuban critics was probably just what he wanted. Few people knew Piñera's polemic bent as well as Lezama, and his observations turned out to be prophetic.

Piñera responded to the negative reviews of *Electra* with a scathing article, "¡Ojo con el crítico . . . !" (Beware of the Critic. . . !), which was published in November in the theater journal *Prometeo*. In the article Piñera warned the literary community to beware of what he classified as the three most dangerous types of critics: the uncultured critic, the Philistine critic, and the failed-artist-turned-critic. He reserved especially emphatic denunciation for Cuba's many frustrated dramatists-turned-critics, who he derided for harboring so much resentment over his success that they found fault with every aspect of his plays: "Su 'constante' . . . es el resentimiento; un profundo resentimiento que lo lleva, sistemáticamente, a negarlo todo en materia de teatro: desde la simple colocación de la bambalina hasta la obra misma que se estrena."[50] (His "constant" . . . is resentment; a profound resentment that causes him to refute systematically everything on the subject of theater: from the simple positioning of the backdrop to the very work that's premiering.) By way of conclusion Piñera insisted that the goal of such "philistines" was to impede the presentation of any dramatic work that would serve to reveal their own failure in the genre.

Piñera's caustic article provoked an immediate and severe response from Luis Amado Blanco, who was at the time the director of La Asociación de Redactores Teatrales y Cinematógrafos (ARTYC). On December 15, 1948, Amado Blanco published his response to Piñera in several Havana newspapers and journals. More than a decade later in 1959, Piñera managed to settle the score with Amado Blanco in the pages of *Revolución*. He summarized the 1948 incident as follows:

> Uno de los acuerdos de ARTYC fue la publicación, en todos los periódicos y revistas de La Habana, de la respuesta de Amado Blanco ("Los intocables," 15 diciembre 1948). Piñera,[51] que se consideraba con el derecho a contestar, acudió inútilmente a los diarios: en todos ellos se le expresó que era acuerdo firme de ARTYC su irradiación total de todo cuanto tuviera relación con las actividades teatrales. En una palabra Piñera se vio convertido, por las iras de Amado Blanco, en un apestado. Y tanto fue así que su pieza "Falsa Alarma" . . . fue precipitadamente retirada del cartel.[52]

> [One of the agreements of the ARTYC was the publication, in all of the newspapers and magazines of Havana, of the response from Amado Blanco ("The Untouchables," 15 December 1948). Piñera, who felt he had the right

to answer, appealed unsuccessfully to the dailies: at all of them he was told that his total irradiation from everything that had to do with theatrical activities was a firm decision of the ARTYC. In a word, Piñera saw himself converted, by the ire of Amado Blanco, into a man infected with the plague. And it was so much so that his play "False Alarm" . . . was quickly withdrawn from the theatre bill.]

Carlos Espinosa-Domínguez has observed that the members of ARTYC urged the editors of *Prometeo* to publish an official apology for Piñera's article.[53] They also wrote letters to various organizations proposing a boycott of Piñera's theater in Havana, where the debuts of *Falsa alarma* and *Jesús* had been announced. Amado Blanco, for his part, spoke with Piñera's brother, Humberto, who he hoped would be able to convince Virgilio to write a letter of apology. The author of *Electra* categorically denied the request, and instead responded to the increasing tension with a letter that he sent to the press. In it Piñera reiterated the major points of "¡Ojo con el crítico!" and with characteristic defiance, refused to back down.

Not surprisingly, Virgilio Piñera never fulfilled the demands of the ARTYC, but as the Cuban theater critic Rine Leal has noted, the scandal did have certain negative consequences. It was largely because of the ARTYC's distaste for Piñera, for example, that *Electra Garrigó* was not staged again in Cuba for nearly ten years. Furthermore, Piñera's profound disillusionment with the Cuban cultural scene made it increasingly difficult for him to function as a writer in Havana. During the nearly two years that he spent in Cuba after his first return from exile he did, however, manage to keep up with his literary endeavors. It was a productive period during which he finished two plays, *Jesús* and *Falsa Alarma*, and began work on his most important novel *La carne de René*.[54] Despite earlier efforts to prevent the performance of Piñera's plays in Cuba, *Jesús* debuted in Havana in October 1950, several months after Piñera's return to Buenos Aires. This play about Jesús García, a humble barber from Camagüey who is mistakenly revered as the son of Christ, remained unpublished until after the triumph of the Revolution. *Falsa Alarma* was published in two consecutive issues of *Orígenes* in 1949, but was not performed until 1957. By April 1950 Piñera could no longer tolerate the asphyxiating cultural climate in Cuba and he decided to return to Buenos Aires, where he would stay for more than four years excluding short visits to Cuba.[55]

RETURN TO EXILE: THE CALM BEFORE THE STORM

From Havana Piñera secured a job at the Cuban consulate in Buenos Aires through his friend Humberto Rodríguez Tomeu, who had been working there for several years. He started his new position in April 1950 and shortly thereafter he traveled with Humberto to France and Belgium where the latter had been sent by the consulate on official business. Soon after his return from Europe, Piñera began to detest the administrative tasks that his job entailed, and he became increasingly frustrated by his cohorts, who he considered provincial and intellectually deficient. From the outset Piñera's second and longest period of exile in the Argentine capital was marked by frustration and seclusion. During these especially difficult years he tended to distance himself from intellectual circles, and he avoided becoming embroiled in major literary scandals.

In May 1952 he made a rare public appearance at a conference on Cuban literature, which had been organized by Borges. In his lecture Piñera took the opportunity to reconfirm his opinion that a national literature still did not exist in Cuba. The talk, entitled "Cuba y la literatura," was one of Piñera's most polemical condemnations of Cuba's cultural climate. In it he argued, through the voice of a fictional student who rebuffs his professor's high opinion of Cuban letters, that his country lacked a national literature:

> Niego que haya tal literatura cubana ya que día a día sufro esa terrible muerte civil del escritor que no tiene una verdadera literatura que lo respalde. . . . No, señor profesor, tomado en rigor no existe por el momento la literatura cubana o si usted se alarma demasiado ante mi ex abrupto puedo concederle esto: Bueno, sí existe la literatura cubana pero . . . sólo en los manuales.[56]

> [I deny that such Cuban literature exists since day after day I suffer that terrible civil death of a writer who doesn't have a true literature that backs him up. . . . No, Mr. Professor, strictly speaking at the moment Cuban Literature doesn't exist, but if you become too alarmed by my sharp observation I can concede you this: OK, Cuban literature does exist but . . . only in the manuals.]

In the same article, which he later read in Havana in 1955 and published in *Ciclón* the same year, Piñera took shots—some obvious, others slightly veiled—at all of his usual targets: the religious tenets and the so-called escapist poems of Lezama and the *Orígenes* group, the "sellout" authors of the *Revista de Avance*, the writers and artists obsessed with European culture, and, of course, the irresolute, spineless literary critics for whom Piñera had developed an especially strong distaste. Reflecting the feelings of bitterness and frustration that had pushed him to leave Cuba for a second time, Piñera equated his country's literary and cultural advancement with the painfully slow march of a turtle, and he lamented the fact that so few of his compatriots had managed, despite their obvious potential, to overcome their literary mediocrity.

Piñera's characteristically negative evaluation of the Cuban cultural scene can be read as a sort of rationalization for his return to Buenos Aires. His second period of exile in the Argentine capital, however, did not live up to the first in terms of both his financial situation and his intellectual pursuits. Without the generous funds from his scholarship he was forced to work full-time at the Cuban consulate, where he hardly made enough to make ends meet. At the same time, he had less opportunities to become involved with the type of intellectual pursuits—translating for Editorial Argos, collaborating with Gombrowicz, meeting with authors and friends—that had made his first visit so satisfying.

Relatively little is known about Piñera's personal life during the early 1950s. The author did, however, leave behind an emotionally charged manuscript that sheds some light on his way of life during that period. In the handwritten text, which he apparently read at a presentation of *La carne de René* in November 1952, Piñera referred to the early years of his second stay in Buenos Aires as a lonely, emotionally unstable period, during which he wrote tirelessly, was intensely bored with his daily routine, lived in near poverty, communicated infrequently with other intellectuals, and had numerous sexual encounters.[57]

It seems that apart from his job at the Cuban consulate, Piñera spent most of his time from 1950–52 writing *La carne de René*. Though he rightly felt that the daring novel was one of his greatest works, he was pessimistic about its prospects in Argentina and the rest of Latin America. As he put it, in the above-mentioned text, "Me carcajeo ante el éxito de *La carne de René*. ¿Traducido a idioma extranjero? Prosigo con convulsas carcajadas." (I roar with laughter at [the idea of] the success of *René's Flesh*. Translated to a foreign language? I continue to laugh convulsively.) Piñera's insecurities were reinforced by the fact that the novel was largely ignored by Argentine literary circles and was virtually unknown among Cuban readers. In fact, *La carne de René* was never widely available in Cuba until its first publication there more than fifteen years after Piñera's death.[58] Apart from occasional comments and critical appraisals from close friends—Witold Gombrowicz, for example, called the novel "una obra visionaria y sombríamente sarcástica"[59] (a visionary and somberly sarcastic work)—*La carne de René* received almost no critical attention. To the best of my knowledge, only two reviews of the novel were published during Piñera's lifetime. A brief but illuminating review—which some critics have speculated was written by Piñera himself—appeared in the Argentine daily *La Nación* on October 1952,[60] and José Rodríguez Feo's article "Una alegoría de la carne" (An Allegory of the Flesh), was published in the first issue of *Ciclón* in 1955.

For a number of reasons *La carne de René* was something of a thorn in Piñera's side. Though he knew that the novel was extremely daring and ambitious, he also realized that he had written it long before its time. In much the same way that the radical originality of his play *Electra Garrigó* had proven to be too hard to swallow for many critics in the late 1940s, *La carne de René* also presented a formidable challenge for contemporary Latin American readers.

The combination of the draining experience of writing *La carne de René* and the lack of readership and critical attention served to discourage Piñera. For nearly two years following the novel's publication he suffered from emotional crises and wrote very little. His literary hiatus was, however, something like the calm before a storm. By the final months of 1953 a literary feud had erupted in Havana. Though the dispute had nothing to do with Piñera himself, it set the stage for his stormy literary comeback.

Ciclón and the Demise of *Orígenes*

Piñera returned to Cuba in September 1953 after winning a plane ticket on Aerolíneas Argentinas.[61] His stay lasted only two months, but given his longtime desire to leave a lasting mark on the Cuban and Latin American cultural scene, he could not have returned to Cuba at a more perfect moment. Just before his arrival in Havana a major literary dispute set into motion the downfall of *Orígenes*. This volatile situation would soon afford Piñera a rare opportunity to advance his own literary career.

The conflict erupted shortly after the publication of the thirty-fourth issue (winter 1953) of *Orígenes*, in which Lezama had included, allegedly without consulting José Rodríguez Feo, who was in Spain at the time of its compilation, a scathing article by his friend and mentor Juan Ramón Jiménez.[62] In "Crítica paralela" (Parallel Criticism), Jiménez denounced a number of his fellow Spanish poets including Jorge Guillén, Luis Cernuda, Pedro Salinas, Gerardo Diego, and especially Vicente Aleixandre, whom Rodríguez Feo had just visited in Spain. Since all of the Spanish poets were considered friends of *Orígenes*, Lezama allegedly tried to convince Jiménez that his attack was not appropriate for the magazine. Jiménez, however, would not be swayed. He argued that Aleixandre had maligned him from the pages of the Spanish journal *Ínsula* and that Guillén and Cernuda had both criticized him in texts published in the previous number of *Orígenes*.[63] Caught off guard by the scandal, Lezama decided that his allegiance to Juan Ramón Jiménez, which dated back to 1936, was too strong to deny the Spanish poet the right to respond to his detractors in the pages of *Orígenes*.

Jiménez's article was especially scandalous for *Orígenes*, which had for the most part managed to steer clear of derogatory criticism and literary disputes. In "Crítica paralela" Jiménez denounced Vicente Aleixandre for allegedly referring to him when he wrote that "un poeta esquisito es siempre un mutilado"[64] (an exquisite poet is always a cripple). In a section of his article entitled "Respuesta concisa: A un mutilado auténtico" (Concise Response: To an Authentic Cripple), Lezama's friend and mentor unleashed an aggressive attack on his fellow Spanish poet and his work:

> Pero supongo que un mutilado corporal verdadero . . . como lo es V.A., no puede escribir poesía esquisita ni siquiera grande, que es la que viene después de la esquisita.
> V.A. es un existencialista de butaca permanente; y que escribe imaginaciones por serie, en álbumes de fantasmas sucesivos. La escritura de V.A. verso o prosa, no es más que una serie de estampas forzadas, sin vida verdadera. . . . (Como la de Guillén y Salinas, es vía muerta).[65]

> [Yet I suppose that a true cripple . . . such as V.A., cannot write exquisite or even grandiose poetry, which comes after exquisite poetry.
> V.A. is a permanent armchair existentialist; and he writes imaginations in serial form, in albums of successive apparitions. The writing of V.A., verse or prose, is nothing more that a series of forced vignettes, without true life. . . . (Like the writing of Guillén and Salinas, it's a dead end).]

Later in his article Jiménez further insulted Jorge Guillén by insisting that he was incapable of understanding his own poetry.[66]

If we can believe his version of the events, Rodríguez Feo was justifiably angry about Lezama's decision to publish "Crítica paralela" while he was in Spain making contacts with some of the same poets that Jiménez insulted in his essay. When he returned to Havana, Rodríguez Feo demanded that Lezama explain in a letter in the next issue of *Orígenes* that he had included "Crítica paralela" without consulting his coeditor. Otherwise Rodríguez Feo, who provided the funding for the magazine, would continue to direct *Orígenes* without Lezama. Lezama resolutely refused to publish any such letter, and he informed Rodríguez Feo that he would continue to direct and publish the journal with those members of the *Orígenes* group who had taken his side.[67]

For the next several months the two directors worked on simultaneous versions of *Orígenes* with their respective groups of supporters. However, in mid-1954, after Rodríguez Feo had edited just two issues of the so-called apocryphal *Orígenes*, Lezama, who had a degree in law, threatened to sue for the exclusive rights to the title of the journal. Though Lezama's move effectively ended *Orígenes*' double life, the journal was doomed without Rodríguez Feo's financial backing. Consequently, only six more issues were published before the journal's official demise in 1956.

Shortly after ceasing to publish his own version of *Orígenes* in mid-1954, Rodríguez Feo decided to create a new journal that he conceived as a final blow to Lezama and his group. It is important to keep in mind that Piñera and Rodríguez Feo did not meet until October 1954, during another of Piñera's brief visits to Havana. However, Rodríguez Feo was familiar with Piñera's literary and critical writings, his contentious relationship with Lezama, and his growing reputation as a provocateur. But perhaps even more importantly, Rodríguez Feo saw great potential in Piñera's connections in Buenos Aires, and he knew that he planned to return early in 1955. For his part Piñera was keenly aware of the clash that had taken place between Lezama and Rodríguez Feo and he surely relished the opportunity to get involved in the polemic. Indeed, it is the opinion of many that when he met Rodríguez Feo (who was in the midst of a court battle with Lezama at the time), Piñera aggressively pushed the idea of forgetting about *Orígenes* and starting a new magazine.[68] Rodríguez Feo might very well have taken on a new editorial endeavor without Piñera's collaboration, but it seems reasonable to assume the latter's eagerness served as an important stimulus to the project, which took off shortly after the two were formally introduced.

The title of the new journal, *Ciclón*, was chosen to reflect what Rodríguez Feo and Piñera envisioned as one of its primary goals: to take the Cuban literary establishment by storm and to blow away any remaining vestiges of Lezama's *Orígenes*. In "Borrón y cuenta nueva" (A Clean Slate), a three-page editorial printed on yellow paper and inserted in the middle of the first issue, Rodríguez Feo declared an intellectual war of sorts on Lezama and the members of the *Orígenes* group who had remained faithful to him. As one critic has noted, Rodríguez Feo's denunciation of Lezama and the *Orígenes* group reflected more than a simple literary or editorial schism.[69] It also underscored the animosity that Rodríguez Feo felt toward Lezama, who he felt had betrayed him.

Rodríguez Feo always maintained that Piñera had nothing to do with the composition of "Borrón y cuenta nueva."[70] It is widely believed, however, that the tempestuous editorial's language and style belie such a claim. To be sure, the bellicose text is loaded with the same type of military terms that Piñera used in his collaborations with Gombrowicz, and the sarcastic tone, caustic humor, the abundance of rhetorical questions, certain vocabulary—"úcases" (ukases)—and catchphrases—"como siempre ocurre" (as always happens)—all suggest Piñera's involvement in its composition.[71] The aggressive opening lines exude an unmistakably Piñeran quality:

> Lector, he aquí a **Ciclón**, la nueva revista. Con él, borramos a **Orígenes** de un golpe. A **Orígenes** que como todo el mundo sabe tras diez años de eficaces servicios a la cultura en Cuba, es actualmente sólo peso muerto. . . . En cuanto al grupo **Orígenes**, no hay que repetirlo, hace tiempo que, al igual de los hijos de Saturno, fue devorado por su propio padre.
> . . . La guerra ya se había declarado hace algún tiempo: hemos guerreado y hemos ganado. Te confesamos que ha sido una guerra corta, casi un paseo militar. ¿Cómo podíamos no ganarla si disponíamos de un arma secreta: **Ciclón**, la nueva revista? [72]

> [Reader, behold **Ciclón**, the new journal. With it, we erase **Orígenes** with one stroke. **Orígenes**, which, as everyone knows is now nothing but dead weight after ten years of efficient service to Cuban culture. . . . As far as the **Orígenes** group is concerned, there's no need to repeat it, it's been a while now since, like Saturn's children, it was devoured by its own father.
> . . . The war had already been declared long ago: we have battled and we have won. We confess to you that it has been a short war, almost a military stroll. How could we not have won it if we had at our disposal a secret weapon: **Ciclón**, the new journal?]

After explaining in detail the events that led up to the scandal and to Rodríguez Feo's decisive severing of ties with Lezama, the authors of the editorial insisted that *Orígenes* had brought about its own downfall by refusing to change with the times: "Esa revista, estéril para nuevos nacimientos, ciega para tomar lo valioso y desdeñar lo superfluo, no tiene otra salida que la de su trampa cultural." (That journal, sterile for new beginnings, blind to taking what is valuable and to disdaining what is superfluous, has no way out other than its cultural trapdoor.)

The advent of *Ciclón* represented something of a watershed in Piñera's career. As the final lines of the editorial suggested, the magazine provided the perfect vehicle through which Piñera and the other contributors could work toward reinvigorating the Cuban cultural climate. Many critics have alleged that *Ciclón* stands out as an irreverent and disrespectful magazine, but the new journal did not simply aim to violate taboos or stir up disputes. Indeed *Ciclón* included original works and translations by an impressively diverse pool of contributors, from up-and-coming Cuban authors (Guillermo Cabrera Infante, Severo

Sarduy, Antón Arrufat), to well-established writers from Latin America, Europe, and the United States. Works by several future Nobel laureates—Vicente Aleixandre (Spain, 1977), Miguel Ángel Asturias (Guatemala, 1967), Octavio Paz (Mexico, 1990), and Salvatore Quasimodo (Italy, 1959)—were published among the pages of *Ciclón*.

There is, of course, some truth to the allegations that the editors of *Ciclón* often tested the limits of modern Latin American sensibilities. In fact, Piñera himself used the magazine as a vehicle through which to disseminate some of his most polemical and controversial personal, literary, and political convictions. It was his idea, for example, to include a segment of Humberto Rodríguez Tomeu's Spanish translation of the Marquis de Sade's *The 120 Days of Sodom* in the first two issues of *Ciclón*. Several pages of this singularly disturbing work, which one critic has called "the most gruesome book ever written,"[73] were published in spite of, or perhaps in response to, the repressive political climate under Batista.

Piñera introduced the translation with a bold defense of the literary value of Sade's licentious and violent writing, which for centuries had been banned in many countries and dismissed as the work of a depraved madman.[74] He argued that, contrary to popular opinion, Sade was not a pornographer, but a great thinker, artist, and moralist who had developed intelligent theories on sexual conduct and erotic love. He further contended that Sade's writings were so valuable that they should be required reading in schools throughout the world.

Like much of his previous critical and creative writing, Piñera's defense of Sade was insightful, well informed, and written before its time. Though by 1955 a number of critics, such as Simone de Beauvoir and Pierre Klossowski, had undertaken serious reexaminations of Sade's writing, Piñera was one of the first writers in Latin America to take up the task. In doing so he challenged the sexual taboos, machismo, and homophobia that permeated Cuban society. Moreover, Piñera's positive appraisal of the French writer demonstrated his knowledge of contemporary scholarly studies on Sade, and it preceded much of the modern criticism that has acknowledged the Marquis' role as an important precursor to such diverse writers as Sigmund Freud, Friedrich Nietzsche, Antonín Artaud, Albert Camus, and the radical *Tel Quel* group of 1960s Paris.[75]

Echoing one of the central motifs in Simone de Beauvoir's classic article "Must We Burn Sade?" Piñera insisted that the Marquis should not be condemned, but respected for his openness toward sexuality, which the Cuban author considered an important aspect of both life and literature: "Estas ciento veinte jornadas son como la culminación paroxística de todos sus escritos sobre la vida sexual del hombre. . . , que, para decirlo de una vez es una de las cuatro patas sobre las que descansa la gran mesa humana."[76] (These one hundred twenty stages represent the paroxysmal culmination of all of his writings on the sex life of man. . . , which, to say it once and for all, is one of the four legs upon which rests the great human table.) Piñera wrapped up his brief commentary by pointing out that if modern readers could only see beyond the supposedly pornographic nature of Sade's writings, they would realize the importance of his daring exploration of human sexuality: "Si debe leerse un escritor como Kafka que expresa, a través del terror, el absurdo de la vida humana, también está en el deber de informarse sobre un escritor llamado Sade que expresa, por medio del terror, la oscura vida sexual del hombre."[77] (If one should read a writer like Kafka, who expresses, through terror, the absurdity of human life, then it is also his obligation to inform himself about a writer named Sade who expresses, by means of terror, man's dark sexual existence.)

Many critics have commented on the polemical nature of Piñera's decision to include passages from *The 120 Days of Sodom* in *Ciclón*. It is surprising, though, that few have ventured beyond the content of Piñera's brief commentary to explore the actual text itself and its relationship to Piñera's own work. Indeed certain aspects of the speech of the Duke of Blangis, which Piñera chose for *Ciclón*, are especially relevant when read in light of Piñera's ongoing attack on religion. From his jabs at Lezama Lima and his Christian cohorts, to the inverted Christ figure in *Jesús*, to the fiercely anti-Catholic tone of *La carne de René*, Piñera often turned Christianity and Catholicism into objects of ridicule.

The venomous passage, which was chosen from a nearly 600-page book, must have especially irritated certain individuals who had often been the butts of Piñera's antireligious sentiment. In the speech the Duke condemns religiosity and he ridicules Christians for their ignorance:

> Habéis visto hasta qué punto se os prohíbe todo lo que pueda tener el aire de un acto de religiosidad cualquiera; os advierto que habrá pocos crímenes más severamente castigados que ése. Sabemos perfectamente que, entre vosotras hay aún algunas imbéciles que no pueden resignarse a abjurar la idea de ese Dios infame y renegar de la religión. . . . Que esas tontas criaturas se convenzan que la existencia de Dios es una locura que hoy en día no tiene sobre la tierra más de veinte sectarios. . . . Si hubiera un Dios y ese Dios tuviera poder, . . . ¿permitiría ese Dios todopoderoso, que una débil criatura como yo . . . se burlara de El, lo desafiara, y lo ofendiera como hago ya a mi gusto a cada momento del día?[78]

> [You have seen with what stringency you are forbidden anything resembling any act of religion whatsoever. I warn you: few crimes will be more

severely punished than this one. It is only too well known that in your midst there are yet a few fools unable to bring themselves to abjure this infamous God and abhor his worship. . . . Let them be persuaded, these stupid creatures, . . . that in all the world there are not twenty persons today who cling to this mad notion of God's existence. . . . Were there a God and were this God to have any power, . . . would this all-powerful God permit a feeble creature like myself . . . to insult him, to flout him, to defy him, to challenge him, to offend him as I do, wantonly, at my own sweet will, at every instant of the day?]79

Readers familiar with Piñera's views on religion will have no trouble imagining the Duke's provocative words as a sardonic speech from Virgilio who, as Cintio Vitier once put it, had a very hostile attitude toward faith and the Catholic Church.80 Shortly after his return to Buenos Aires in 1955, Piñera referred to the Sade text in *Ciclón* in a letter to Rodríguez Feo with typical impudence, indicating his delight that his article and Sade's passages had scandalized his target audience: "Por lo que veo no redujiste en nada el texto de Sade. Es tan fuerte que fortalece a la revista, y se escuchan los quejidos de horror de los 'exquisitos místicos.' "81 (From what I see, you didn't reduce the Sade text at all. It is so powerful that it strengthens the journal, and one can hear the moaning of the "exquisite mystics"). The so-called exquisite mystics were, to be sure, the defunct *Orígenes* group's growing Catholic contingent, which by then included Cintio Vitier and Fina García Marruz who had converted in 1953.

Piñera and Rodríguez Feo were thrilled that the publication of the texts had provoked reactions from other groups in Cuba as well. In April 1956, for example, an editorial demanding the closure of *Ciclón* — for being an immoral and pornographic publication — was read over Cuban radio. Such denunciations of the magazine only served to strengthen the force of the storm.

In their own right the Sade texts in *Ciclón* encourage the reader to explore the little-studied influence of the Marquis' works in Piñera's own writings. The irreverent speeches of the Duke, for example, are echoed by the blasphemous sermons by Cochón in *La carne de René*. This deranged, Jesuit dropout preaches vengeance against the Catholic Church in polemical and provocative sermons that exude an unmistakably Sadean tone.82

In the fifth issue of *Ciclón* Piñera published another article that challenged Cuba's conservative cultural and social establishment. In his essay "Ballagas en persona," written one year after the death of his longtime friend and fellow poet Emilio Ballagas (1910–54), Piñera condemned certain Cuban intellectuals — especially Cintio Vitier — for painting a disingenuous portrait of the homosexual poet after his untimely death. Piñera argued that Ballagas's supposed friends had transformed him into a model of Cuban conservative morality instead of discussing his homosexuality and the inner turmoil that it had caused him throughout his life.

> Ellos le han cambiado en otra cosa que no fue en la tierra; espejo de buenas costumbres donde puede asomarse sin riesgo alguno.
> Pero hay todavía más, hay más fango perfumado por remover. Sus amigos nos dicen: "He aquí a un artista, también a un buen hombre; he aquí a un sólido pilar de nuestra sociedad; vedlo con su amante esposa, con su adorado hijo; vedlo buen católico y hasta buscador infatigable de la Gracia."[83]

> [They have turned him into something that he never was on earth; mirror of good manners that one could look into with no risk whatsoever.
> But there is more still, there's more perfumed mire to remove. His friends tell us: "Here is an artist, also a good man; here is a solid pillar of our society; look at him with his loving wife, with his adored son; look at him, a good Catholic, and even an indefatigable seeker of Grace."]

Piñera contended that such concerted efforts to underscore Ballagas's role as a perfect husband, father, and Catholic served only to deny his homosexuality and mask a defining characteristic of both his personality and his art. In the highly autobiographical article, Piñera implicitly condemned Cuba's *machista* society for creating an environment in which some homosexuals and bisexuals felt compelled to assume essentially false identities in order to escape ridicule and repression. Piñera's most passionate criticism was aimed at Vitier and his prologue to the recently published *Obra poética de Emilio Ballagas* (Poetic Work of Emilio Ballagas).[84] Piñera insinuated that because of his adherence to certain moral and religious tenets (Vitier had converted to Catholicism two years earlier), the author chose to evade the topic of homosexuality. For Piñera this was evidence enough that Vitier had not understood or properly interpreted Ballagas's poetry. Piñera insisted, in fact, that Vitier had even failed to answer the most significant question that he had posed in his fifty-page essay: *"¿Qué tragedia es ésa que el adolescente ha vislumbrado en su meditación o su presentimiento?"*[85] (*What is the tragedy that the adolescent has glimpsed in his meditation or his presentiment?*)

In Piñera's mind the answer to Vitier's question was painfully obvious. The so-called tragedy that Vitier referred to was Ballagas's closeted homosexuality. Piñera argued that in order to understand Ballagas's poetry, one had to take his homosexuality into account:

> Si los franceses escriben sobre Gide tomando como punto de partida el homosexualismo de este escritor; si los ingleses hacen lo mismo con Wilde, yo

no veo por qué los cubanos no podamos hablar de Ballagas en tanto que homosexual. ¿Es que los franceses y los ingleses tienen la exclusiva de tal tema?[86]

[If the French write about Gide taking the writer's homosexuality as a point of departure; if the English do the same with Wilde, I don't see why we Cubans can't speak about Ballagas in terms of his homosexuality. Or is it that the French and English have exclusive rights to such a theme?]

As Santí has noted, Piñera's discussion of Ballagas's bisexual anguish, which the latter translated into moral guilt, was perhaps the first of its kind in Cuba.[87] Through his explication of Ballagas's moral struggle with his sexual identity, Piñera underscored the proliferation of misinterpretations of Ballagas's poetry. At the same time the polemical essay called attention to a national illness of sorts, that is, the prevalence of a *machista* mentality that had led the intellectual community to disregard homosexuality as a valid subject of art and literature.

It is important to keep in mind that Piñera's insistence that Ballagas's sexual orientation was a key to interpreting his poetry served as an implicit suggestion about how to read and understand his own work. To be sure, certain themes discussed in the article closely parallel some of those found in Piñera's own life and writings: the constant struggle between mind and body, self-rejection and marginalization by society, and the nausea provoked by inner turmoil.

Piñera's interpretation of Ballagas's treatment of heterosexual love in the poem "Psalmo" (Psalm) is especially revealing. He understood the sexual anguish expressed in the poem in much the same way that he had presented a similar theme in *La carne de René*. According to Piñera's reading of "Psalmo," the poetic voice says that a woman looks for him, when in reality it is he who looks for her but fears the encounter. Piñera adds that "La nausea alcanzó su punto alto cuando Ballagas fue tocado por las flechas del amor."[88] (The nausea reached its climax when Ballagas was touched by the arrows of love.) In much the same way the sexually confused protagonists of *La carne de René* (1952) and *Pequeñas maniobras* (1963) are overcome by feelings of anguish and nausea when they are confronted by the women who at once attract and disgust them. Just like Ballagas's poetic voice, who speaks of the repugnance caused by the "brief pleasure" that he begs for, René and Sebastián at once seek and flee from sexual encounters with women.

The anguish felt by Ballagas, and perhaps also by Piñera, had been reinforced by a culture of conformity and supposed moral steadfastness, which frowned on difference and sincerity. Piñera's opinion was likely shared by many, but he was one of the few brave enough to express it so frankly.

CICLÓN IN BUENOS AIRES

In addition to serving as a vehicle for publishing much of his own work, *Ciclón* also afforded Piñera the opportunity to become more involved in the Argentine literary scene when he returned to Buenos Aires early in 1955. During his third period of exile in the Argentine capital Piñera functioned largely as a correspondent for *Ciclón*, for which he managed to acquire an impressive collection of contributions from many of that country's most important writers, including Adolfo Bioy Casares, Jorge Luis Borges, José Bianco, Silvina Ocampo, Ernesto Sábato, and Julio Cortázar.[89]

Through his connection with Rodríguez Feo, who was by then widely known among Latin American literary circles, Piñera met José Bianco in April 1955.[90] As the acting director of *Sur*, Bianco proved to be an invaluable connection in Buenos Aires. Bianco not only helped Piñera acquire articles for *Ciclón*, but he also published several of the Cuban author's essays, book reviews, and stories in *Sur*. It was also largely because of Piñera's subsequent friendship with Bianco that *Cuentos fríos* was published by Editorial Losada, one of Argentina's premiere publishing houses. Bianco was likewise instrumental in the publication of *El que vino a salvarme* (The One Who Came to Save Me), for which he wrote the excellent prologue, "Piñera narrador."[91]

Piñera's prolific correspondence with José "Pepe" Rodríguez Feo, who was in Havana serving as director and financier of *Ciclón*, offers a rich source of information about his experiences during this period in Buenos Aires.[92] In their earlier letters Piñera and Rodríguez Feo expressed their conviction that they had won a major battle against Lezama and *Orígenes*. In one from March 1955, for example, Rodríguez Feo referred to his severing of ties with Lezama as follows: "No hay marcha atrás. ¡Nunca! Lezama se desintegra; tengo varias firmas nuevas, [escritores] jóvenes. Creo el '55 es nuestro año consagratorio."[93] (There is no retreat. Never! Lezama is disintegrating; I have new signatures, young [writers]. I think '55 is our hallowed year.) For his part Piñera revealed a palpable sense of contentment when he referred to the inevitable collapse of *Orígenes* and the impact it would have on Lezama and his literary circle. "Con tantos triunfos de Ciclón," he wrote, "supongo que Lezama y Cía. estarán como pulverizados. Vi el último número de *Orígenes*. Tristísimo."[94] (With Ciclón's many triumphs, I suppose that Lezama and Co. will be practically pulverized. I saw the last number of *Orígenes*. Pathetic.)

Piñera was especially proud of *Ciclón*'s success in Buenos Aires, which was in large part due to his own efforts. He insisted in many letters that intellectuals in Argentina were crazy about the journal, and he corroborated his claims by citing the number of copies that had been sold in local bookstores. At times he even went so far as to suggest that *Ciclón* was more significant than *Sur*. Piñera often recounted the reactions of the literary community to specific texts that appeared in the pages of the journal. In one letter, for instance, Piñera described José Bianco's reaction to the impressive variety of texts by French writers in *Ciclón*. Piñera's snooty tone underscored the pleasure he felt when he learned that many of the authors had never been published in *Sur*.

> Bianco me preguntó muy sorprendido si nosotros estábamos autorizados para publicar esos magníficos textos franceses, y lo puse en su lugar. Le contesté elegantemente que Queneau era amigo tuyo a través de Carpentier, que el texto de Merle había sido autorizado por el propio Merle . . . que lo Torma había sido autorizado por el director de los cuadernos de *Patafísica*. Murena, que estaba presente, me preguntó si la revista se vendía en Bs.As. También lo puse en su lugar.[95]

> [Bianco asked me with much surprise if we were authorized to publish those magnificent French texts, and I put him in his place. I answered him elegantly that Queneau was a friend of yours through Carpentier, that the text by Merle had been authorized by Merle himself . . . that Torma's article had been authorized by the journal *Patafísica*. Murena, who was also there at the time, asked me if the magazine was for sale in Buenos Aires. I also put him in his place.]

Piñera also chronicled the reaction of Argentine authors to his own publications in *Ciclón*. He reported that his article "Ballagas en persona" was very well received, and he claimed that his story "El gran Baro" (The Great Baro), which he read to a nearly blind Borges in the latter's home, had made quite an impression on the author of *Ficciones*: "No puedes imaginar los elogios que le hizo"[96] (You can't imagine the tributes he paid it), he boasted.

Some of the most colorful details in Piñera's letters to Rodríguez Feo concern his persistent attempts to secure collaborations from Borges, who was at the time having difficulties with his literary pursuits due to serious problems with his vision. By 1955 Borges had already had eight eye operations, and his doctor had advised him not to read or write. As James Woodall has noted, his increasing blindness made him more dependent on others, especially his mother, Leonor Acevedo.[97]

Though Piñera often worried that he was being overly persistent with Borges and his mother, his determination to send an original Borges text to Rodríguez Feo paid off. After less than a month in Buenos Aires he had already sent Borges's first collaboration to Havana. In a letter dated March 16, 1955, Piñera gave a fascinating account of how he had obtained the short text "Inferno, I, 32" from Borges:

> Ha sido, como se dice, una pica en Flandes conseguir esta colaboración. Piensa que no quiere soltar nada con nadie. Entre otros motivos porque tiene poquísimo o nada para publicar. Los cuatro meses de lucha con la vista le han impedido escribir. Él ha estado muy amable con nosotros. Me invitó a tomar el té, y después de las generalidades de rigor, le pedí algo para *Ciclón*. En seguida me dijo que no podía negarme nada y que tenía mucho gusto de colaborar en tu revista. Me hizo la advertencia que sólo podría darme el único texto inédito que tenía por el momento, que era bien corto y que si preferíamos que más extenso tendríamos que esperar a que él recuperase enteramente. Yo le dije que (pensando en lo de más vale pájaro en mano . . .) a nosotros nos interesaba ese texto, aunque corto, valioso etc. etc. . . . Sólo me hizo una exigencia: que cuando esté la prueba de plana se la mandes para él corregir personalmente la prueba. Es absolutamente necesario que esa prueba llegue a sus manos sin una errata, y lo más importante: que cuando aparezca el texto en *Ciclón* no tenga *ninguna errata*. . . . Querido Pepe, ya tenemos la puerta abierta con Borges.[98]

> [It has been, as they say, a major accomplishment to get this collaboration from Borges. He's decided that he doesn't want to give anything to anybody. Among other reasons, because he has little or nothing to publish. These four months of struggle with his vision have kept him from writing. He has been very kind to us. He invited me to have tea, and after the essential niceties, I asked him for something for *Ciclón*. Immediately he said he couldn't possibly turn me down, and that it would be a pleasure to collaborate in your magazine. He warned me that he could only give me the one unpublished text that he had at the moment, that it was very short, and that if we preferred something longer we would have to wait until he had fully recuperated. I told him (thinking that a bird in the hand is worth two in the bush) that we were interested in his text, which though short, was estimable, etc. etc. . . . He only made one demand: that when the page proofs are ready, you send them to him so that he can correct them personally. It is absolutely necessary that the proofs arrive in his hands without any printer's error, and even more importantly: when the text appears in *Ciclón* that it has *no misprints*. . . . My dear Pepe, we now have the door opened with Borges.]

Piñera's letter calls attention to the fact that *Ciclón*'s success owed much to both his persistence and his preoccupation with editorial details. Piñera was very sensitive to what he claimed were differing attitudes among intellectuals in Havana and Buenos Aires, and he felt that *Ciclón* had to be free of errors if it were to be taken seriously by Argentine intellectuals who were used to professional, well-organized publications like *Sur*. "Tu sabes lo anárquico que es el cubano," he complained to

Rodríguez Feo on one occasion. "No conoce el método. Por favor, procura que no salgan erratas. Los argentinos, que son minuciosos, no perdonan esas fallas."[99] (You know how anarchical Cubans are. They don't know the method. Please, be sure that there are no misprints. The Argentines, who are very picky, don't pardon such mistakes.)

Borges's short text appeared in May 1955 in the third issue of *Ciclón*, and Piñera rightly considered its publication to be an indication not just of his own achievement—especially given the fact that Borges had never contributed to *Orígenes*—but also of the magazine's potential to be one of Latin America's most important literary journals.

Upon returning to Buenos Aires in November 1955, after a five-month stay in Cuba,[100] Piñera was quick to return to his routine of working to secure collaborations for *Ciclón*, which by then had won the respect of the Argentine intelligentsia that the Cuban author so much wanted to impress. One of his major goals was to acquire a second piece from Borges for a special issue to be dedicated to the Spanish philosopher José Ortega y Gasset (1883–1955). Despite his initial confidence—just a week after arriving in Buenos Aires he wrote to Rodríguez Feo that he had already convinced Borges to write an essay for the issue on Ortega—procuring the essay proved to be one of Piñera's great challenges of the *Ciclón* years. The experience pushed his patience to its limit, but again his persistence paid off in the long run. In several letters he made reference to his indefatigable efforts to obtain "Nota de un mal lector" (Note from a Poor Reader), a one-page essay on Ortega y Gasset that took the Argentine author nearly four months to hand over. Piñera often noted that dealing with Borges, who in addition to directing the National Library had recently accepted a professorship in Germanic literatures, had become increasingly difficult.

In his humorous recounting of his interactions with Borges, Piñera emphasized the crucial role that the Argentine author's mother played in her son's life. In fact Piñera insinuated on occasion that it was largely because of her that Borges ever got anything done at all. After dealing with mother and son for weeks Piñera wrote to Rodríguez Feo on Christmas Eve 1955: "Lucho a brazo partido con Borges para que acabe por entregarme su colaboración. Me da cortas y largas. Ayer la madre me dijo que me lo entregaría sobre el día treinta."[101] (I fight hand-to-hand with Borges to get him to hand over his article once and for all. He gives me all sorts of excuses. Yesterday his mother told me that he would give me the article around the 30th). The following week an increasingly anxious Piñera was still waiting for the collaboration from Borges, and he wrote again: "La señora madre quedó en llamarme para el día 31 y no lo ha hecho todavía. ¿Qué hacer? . . . La señora dice que Borges está muy ocupado y que ya entregará el artículo."[102] (His mother said she would call me on the 31st, but she hasn't done it yet. What to do? . . . The señora says that Borges is very busy and that he will soon hand over the article.) When another week passed, and Piñera still hadn't received the article, he sent his friend Graziella Peyrou to speak with Borges's mother. His account of their meeting—reminiscent in its comic undertones of a scene from one of his dramatic works—captures perfectly Leonor Acevedo's central role in Borges's affairs:

> Por intermedio de Graziella he sabido el último . . . George empezará el ensayo sobre Ortega mañana. . . . (Graziella pregunta: Pero señora, ¿no cree usted que Borges no querrá escribir sobre Ortega habiéndolo hecho ya para *Sur*? Respuesta de la señora: ¡Eso no es cierto, querida; George no ha escrito nada para *Sur*; su compromiso es para *Ciclón* y él tiene mucho gusto en hacerlo. Pausa. Además, no se trata de si le gusta o no le gusta. Para él es una obligación sagrada pues ha empeñado su palabra a Virgilio Piñera. Graziella: Señora, pero me consta que R. Feo está demorando el número de *Ciclón*. Señora: Que no se apure, en estos días tendrá el ensayo).[103]

> [By way of Graziella I have found out the latest . . . George will begin the essay on Ortega tomorrow. . . . (Graziella asks: But ma'am, don't you suppose Borges will not want to write about Ortega, since he's already done so for *Sur*? The señora's response: That's not true, my dear; George has not written anything for *Sur*; his commitment is to *Ciclón*, and he is honored to comply. Pause. And besides, it's not a matter of whether he wants to or not. For him it is a sacred obligation since he has given his word to Virgilio Piñera. Graziella: Ma'am, I know for sure that R. Feo is holding up the issue of *Ciclón*. Señora: Don't fret, shortly you will have the essay).]

As James Irby once observed, Borges and his mother had a rather uncommon relationship. "Those who don't know Borges is single think, seeing him and his mother together, that they are man and wife. . . . She calls her son 'Georgie,' looks after him constantly, and organizes his life. In all aspects of daily and practical life, his relation to her is one of almost complete dependency particularly since his sight is gone; she reads him the books he can't read; she is his scribe for correspondence and writings."[104] José Bianco, who put it more poetically, observed that Borges's mother was like a rope that kept a kite from flying away. Without her, Bianco mused, "this man, so alien to life's realities," would have been lost in the clouds.[105]

Back in Cuba Pepe had more patience than Piñera did with the sightless Argentine man of letters, and he zealously declared his determination to procure a text by Borges, whose reputation was rapidly growing among Latin American literary circles: "*Ciclón* espera a . . . Borges hasta el Juicio Final."[106] (*Ciclón* waits for . . . Borges until the Final Judgment). After months of nagging, an increasingly frustrated Piñera finally got the article at the beginning of February. He blamed what he referred to as Borges's "typical slowness" not just on his problems with his vision, but also on the fact that he was overcommitted at the Biblioteca Nacional and with his new teaching position.

According to Piñera, Borges's unenthusiastic evaluation of the work of Ortega y Gasset in his 500-word article ruffled feathers among members of the largely pro-Ortega *Sur* group. In the essay, which to the best of my knowledge has not been published elsewhere, Borges made two basic points. First, he declared that while he had established a sort of "friendship" with the works of the great Spanish philosopher, Miguel de Unamuno, he found Ortega's writings somewhat bothersome:

> Algo me apartó siempre de su lectura, algo me impidió superar los índices y los párrafos iniciales. Sospecho que el obstáculo era su estilo. Ortega, hombre de lecturas abstractas y de disciplina dialéctica, se dejaba embelesar por los artificios más triviales de la literatura.[107]

> [Something pushed me away from reading his work, something hindered me from going beyond the tables of contents and the introductory paragraphs. I suspect that the obstacle was his style. Ortega, man of abstract readings and dialectic discipline, let himself be enchanted by the most trivial artifices of literature.]

Borges's second major point in the brief essay was that he didn't understand why Ortega was considered by so many to be such an important author and intellectual. His concluding statement was especially blunt—"Quizá algún día no me parecerá misteriosa la fama que hoy consagra a Ortega y Gasset"[108] (Perhaps some day the fame that consecrates Ortega nowadays will not seem so mysterious to me)—and it likely upset those among his Argentine cohorts who greatly revered the writings of the Spanish author.

Always the polemicist, Virgilio Piñera was delighted when Borges's contribution to *Ciclón* caught the attention of the Buenos Aires intellectual community. The publication of "Nota de un mal lector" was a major success for the magazine, and according to Piñera's own report that issue of *Ciclón*—which also included essays on Ortega by María Zambrano and Guillermo de Torre—was in hot demand once the news of Borges's article got out. Piñera further noted in other letters to Pepe that José Bianco was afraid that Borges would want to publish a similar essay in *Sur*, and that Victoria Ocampo, who had reportedly been involved in a long relationship with the Spanish writer, would be especially upset by the article.

Shortly after the publication of "Nota de un mal lector" Piñera and

Rodríguez Feo decided, in a rare moment of restraint, that it was in the best interest of their increasingly popular journal to try to avoid further offending the *Sur* group. Their editorial discretion created tension with Witold Gombrowicz, who had hoped to publish provocative excerpts from his diary in *Ciclón*. It is worth noting here that Gombrowicz had already angered many Argentine authors from the pages of *Ciclón* with his article "Contra los poetas" (Against Poets). In this typically sardonic essay Gombrowicz declared, among other things, that poetic excess drove him crazy, that poets were mostly concerned with praising themselves and each other, and that few of them really knew anything about their art. To prove this last point, Gombrowicz told of how he often rearranged the verses in famous poems and then recited them to "great poets" who, he insisted, never noticed the difference. Piñera was convinced that if Gombrowicz were to aim his criticism at specific Argentine authors, *Ciclón* would meet with certain doom in Argentina. In order to avoid such a scenario he and Rodríguez Feo decided not to publish the passages from Gombrowicz's diary. The decision was not taken lightly by the Polish author, who felt betrayed by the man with whom he shared many of his polemical views on art and literature.

The *Ciclón* years were among the most productive and fulfilling of Virgilio Piñera's long literary career. The magazine at once represented for Piñera a vehicle through which to express his provocative opinions, a place to publish his own creative writings, and a springboard for exciting intellectual endeavors. Despite keeping quite busy in Buenos Aires with his writing and with duties related to the magazine, however, Piñera was often beleaguered by pessimism and gloominess during his final years in the Argentine capital. In his correspondence with Rodríguez Feo, he frequently referred to his delicate emotional state, which was exacerbated by his preoccupation with Argentina's increasingly fragile political situation. In a letter written in November 1955, just days after his return from a five-month stay in Cuba, Piñera suggested, for example, that his depressed state was at least due in part to his fear that Argentina was headed for a civil war.

> Estoy bastante deprimido pues bien sabes que esta ciudad no la trago con sus brumas y sus tristezas. . . . Además lo político es muy malo. Ya estarás enterado del cambio de Lonardi a Aramburo [*sic*].[109] En el fondo el país está gobernado por los militares. Hay conatos de huelga que no sabemos cómo sofoca el gobierno pero que probablemente serán reprimidos todos sangrientamente, como es típico de esos casos. Todo el mundo habla de la posibilidad de una guerra civil.[110]

[I'm quite depressed, as you well know I can't stand this city with its mists and its gloominess. . . . Moreover the political situation is very bad. You must already be aware of the change from Lonardi to Aramburu. Basically, the country is being governed by the military. There are attempts to strike that we don't know how the government quells, but everyone will probably be repressed bloodily, which is typical in these cases. Everyone speaks of the possibility of civil war.]

To make matters worse, Piñera lost his job at the Cuban consulate in February 1956, and was thus left in Buenos Aires without a reliable source of income. Had it not been for the financial support of Rodríguez Feo, one of Piñera's most important and well-known books, *Cuentos fríos*, would surely not have been published in Buenos Aires later that year. The publication of this collection of short stories by Losada, one of Latin America's most prominent publishing houses, was something of a breakthrough in Piñera's career given that it made the many texts available to a much larger and more diverse reading public than any of his previous publications had enjoyed.

According to his own account, *Cuentos fríos* was very well received in the Argentine capital. It was favorably reviewed in *Sur* and in *Ciclón*, and a number of Piñera's friends and acquaintances—Gombrowicz, Borges, Adolfo Bioy Casares, and Silvina Ocampo to name just a few—praised his highly original stories. In a letter to Rodríguez Feo, Piñera referred to the popularity of the collection in typically immodest terms: "¿Sabes que Losada está chocho con los cuentos? Y todo el mundo. Al fin, después de diez años, se dan cuenta con qué huésped contaban."[111] (Do you realize that Losada is crazy about the stories? As is everybody. Finally, after ten years, they realize what a guest they've been dealing with.) Piñera's comment underscores the fact that, despite his tendency to mock the Argentine intelligentsia and to downplay his own interest in fame, he was determined to earn the respect of one of Latin America's most elite literary communities and to make a name for himself in Buenos Aires.

Shortly after the publication of *Cuentos fríos*, Piñera returned once again to Havana, where he would end up staying until March 1958. It is important to point out that Piñera arrived just before the precarious political situation in Cuba was about to take a drastic turn for the worse. The events of the following months would end up having a dramatic impact on the future of *Ciclón*, and consequently on Piñera's literary career.

From exile in Mexico Fidel Castro had organized and consolidated the July 26 Movement, and at the end of November 1956 he and eighty-two supporters traveled to Cuba on a yacht called *Granma* with the intention of starting an insurrection in Oriente Province. After the rebels were badly defeated on December 2 by Batista's forces—who had learned of the planned invasion beforehand—Castro and about a dozen surviving supporters escaped and took refuge in the Sierra Maestra mountain range in eastern Cuba. There they planned their campaign of guerrilla warfare against Batista and his supporters. By early 1957 Batista's police forces had begun launching assaults in Cuba's urban centers. University students and professors were often singled out for their involvement in organized protests against his regime, and many of them were executed by Batista's police. Their bodies were frequently displayed in public plazas to deter further antigovernment rallies.

After completing just two issues of *Ciclón* in 1957 Rodríguez Feo, moved by the tragic circumstances in Cuba, suspended publication of the magazine. Two years later in the first and only number of *Ciclón* published after the triumph of the Revolution, the magazine's director defended his decision in an emotional editorial entitled "La neutralidad de los escritores" (The Writers' Neutrality):

> En el mes de junio de 1957 se suspendió la publicación de esta revista porque en los momentos en que se acrecentaba la lucha contra la tiranía de Batista y morían en las calles de la Habana y en los montes de Oriente nuestra juventud más valerosa, nos pareció una falta de pudor ofrecer a nuestros lectores "simple literatura."

> [In June 1957 publication of the journal was suspended because, at a time when the fight against the tyranny of Batista was intensifying, and our most courageous young people were dying on the streets of Havana and in the mountains of Oriente Province, it seemed inappropriate to us to offer our readers "simple literature."]

Rodríguez Feo's unexpected decision to discontinue publication of *Ciclón* was especially devastating for Piñera, who had worked tirelessly for more than two years recruiting collaborators and writing and translating texts for the magazine.

The premature demise of *Ciclón*, whose success Piñera rightly felt was due in large part to his own hard work, left him deeply disappointed. He managed to keep busy in Havana, however, putting the finishing touches on a new play, *La boda* (*The Wedding*), which he had written for the next issue of *Ciclón*,[112] and preparing for the premiere of *Falsa alarma*. The latter play, which Piñera had written nearly a decade earlier, opened on June 28 in the Havana Lyceum as part of a series of Cuban theater of the absurd that was under the direction of Julio Matas. During the same period Piñera also began work on his novel

Pequeñas maniobras (Little Maneuvers), which he published in Havana in 1963.

By the end of summer 1957 Piñera had finished *La boda*, and he began making arrangements for its production in Havana. The Cuban theater director Adolfo de Luis feared that the play was too scandalous for contemporary Cuban audiences, but given the fact that a Havana theater festival was already being planned for February 1958, and two of Piñera's plays—*Electra Garrigó* and *Los siervos*[113]—were on the program, he agreed to direct it.

La boda premiered on February 15, 1958, in the Teatro Atelier. The event was fraught with problems, and the play ended up meeting with the public disapproval that Adolfo de Luis had foreseen. As Piñera reported in a letter to Humberto Rodríguez Tomeu, there was a blackout in the theater before the show, the actors were unimpressive, and many of the performers resisted saying "tetas," a word that appears scores of times in the play.[114] In a public talk given after the premiere of *La boda*, and published some three years later in *Lunes de Revolución*, Piñera poked fun at the conservative values of Cuban actors: "sobre todo en el campo femenino . . . tenemos un compuesto de actriz y niña de su casa, cómico a la vez que patético"[115] (above all in the feminine camp . . . we have a composite of actress and mama's girl, at once comical and pathetic).

As if to confirm Piñera's complaints about the stuffy, ultraconservative climate in Cuba, a group of Catholic youth tried to organize a boycott against *La boda*.[116] This incident, which must have seemed to have come straight from one of his absurdist texts, was one of many indications that Cuba still suffered from the cultural stagnation and backwardness that had pushed him into exile several years earlier.

On March 13, 1958, after a visit that had lasted far longer than he originally planned, Piñera returned once more to Buenos Aires. During his last difficult months in Argentina Piñera fell into another emotional crisis, but he kept himself busy with his writing. He reported to Rodríguez Feo in April of that year, for example, that he had finished his novel "La última conspiración" (The Last Conspiracy)—an early title for *Presiones y diamantes* (Pressures and Diamonds)—and added that he planned on submitting it to a literary contest sponsored by Editorial Losada.[117] Around the same time he published a masterful story, "La gran escalera del palacio legislativo" (The Great Staircase of the Legislative Palace) in *Sur*. With typical sarcasm he boasted that "Silvina está chocha con este cuento, me dijo que ella hubiera querido escribirlo, que si soy un genio, etc."[118] (Silvina Ocampo is crazy about this story, she told me she would have loved to have written it, that I'm a genius, etc.) Despite such bursts of humorous self-adulation, however, Piñera's spirits were low and his attitude toward his writing became increasingly negative. After almost twelve years in exile in Argentina he had still not achieved the recognition that he felt he deserved.

By the final months of 1958 Piñera even began to have doubts about the value of his career as a writer, which he had always held to be an admirable vocation. "Cuando esté bajo tierra," he wrote to Pepe back in Havana, "dirán de mí: ese tonto se sacrificó nada menos que por la literatura . . . Pasó hambre, frío, vejaciones y demás por algo tan estúpido como la literatura."[119] (When I'm dead and buried, they will say of me: that fool sacrificed himself for nothing less than literature . . . he endured hunger, cold, annoyances and more for something as stupid as literature.) A few months later Piñera wrote the following prophetic words to his sister Luisa: "Créeme que ansío la paz, acabar de fijarme en Cuba."[120] (Believe me, I crave peace, to establish myself in Cuba once and for all.) The melancholic, wistful tone of both letters clearly suggested that Piñera was ready for his definitive return from exile, and indeed by the final days of September 1958 he was on his way home. What he could never have imagined was that, in spite of his best efforts in the years to come, he would never set foot on Argentine soil again.

3
Disillusion to Revolution and Back Again (1958–79)

> Pues me fui de Habana empujado por la necesidad y me iré de Bs. As. empujado por lo mismo. No estoy loco ni soy caprichoso. Ocurre que no me gusta estar todo el tiempo en la misma prisión y cada cierto tiempo elevo a la Superioridad un escrito pidiendo que me transfieran de mazmorra.
>
> [Well, I left Havana pushed by necessity and I will leave Buenos Aires for the same reason. I'm neither crazy nor capricious. It happens that I don't like being in the same prison all the time, and every so often I submit a document to the Warden asking for a change of dungeons.]
>
> —Virgilio Piñera[1]

> ¿A quién tememos? ¿qué autoridad es la que tememos vaya a asfixiar nuestro espíritu creador?
>
> [Who are we afraid of? What authority do we fear is going to stifle our creative spirit?]
>
> —Fidel Castro, "Palabras a los intelectuales"[2]

UPON HIS ARRIVAL IN HAVANA IN SEPTEMBER 1958 PIÑERA WITNESSED, as he had on previous visits during his lengthy exile, that few things in his homeland had changed for the better. By the time of Piñera's return, Cuba was besieged by social, economic, and political crises, and the cultural scene, which had been all but stifled by the repressive Batista regime, was in dire straits. Since Piñera's last visit in early 1958 Cuba's political situation had grown especially tense, and violent conflicts between Batista's forces and the rebels in the Sierra Maestra were becoming more frequent. In the midst of the turmoil, Piñera observed that his own family seemed to reflect the political, economic, and social stagnation that had dominated the island since his initial voyage to Argentina some twelve years earlier. As he pointed out later in the introduction to his *Teatro completo*, for example, his house at Panchito Gómez 257 still had the same weather-beaten furniture and his family continued to suffer from the economic difficulties that had plagued them since their arrival in Havana in the 1930s.

Piñera responded to his family's pitiable circumstances and to the misery and frustration that had plagued Cuba during the Batista years with his play *Aire frío* (*Cold Air*), which he wrote in the final months of 1958.[3] *Aire frío* is unique among Piñera's dramatic works for its highly autobiographical content. The play chronicles the daily life of a Cuban family during a roughly twenty-year period between 1940–58. The trials and tribulations of the Romaguera household reflect many of the experiences of Piñera's own family during the same period, and Oscar, the aspiring poet who decides to look for better opportunities in Buenos Aires, shares much in common with Piñera himself. Writing the play represented something of a catharsis for Piñera, who felt overwhelmed by the precarious circumstances of both his country and his family upon returning to Cuba.

Months earlier, in a rather prophetic letter sent from Buenos Aires to his sister Luisa, Piñera had referred to a strong desire to write a humble and deeply personal work: "Siento que tengo algo en el pecho, lo más importante que todavía no he puesto en mi obra . . . Espero ese día glorioso y amargo en que escribiré con la humildad."[4] (I feel like I have something in my heart, the most important thing that I have yet to put in my work . . . I long for that glorious and bitter day when I will write with humility.) His response to this need was *Aire frío*, which is arguably his most moving and sincere work.

THE BIG BREAK: *REVOLUCIÓN* AND *LUNES*

Like so many of his fellow writers, Virgilio Piñera welcomed the triumph of the Revolution. Batista's flight from Cuba early on New Year's Day 1959 and Castro's victorious march into Havana a week later were cause for enthusiasm on numerous fronts. Many intellectuals, for example, saw the events of the opening day of 1959 as auspicious signs that Cuba had emerged from the frustration and the rampant corruption of the Batista years. Piñera's initial response to his country's newfound sense of nationhood was at once enthusiastic and cautious. Throughout the opening months of the Revolution he expressed his opinions in numerous articles and editorials. In early January he began to work with Rodríguez Feo on an issue of *Ciclón*, the only one that would be published after the triumph of the Revolution. Much like the inaugural issue in 1955, this one contained a scathing editorial, "La Neutralidad de los Escritores" (The Writers' Neutrality), which was penned by Rodríguez Feo. The director of the magazine opened by explaining

Ciclón's silence since June 1957, but his main purpose was to denounce numerous Cuban writers who, despite claims of "neutrality," had allegedly supported Batista's cultural programs in various ways.

After deriding several artists and writers—Salvador Bueno, Gastón Baquero, Jorge Mañach, Humberto Piñera, Lezama among others—for their alleged intellectual collaboration with Batista's government, Rodríguez Feo suggested that such individuals did not deserve the respect of the new generation of revolutionaries. He stressed the paramount importance of being wary of any writer who, in the name of personal interests or political indifference, had claimed to be neutral but continued to lend their support to a corrupt cultural program. Rodríguez Feo's inclusion of Lezama in this list attests to the animosity that still existed between the two in 1959, and his inference that Lezama was somehow colluding with the Batista regime was of course highly exaggerated. According to Mariano Rodríguez, there was talk among Lezama's detractors that his most recent book of poems, *Dador*, was "stained with the blood of the people" since he had financed it in part with his minimal salary as a government employee at a Havana prison.[5]

In the same number of *Ciclón* Virgilio Piñera published "La inundación" (The Flood). In this provocative article, which set the tone for his polemical cultural criticism in the early years of the Revolution, Piñera poked fun at the tide of young authors who had emerged since the triumph of the Revolution: "En estos días del triunfo revolucionario—mitad paradisíacos, mitad infernales—no podían faltar en la gran inundación los escritores. Me sorprendió grandemente que en vez de una gota de agua aportaron Nilos y Amazonas."[6] (In these days of revolutionary triumph—half heavenly, half infernal—there could not have been a lack of writers in the great flood. But I was greatly surprised that instead of a drop of water, Niles and Amazons appeared out of nowhere.) With characteristic derision Piñera observed that Cuba had spawned more writers in a couple of days than it had in the previous five decades, and he expressed his surprise that these so-called writers of the Revolution, who had written little or nothing, suddenly had become the most outspoken proponents of Cuban culture.

Piñera warned that genuine cultural promoters of the Revolution should beware of giving too much importance to this ilk of pseudowriters since they were often nothing but journalists or professors who had little interest in good literature. In his strangely prophetic closing remarks Piñera underscored the importance of good writers for the success of the Revolution: "El buen escritor es, por lo menos, tan eficaz para la Revolución como el soldado, el obrero o el campesino."[7] (The good writer is at least as useful for the Revolution as the soldier, worker, or peasant.) Ironically, just over two years later Fidel Castro's infamous "Words to the Intellectuals," which officially challenged commonly held notions of artistic freedom in Cuba, would give Piñera's observation a new and unexpected significance. In the meantime, however, Piñera's influence among Cuban intellectuals would grow and his writing would take on a level of importance that he had scarcely imagined.

In January 1959 Piñera began to collaborate in the newspaper *Revolución*, which had been founded clandestinely by Carlos Franqui in the mid-1950s. By June 1959 Piñera was a frequent contributor to the newspaper, at times writing more than one article per week. Later that year Piñera also began to contribute on a regular basis to *Lunes de Revolución*, the newspaper's artistically imaginative literary supplement, which was directed by Guillermo Cabrera Infante. In the words of Raymond D. Souza, "*Lunes de Revolución* was the most innovative, broadly based, and integrative journal in Cuba. There wasn't another intellectual supplement like it and there never was another after its demise. Reflecting the eclectic aesthetic concerns of both its founder and its editor, it was interested in all the arts as well as political and theoretical writings."[8]

Piñera relished the opportunity to express his ideas and opinions in articles and editorials in both publications. His essays, which tended to stand out for their provocative tone, varied widely in subject matter; from calls to literary and cultural reform, to spirited praise for the Revolution, to a reevaluations of nineteenth-century Cuban literature, to candid and aggressive criticism of Cuban writers, journals, publishing houses, and cultural institutions. As Antón Arrufat has pointed out, Piñera's involvement with *Revolución* and *Lunes* placed him on the cutting edge of Cuban culture. From *Ciclón* and its circulation of several hundred copies, Piñera stepped up to *Revolución* and *Lunes*, which reached hundreds of thousands of readers.[9] The change was at once dramatic and encouraging for Piñera, who had always wanted to leave a lasting mark on the Cuban cultural scene. In 1959 alone he wrote some fifty essays and editorials for the newspaper and its supplement, and by July, he had his own column, "Puntos, comas, y paréntesis" (Periods, Commas, and Parentheses). From then until July of the following year he signed his editorials with the pseudonym "El Escriba" (The Scribe).[10]

In several of his early essays Piñera underscored his conviction that the Revolution had brought and would continue to bring positive cultural and social reforms. At the same time, though, he exhorted his readers to be patient and cautious, since he felt that unbridled change in the past had too often brought little more than cultural and social decadence. Piñera penned his first editorial in *Revolución*, "Nubes amenazadoras" (Threatening Clouds), just days after Castro's triumphant march into Havana. In it he contended that as a result of the social, economic, and cultural problems that had plagued the island for nearly forty years, many Cubans suffered from a collective sense of fear and insecurity about their future. He insisted that in light of the constant political turmoil of the past, Cubans were still troubled by a question that they had asked many times since the establishment of the republic: "¿Esta [revolución] de ahora será como las otras de antes?"[11] (Will this [revolution] be like the ones before it?) In the same article Piñera called attention to the widespread hunger in Cuba, and he lamented the fact that no government in the past had been able (or willing) to take on the challenge of eliminating this chronic social ill: "viene planteándose, desde la instauración de la República, esta pregunta angustiosa: ¿Comeré hoy? . . . Porque digámoslo sin cortapisas: . . . el tirano a perpetuidad de esta isla ha sido y continúa siendo el hambre."[12] (Since the beginning of the Republic, the following distressing question has been asked: Will I eat today? . . . Because, let's put it frankly: . . . the perpetual tyrant of this island has been and continues to be hunger.) Even though Piñera conceded at the end of the editorial that his readers had many good reasons to be enthusiastic and encouraged them not to lose faith, the predominant tone of this inaugural publication in *Revolución* is one of guarded optimism.

As the months passed and Piñera's own situation continued to improve, his editorials became more optimistic and his praise for the Revolution more frequent. Piñera wrote many editorials about the positive changes in Cuba's literary and cultural scene that had come about since the triumph of the Revolution. In "Balance cultural de seis meses" (Sixth-Month Cultural Balance-sheet) for example, he lauded the improvement of the situation of Cuban writers and artists: "El escritor—el artista cubano en general—lo está pasando mejor con la Revolución y si las cosas siguen como hasta el presente, su status irá mejorando."[13] (The writer—the Cuban artist in general—is doing better with the Revolution, and if things continue as they have up to now, his situation will keep getting better.) In the same essay he noted enthusiastically that for the first time in the country's history many Cuban authors—including himself—were making a decent living from their work.

Piñera felt especially satisfied with the improvement of the economic lot of writers in Cuba, not so much because he felt like he deserved to be paid for his writing—indeed he had always been willing to sacrifice so much for his career—but because it signified that literature was finally being taken seriously in Cuba. We should recall that one of the first things that had impressed Piñera about the literary scene in Buenos Aires in 1946 was that writers were actually paid for their contributions to newspapers and journals. When Piñera began to receive decent wages for his contributions to *Revolución* and *Lunes*, then, it must have felt like Cuba had begun to advance toward the cultural sophistication he had left behind in Buenos Aires.

In a handful of his editorials in *Revolución* Piñera kept tabs on the progress or decadence of various Cuban cultural institutions. In "El Teatro Nacional funciona" (The National Theater Works), for instance, he extolled the government's efforts to build a national theater. As one of the country's foremost dramatists Piñera had an obvious vested interest in the project, and he admitted that he, like other theater enthusiasts, was anxiously awaiting the building's completion. He reserved special praise for the theater's director, Isabel Monal, for encouraging the production of works in the unfinished structure instead of waiting until its completion: "Entre esperar dos años para sentar al público en lunetas de peluche, o empezar sentándolo en sillas de tijera, Isabel Monal, con verdadero sentido revolucionario, optó por la segunda solución."[14] (Between waiting two years to accommodate the public in plush seats, or to begin sitting them in folding chairs, Isabel Monal, with true revolutionary spirit, opted for the second solution.)

A visit to Cuba's National Library in July, on the other hand, inspired a rather testy editorial in which Piñera criticized his compatriots' apathy toward reading and literature. In "Visita a la Biblioteca Nacional" (Visit to the National Library) he complained that during a stroll through the library he saw just a handful of patrons in a central reading room with space for more than two hundred. Piñera likewise marveled at the fact that despite holdings of nearly a million volumes, the library felt more like a pantheon of mummified books than a place for study and learning. Like he did in so many other editorials, Piñera took advantage of this one to exhort cultural reform, and he warned with revolutionary gusto that if Cubans remained indifferent to reading and literature, a precious national treasure would continue to waste away as it had under Batista and his predecessors.

As an author who had been deeply affected by the cultural stagnation that reigned in Cuba during the first half of the twentieth century, Piñera urged young writers to take part in an exciting revival of Cuba's literary scene. He advised young authors that insincere participation in the revolutionary process could result in the loss of the precious ground gained in the first months of the Revolution: "estamos en ese punto crítico en que una oclusión, por leve que sea de nuestra vida cultural, nos pondría en peligro de muerte. . . . Si desaprovechamos la ocasión o si nos la malogran, retrasaremos nuestro reloj cultural en cincuenta años."[15] (We are at that critical juncture in which even the slightest occlusion of our cultural life would put us at risk of death. . . . If we don't take advantage of the occasion or if we waste it, we'll turn our cultural clock back fifty years.)

Piñera was careful to point out, though, that the major literary reform that he envisioned would require a concerted effort and plenty of revolutionary spirit. Echoing his observations in "La inundación," he argued in "Cambio de frente politico" (Change of the Political Front) that the publication of a few propagandistic "poemitas" simply would not suffice. Likewise, in "La reforma literaria" (Literary Reform) he pointed out that good literature required an increasing political awareness and the rejection of clichés. Harking back to his frequent negations of the existence of a national literature and his criticism of the hermetic and escapist qualities of Cuban poetry, Piñera encouraged the young authors to stay in touch with contemporary political, social, and cultural realities. Doing otherwise, he warned, would increase the possibility of another cultural catastrophe.

One of Piñera's most passionate editorials, "El arte hecho revolución, la revolución hecha arte" (Art Turned Revolution, Revolution Turned Art) underscores his ardent support of the Revolution. In this article from November 1959, Piñera praised the Revolution for having greatly improved the lot of writers in Cuba, and he called on his cohorts to support the Revolution in their works and in their daily lives. Piñera insisted that "el nuevo escritor de nuestro momento debe y tiene que vivir en peligro, comprometerse mañana, tarde y noche y . . . expresar en su obra la hermosura viril de la revolución"[16] (the new writer of our times should and must live in danger, commit himself morning, afternoon, and night and . . . express in his art the virile splendor of the Revolution). It is ironic that, in his impassioned declaration of what he thought the Revolution expected of its writers, Piñera advocated the very ideals that would end up damning him and other authors once Cuba became associated with Marxist-Leninist ideology. "¿Qué quiere, pues, la Revolución de nosotros, escritores, poetas, pintores, músicos, escultores? . . . Pues quiere que todos . . . la afirmen, la expresen, la representen, la hagan, cada vez más, Revolución plena, Revolución confirmada, Revolución permanente."[17] (What, then, does the Revolution want from us, writers, poets, painters, musicians, sculptors? . . . Well, it wants everyone . . . to express it, represent it, and make it an increasingly more complete Revolution, endorsed Revolution, permanent Revolution.)

In many other articles, such as "Llamamiento a los escritores" (Call to Writers), "La Revolución se fortalece" (The Revolution is Getting Stronger), "Señales de los tiempos" (Signs of the Times), and "26 de Julio" (July 26), Piñera also expressed his enthusiastic support of many of the Revolution's programs and ideals. It is important to keep in mind, however, that in his creative writing Piñera did not tend to affirm, express, or represent the new revolutionary spirit as he so often encouraged other writers to do. This so-called lack of commitment would end up ensuring Piñera's precipitous fall from grace in the final months of 1961.

From the pages of *Revolución* Piñera also stressed the need for the creation of a national press and the foundation of respectable publishing houses. In "Algo pasa con los escritores" (Something is Happening to Our Writers), he lamented the fact that Havana had nothing that could rival the well-organized enterprises of Mexico City, Buenos Aires, and other large Latin American cities. Indeed, until the founding of Ediciones R in 1961, Cuba did not have a single publishing house that paid authors for their contributions. Without such establishments, Piñera cautioned, Cuba would remain trapped in an atmosphere of amateurism and would never measure up to countries with more developed cultural infrastructures.

Piñera was likewise deeply concerned with the lack of quality literary journals and periodicals in Cuba, and he frequently challenged his readers to take up the task of creating new ones. In his editorial "Exhortación a Rodríguez Feo" (Exhortation to Rodríguez Feo) for instance, Piñera called on his longtime friend to revive *Ciclón*, while in "Espejismo de revistas" (Mirage of Journals) he bemoaned the scarcity of reviews, magazines, journals, and literary pamphlets in Cuba. In his mind it made little sense that the Cuban Revolution had spawned such a limited number of new publications, especially given the fact that Cubans were finally free to express their opinions. As he put it, "Si el pensamiento se mantuvo ahogado por años es lógico que se manifieste profundamente con la llegada de la libertad de expresión."[18] (If thought was kept pent up for years, it is logical that it show itself profoundly upon the arrival of freedom of expression.)

Given his affinity for stirring up the literary community, it is not surprising that even after advocating the creation of such publications, Piñera did not hesitate to criticize new magazines when he found them to be insufficient or uninspiring. In fact, a week after his plea in "Espejismo de revistas," Piñera wrote a scathing review of *La Nueva Revista Cubana* (The New Cuban Review) whose first numbers were under the direction of Cintio Vitier. Piñera accused Vitier's fledgling magazine of failing to reflect Cuba's new and exciting reality, and he added that he was especially turned off by its overly respectful tone. In a clever reference to *Ciclón*, Piñera complained that *La Nueva Revista Cubana* "no levantaría vientos y tempestades" (wouldn't stir up winds and storms),[19] and he quipped that reading the dull publication was about as exciting as drinking a glass of lemonade. Piñera had a similarly negative impression of the long-running *Diario de la Marina*, which was directed by Gastón Baquero. On several occasions he lambasted the magazine for, among other things, its supposedly low editorial standards, its incompetent director, and the poor quality of its publications.[20]

Since Piñera took great pride in his reputation as a polemicist, he often took advantage of his column in *Revolución* to reinforce his role as the relentless provocateur of the Cuban intellectual community. He challenged, indeed at times even attacked, everyone from little-known authors such as the young Cuban playwright Wilberto Cantón ("¡Cuán gritan esos malditos!" [How Those Devils Scream!]), to important literary and cultural figures. Among his most frequent targets were Cintio Vitier ("Espejismo de revistas" [Mirage of Reviews], "Hablemos de excesos" [Let's Talk About Excesses]), and Gastón Baquero ("El Baquerismo literario" [Literary Baquerism]), but on occasion he also poked fun at other Cuban authors such as Alejo Carpentier, Nicolás Guillén, and Heberto Padilla. It is noteworthy that despite his notorious confrontations with Lezama in the past, Piñera rarely criticized him in *Revolución* or *Lunes*. In fact, in various articles, "Veinte años atrás" (Twenty Years Ago) and "Más Miscelánea" (More Miscellanea), for example, Piñera pointed out Lezama's central role as an innovator of Cuban and Latin American poetry.

For the most part, though, praise was outweighed by ridicule in the scores of essays and editorials that Piñera wrote for *Revolución* and *Lunes*, and in one of his most contentious articles, "Las plumas respetuosas," he admitted with characteristic candor that he very much enjoyed his role as a disrespectful author. In the same article he defined so-called respectful writers, and listed the key ingredients of their work: Catholicism, frequent reference to the mystics, *preciosismos*, smoke screens and other forms of deception, flattery, and cowardice. Piñera declared that his frequent insolent critiques of his fellow writers were necessary since through them he underscored the need for cultural reform. Since respectful authors and critics were afraid of sacrifice and compromise, he contended, there was no place for them in the Revolution.

> Ojalá esta Revolución traiga un soplo renovador al campo cultural. . . . Que de una vez por todas barra . . . con los críticos respetuosos, que tampoco saben nada de nada y, más que todo eso, con los escritores respetuosos cuya sabiduría se ha empleado todo el tiempo en repartir altas dosis de respeto a la juventud desorientada.[21]

> [Let's hope that this Revolution brings a renovating breath to the literary sphere. . . . That once and for all it does away . . . with respectful critics,

who don't even know anything about anything, and in addition to all that, with respectful writers whose wisdom has always been employed in handing out high doses of respect to our disoriented youth.]

A well-known tiff between Piñera and Heberto Padilla erupted in December 1959 after the young and aspiring poet wrote a feisty response to Piñera's article "Veinte años atrás," which had been published in *Revolución* two months earlier. In that article, Piñera extolled the poetry of José Lezama Lima, and referred to the great poet as one of the only innovative Cuban writers of the twentieth century. Piñera pointed out that with *Enemigo rumor* (1941) Lezama had broken the mold by writing extraordinarily original poems. For his part, Padilla argued in "La poesía en su lugar" (Poetry in Its Place) that Lezama was not the innovator that Piñera claimed he was.[22] Instead, Padilla insisted that *Enemigo rumor* represented a one-hundred-year step backward, and he added that Lezama and most of the other *Orígenes* poets had written largely escapist texts that had nothing to do with the country's social or political reality. Padilla went on to argue that *Orígenes* was nothing but an ordinary journal that had no direction whatsoever, and he claimed that many of those associated with the group—including Piñera himself—would have been much better poets had they not bowed to the influence of Lezama.[23]

Piñera was not one to leave a challenge unanswered. He responded to Padilla's intransigent article in the next number of *Lunes*. He began "Cada cosa en su lugar" by noting that Padilla seemed to have usurped the role of "lobo feroz" (big, bad wolf) that Piñera himself had played for so many years. Piñera advised Padilla, though, that he had clearly not learned to play the part:

> Pues Padilla . . . trata de poner a la poesía cubana en su lugar. . . . Es claro, Padilla hace sus primeras actuaciones de lobo feroz y se advierte de entrada que no está bien interiorizado con su papel. Su apreciación del fenómeno poético cubano entre 1936–1958 queda, justamente, un poco fuera de lugar.[24]

> [Well then, Padilla . . . tries to put Cuban poetry in its place. . . . It's clear, Padilla puts on his first performance as the big, bad wolf and from the get-go one notices that he is not well familiarized with his role. His critical appreciation of the phenomenon of Cuban poetry from 1936–1958 comes off as being, precisely, a bit out of place.]

Piñera took exception to Padilla's claim that he had let Lezama's poetic impact annul his own poetic intuition. While he admitted that in his formative years he had penned poems that were greatly influenced by

Lezama, he added that by 1940 he had given up his submissive position. As he put it, "me quité la piel de oveja para asumir mi papel de lobo feroz."[25] (I took off my sheep's clothing in order to assume my role as the big, bad wolf.) Thus began his unofficial vocation as a provocateur, which he underscored by citing several examples of his "insumisión eterna" (eternal rebelliousness) since 1941, such as his break from *Espuela de Plata* and subsequent foundation of *Poeta*, his poem "La isla en peso" (1943), and a letter in which Piñera derided Gastón Baquero for choosing a career as a journalist.

"Cada cosa en su lugar" is one of Piñera's most interesting articles and in it the reader will find many of the trademarks—biting wit, sarcasm, derisive putdowns, self-promotion, and arrogance—of his unique approach to literary and cultural criticism. In this key article, and in many others for that matter, Piñera declared not only that he enjoyed his self-proclaimed role as a provocateur, but also that his incessant instigation greatly benefited the Cuban cultural scene: "En nuestra incipiente literatura . . . este rol de lobo feroz ha sido muy beneficioso. A qué cumbres de estupidez no llegaríamos si, de vez en cuando, estos animables [*sic*] temibles no hicieron su aparición en el campo literario cubano. Seríamos nada más que un rebaño de mansas ovejitas."[26] (In our insipient literature . . . this role of the big, bad wolf has been very beneficial. To what heights of stupidity would we arrive if these terrifying animals didn't make an appearance on the Cuban literary scene. We would be nothing but a flock of tame little lambs.)

Piñera's role as a polemicist did have certain drawbacks. Despite his routine declarations that he enjoyed stirring up the literary community, he managed to create plenty of adversaries among Cuba's cultural and political circles. On a number of occasions Piñera's commentaries provoked heated responses from his readers.[27] His aggressive critical style and numerous personal attacks of influential social and cultural figures not only perturbed the individuals themselves, but also many of their supporters.

Eventually Piñera's provocations would catch up to him. In the meantime, though, he enjoyed his prestigious spot in the limelight and continued to have confidence in the importance of his role in the Revolution. In February 1961 he made the following observation, which underscored his firm conviction that he had played an instrumental role in Cuba's cultural reform: "Ahora estoy en terreno favorable. La Revolución me ha dado carta de naturaleza. Los años que me quedan de vida no volverán a confrontarme con tales humillaciones."[28] (Now I'm on favorable ground. The Revolution has thoroughly accepted me. The years of life that I have before me will never again confront me with such humiliations.) Ironically, Piñera's days of glory were numbered, and his most humiliating moments were to come very soon.

Fleeting Days of Glory

Piñera's assiduous collaboration in *Revolución* and *Lunes* filled him with a sense of importance that he had rarely felt throughout his long literary career. It was, however, a very demanding job that at times pulled him away from other literary endeavors. In his correspondence with Humberto Rodríguez Tomeu, who was still living in Argentina, he griped that his involvement with *Revolución* and *Lunes* was pushing him to the limit.[29] He complained, for example, that Guillermo Cabrera Infante—the magazine's director—called too many time-consuming meetings with the editorial staff. Furthermore, Piñera noted that his responsibilities with *Lunes* had increased significantly after Cabrera Infante named him director of Ediciones R, a new publishing house under the auspices of the magazine. His duties with the Ediciones R were varied and kept him extremely busy. In June 1960 he wrote to Humberto to describe the overwhelming responsibility of his new position: "Tenemos que dejar listos cinco libros para el próximo Congreso de Escritores a celebrar la última semana de junio. . . . Imagina: he tenido que leerlos todos, hacer correcciones, escribir solapas, etc."[30] (We have to have five books ready for the next Writers' Congress to be celebrated the last week of June. . . . Imagine: I have had to read all of them, make corrections, write flap notes, etc.)

Piñera's *Teatro completo*, a collection of eight plays written between 1941–60, was one of his earliest projects with Ediciones R. Though Piñera announced in a letter to Humberto that it would be completed by June 1960, the book turned into a rather complicated undertaking. As it turned out, the finished product, complete with a lengthy introduction by Piñera and sixteen pages of photographs, was not available in bookstores until March of the following year.[31] Despite a complicated editorial history, the timing of the publication of *Teatro completo* was opportune in many ways. By 1961 Piñera had become widely known as a major figure of Cuban theater. Since his return to the island in 1958 he had written three new plays: *Aire frío*, *El flaco y el gordo* (The Skinny Man and the Fat Man), and *El filántropo* (The Philanthropist). *Electra Garrigó*, which he had written nearly twenty years earlier, had not been previously published but was performed repeatedly in the 1960s, received rave reviews, and quickly turned into something of a Cuban classic.

When the play opened for the third time at the Teatro Prometeo in

February 1960, performances sold out and extra seats were packed into the aisles: "Electra va muy bien" (Electra is going very well), Piñera wrote to Humberto several weeks later. "El domingo pasado se llenó de tal modo que pusieron sillas de tijera. . . . Mañana sábado irá Sartre a verla."[32] (Last Sunday it filled to such an extent that they set up folding chairs. . . . Tomorrow Sartre will go to see it.) In a postscript to the same letter Piñera made reference to a newspaper photo of Jean-Paul Sartre attending the play, which he had enclosed. He reported that Sartre was crazy about the play and was making plans to bring it to Paris, and added that Fidel Castro was expected to attend a performance of *Electra Garrigó* the following weekend.

Unfortunately, Sartre never brought the play to Paris, and Castro never showed up on the expected date. But these were the glory days for Virgilio Piñera, and at least for the time being such matters were of minimal importance. *Electra* was performed for equally enthusiastic audiences in the theater of the recently founded Casa de las Américas in March 1961, where 2,000 tickets were sold in just three nights. It was also performed for enthusiastic audiences at the National Theater in April. On top of the unprecedented popular success of his play, Piñera was being paid to write theater for the first time in his life, and venues began to commission him to write new works. In March 1960, for example, the National Theater commissioned a play for the grand opening of the Sala Covarrubias. Piñera immediately began writing *El filántropo*, which he based on the story of the same name. He finished this lengthy dramatic work in just a few weeks. Though its premiere on August 20, 1960, was met with mixed reviews, the play was performed twenty times and was shown on Cuban television in October. The play's budget was high for the time, and something playwrights like Piñera were not used to, as he clearly indicated in a letter to Humberto: "Ayer fuí al teatro para lo del presupuesto de la representación de *El Filántropo*. Me parecía estar soñando. Presupuesto: siete mil pesos."[33] (Yesterday I went to the theater to find out about the budget for the representation of *El filántropo*. It seemed like I was dreaming. Budget: seven thousand pesos.) Piñera's one-act play "La sorpresa" (The Surprise), also commissioned by the National Theater, premiered on June 27, 1960.

Piñera's success during these early stages of the Revolution came to him as somewhat of a surprise. After the premier of "La sorpresa" he joked in a letter to Humberto that he hardly knew what to do with all the money he had earned from his plays. "¿Te acuerdas de aquellos tiempos en que gastar un peso de más significaba un desequilibro horrible? . . . [Ahora] tengo dinero que no sé en qué gastar."[34] (Do you remember those times when spending an extra peso resulted in a horrible imbalance? . . . [Now] I have money and don't know what to spend it on.) In a matter of months Piñera had become a professional writer and a star of the budding Havana theater scene. As one critic aptly put it, 1960 was the glory year of Virgilio Piñera, who had once complained that he would never be able to enjoy anything in life.[35]

Falling from Grace

Unfortunately, Piñera's days of glory and his revolutionary exuberance would soon begin to fade. As Fidel Castro gradually consolidated his control of Cuba, signs of the country's new political direction began to concern many groups who feared losing freedoms that they had gained since the triumph of the Revolution. Castro's declaration in 1960 that there would be no presidential elections, and his increasingly aggressive courtship of the Soviet bloc, further raised fears among certain intellectual circles that Cuba was heading toward Stalin-era cultural and social repression.[36]

Castro's harsh treatment of his opponents also began to alarm some groups. Batista officials and other political dissidents, including some of Castro's former supporters in the Sierra Maestra campaign, were imprisoned or executed. Huber Matos, a former Castro adherent who had expressed concern over the leader's growing power, was sentenced to a twenty-year prison term. Likewise, the revolutionary leader Camilo Cienfuegos disappeared in a small private plane shortly after publicly condemning the treatment of Matos.

Both Thomas and Rogozinski have suggested that by early 1961 some 2,000 of Castro's opponents had been executed.[37] Just over three years later, the official number of Cubans who were in jails and camps for political crimes was nearly 15,000, and in 1965 Castro admitted in an interview with Lee Lockwood that the number of political prisoners in his country was approaching 20,000.[38] In the same interview Castro partially explained the reasons for the high number of prisoners with a characteristic observation. He noted, as he had many times since 1959, that "In a revolutionary process, there are no neutrals; there are only partisans of the revolution or enemies of it." Castro added that as long as there was counterrevolution, "the revolutionary tribunals will have to exist in order to punish" those involved in activities against the Revolution.[39]

Such issues served to polarize the country, and it became increasingly difficult (and risky) to claim neutrality. The expression "con Cuba o contra Cuba" (for Cuba or against Cuba) became an official slogan of the Revolution in the early 1960s, and many writers, artists, and intellectuals began to lose faith in the government and to distance themselves from the political mainstream. As Louis A. Pérez has pointed out, in this increasingly tense climate, opposition newspapers and radio stations were taken over or shut down by the government.[40] Some collaborators in *Revolución* and *Lunes* began to question the changes, but those publications themselves eventually became victims of the government's strict new laws and regulations. According to Carlos Franqui, who had participated in the Sierra Maestra campaign with Castro and served as director of *Revolución*, "a general crackdown was taking place" and many of the newspaper's contributors "were going against the tide of events, in part because we believed that as an integral part of the literary campaign, cultural literacy was something that should be totally free of controls."[41] The government, however, felt differently.

The year 1961 was a watershed year for the Cuban Revolution, but the new political climate that emerged did not bode well for many artists and intellectuals. In fact, many authors began to feel ill at ease in the midst of an increasingly stifling intellectual atmosphere. On the political front, 1961 was an especially significant year. In April Castro made his first public statement concerning the socialist nature of the Cuban Revolution, and later that year he made one of his most famous declarations on state television: "I am a Marxist-Leninist and shall remain a Marxist-Leninist until the day I die." The statement served to heighten many intellectuals' well-founded fears of imminent cultural repression. Shortly after Castro's April declaration, a group of Cuban exiles, with support from President Kennedy and the CIA, took part in a disastrous invasion at the Bay of Pigs. Within two days Castro and his followers had quashed the invaders, and he declared a total victory against Yankee imperialism.

In an interesting letter to Humberto, Piñera described the tense atmosphere in Havana after the Bay of Pigs attack. The most interesting aspect of the letter is his reference to the drastic measures taken by the Castro government to round up suspected counterrevolutionaries:

No puedo contarte de la angustia de estos días con la invasión . . . El gobierno se vio obligado a una medida drástica: encerrar a miles de personas sospechosas de contrarrevolución. Como dijo el propio Fidel, en la redada cayó mucha gente inocente . . . , pero que en la natural confusión fueron tomados.[42]

[I can hardly describe the anguish of these days with the invasion . . . The government felt obligated to take a drastic measure: to incarcerate thousands of people suspected of counterrevolution. As Fidel himself said, many innocent people went down in the roundup . . . , but that in the natural confusion they were taken.]

It should not be overlooked that even after the roundup of suspected counterrevolutionaries, Piñera still supported Castro and the Revolution. Like many Cubans he felt that his country had been turned into a victim of American imperialism. In his correspondence with Humberto he frequently complained about the United States and its dealings with Cuba. In one letter he asked, for example, "¿Has visto el Kennedy como nos trata? Qué se habrá creído."[43] (Have you seen how Kennedy treats us? What does he think he is?)

Piñera's faith in Castro's government would soon change, however, as would his personal circumstances. It was shortly after the inauspicious events of the Bay of Pigs invasion that *P.M.*, a short film directed by Orlando Jiménez Leal and Sabá Cabrera Infante (Guillermo's younger brother), was turned into the perfect pretext for the increasingly testy Castro government to clamp down on the country's intellectuals and artists. The seventeen-minute film is an experiment in Free Cinema. It depicts scenes of nightlife in Havana neighborhoods populated by mostly the black and mulatto lower class.[44] According to Michael Chanan, the term Free Cinema was first used in London in 1956, and its practitioners "offered up . . . simple fragments of daily reality, modest film essays on things close to common experience. They wanted to use film," he adds, as "a testimonial that brought a living document to the screen."[45] *P.M.* has no dialogue and focuses on scenes of revelry—dancing, drinking, and music playing, and even a brief scuffle over a woman—in a number of bars and clubs in the Cuatro Caminos and Playa de Marianao sections of Havana. As the night wears on and the crowds in the bars begin to thin out, the atmosphere of the film becomes more melancholic. As Guillermo Cabrera Infante has pointed out, a somber bolero—"Canción por la mañana" (Song for the Morning)—sung by Vicentico Valdés (1921–1995)—lends an air nostalgia and solitude to the final minutes of *P.M.*[46]

It was largely the film's depiction of the supposedly seamy side of Cuban reality in the midst of the heroic events of the Revolution that some Cuban officials found distasteful. Despite the fact that the film had been shown on Cuban television without incident or complaint, Alfredo Guevara—who was the acting head of the Instituto Cubano de Arte e Industria Cinematográficos (ICAIC)—denied the directors' request for permission to show it in a Havana theater in May.[47]

After the banning and confiscation of *P.M.*, scores of artists and intellectuals—including Virgilio Piñera—signed a manifesto that reaffirmed their solidarity with the Revolution, but called for greater artistic freedom. "Manifiesto de los intelectuales y artistas" (Manifesto of the Intellectuals and Artists) was published in *Lunes* on June 11, 1961. The text began on page seventeen with the following statement:

> Los intelectuales, escritores y artistas cubanos queremos afirmar por este medio nuestra pública responsabilidad ante la Revolución y el pueblo de Cuba, en una época cuyo sentido profundo es el de la lucha unida para alcanzar la completa independencia de nuestra patria como nación.
>
> Estamos seguros de que el triunfo de la Revolución ha creado entre nosotros las condiciones necesarias para el desarrollo de la cultura nacional; una cultura liberadora, libre en sí misma y por tanto capaz de servir y estimular el avance revolucionario.

> [The intellectuals, writers, and artists of Cuba want to affirm by this means our public responsibility to the Revolution and the Cuban people, in an era whose profound sense is one of united struggle to achieve the complete independence of our country as a nation.
>
> We are confident that the triumph of the Revolution has created among us the necessary conditions for the development of national culture; a liberating culture, free in its own right, and for that reason capable of serving and stimulating revolutionary advance.]

The document's ninety-two signatories confirmed their integral role in the revolutionary process, and they outlined their plan of action for the immediate future. In the concluding statement they contended that all artists should be able to express their support of the Revolution in any way that they considered appropriate, and they encouraged the organization of a national conference at which such issues could be addressed.

Allegedly as a means to ease the growing tension instigated by the banning of *P.M.*, the government responded by organizing a series of meetings with Cuban intellectuals on three consecutive Fridays—June 16, 23, and 30—in the Biblioteca Nacional José Martí. As Raymond Souza has so aptly put it, "An affair that apparently started out as a minor matter was soon recognized as an attack against anyone associated with *Lunes*."[48]

A now legendary anecdote has it that on the first day of meetings, before the official commencement of the sessions, Cuban president Osvaldo Dorticós, with Castro at his side, invited those present to express their concerns. According to Guillermo Cabrera Infante's oft-cited version of the story, Virgilio Piñera was the only one to stand up. "Suddenly out of the blue alert: a timid man with mousy hair, frightened voice and shy manners . . . said that he wanted to speak. It was Virgilio Piñera. He confessed to being terribly frightened. He didn't know of what, but he was really frightened almost on the verge of panic."[49]

Ironically, just four months earlier Piñera had declared in an editorial in *Revolución* that he was on favorable ground as a firm supporter of the Revolution, and he added that he would never again be faced with the type of humiliation that he so often suffered during the Batista years.[50]

It is indeed somewhat disconcerting that these words came from the same man that found himself confessing in June 1961 that he, like so many others in the room, was afraid of what the future held in store for Cuban intellectuals. Perhaps Fidel Castro was referring to Piñera himself when he addressed the fears expressed by certain individuals on the first day of the meetings. "Había ciertos miedos en el ambiente y algunos compañeros han expresado esos temores" (There were certain apprehensions in the air and some comrades have expressed those fears),[51] he observed as he set out to define the ideological and cultural norms to be followed by the writers and artists of the Revolution.

In "Palabras a los intelectuales" Castro focused on freedom of artistic expression, an issue that many authors rightly feared had taken a backseat to other supposedly more important ideals of the Revolution. His strong words were clearly aimed at the collaborators of *Lunes* who, in the eyes of the government, had strayed too far from the social, cultural, and political mainstream. It was the government's feeling that their liberal attitudes about artistic freedom had to be kept in check. In his introductory comments of the address Castro outlined the basic problem at hand: "El problema que aquí se ha estado discutiendo y vamos a abordar, es el problema de la libertad de los escritores y de los artistas para expresarse. . . . El punto más polémico de esta cuestión es: si debe haber o no una libertad de contenido en la expresión artística."[52] (The issue that you've been discussing and that we are going to take up, is the issue of the freedom of writers and artists to express themselves. . . . The most polemical point of this matter is: should or should there not be freedom of content in artistic expression.)

Castro added that the question of freedom of content should only pose a problem to those who were not sure of their revolutionary convictions, and he noted that such individuals were likewise the only ones who represented a real threat to the Revolution. With typically unforgiving bluntness, Castro made it clear during his infamous speech that the notion of freedom of artistic expression had taken on a new meaning in Cuba: "Esto significa que dentro de la Revolución todo; contra la Revolución nada. Contra la Revolución nada, porque la Revolución tiene también sus derechos y . . . nadie puede alegar con razón un derecho contra ella."[53] (This means that within the Revolution everything; against the Revolution, nothing. Against the Revolution nothing, because the Revolution also has it rights and . . . no one can invoke with reason a right against it.)

Castro's words underscored the fact that in Cuba neutrality was not permissible in politics or in literature. In other words, one was either for the Revolution or against it, and works of art or literature that did not directly support the Revolution and its goals would therefore be deemed counterrevolutionary. Such a notion mirrored Castro's vision of a "new man" in Cuba who would be motivated in every way by a revolutionary spirit. As one historian put it, "In addition to behaving correctly, this new man also would be filled with revolutionary fervor expressed through selflessness, sacrifice, and unswerving loyalty to the government."[54]

It is not hard to imagine why Virgilio Piñera would have found Castro's words so troubling. For more than two years he had defended many of the causes of the Revolution and had praised the ever-increasing freedoms enjoyed by authors and artists in Cuba under the new regime. We must recall that in many of his early editorials in *Revolución* and *Lunes* Piñera had praised the Revolution's promotion of Cuban culture and even the newfound freedom of expression in revolutionary Cuba. He wrote in "Literatura y Revolución" (Literature and Revolution), for example, that "la propia Revolución no ha pensado por un momento en dar pautas al escritor, en consignarlo a escribir lo que ella quiera"[55] (the Revolution itself has never considered for a moment setting guidelines for the writer, in making him write what it wants). But Castro's words undermined his enthusiasm by confirming that the freedom of expression that Piñera had envisioned as a central part of Cuba's cultural reform during the Revolution suddenly had become implausible.

Shortly after the June meetings Piñera embarked on a monthlong trip to Europe. There he met up with Humberto and the two traveled in a number of countries. By the time of his return to Cuba in mid-September, the government had taken even tighter hold on the reigns of the country's cultural and social scene. *Lunes*, for example, was shut down in October—ostensibly because of a lack of paper—and all other modes of popular and cultural expression fell under strict scrutiny. The closure of *Lunes* was by then, of course, a foregone conclusion since the government had made clear its opposition to all forms of so-called ideological nonconformity. Interestingly enough, Piñera himself had once declared that "lo revolucionario de 'Lunes' se fundamenta en el derecho que tiene todo escritor de expresar su pensamiento" (the revolutionary aspect of "Lunes" is based on the right that every writer has to express his thoughts).[56] It was precisely this sort of attitude that ended up insuring the magazine's demise.

It is important to add that *Lunes* was also known as a haven for homosexuals,[57] which surely made the magazine and its staff all the more unpalatable to Cuban government officials who considered homosexuality to be a sign of divergence from socialist ideals. In his study of homosexuality and the Cuban Revolution, Marvin Leiner has observed that with the emergence of Marxism-Leninism, which had long espoused a certain puritanism and cultural rigidity, the Cuban campaign against bourgeois decadence began to concentrate on so-called moral violations. "Not only was the corruption of prostitution condemned, but also any notion of sexual freedom or changes that endangered the traditional family institution."[58] It was a commonly held belief, Leiner adds, "that male homosexuals could not, by their nature" achieve the status of Cuba's "new man"—a courageous, selfless individual willing to fight for the Revolution.

It was inevitable, then, that Piñera would eventually become a victim of the crackdown on sexual deviance. On October 11, 1961, he was arrested for an alleged violation of revolutionary morality, in a bar near his beach house in Guanabo. The arrest took place the morning after the infamous Night of the Three P's, a Marxist-moralist operation that aimed to rid the city of prostitutes, pimps, and pederasts. According to Carlos Franqui this was "the first massive socialist raid of the Cuban Revolution."[59] Through the intervention of Franqui and other friends, Piñera was released quickly, but the experience crushed his spirits and filled him with intense fear. Upon returning to his beach house, he found that it had been searched and locked by the authorities. Though he was eventually given permission to return, his fear of living alone and of being arrested again moved him to abandon the house.

In a letter written to Humberto shortly after his arrest Piñera did not mention the incident—probably out of fear that his letters were being intercepted by the authorities—but he clearly underscored his disturbed emotional and physical state. It is especially interesting to note his attempts to justify his decision to abandon the beach house in Guanabo that the two of them had once lived in together.

> Tienes razón en quejarte de mi irregularidad en escribirte pero si supieras lo malo que he estado. Tengo el hígado a la miseria y hasta me repitió la neuritis que tuve en Buenos Aires. . . . En estos días tomaré un apartamento en la Habana. Lo he decidido pues acá en Guanabo estoy muy solo y Luisa no puede atenderme como es debido. . . . voy a estar más tranquilo.[60]

> [You are right to complain about my irregularity in writing to you, but if you knew how ill I have been. My liver is in wretched shape and I even had a relapse of the neuritis that I suffered in Buenos Aires. . . . Soon I will take an apartment in Havana. I have decided to do so because here in Guanabo I am very lonely and Luisa can't attend to me as is necessary. . . . I'll be more relaxed.]

By the end of January 1962 Piñera had abandoned his beach house and moved into an apartment adjacent to that of José Rodríguez Feo at the corner of Calle "N" and Calle 27, in the Vedado district of Havana.

The move to el Vedado, the recent demise of *Lunes*, and his arrest a few months earlier greatly dampened Piñera's spirits and precipitated another emotional crisis. "Qué manera de cambiar la vaca por la chiva" (What a way to exchange the cow for the nanny-goat), he complained to Humberto, referring to the difference between his tiny apartment and his spacious beach house. "Ya estoy que ni hago planes ni quiero conversar nada."[61] (I'm in such a state that I don't make plans and I don't want to converse at all.) During this period Piñera's prolific correspondence with Humberto started to take on a more negative tone. In his letters—which became less frequent with the passing of the years—he chronicled his own downward tumble amid the increasingly repressive atmosphere of revolutionary Cuba.

By early 1962 Piñera's lifestyle began to change as drastically as his living quarters had. His highly visible and prestigious position as a collaborator for *Revolución* and *Lunes* was replaced by a less significant, but respectable, job as an editor and translator for the Editorial Nacional.[62] Piñera also wrote a handful of articles, poems, and stories for two new journals, *Unión* and *La Gaceta de Cuba*, but he no longer had a viable outlet for the publication of provocative editorials like those he had written on a nearly weekly basis since June 1959.

Despite the decline of his personal circumstances and the government's increasing determination to limit the influence of homosexuals on art and culture, Piñera continued to write and to hope that his circumstances would improve. A rare moment of glory came with the premier of *Aire frío* on December 8, 1962. The concern that Piñera had voiced in his introduction to his *Teatro completo*—that is, that the public would not tolerate such a long play[63]—turned out to be unfounded. The staging of the play, which he had written more than three years earlier, was a resounding success. Performances sold out nightly and Piñera was overwhelmed by both the effusive popular and critical reception of the play.

> Ha sido un success tan grande que las colas para verlo son impresionantes. Tuve que salir a escena y el público entero se puso de pie para gritarme bravo y aplaudir. . . . La gente llora, suspira, y le parece poco las tres horas y media que dura la pieza.[64]

> [It has been such a success that the lines to see it are impressive. I had to go out on stage and the entire audience got on their feet to shout bravo to me and to applaud. . . . People cry, sigh, and the three and a half hours that the play lasts seem short to them.]

In another letter written more than a month later he reported that performances were still selling out nightly, and added that the French critic Claude Couffon had seen the play and had compared it to works by Eugène Ionesco and Samuel Beckett.[65]

Unfortunately such grand moments were far outnumbered by disappointments and setbacks. Plans to perform *La boda* in Vienna in 1962, for example, never materialized, and in September 1963 Piñera's spirits were crushed when he learned that a personal invitation to attend a major theater festival in Edinburgh, Scotland, in August of the same year had supposedly been opened too late by the secretary of the UNEAC. In a letter to Humberto, Piñera expressed his great disappointment and suggested that the unfortunate incident was not a mistake:

> Esta carta llegó a la Unión el 2 de agosto y ¡agárrate! Fue abierta el 5 de septiembre.... Me dice Guillén que la culpa es de la secretaria que no no [*sic*] abrió la correspondencia....[66] Es, como comprenderás, una excusa como otra cualquiera.[67]

> [This letter arrived at the Union on August 2 and, brace yourself! It was opened on the 5th of September.... Guillén tells me that it was the secretary's fault since she didn't open the correspondence.... It is, as you will understand, an excuse like any other.]

To underscore the increasingly difficult nature of everyday existence in Cuba, Piñera noted in the same letter that one of the only bright moments of recent days had come when he received, by post from a friend in London, a high-quality nylon toothbrush. With a mix of bitterness and humor he added that it was the first decent toothbrush he had had since living in Buenos Aires.

By the mid-1960s, disappointment and disillusion had become facts of life for Piñera. Though he published a number of works during that time, it became increasingly apparent that attempts were being made to lessen his influence in the Cuban cultural community. In 1964 he lost his position as director of Ediciones R as well as his job at the Editorial Nacional, and was given a position of minimal influence as a translator at the Imprenta Nacional.

In September 1964 Piñera managed to travel to Europe where he made arrangements for the translation of several of his works. In Italy, for example, he signed a contract with Editore Feltrinelli for the translation rights to his short stories, *La carne de René*, *Teatro completo*, and *Pequeñas maniobras*. Likewise, through a contact with the Spanish writer Juan Goytisolo, he set up a deal with Éditions Gallimard for the rights to *Cuentos fríos*.[68] He later traveled to Belgium where he visited Guillermo Cabrera Infante, who was serving as the Cuban cultural attaché to that country. With Cabrera Infante Piñera traveled to Paris in early December 1964, where they met with fellow Cuban authors Heberto Padilla, Pablo Armando Fernández, and Carlos Franqui.[69] In Paris Franqui warned Piñera about the increasing repression of homosexuals in Cuba and informed him that the government had plans to establish camps where individuals who were considered unproductive or nonconformist would be sent for rehabilitation.[70]

Franqui encouraged Piñera not to return to Cuba, but the latter felt obligated to go back immediately, largely because he had recently received a letter from his sister Luisa who begged him to help her sort out problems with their ailing father. In a letter sent to Humberto from Madrid Virgilio explained his reasons for deciding to go back to Cuba: "Decidí regresar. Yo sé que me acusarás de vacilación y de pensar demasiado en la familia, pero así soy y además estoy cansado de tanto luchar."[71] (I decided to return. I know that you're going to accuse me of indecision and of thinking too much about my family, but that's how I am, and besides, I'm tired of so much struggle.) He further explained that another exile in Buenos Aires, though tempting, was out of the question for the moment since such a move might hurt his chances to publish his works in Europe given that his potential publishers supported the Revolution. In December Piñera returned to Cuba unaware, to be sure, that he would never leave the country again.

By the time of Piñera's return to Cuba in early 1965, the situation that Carlos Franqui had warned him about had materialized, and as Marvin Leiner has noted, "homophobia had reached a level of organized repression."[72] In the province of Camagüey the government had established Unidades Militares para la Ayuda de Producción (UMAP), to which so-called dissidents, homosexuals, and other socially marginalized individuals were sent to be "rehabilitated." The UMAP continued to operate through 1967, when they were finally shut down due to increasing local and international pressure. During these difficult years Piñera frequently suffered from depression and anxiety, and at times he greatly feared being arrested again.

The Spanish writer Juan Goytisolo, who visited Cuba in 1967, has offered a moving portrait of Piñera in the mid-1960s. In his autobiographical work, *Realms of Strife*, he describes a brief meeting with Piñera at the Hotel Nacional in Havana:

> His worsening physical state, the signs of a life of panic and distress were quite visible. Frightened like someone on the run, he wanted to go out into the garden to speak freely. He related in detail the persecution of homosexu-

als, the way they were being spied on and rounded up. . . . Despite repeated moving evidence of attachment to the revolution, Virgilio lived in constant fear of betrayal and blackmail. . . . When we bid farewell, I found the impression of moral solitude and misery emanating from his person quite unbearable.[73]

In his correspondence with Humberto Rodríguez Tomeu, Piñera chronicled his gradual downfall. Certain themes are repeated almost obsessively in the letters written after 1962. References to his emotional instability, his increasing pessimism, his advancing age (he mentions his birthday, August 4, with surprising frequency), and encroaching death are especially numerous.[74]

In much the same way that his personal correspondence reveals the emotional turmoil that beleaguered him throughout the later years of his life, many of Virgilio Piñera's creative writings reflect his ever-increasing fears and tensions. For instance, *El no* and "Rebelión de los enfermos" (Rebellion of the Sick), both written in 1965, can be interpreted as very personal responses to the Cuban government's adoption of ideologies that not only condemned all types of nonconformism but also touted socialism's supposed ability "to cure vices and restore people's health."[75] *El no*, which is discussed at length in chapter 7, is somewhat autobiographical in its presentation of individuals who refuse to accept an ideology that they do not espouse even though they know that they risk being punished for their nonconformity.

"Rebelión de los enfermos," which was originally published in the Cuban journal *Unión* in 1965, can also be seen as a reaction to the ever-increasing repression of homosexuals and nonconformists in Cuba in the 1960s. Indeed, through this masterful story, in which seemingly normal and healthy citizens are forced to take refuge in a hospital where they are separated from the rest of the population, Piñera criticized Cuban homophobia and parodied the government's decision to send so-called socially deviant individuals to the UMAP for rehabilitation.

Piñera's play *Dos viejos pánicos* (Two Panicked Old Folks), which was awarded the prestigious Casa de las Américas Prize in 1968, also reflects many of the author's fears and preoccupations during his later years. The play's sole protagonists are an elderly couple, Tabo and Tota, who are prisoners of a fear that has overwhelmed them for most of their lives. Despite being one of Piñera's most widely acclaimed plays, *Dos viejos pánicos* was something of a thorn in Piñera's side. Shortly after its publication, the play was deemed counterrevolutionary and it was thus banned in Cuba during Piñera's lifetime.[76]

Piñera's sense of fear was no doubt heightened by the events of the final months of 1968, when two of his friends and fellow authors, Heberto Padilla and Antón Arrufat, became embroiled in a literary scandal that would eventually provoke intense international criticism of Cuba's increasingly severe cultural repression. Padilla's troubles with Cuban officials had started a year earlier, after he published a favorable review of Guillermo Cabrera Infante's novel *Tres tristes tigres* (*Three Trapped Tigers*). Cabrera Infante had officially defected from the Revolution and was living in exile in London. Since the author of *Tres tristes tigres* was considered an enemy of the state, Padilla's review of the novel was considered to be an implicit defense of a traitor. Shortly after publishing the review, Padilla was invited to teach at a French university, but he was denied permission to leave the country.

In October 1968 Padilla and Arrufat were awarded the UNEAC prize, for poetry and theater respectively, by a jury of Cuban and foreign authors.[77] However, members of the writers' union who had not taken part in the decision denounced Padilla's book of poems *Fuera del juego* (*Sent off the Field*) and Arrufat's play *Los siete contra tebas* (*The Seven Against Thebes*) and accused both authors of counterrevolutionary writing. These members of the UNEAC initially aimed to have the books banned, but they eventually conceded to publish both works with a defamatory introduction. Despite both authors' compliance with the UNEAC's unreasonable terms, the expense-paid trips abroad that were supposed to be part of the prizes were denied, and neither of the authors was permitted to leave the country. In the official journal of the Cuban military, *Verde Olivio*, derogatory articles condemned both men.

J. M. Cohen, a member of the jury that awarded the prizes, has noted that "Padilla was characterized as a counter-revolutionary" and "a vain and perverse critic."[78] Antón Arrufat, for his part, was labeled as an enemy of the Revolution and denounced for being a homosexual. By the end of 1968, the scandal around the incident had quieted down. However, the worst was yet to come.

The Final Decade: Official Silence and Death

Throughout his final decade of life, Piñera suffered from emotional crises and feared run-ins with Cuban officials who had greatly restricted his freedoms as a writer and a participant in cultural activities. After the publication of his collected poetry, *La vida entera* (*My Whole Life*) and the premiere of his experimental musical comedy *El encarne* (*The Hunting Bait*), both in 1969, none of his works were published or performed in Cuba until nearly eight years after his death. His name was rarely uttered in public, his works were conspicuously left out of anthologies of Cuban literature, and he was gradually removed from official lists and library card catalogues. According to some accounts, Piñera underwent periodic harassment by military and police officials.

In March 1971 Cuba's intellectual community was put on the defensive, so to speak, when the Padilla case resurfaced and drew major international scrutiny to socialist Cuba's ever-tightening control of cultural and intellectual life. In March 1971, some three years after the controversial publication of *Fuera del juego*, Padilla was arrested, along with his wife, Belkis Cuza Malé, and a French painter. When the officials searched Padilla's French friend, they allegedly found incriminating letters written by the poet to his friends abroad.[79] Padilla was charged with conspiracy against the Cuban government and jailed for nearly forty days.

Shortly after Padilla's arrest, many of Castro's well-known European and Latin American supporters composed a letter to him and published it in the Parisian daily *Le Monde* on April 9. In it they expressed their disillusion with the Cuban government's treatment of Padilla: "the use of repressive measures against intellectuals and writers who have exercised the right of criticism within the revolution can only have deeply negative repercussions among the anti-imperialist forces of the entire world, and most especially in Latin America, for which the Cuban revolution is a symbol and a banner."[80]

The letter did not have its desired effect. While in prison Padilla was forced by government officials to write a 4,000-word statement in which he not only denounced his supposedly counterrevolutionary verse in *Fuera del juego*, but also confessed to an almost laughable series of "transgressions" against the Revolution. According to Maurice Halperin, Fidel Castro was personally involved in "this shady business," and he correctly figured that "the confession would be easy to come by."[81] Upon his release from prison on April 27 Padilla read the twenty-five-page document to a group of authors and intellectuals at the headquarters of the UNEAC. Many of those present were implicated in Padilla's supposed conspiracy against the Revolution. Although Virgilio Piñera was not mentioned, his association with many of the named individuals proved to be sufficient grounds for concern.

The timing of Padilla's arrest coincided with the First National Congress on Education and Culture, which was held at the end of April 1971. During the Congress it was declared, among other things, that any expression of bourgeois ideology would be condemned. In the closing speech of the conference, Fidel Castro personally denounced the intellectuals who had signed the letter of condemnation in *Le Monde*. According to Halperin, Castro's words revealed "his deep personal resentment against those whom he had invited to Cuba at considerable expense to praise him, but who finding less and less to praise over the years instead criticized him, however gently and considerately in most cases."[82] The following excerpt from Castro's bitter invective against his foes is illustrative of his growing antipathy for foreign intellectuals:

> [Cuba] will furnish no pretexts for brazen pseudoleftists who hope to win their laurels living in Paris, London, or Rome. Some of them are shameless Latin Americans who, instead of taking their posts there in the trench of the struggle, (APPLAUSE) live in bourgeois luxury millions of miles from problems, cashing in on the measure of fame they won. . . .
> But as far as Cuba is concerned, they will never again—never!—be able to use her, not even pretending to defend her . . . Now you know it bourgeois intellectuals and bourgeois libelants, agents of the CIA and intelligence services of imperialism . . . you will not be allowed to come to Cuba just as UPI and AP are not allowed to come (APPLAUSE). Our doors will remain closed indefinitely (APPLAUSE) ad infinitum![83]

On May 20 a second letter to Castro was published in *Le Monde* and signed by more than sixty writers and intellectuals. In this second document the signers expressed their "shame" and "cholera" over the circumstance surrounding Padilla's forced confession. They compared the scene in the UNEAC to the most sordid moments of Stalinism, and concluded by declaring their desire to see the Revolution, which they had once considered to be a model of socialism, return to a righteous path.

The ire of the international intellectual community was also stirred by the unequivocally antihomosexual tone of the First National Congress on Education and Culture, which had officially recognized "the social pathological character of homosexual deviations" and determined "that all manifestations of homosexual deviations are to be firmly rejected and prevented from spreading."[84] The declaration further stated that homosexuals and other so-called sexual deviants would not be permitted to have any influence on the younger generations and that individuals whose morals did not correspond with those of the revolution would be banned from any group or organization officially representing Cuba.

It was certainly no coincidence that it was precisely around the time of these events that Piñera and his writings were officially condemned. As Reinaldo Arenas has noted, after the April Congress the publication of works by homosexual writers in Cuba was essentially illegal.[85] Furthermore, by virtue of a new revolutionary law according to which all artistic work belonged to the national patrimony, writers like Piñera were denied the right to publish outside of Cuba or to travel abroad.

In spite of growing official pressure, Piñera and his ever-shrinking circle of friends did their best to persevere in their intellectual endeavors and to lead lives with some semblance of normalcy. By 1971 Piñera had been relegated to an insignificant job as a translator for the Instituto del Libro, but he continued to write avidly, and frequently met with small groups in secret *tertulias* where he read and discussed his most recent writings.[86] Among the participants in the clandestine meetings were Piñera's close friends Antón Arrufat and José Rodríguez Feo and many young writers such as Abilio Estévez, Reinaldo Arenas, and Roberto Valero, for whom Piñera served as something of a mentor.

During his final years Piñera also met regularly with Lezama, with whom he had rekindled a harmonious relationship soon after the publication of *Paradiso* in 1966.[87] Reinaldo Arenas correctly points out in *Antes que anochezca* that the rapprochement between these two great Cuban authors was at least partially due to their common suffering in their final years.[88] It should not be overlooked, however, that Piñera was deeply moved by Lezama's masterpiece, which revived in him feelings of personal and intellectual accord with the man whom he had once considered to be a kindred spirit. We should recall that the initial hostility between Piñera and Lezama was largely a product of Piñera's allegation in 1941 that his literary cohort had betrayed both their friendship and their unique intellectual bond by choosing Ángel Gaztelu, a Catholic priest, instead of Piñera to codirect *Espuela de Plata*. Piñera, who felt that he should have been given the position, interpreted Lezama's decision not only as a sell-out to tradition, but also as an implicit disavowal of their shared heterodox views and subversive inclinations. Much of the tension between the two authors from that point on, then, was a product not so much of Piñera's distaste for Lezama's poetry (as Piñera often claimed it was), but of his opinion that Lezama's writings did not sincerely reflect his more intimate personal and literary convictions.

Paradiso, with its candid treatment of eroticism and homosexuality and its deeply intimate tenor, had a dramatic impact on Piñera. Indeed, he embraced the controversial novel as a testament to one of his own central literary tenets, that is, that sexuality should be seen as a vital component of life and of artistic expression. But Piñera also took pleasure in the fact that because *Paradiso* represented Lezama's symbolic blow to tradition, it would assure his legacy as a writer who, like Piñera himself, had dared to challenge the moral mainstream. Since Piñera saw great merit in defying the literary establishment, even when it meant jeopardizing his own reputation as a writer, he had tremendous respect for Lezama's courageous decision to publish a work that he surely knew would scandalize so many among Cuba's intellectual community, especially certain members of the *Orígenes* group.[89]

In "El hechizado" (The Bewitched), a beautiful poem that he wrote on the day of Lezama's death, Piñera offered the following poignant tribute to his dear friend and his courageous novel:

> Por un plazo que no puedo señalar
> me llevas la ventaja de tu muerte:
> lo mismo que en la vida, fue tu suerte
> llegar primero. Yo, en segundo lugar.
>
> Estaba escrito. ¿Dónde? En esa mar
> encrespada y terrible que es la vida.
> A ti primero te cerró la herida:
> mortal combate del ser y estar.
>
> Es tu inmortalidad haber matado
> a ese que te hacía respirar
> para que el otro respire eternamente.
>
> Lo hiciste con el arma *Paradiso*.
> —Golpe maestro, jaque mate al hado—
> Ahora, respira en paz. Vive tu hechizo.[90]

[By a space of time I cannot specify / you are ahead of me in your death: / just like in life, it was your destiny / to come in first. I, in second place. / It was written. Where? In that choppy / and terrible sea that is life. / It closed your wound first: / mortal combat of Being and being. / It is your immortality to have killed / the one who made you breathe / so that the other could breathe eternally. / You did it with that weapon, *Paradiso*. / —Master stroke, checkmate against fate— / Now, breathe in peace. Your spell lives.]

Piñera's heartfelt text attests to his renewed deference to Lezama and his literary legacy. To be sure, if as a young and aspiring poet Piñera had viewed Lezama as a master of sorts, in the final years of his life he bowed to Lezama's undeniable greatness as a novelist and to his momentous, forty-year career as a Cuban cultural icon. In the final stanzas of "El hechizado" Piñera suggests that in writing *Paradiso* Lezama had effectively unleashed his subversive self from the constrictive reigns of convention, a masterly achievement that would at once assure an eternity of peaceful breathing (a clear reference to Lezama's asthma) and his lasting legacy as the charmed author of enchanted texts.

Lezama's death, which came just five days after Piñera's sixty-fourth birthday, represented a great personal loss and the end of an era, and it left Piñera feeling emotionally distraught: "Piensa en el estado que me ha sumido esa muerte," he wrote to Humberto, "que además de ser un aviso—no al lector, sino al escritor—es todo un desgarramiento"[91] (imagine the state in which I have been plunged by his death, which in addition to being a warning—not to the reader, but to the writer—is a real upheaval).

3: DISILLUSION TO REVOLUTION AND BACK AGAIN (1958–79)   115

Despite bouts of despair and hopelessness, Piñera wrote tirelessly in his final years and completed several short plays, stories, and a book of poems. Though he was distressed by the fact that the publication of his works was forbidden, Antón Arrufat insists that Piñera was also convinced until the day he died that he had made the right decision to stay in Cuba, and he believed that one day his period of imposed silence would end.[92] However, it is important to point out that Piñera's correspondence and certain works from the period reveal the somber mood of a man who felt a deep sense of doom in a repressive society. In a letter to Julia Rodríguez Tomeu, for example, Piñera's empty, desperate tone underscored the monotony and frustration that troubled him in his final years: "no tengo deseos de escribir, ni sobre nada ni a nadie. Mi vida está por terminar, he luchado mucho y estoy cansado de luchar. Me dejo ir, eso es todo. Los días son iguales como gotas de agua."[93] (I don't have any desire to write, not about anything or anybody. My life is coming to an end, I have fought much and I am tired of fighting. I let myself go, that's all. The days are identical like drops of water.)

In 1979 Piñera experienced two significant run-ins with the Cuban State Security agents. According to Barreto, in May of that year a French friend of Piñera's was caught trying to leave the country with a number of his manuscripts. Following the incident, Piñera was severely reprimanded by the authorities, who warned him to avoid further trouble.[94] Heberto Padilla has similarly described how in early October 1979, just weeks before Piñera's death, members of the Cuban Seguridad de Estado entered his apartment in el Vedado, accused him of counterrevolutionary activity, confiscated a number of copies of his published works, and warned him not to associate with foreigners or to meet in certain literary circles.[95]

Both incidents left Piñera so terrified that Cabrera Infante has suggested that his sudden death on October 19, 1979, was a result of his intense fear.[96] In two somewhat exaggerated accounts of Piñera's death, Reinaldo Arenas suggests that Piñera could have been killed by Cuban security agents.[97] Though both anecdotes have added to the growing legend surrounding Piñera's life and works, the official story, and the most credible one, is that Virgilio died alone of a heart attack in his apartment in Havana.

Piñera's obituary in *Granma*—laughably brief and buried among three articles about different cultural activities in Havana—attests to the relative oblivion into which he died:

Efectuado el sepelio del escritor Virgilio Piñera
Ayer en horas de la tarde se efectuó el sepelio del escritor Virgilio Piñera

(1912–1979), en el cementerio de Colón, en La Habana. Dramaturgo, novelista, cuentista, poeta y crítico, Piñera produjo una extensa obra literaria. Virgilio Piñera falleció repentinamente el jueves a consecuencia de un colapso cardíaco; al morir trabajaba en la esfera editorial del Ministro de Cultura.[98]

[Writer Virgilio Piñera Buried
Yesterday in the afternoon the writer Virgilio Piñera (1912–1979) was buried in the Colón Cemetery in Havana. Dramatist, novelist, short story writer, poet, and critic, Piñera produced an extensive literary oeuvre. Virgilio Piñera passed away unexpectedly Thursday from a cardiac arrest; at the time of his death he was working in the editorial division of the Ministry of Culture.]

A similarly terse obituary published in *La Nación* the same day referred to this major Cuban author as an adversary of the Revolution who had fallen out of official government favor after the publication in 1967 of his third novel, *Presiones y diamantes*.

According to Barreto et al.,[99] on the night of Piñera's funeral his brother Juan Enrique was warned that government security officials were planning to search Virgilio's home for incriminating materials. The house had already been ransacked by the time Juan Enrique and some of Piñera's friends arrived at the residence later that evening, but most of the papers that Piñera had left in a closet had not been disturbed. The majority of the manuscripts that were confiscated by the authorities and kept in a special file in the National Library were eventually returned to Piñera's family.

Piñera left behind an impressive amount of writing—some eighteen boxes of manuscripts according to several accounts—including a completed book of poetry (*Una broma colosal* [A Colossal Joke]), numerous short stories (collected in *Muecas para escribientes* [Grimaces for Copyists] and *Un fogonazo* [*An Explosion*]), a handful of completed plays (*Teatro inédito* [Unpublished Theater]), several dramatic works in process (*Teatro inconcluso* [Unfinished Theater]), and a variety of miscellaneous manuscript materials. Nearly a decade would pass, however, before the publication of any of these works was allowed in Cuba.

The publication of numerous editions and translations of Virgilio Piñera's writings in the late 1980s spurred a dynamic resurgence in scholarly interest in his life and work. Critical essays on his short stories and plays have become especially numerous, and his novels and poetry have been the subject of several studies. In the past few years, new editions of many of Piñera's works by major publishing houses in Spain and Latin America have served to strengthen his stature as a major contemporary writer. Despite this renewed interest, however, Virgilio Piñera has still not earned the place that he deserves among the great figures of twentieth-century Latin American writers and intellectuals. Moreover, among English-speaking audiences Virgilio Piñera is still a little-known literary figure. It is my expressed hope that the present study will serve not only to familiarize a broader audience with the life and works of Piñera, but also to inspire other scholars of Latin American letters to shed more light on one of the great authors of our time.

II
Writing from the Margin

Virgilio Piñera, Guanabo, Cuba, 1954. Photo courtesy of Princeton University Library, Department of Rare Books and Special Collections.

4

Tales of Absurd Hope and Senseless Logic: Virgilio Piñera's Early Stories

> There is so much stubborn hope in the human heart. The most destitute men often end up by accepting illusion.
> —Albert Camus, *The Myth of Sisyphus*[1]

> En *Cuentos fríos* Virgilio Piñera . . . quiere hacer palpable la locura cósmica del hombre que se devora a sí mismo mientras rinde tributo a una lógica insensata.
>
> [In *Cold Tales* Virgilio Piñera . . . wants to make palpable the cosmic madness of the man who devours himself while he pays tribute to a senseless logic.]
> —Witold Gombrowicz[2]

AMONG NON-SPANISH-SPEAKING AUDIENCES VIRGILIO PIÑERA IS PERhaps best known as a writer of singularly original short fiction. This is largely due to the fact that, since his death in 1979, major collections of his stories have been published in English, French, Portuguese, and Italian, while most of his works in other genres have still not been translated. Among Spanish speakers, Piñera's ever-growing fame as a writer of short fiction has largely resulted from the publication of numerous comprehensive collections of his unique tales in Latin America and Spain over the last two decades.[3] Moreover, while Piñera's name and his stories were long excluded from anthologies of Latin American short fiction, in recent years the inclusion of his stories in such collections—in Spanish and in translation—has become a relative commonplace.

As is often the case with writers as eccentric and inimitable as Virgilio Piñera, the Cuban author's stories have been subjected to multiple interpretations, and much effort has been made to classify them. Contemporary reviewers and critics have referred to Piñera's short fiction as absurd, grotesque, fantastic, existentialist, Goyaesque, and neobaroque, and have employed contradictory terminology—tropical and cold, tragic and farcical, horrifying and humorous, irrational and cerebral—in their attempts to elucidate them.[4]

In terms of literary affinities and influence, studies of Piñera's short fiction frequently refer to the Cuban author's debt to Franz Kafka. It should be noted, though, that discussions of Kafka's influence on Piñera have been largely schematic if not superficial, and no critic has taken up the task of a comprehensive comparative study of the two authors' short fiction.[5] Piñera's stories have also been likened to those of other Latin American authors such as Julio Cortázar and Felisberto Hernández.[6] However, it is important to point out that Piñera's alleged affinity with these writers is not so much a product of literary influence, but rather of a shared fascination with the realms of the fantastic and the absurd. In short, even a cursory reading of Piñera's remarkably diverse stories reveals that more often than not they defy facile comparisons and categorization. Perhaps Guillermo Cabrera Infante put it best when he insisted in the introduction to *Cold Tales* that "Virgilio Piñera's short stories are far from any received notion in literature."[7]

Piñera himself often described his work with contradictory or ambiguous terms. In the oft-cited introduction to his *Teatro completo*, for example, he summed up one of the defining characteristics of his literary production with the following observation: "Nada como mostrar a tiempo la parte clownesca para que la parte seria quede bien a la vista. Ya se ve en mi obra: soy ese que hace más seria la seriedad a través del humor, del absurdo y de lo grotesco."[8] (There's nothing like showing in due course the clownesque side of things so that the serious side stands out. It can be seen in my work: I am the one who makes seriousness more serious through humor, the absurd, and the grotesque.)

Just as Piñera referred to his works as "absurd" and "grotesque" on many occasions, modern critics have called attention to the "cruelly absurd reality" of Piñera's stories, to his "rebellion against the absurd" and to his predilection for "grotesque humor," "grotesque situations," and "grotesque themes and imagery."[9]

While few would question the appropriateness of employing these terms to describe Piñera's singular stories, it is important to point out that "absurd" and "grotesque" are somewhat problematic concepts given that they have come to be synonymous with a vast range of emotions and ideas. The absurd, for example, is at once a philosophical concept that denotes a fundamental lack of reason and meaning in human existence, and a term that forms the basis for the existentialist notion that "man is thrown into an alien, irrational world in which he must create his own identity through a series of choices for which there are no guides or criteria."[10] We should add, furthermore, that the literary movement known as the theater of the absurd, which grew out of the philosophy of existentialism, became popular in Europe and the Americas in the 1950s and 1960s, and Piñera himself is widely hailed as one of its first practitioners in Latin America.[11] Like his absurdist dramas, which tend to emphasize the purposeless and irrational nature of human existence, Piñera's short stories often focus on the protagonists' struggle to find order and meaning in an illogical universe. Finally, in keeping with modern usage of the word, many modern critics of Piñera's works, including myself, have tended to employ the term "absurd" rather freely to connote the "ridiculous," "preposterous," and "bizarre" qualities of his writings and the unique notions that they express.

The term "grotesque" has similarly been drawn on to explain everything from the shocking images and situations to the air of incongruity and irrationality that permeate Piñera's stories. Much like the grotesque world that Wolfgang Kayser describes in his classic study on the grotesque, Piñera's fictional universe "is—and is not—our own world."[12] It is at once familiar and strangely foreign, amusing and ominous. "The grotesque" as it applies to Piñera's work is a paradoxical concept that evokes the range of emotions that Wilson Yates—inspired by Kayser, to be sure—sees as the signature elements of the grotesque in art and literature:

> When we encounter the grotesque, we are caught off guard, we are surprised and shaken, we have a sense of being played with, taunted, judged. It evokes a range of feelings, feelings of uneasiness, fear, repulsion, delight, amusement, often horror and dread, and through its evocative power it appears to us in a paradoxical guise—it is and is not of this world—and it elicits from us paradoxical responses.
>
> ... We laugh at its comic features while sensing its dark implications; we are fascinated and attracted to its power while being threatened by it and compelled to repudiate it; we experience its denial of our canons of truth while glimpsing a truth that our canons deny us.[13]

Cuban Hunger Artists: Creators of Sustenance and Nonconsumption

In many of Piñera's best stories the absurd and the grotesque reveal themselves through the protagonists' futile attempts to transcend their physical and mental afflictions. In "La carne" (Meat) and "La cena" (Supper) for example, the protagonists' laughably fanciful methods of combating impending starvation—consuming their own flesh and ingesting an invisible banquet of intestinal gases—typify Piñera's penchant to exploit absurd situations and grotesque metaphors in his endeavor to bring about paradoxical responses from the reader. When confronted with the bizarre behavior of Piñera's characters, we are usually caught off guard and thus not quite sure if we should cringe with disgust or let out a hearty chuckle.

The reader's ambivalent feelings toward many of Piñera's early stories is, in large part, triggered by Piñera's depiction of the human body as a locus of both tragedy and comedy. In "La carne" and "La cena," situations that we know would involve tremendous physical and emotional stress are downplayed to such an extent and treated so matter-of-factly that they become commonplace. When the stoic protagonists of "La carne" embrace self-cannibalism as a reasonable means to overcome their hunger, for example, they turn corporeal anguish into a laughing matter. Likewise, the scenario of "La cena"—ten men on the verge of agonizing death by starvation inhale the smells of burps and farts and claim to have been blessed with a cornucopia of abundance—is at once hilarious and pathetic. Both stories are emblematic of Piñera's deep appreciation of two important notions that David Morris describes in *The Culture of Pain*: first, that human bodies are, from a comical point of view, "almost inherently funny," and often serve as the common ground for tragedy and farce; and second, that comedy is an especially effective defense against pain.[14]

The third-person narrator of "La carne"[15] begins by recounting, with few details and in a cool tone that suggests little cause for concern, how the members of an anonymous town coped with the sudden scarcity of meat.

> Sucedió con gran sencillez, sin afectación. Por motivos que no son del caso exponer, la población sufría de falta de carne. Todo el mundo se alarmó y se hicieron comentarios más o menos amargos y hasta se esbozaron ciertos propósitos de venganza. Pero, como siempre sucede, las protestas no pasaron de meras amenazas y pronto se vio aquel afligido pueblo engullendo los más variados vegetales. (38)[16]
>
> [It happened simply, without pretense. For reasons that need not be explained, the town was suffering from a meat shortage. Everyone was alarmed, and rather bitter comments were heard; revenge was even spoken of. But, as always, the protests did not develop beyond threats, and soon the afflicted townspeople were devouring the most diverse vegetables.] (9)[17]

It is important to keep in mind that in many societies in which meat is a staple of the daily diet, shortages of it often precipitate fear of starvation.[18] The villagers in Piñera's story are understandably alarmed by the meat shortage, then, because it forces them to subsist on plant foods that they are not used to eating in order to avoid what they perceive as certain starvation.

The narrator's suggestion that the meat-loving villagers' dissatisfaction with their vegetarian diet lead them to consider acts of revenge calls attention to the story's very subtle political undertones. Though it is certainly true that "La carne," like the majority of Piñera's stories, is devoid of specific Cuban references, it is not unreasonable to read the seemingly outlandish text in light of that island's sociopolitical reality of the early 1940s. During that time meat shortages in Cuba were very common. As R. Hart Phillips has observed, unusually high beef prices in the United States led to huge price increases in Cuban beef during the war years. By 1943, the year in which Piñera penned his story, "cattle producers and butchers protested these prices and beef vanished. Five months passed in Havana without any beef being put on sale except on the black market."[19]

Despite the obvious pitfalls of lending credence to an author's explanations of his/her own work, Piñera's remarks about "La carne" are worth bearing in mind. In a 1956 interview following the publication of *Cuentos fríos*, for example, Piñera made the following observation: "Por esa época faltaba la carne en La Habana. Entonces yo escribí el cuento 'La carne.' Pero no sólo faltaba sino que de haber estado llenas las carnicerías, no tenía un centavo para comprarla. . . . Entonces protesté y mi protesta fue ese cuento."[20] (In those days there was a lack of meat in Havana. Therefore I wrote "Meat." But it wasn't just that it was lacking, for even if the butcher shops had been full, I didn't have a cent to buy it. . . . So I protested, and my protest was that story.) Likewise, in an article published several years later in *La Gaceta de Cuba*, Piñera declared that "La carne" was at least in part motivated by his anger at the Cuban government's policy of sending cattle to the United States during World War II, which resulted in meat shortages throughout the island.[21]

While "La carne" can be read as a highly distorted sociopolitical allegory about the problem of physical hunger in Cuba, however, the reader must be careful not to take Piñera too literally. Even if "La carne" is not completely dislocated from Cuban reality, as many critics have assumed, reading the story as nothing but a hyperbolic piece of social realism would be a disservice to a masterful text that is in many ways emblematic of Piñera's highly original and imaginative short fiction.

On a more universal level, the predicament of the hungry villagers in "La carne" serves as a metaphor for the futility of modern man's efforts to overcome the difficulties that turn human existence into a constant struggle. The starving villagers' desire for meat symbolizes a sort of metaphysical hunger, a longing for a more substantial and meaningful existence. The lack of desirable options available to the people—which is embodied in the vegetable matter that they are forced to gulp down—suggests their lack of control over their own destinies.

According to Carmen Torres-Robles's reading of the story, the townspeople see the vegetables as a viable solution to their problem.[22] However, it seems to me that when the narrator speaks of "the most diverse vegetables" he is not referring to the kind of "vegetables" that one would normally eat. Rather, he implies that the starving individuals were forced to consume whatever organic and plant matter they could get their hands on.[23] Piñera's use of the verb "engullir," which suggests gulping down ravenously without chewing, not only underscores the people's great hunger, but also implies that they find the odd variety of plant foods unappetizing.

One member of the village, at once moved by both his aversion to the new diet and his overwhelming hunger for a succulent piece of meat, dreams up a preposterous solution to a problem that his fellow villagers had considered unsolvable:

> Sólo que el señor Ansaldo no siguió la orden general. Con gran tranquilidad se puso a afilar un enorme cuchillo de cocina, y, acto seguido, bajándose los pantalones hasta las rodillas, cortó de su nalga izquierda un hermoso filete. Tras haberlo limpiado lo adobó con sal y vinagre, lo pasó—como se dice—por la parrilla, para finalmente freírlo en la gran sartén de las tortillas del domingo. Sentóse a la mesa y comenzó a saborear su hermoso filete. (38)

> [Only Mr. Ansaldo didn't follow the order of the day. With great tranquillity, he began to sharpen an enormous kitchen knife and then, dropping his pants to his knees, he cut a beautiful fillet from his left buttock. Having cleaned and dressed the fillet with salt and vinegar, he passed it through the broiler and finally fried it in the big pan he used on Sundays for making tortillas. He sat at the table and began to savor his beautiful fillet.] (9)

The narrator's matter-of-fact relation of Alsaldo's stoic determination to subsist on his own flesh is an essential element of the story's shock effect, and it is emblematic of the type of absurd and grotesque elements in Piñera's writing that tend to elicit contradictory responses.[24] Ansaldo's cheerful attitude toward self-mutilation, despite the inevitably tragic outcome of such conduct, underscores how Piñera cleverly turns the body into the locus of tragedy and farce. The human backside, moreover, has especially great comic potential, and no matter how much the notion of slicing off a piece of our own flesh might disgust us, it is hard to resist letting out at least an uneasy chuckle when we are faced with this image of a delusional man who drops his drawers and, with utter aplomb, shaves a fillet from his buttock.

Torres has correctly noted that Ansaldo's outrageous conduct is made more comical by "the narrator's effort to present it as an aesthetic act."[25] It is quite amusing that by seasoning and cooking the flesh from his buttock—which the narrator incongruously describes as "his beautiful fillet"—Ansaldo manages to turn it into a mouthwatering dish that resembles the type of fare that the villagers most crave. When a starving neighbor sees and smells the succulent rump steak, he does not notice Ansaldo's mutilated backside. Instead he fixes his gaze on the sizzling meat, which he understandably sees as a potential remedy to his own suffering.

The situation becomes all the more comical when Ansaldo, responding to an enthusiastic request from the mayor, publicly demonstrates his method of filleting on a lifelike cast of his own behind, which he hangs from a meat hook in the town square. According to the narrator, all of the villagers were enlightened by Ansaldo's example, and thus began to cut flesh from their own buttocks. The narrator inadvertently calls attention to the paradoxical nature of the event when, after referring to it as a "glorioso espectáculo" (glorious spectacle) (39), he admits that he prefers not to go into details, ostensibly out of fear that a graphic account would be too shocking.

We should add here that the lack of surprise in both the narrator's description of the events and the characters' reactions to them serves to make the circumstances seem especially incongruous. Here Piñera's brilliant storytelling technique is reminiscent of Kafka, whose works often involve a narrator like the one in "La carne" who recounts bizarre situations with a masterful combination of lucidity and cold detachment. Summarizing a similar characteristic of Kafka's fiction, Albert Camus pointed out that "by an odd but obvious paradox, the more extraordinary the character's adventures are, the more noticeable will be the naturalness of the story: it is in proportion to the divergence we feel between the strangeness of a man's life and the simplicity with which that man accepts it."[26]

Reflecting this notion, the narrator of "La carne" notes, for example, that apart from some insignificant protests from the town's most educated residents, the villagers all enthusiastically embraced the practice of self-consumption, which they immediately began to refine in an attempt to introduce some variety to their diet. Simple fillets of buttock soon lost popularity to more succulent dishes like lip fritters, roasted tongue, and broiled fingertips, which the narrator comically insists gave rise to the saying "para chuparse la yema de los dedos" (39) (finger-licking good) (10).

It is especially notable that in his account of the villagers' mutilation and consumption of their own bodies, the narrator leaves out descriptions of wounds and physical pain. The villagers' apparent invulnerability to corporeal suffering brings to our attention Piñera's keen awareness of the comic potential of bodies in distress. Much like the cartoons and slapstick comedies that were popular during the wartime era (the Three Stooges immediately come to mind), in which pain is mysteriously absent when we most expect it, Piñera's stories often stand out for their portrayal of individuals who are impossibly impervious to brutal physical violence.

David Morris has pointed out that the "strange absence of pain in situations that everyone recognizes as painful constitutes an important sign that we have entered the comic world."[27] This notion is clearly exemplified in "La carne" and a number of other absurdist stories that Piñera penned in the 1940s. In "La caída" (The Fall), for example, two mountaineers are dismembered and smashed to bits during a catastrophic fall. The narrator/protagonist recounts the tumble with laughable, mathematic precision, but makes no mention whatsoever of physical suffering. By the end of their mishap, the narrator and his companion have been reduced to a pair of eyes and a beard resting on a grassy plain, but the narrator calmly declares that they are delighted to have preserved the only body parts that they truly cared about. In "Las partes" (The Parts) the narrator nonchalantly describes how his neighbor, after a gradual process of self-dismemberment, created an artistic composition by nailing his severed body parts (with the exception of his head) to his apartment wall. But even when the neighbor asks the narrator to place his head in the empty part of the arrangement, which the latter gladly does by fixing it to the wall with an enormous metal spike, no mention is made of pain. With utter coolness the narrator ends his tale by noting that he left with his neighbor's cape, since it would have been of no use to him.

The impossibly robust characters in Piñera's works are in many ways highly contrived monuments to the strength and endurance of the human body and spirit. Their perseverance in the midst of tragedy calls attention to a universal truth that permeates Piñera's work, that is, that human beings can be subjected to unbelievable horrors and still engage in a stubborn fight for survival. Characters like Ansaldo and the other villagers in "La carne" are celebrations of what Morris refers to as the "perverse energy in bodily life that manages to overcome every effort to deny or subdue it."[28] Oblivious to the inevitably tragic consequences of their self-destructive behavior, they refuse to admit that life has nothing better to offer them. Instead of eking out a miserable existence on repugnant "vegetables" they choose, in a sort of absurdist carpe diem, to enjoy their much-loved meat while they can. The narrator emphasizes the villagers' steadfast determination to endure when he declares that, despite a local anatomist's expert opinion that the supplies of edible flesh could not last indefinitely, they chose not to focus on their imminent deaths, but rather on the immediate goal of filling their bellies: "lo que importaba era que cada uno pudiese ingerir su hermoso filete (39) (what mattered was that each person could eat his beautiful fillet [10]).

Throughout his account the narrator attempts to cast the era of the meat shortage in a largely positive light by referring to the period in the village's history as "aquella agradable jornada" (that pleasant period), and by employing words such as "hermoso" (handsome), "delicioso" (delicious), and "pintoresco" (picturesque) to describe the practice of self-consumption. However, toward the end of the narration he seems to concede that not all of the incidents were as amusing as he has led us to believe. After witnessing a ballet dancer dissect his big toe and then swallow it raw, for example, he insinuates that a group of onlookers was overcome with dread:

> Éste, por respeto a su arte, había dejado por lo último los bellos dedos de sus pies. . . . Ya sólo le quedaba la parte carnosa del dedo gordo. Entonces invitó a sus amigos a presenciar la operación. En medio de un sanguinolento silencio cortó su porción posterior y sin pasarla por el fuego la dejó caer en el hueco de lo que había sido en otro tiempo su hermosa boca. Entonces todos los presentes se pusieron repentinamente serios. (39–40)

> [Out of respect for his art, he had left his beautiful toes for last. . . . There now remained only the fleshy tip of one big toe. At that point he invited his friends to attend the operation. In the middle of a bloody silence, he cut off the last portion, and, without even warming it up, dropped it into the hole that had once been his beautiful mouth. Everyone present suddenly became very serious.] (11)

By making his meal into a public spectacle, the dancer turns the witnesses into unwitting participants in a gruesome act that brings them face-to-face with their collective savagery. More importantly, though, the villagers, who have grown accustomed to fried, seasoned fillets of buttock and lip fritters prepared according to local culinary customs, are shocked because their comrade eats his flesh without cooking it. Indeed, it is commonly held that cooking animal flesh before consuming it separates humans from the world of beasts since the process symbolically changes it "from a corporeal substance to an artifact of culinary culture."[29] When the dancer eats raw flesh, then, he crosses the symbolic threshold that the rest of the villagers had managed to avoid through preparing and cooking their flesh before eating it.

The narrator's ironic tone at the end of the story is important since it suggests his heightened awareness that his matter-of-fact account is unconvincing. Realizing that his audience will not swallow his ludicrous claim that the villagers' happiness had not been undermined by the terrible incidents he has described, he makes a feeble attempt to rationalize his obvious indifference to their plight:

> ¿De qué podría quejarse un pueblo que tenía asegurada su subsistencia? El grave problema de orden público creado por la falta de carne, ¿no había quedado definitivamente zanjado? Que la población fuera ocultándose progresivamente nada tenía que ver con el aspecto central de la cosa, y sólo era un colofón que no alteraba en modo alguno la firme voluntad de aquella gente de procurarse el precioso alimento. (40)

> [For how could a town that was assured of its subsistence complain? Hadn't the crisis of public order caused by the meat shortage been definitively resolved? That the population was increasingly dropping out of sight was but a postscript to the fundamental issue and did not affect the people's determination to obtain their vital sustenance.] (11–12)

After posing intriguing questions whose answers would serve to elucidate the psychological, social, and political issues behind the grim situation of the starving villagers, the narrator declares that further consideration of the matter would be contemptible and inappropriate. His apparent disinterest in the deeper implications of the meat shortage echoes his declaration at the beginning of the story that explaining its causes would be pointless.

The narrator's apathy toward the villagers' patently desperate dilemma and his irrational claim that they had found a practical solution to it underscores the fundamental absurdity of his account. At the same time it serves to expose the social criticism that lurks below the story's surface. The narrator's alarming callousness toward the human misery that he describes suggests a parody of the tendency of modern societies, like 1940s Cuba, to turn a blind eye to the physical and metaphysical hunger of the people. Gilgen has correctly pointed out that Piñera's absurdist stories are not especially effective as direct social protest because they are by and large highly abstract and lack specific historical references.[30] This does not mean, though, that the reader must disregard the possibility that through texts like "La carne" Piñera indirectly exposed and censured certain aspects of Cuban society.

Even though it would be disingenuous to suggest that "La carne," or any of Piñera's stories for that matter, is an explicitly sociopolitical text, it is important to keep in mind when reading the story that in his early years as a writer Piñera was deeply troubled by what he perceived as the Cuban government's total indifference toward the physical hunger and metaphysical malaise of so many of the island's inhabitants. Moreover, it is widely known that Piñera's own circumstances during the early 1940s were especially precarious: he had almost no money and more often than not had little to eat. Through the narrator's deliberate evasion of the causes and implications of the villagers' hunger, then, we can perceive not just Piñera's absurdist vision of man's predicament in a harsh and indifferent universe, but also his embedded condemnation of the overwhelming callousness of his own society, which he found difficult to accept and nearly impossible to explain from a realist perspective.

In "La cena" Piñera again presents hunger as both a source of human suffering and a catalyst of what we might call irrational resourcefulness. The starving protagonists of "La cena" claim to assuage their hunger pangs by screaming out the names of national dishes as they "ingest" an invisible banquet of intestinal gases. Despite the story's obvious humor, it was clearly not conceived as a purely comical text. Even though the copious belches and farts are bound to evoke our laughter, they also call attention to the wretched circumstances of ten malnourished men whose hunger has had a profound impact on their material and emotional existence.

Through this highly original story Piñera debunks the myth that our minds can free us from our suffering by positing that the dehumanizing powers of poverty and starvation far outmatch the fancies of the imagination. Much like the narrative technique employed in "La carne," the matter-of-fact tone of the narrator/protagonist of "La cena," who presents his pitiable circumstances with incongruous levity, is a crucial component of the story's overall air of absurdity.

> Como siempre sucede, la miseria nos había reunido y arrojado en el reducido espacio de los consabidos dos metros cuadrados. Allí vivíamos. Sabía que no comería esa noche, pero el alegre recuerdo del copioso almuerzo de la mañana impedía briosamente toda angustia intestinal. Tenía que hacer un largo camino, pues del Auxilio Nocturno—a donde había ido al filo de las siete a solicitar en vano la comida de esa noche—a nuestro cuarto mediaban más de cinco kilómetros. Pero confieso que los recorrí alegremente. Aunque ya nada tenía en el estómago del famoso almuerzo, me acometían a ratos los más deliciosos eructos que cabe imaginar. (40)[31]

> [As always happens, misery had brought us together and thrown us into the reduced space of those familiar two square meters. That's where we lived. I knew that I wouldn't eat that night, but the pleasant memory of my plentiful, midday lunch resolutely impeded any intestinal anguish. I had to make a long trek, since the distance from the Night Relief Center—where I had

gone at precisely seven to solicit in vain that night's meal—to our room measured more than five kilometers. But I must confess that I walked them happily. Even though by then I didn't have anything in my stomach from my splendid lunch, I was overcome at times by the most delicious belches that one could imagine.][32]

In his description of his situation the narrator/protagonist intimates that he and the characters are victims of circumstances that are beyond their control. The catchphrase "Como siempre sucede"—which is also used in the opening lines of "La carne"—suggests that the protagonists see their misery as a fact of life that they are powerless to change. Moreover, by pointing out that he was unable to find a meal even at an established aid station that is meant to provide for those in need, the narrator suggests that he and his famished companions have been abandoned to their fate.

One of the most attention-grabbing aspects of "La cena" is how the narrator, despite his obvious lack of motive for good cheer, infuses his account with optimism. As the reader of Piñera's stories comes to expect, though, his incongruous high spirits are not meant to suggest the acceptance of his misery, but rather a categorical denial of it. In many ways, the narrator's attitude embodies what Piñera saw as a typical Cuban approach to dealing with tragedy:

> A mi entender el cubano se define por la sistemática ruptura con la seriedad entre comillas. . . .
> Como todos los cubanos yo evadía la realidad, y no tanto la evadía como le hacía resistencia a través del elemento cómico apuntado.[33]

> [The way I see it, Cubans can be defined by their systematic rupture from so-called seriousness. . . .
> Like all Cubans I evaded reality, and I didn't so much evade it as I resisted it by way of a sharp comic element.]

The narrator's ironic use of words such as "alegre," "copioso" and "famoso" to describe what was surely a meager lunch, and his insistence that the memory of the distant meal resolutely overpowered his hunger pangs, exemplify how comedy functions as an imperfect vehicle of evasion in the story. To be sure, even though his optimism is oddly humorous, it also evokes a sense of pity since we know that destitution cannot be overcome by simple good cheer. Moreover, while his "delicious" belches are humorous in their own right, they are also emblematic of the story's biting irony. The reader knows, for instance, that burping, especially on an empty stomach, does not taste good. Moreover, it is obvious that recalling a meal in the midst of hunger pangs would not alleviate them. A similar irony is further exploited later in the story when the narrator makes the ludicrous claim that he and his nine companions manage to alleviate their hunger be inhaling the "mouthwatering" odors of their own intestinal gases.

When he arrives at his living quarters the narrator is met with a veritable orchestra of noises caused by the grumbling stomachs and chronic flatulence of his companions. His exaggerated description of the bodily sounds is a fine example of how Piñera makes use of humor and the body to call attention to the tragic side of human existence: "Uno era como el aire que se escapa de los tubos de un órgano cuando él que lo toca abre todas las llaves del mismo; el otro se parecía a ese chillido seco y prolongado que emite una mujer frente a una rata, y el tercero podía identificarse al cornetín que toca la diana en los campamentos (49). (One was like the sound of air escaping from the tubes of an organ when the one playing it presses all the keys at once; the second sounded like the dry, prolonged screech that a woman lets out when she sees a mouse; the third could be compared to a cornet that plays reveille at military camps.)[34]

This situation takes a bizarre turn when the men, who are laying faceup in their respective cots, begin to shout out the names of national dishes whose aromas are supposedly evoked by the gases emanating from their bodies: "'¡Carne con papas!', '¡arroz con camarones!', '¡rabanitos!'" (49) (Meat and potatoes!, Rice with shrimp!, Radishes!). For his part, when he sniffs an odor that reminds him of his own favorite dish he cries out "¡Empanadillas, enpanadillas!" (50). With a sardonic tone that belies his supposed satisfaction, the narrator insists that the appetizing smells made for a Roman feast that they all enjoyed so much that their nostrils dilated dramatically from their intense sniffing.

One critic has pointed out that during their olfactory feast the hungry men conjure up memories of their most recent meal,[35] but the narrator's own words—"hacia tanto tiempo que la abundancia no nos visitaba" (50) (It had been so long since abundance had visited us)—imply that they are merely dreaming of dishes that they rarely or never eat. To be sure, we are meant to understand that the ten hungry men crave meat, shrimp, and *empanadillas* precisely because they have not eaten anything but unappetizing fare for so long.

Despite the air of levity and the grotesque humor that permeates the story, certain observations in the narrator's account contradict his delusional claims that he and his companions have enjoyed and benefited from their imaginary feast. In the midst of the tumultuous orchestra of bodily emissions and sniffing noses, for example, the narrator pauses to reflect on the bizarre scene. His solemn remark serves as a poignant admission that the fancies of the imagination are no match for the accumulated miseries that the men have endured: "En verdad aquel olor excitaba el apetito . . . pero todavía me detuve un instante para observar aquellas caras de una beatitud hace mucho tiempo desaparecida" (50). (In truth, that odor excited the appetite . . . but I nonetheless stopped an instant to look at those faces whose beatitude had long ago disappeared.)

The narrator's evocation of this pathetic image of ten faces that have lost all signs of serenity and blessedness is significant for two reasons. First of all, it underscores the dehumanizing power of hunger. Secondly, it reveals the story's subtle mockery of religious faith, which becomes more apparent when the narrator sarcastically claims in the next paragraph that he interpreted the invisible banquet as a sign of God's goodness:

> Pensé que no estábamos dejados, como se dice, de la mano de Dios, al ver cómo el cuerno de la abundancia se derramaba sobre nosotros. Pero no había tiempo que perder en reflexiones, pues a medida que el entusiasmo crecía los platos se iban multiplicando. Eran tantos que era casi imposible devorarlos cabalmente a todos. (50)

> [I thought that we weren't abandoned, as they say, by the hand of God, upon seeing how the horn of plenty spilled out before us. But there was no time to waste in reflections, as our enthusiasm grew the plates continued to multiply. There were so many, that it was practically impossible to devour them all properly.]

The derisive tone of the narrator's remarks belies his supposed feelings of gratitude, just as the absurd image of a cornucopia of succulent vittles is wittily undermined by his own admission that "los platos eran devorados sin que nadie manifestase signos de hartura" (50) (the dishes were devoured without anyone showing any signs of fulfillment). His comments also reveal the utter hopelessness of a man who feels forsaken by a cruel God who has left him to live in a society that is indifferent to his misfortunes.

In the story's poignant conclusion the narrator definitively debunks the notion that one can live off of the fruits of the imagination. With a melancholic tone that seems more in keeping with his circumstances, he effectively concedes defeat with his closing observation: "Pronto la habitación fue nada más que un ruido y un olor que diez patéticas narices aspiraban acompasadamente. No importaban tales excesos; aquella noche al menos, no pereceríamos de hambre" (50). (Soon the room was nothing but noise and odor that ten pathetic noses sucked in rhythmically. But such excesses didn't matter; that night, at least, we wouldn't die of hunger.)

While Carmen Torres-Robles is correct to point out that the protagonists in "La cena" dream up the invisible banquet as "a defense mechanism from their impending annihilation," she misrepresents the story's highly pessimistic tone by suggesting that "through the imagination and the materialization of the image 'living off thin air' what could be a form of anguish becomes, for the ten members of the shelter for the poor, a true banquet."[36] Marta Morello-Frosch follows a similar line of thinking by insisting that "what could have been a torment of Tantalus becomes . . . a true bellyful of meals remembered individually and enjoyed communally. . . . These men literally manage to live off of thin air."[37]

The story's message is far more pessimistic than Torres-Robles and Morello-Frosch suggest. The characters' hunger is still very real and their so-called "Roman feast" has not improved their plight in any way. Furthermore, through his trademark use of caustic irony, Piñera implicitly warns the reader to take little stock in the supposed happiness or well-being of his miserable characters. The narrator, for instance, might express confidence that he will endure another night without succumbing to hunger and ever-encroaching death, but this does not suggest that his imaginary meal has extended his pathetic existence. Rather, his sobering observation at the end of his account suggests his realization that his imagination has proven to be of little use in his quest to evade the reality of his impending doom.

Once the reader sees through the comic elements of "La carne" and "La cena," it becomes apparent that the underlying message of both stories is that human suffering cannot be remedied by fantastic solutions. In both stories the tragic side of absurdity overshadows the signature comic elements once we come to realize that the protagonists have no viable escape from their irremediable dilemmas.

On Minutiae and the Evasion of the Meaningful

As we have seen, the protagonists of Piñera's stories stand out for the peculiar ways that they react to their surroundings and to the daunting circumstances that they face. Many of the unstable individuals who narrate and populate his short stories, for instance, exhibit a marked tendency to become entangled in a web of trivialities or to focus an inordinate amount of energy on inconsequential matters while they blissfully ignore the ominous implications of their attitudes and actions. "La caída" once again serves as an emblematic example among Piñera's stories as it offers a graphic and exaggerated illustration of this notion. While the two mountaineers tumble out of control down a precipitous slope, losing their body parts as they go, they are not in the least bit preoccupied with their impending doom. Rather, each man becomes obsessed with preserving what he considers his most aesthetically pleasing physical feature. The narrator/protagonist explains their preposterous fixations as follows:

> Como mi única preocupación era no perder mis ojos, puse todo mi empeño en preservarlos de los terribles efectos de la caída. En cuanto a mi compañero, su única angustia era que su hermosa barba . . . no llegase a la llanura ni siquiera ligeramente empolvada. (35–36)

> [Because my sole concern was to avoid losing my eyes, I put all my effort into preserving them from the terrible effects of the fall. As for my companion, his only worry was that his beautiful beard . . . reach the plain intact, not even slightly dusty.] (6)

"La caída" can be read as a sort of allegory of the arrogant, self-absorbed man's fall from grace given that it is largely the protagonists' preoccupation with their physical beauty (each one covers his companion's prized "part" with his hands) that prevents them from stopping their destructive downward tumble.

In the characteristically brief "El parque" (1944), consequential issues take a backseat to senseless arguments that serve to polarize the members of an anonymous town. The narrator begins by recounting how the town's officials had devoted an excessive amount of time and energy to debating the shape of the town's central plaza. The story's opening lines are illustrative of Piñera's fascination with the human propensity to become engrossed in banality:

> Siempre se había discutido con viva pasión si el parque era rectangular o cuadrado. El sabio del pueblo afirmaba que era una de tantas ilusiones ópticas muy frecuentes en toda la tierra; opinión que apoyaba el agrimensor afirmando que cualquier transeúnte que viniera en dirección al parque por su lado norte lo vería rectangular, pero que, asimismo, otro que lo hiciera por su lado este lo vería cuadrado. (82)

> [It was always argued with great passion whether the park was rectangular or square. The town sage maintained it was one of many optical illusions common throughout the world; an opinion supported by the surveyor, who affirmed that to any passerby approaching from the north it would appear rectangular, whereas to someone coming from the east, it would appear square.] (55)

Echoing the expert anatomist in "La carne" who wastes his time calculating how long his fellow villagers will be able to continue the practice of self-consumption before their reserve flesh runs out, the town sage and the surveyor squander their intellectual capacities quibbling over a senseless matter while they disregard an issue of considerable significance, that is, the fact that the term "park" is a euphemism for what is actually a gigantic mausoleum that encloses the remains of four of the town's citizens:

> Sobre todo, lo que hacía el orgullo de los habitantes de M. era el magnífico piso de granito gris que cubría los doscientos metros—rectangulares o cuadrados—del parque. Ayudaba a prestarle mayor solemnidad la total ausencia de arbolado. En el centro se levantaba algo así como una columna retorcida. . . . Se le llamaba humorísticamente el Monumento a los Obreros del Ramo de Marmolería y Piedras de Pavimentación. Se contaba que los obreros encargados de accionar las máquinas pulimentadoras del granito las habían manejado en la última jornada de trabajo con tal ardor, con tal devoción ciudadana, que al llegar los cuatro obreros y las cuatro máquinas, desde los cuatro ángulos de la plaza hasta su centro, chocaron para ser inmediatamente cubiertos por una gigantesca columna de granito líquido que resolvió el espinoso problema de orden público de la putrefacción de los cuerpos y el enmohecimiento de las máquinas. (82)

> [Above all, the inhabitants of M. were proud of the magnificent expanse of gray granite covering the two hundred—rectangular or square—yards of the park. The total absence of trees helped lend a greater solemnity to the park. In its center stood something rather like a twisted column. . . . It was humorously referred to as the Monument of the Marble and Cobblestone Workers. It was said that the workers in charge of operating the granite-polishing machines were, on the last day of the job, working the machines with such ardor, such patriotic devotion, that when the four workers and the four machines reached the center from the four corners of the plaza, they collided and were immediately encased in a huge column of liquid granite that eliminated the vexing public sanitation problem of putrefying bodies and rusting machines.] (55–56)

The narrator's description of the monument in the center of the so-called park and the tragedy that led to its formation is especially peculiar since it raises more questions than it answers. First of all, the reader is bound to wonder why the narrator finds the monument's name so humorous, given that it seems to reflect appropriately the fact that it contains the decomposed bodies and destroyed vehicles of the construction workers. Moreover, it is not clear why the bodies and the machines would have represented a public problem if they had not been encased in stone. As is often the case in Piñera's stories, the narrator brings up important issues without sufficiently expounding upon them, thus leaving the reader with questions that will never be answered. In fact, just when the account begins to get interesting, the narrator turns his attention to senseless details.

> De pronto y bajo un sol terrible—eran aproximadamente las tres de la tarde—T. avanzó destocado, de izquierda a derecha y de norte a sur. Al llegar al espacio inmediatamente anterior al monumento conmemorativo, vio a D. que, viniendo del oeste, sombreaba un tanto con su cuerpo la mitad derecha de su cara. Un poco más allá las excretas de un perro probaban que el basurero no había pasado todavía. (82–83)

> [Suddenly, under a terrible sun—it was approximately three in the afternoon—T. walked hatless from left to right and from north to south. Arriving at the space directly in front of the commemorative monument, he saw D. coming from the west, the right side of his face darkened by his shadow. A little further on, the excretions of a dog showed that the street cleaner had not yet passed.] (56)

The laughable exactitude of the language in the story's closing paragraph serves a double purpose. First, the narrator's mathematically precise description of a mundane encounter between two men taking a walk in the park echoes the senseless debate over its shape. Second, through his incongruous observations the narrator, like so many characters in Piñera's works, effectively strips language of its traditional utilitarian function, thereby reinforcing the story's overall air of absurdity. We should recall here that language's loss of meaning and functionality is a signature element of absurdist literature that Piñera himself recognized in the classic foreword to *Cuentos fríos*: "En realidad, dejamos correr la pluma entusiasmados. De pronto las palabras, las letras se entremezclan, se confunden; acabamos por no entender nada . . . Y entonces, espontáneo, ruidoso, brota ese misterioso balbuceo: ba, ba, ba, ba . . ." (n.p.). (Instead, full of enthusiasm, we let the pen run freely. Soon, the words, the letters run together, becoming confused; in the end, we understand nothing . . . And then, a mysterious babbling, spontaneous and noisy, bursts forth: ba, ba, ba, ba . . . [3].) The casual reference to a pile of feces in the story's final line at once reinforces the story's nonsensical tone and serves as a vulgar metaphor for the senseless babble—"mierda" or "bullshit," if you will—that fills the narrator's account.

Though Barreto is correct to point out that in "El parque" Piñera rejects plot in favor of description, her assertion that the story is about "absolutely nothing" exaggerates the point. According to her reading, "'The Park' is merely the description of a plaza, which gives rise to arguments of a geometrical nature . . . Nothing more."[38] Indeed, Barreto's failure to acknowledge the story's deeper implications echoes the superficial interpretation of reality that Piñera parodies in so many of his early stories. The problem with the townsfolk's mixed-up way of seeing things is precisely their refusal to look beyond the surface, which leads them to fixate on squares and rectangles instead of reflecting on the significance of the massive tomb that holds the remains of their fellow citizens.

"La boda" (1944) is similar to "El parque" in terms of its implicit parody of the tendency of the individual in modern society to evade reality by concentrating on trivialities. The story's central irony springs from the fact that the wedding announced in the title is of no consequence to the narrator who fixates on comically precise details—the exact position of the bride's dress as she enters the sanctuary, the angle of her shoulders in relation to objects in the church, the number of pews that she passes, the stains on the church's marble floor—and fails to describe or even mention the ceremony itself. The narrator's brief account is as nonsensical for what it includes as for what it leaves out:

> A una señal, el altar se iluminó, mientras el pie derecho de la novia penetraba en el templo. Cuando el extremo de la cola de su vestido tocó justo el sitio donde su pie derecho había marcado una levísima huella, se pudo observar que dejaba atrás treinta cabezas de águila que formaban el tope de otras tantas columnas situadas en el atrio. Así que una vez llegada la novia ante el oficiante, el extremo de su cola vino a quedar separado de su cuerpo por una distancia de treinta cabezas de águila. Claro que la distancia parecía un tanto mayor a causa del ángulo que se formaba de los hombros al suelo.... El piso, de mármol, estaba un poco manchado. También las cintas limitadoras dejaban ver un pequeño ángulo por el vacío existente entre asiento y asiento. Pero ya la novia iniciaba la salida apoyando suavemente su pie izquierdo en el primer peldaño de la graciosa escalinata que conducía hasta el altar. (86)

> [At a signal, the altar was illuminated, as the right foot of the bride crossed the threshold of the temple. When the end of her train touched precisely the point where her right foot had left its very slight print, it could be seen that in the atrium behind her thirty eagle heads crowned as many columns. In this way, once the bride had arrived in front of the minister, the end of her train came to rest at a distance of thirty eagle heads from her body. Of course, the distance appeared slightly greater due to the angle her shoulders formed with the floor.... The floor—made of marble—was slightly stained. In addition, the ribbons lining the aisle hung a little slack due to the space between the chairs. But already the bride was beginning her exit, lightly supporting her left foot on the first step of the stairway that led up to the altar.] (59)

This passage embodies what Gombrowicz referred to as the "senseless logic" that pervades Piñera's stories. While we immediately recognize the pointlessness of the narrator's observations, we are at the same time struck by his curious lucidity and exactness, which serve to confer a certain air of validity to his descriptions.

It is especially interesting that the minute details caught by the observer's eye are all related to the bride's entrance and exit. Everything that presumably happens in between these two moments—the Mass, the exchange of vows, the priest's blessing—is edited, so to speak, from the narrator's account. And even though the descriptions focus exclusively on things that most people would not notice, such as the light impression in the carpet left by the bride's feet and the angles created by the positions of various objects in the church, the narrator goes to great pains to make them seem significant.

Read Gilgen has observed that by treating trivialities as if they were extremely important, Piñera at once "capture[s] the essence of absurdity" and illustrates the monotonous nature of daily routine. "The reader," Gilgen adds, "is forcefully reminded that much of the drama he experiences is almost always equally unimportant."[39] But "La boda," like the other stories that we have discussed, presents multiple interpretive possibilities. It can also be read, for example, as a mockery of a materialistic society's tendency to place great importance on the superficial aspects of otherwise meaningful events. To be sure, the falsely dramatic atmosphere that Piñera creates in this brief narrative reads something like a report in a newspaper society page, where descriptions of wedding dresses, decorations, and ornate temples typically overshadow details about the deeper, spiritual component of the sacrament of marriage. It is especially noteworthy that in this early story Piñera subtly turns matrimony into an object of ridicule when we consider the fact that in many of his later works—*La boda* (1957), *Pequeñas maniobras* (1963), *El no* (1965)—marriage is presented as a bankrupt institution in a society that sees it as a social obligation rather than a personal commitment.

Several of Piñera's early stories can be read as highly exaggerated parodies of what he often claimed had become an increasingly prevalent trend among modern writers and artists, that is, the tendency to put more emphasis on form than content. In an article in the second number of *Poeta*, for example, Piñera alluded to this subject by accusing ex-members of the recently disbanded *Espuela de Plata* group of failing to recognize a "literary shortcoming" that Piñera himself claimed to have surmounted: "nuestra asombrosa disposición para dotarnos de un instrumento de decir..., que, contra toda trabazón lógica proponía, antes que 'el qué decir' el 'cómo decir' . . ."[40] (our astonishing disposition to endow ourselves with an instrument of expression..., which, against all logical coherence, put forward, before "what to say," the question of "how to say it" . . .). In "El País del Arte," one of his most important essays from the 1940s, Piñera was even more direct in his criticism of this artistic mentality that he found increasingly unpalatable:

> Esto es el colmo de la locura y de la desdicha, pero no es menos una amarga realidad en nuestros medios cultos: hasta un ensayista, que es, formalmente, el menos artista de todos los artistas, se preocupa tanto con la forma artística de su ensayo, que sacrifica el contenido a la ornamentación; el asunto en sí a la mera palabra. (38)

> [This is the height of craziness and misfortune, but it is nonetheless a bitter reality of our cultured methods: even an essayist, who is formally the least artistic of all artists, concerns himself so much with the artistic form of his essay that he sacrifices the content to ornamentation; the main theme itself to the mere word.]

We must keep in mind that throughout his career Piñera relished the opportunity to mock Cuban intellectual circles and literary trends. In his early years as a struggling writer in Havana Virgilio Piñera was keenly aware of the fact that his audience was limited to a reduced number of Cuban readers (none of Piñera's first three books exceeded 150 copies) who would have had no problem deciphering the acerbic critical undertones of his absurdist stories.

Notwithstanding the thematic and stylistic similarities that it shares with many of his early stories, "El álbum" is unique among the short fiction published in *Poesía y prosa* both in terms of its length and its character development. In this twenty-page tale, the narrator/protagonist, who is initially presented as a man with a sense of purpose and a firm grip on reality, completely loses touch with the meaning of his existence when he becomes entangled in the absurd world of a guesthouse and its eccentric inhabitants. "El álbum" is especially illustrative of how the grotesque and absurd elements of Piñera's writings serve to create environments and characters that seem to be at once part of our world and strangely foreign to it. The text is, in fact, deeply troubling precisely because it fits within the realm of possibility while it teeters precariously on the lunatic fringe. Daniel Balderston has noted that the most disquieting aspect of "El álbum" is its distorted perspective. As he astutely points out, an inordinate amount of time is wasted describing trivialities while the presence of the horrendous and absurd is hardly acknowledged by either the narrator/protagonist or the other characters.[41]

The narrator begins his tale by recounting his strange experiences on his first day as a resident in the guesthouse, where he has just moved in order to be closer to the home of a blind man who has hired him to work as his personal reader. Despite his best efforts to make it to his new job, the increasingly frustrated narrator finds it impossible to escape the confines of his new home.[42] Each time he tries to make an exit he is accosted by a different resident of the house, each of whom seems determined to make him stay for an event that is scheduled to take place in the main dining room of the guesthouse later that evening: the landlady's exhibition of the snapshots in her gigantic wedding album.

The doorman, who has turned the wildly popular album sessions into a lucrative scam, assails the unsuspecting narrator as he heads out the door with a high-pressure pitch to convince him to buy a ticket for the best seat in the house. The narrator is understandably disinclined to fall for such a scam, but the doorman is quick to point out that the other residents of the house would not even dream of missing out on such a grand occasion. According to him, all of the nearly one hundred residents willingly put their work and other obligations on hold until the exhibitions, which have been known to last more than six months, have concluded. He notes, moreover, that many of the boarders would literally kill for the opportunity to occupy the seat of honor.

The narrator is shocked that anyone would make radical changes in their daily lives or resort to such drastic measures in order to be able to contemplate the wedding photos of a stranger. The doorman, however, with a matter-of-factness that is at odds with his disconcerting remarks, responds to the narrator's surprise with additional unsettling details about the album sessions.

> "¡Oh, eso no es nada! . . . Por ejemplo: si se sabe que la sesión va a durar meses los huéspedes de la gradería hacen una comida cada dos días y dan curso a sus naturales necesidades en el mismo sitio en que se encuentran. A veces la gente del barrio se ha quejado a la sanidad; usted se imagina, el hedor que sale de la casa, a pesar de tenerla herméticamente cerrada, es insoportable. ¡Pero . . . todo es poco sacrificio con tal de tener el supremo placer de contemplar el álbum de la señora y escuchar sus explicaciones!" (66–67)

> ["Oh, that's nothing! . . . For example: if it's known that the session is going to last for months, the lower-class boarders fix meals every two days and let natural necessities run their course in the very seats that they sit in. At times, people in the neighborhood have complained about the sanitation; you can imagine the stench rising from the house—in spite of it being hermetically sealed—is unbearable. But . . . all this is a small sacrifice compared to the supreme pleasure of contemplating the lady's album and listening to her explanations!"] (40)

4: TALES OF ABSURD HOPE AND SENSELESS LOGIC 143

Given that Piñera's characters rarely seem to be affected by shocking circumstances, the narrator's dumbfounded response—"¡un álbum no es razón bastante para que toda una casa de huéspedes se exponga a los peligros del hambre y de la peste!" (67) [an album is not sufficient cause for a whole boarding house to be exposed to the dangers of hunger and plague! [40])—at first seems anomalous. However, it is important to point out that in a matter of hours he disregards his disgust and his sense of propriety by cheerfully embracing the deranged behavior of the other residents:

> También me convencieron de que no constituía vergüenza ninguna defecar sobre el asiento en que me encontraba. Defequé, pues, copiosamente sobre mi butaca, mientras la jovencita a mi lado me ofrecía un pedazo de carne asada, y yo, en justa reciprocidad, la obsequiaba con un trozo de pollo frío. (80)

> [They also convinced me that it was no disgrace to defecate on the seat in which I sat. So I defecated copiously all over my seat while the young woman to my side offered me a piece of roast, and I, in the spirit of reciprocity, presented her with a portion of cold chicken.] (53)

As we have noted, Virgilio Piñera frequently exploited the absurd and the grotesque for their inherent ability to leave the reader feeling ambivalent about his texts. Though laughter is a viable response to the passage cited above, its comic potential comes not so much from the presence of excrement, but rather from the characters' casual attitude toward it. The incongruity between the narrator's initial repulsion to the idea of defecating in public and his frank, cheerful discussion of his bowel movements just a few pages later is indeed at once disturbing and humorous.

In his study on the modern satiric grotesque, John R. Clark points out that the satirist often employs scatological humor precisely because so-called polite society considers fecal matter to be unsavory, offensive, and forbidden. According to Clark, "proud, self-delusional man ever aspires to elevate himself and his dignity, whereas the satirist destroys such upward mobility by reducing man to a defecating animal before our eyes."[43] By reducing the narrator to just such a defecating beast after having presented him as the character with a seemingly normal sense of direction and purpose, Piñera further calls attention to the fruitlessness of his attempts to make something of his life. Indeed, despite his determination to keep his commitment as a reader for a wealthy blind man, the weak-willed narrator becomes a prisoner of his irrational surroundings. This incongruity between the narrator's aspirations and the pathetic reality of his existence is a key component of the air of absurdity that permeates the story.

It is highly symbolic that the narrator and his companions take care of their biological necessities while they attend the album session, which is allegedly seen as a deeply inspiring and artistic event. The introduction of excrement in the room where the contemplation of the photos takes place serves both to undermine the activity's supposed lofty character and to emphasize its absurdity. In this sense, "El álbum" recalls Piñera's disdain for what he saw as a predisposition among modern cultural circles to turn the discussion and contemplation of works of art into banal, senseless activities. In his provocative article "El País del Arte," for instance, Piñera ridiculed the tendency among so-called connoisseurs to ignore a work's true worth by focusing solely on its superficial qualities:

> Entonces se llega a los detalles. ¡Dios mío, los detalles! Y los detalles hacen multiplicar y quintaesenciar las exclamaciones: ¡Ah!, ¡Oh!, ¡Estupendo!, ¡Estupendísimo!, ¡Qué cosa!, ¡Notable!, ¡Maravilloso! Y como el pintor sigue encontrando detalles y como ya también los encuentran los invitados, ocurre que el cuadro se vuelve un detalle, y como el detalle lleva al detalle, todos se dan a encontrar un detalle en lo que les rodea; la casa se hace detalle, detalle los seres allí reunidos, la vida detalle y . . . ¡horror! el Arte, un detalle, lleno él mismo de graciosos y suculentos detalles. (36)

> [Then one arrives at the details. My God, the details! And the details make the exclamations refine and multiply. Ah!, Oh!, Stupendous!, Really stupendous!, What a sight!, Remarkable!, Marvelous! And since the painter keeps finding details and given that the guests also find them, it happens that the painting becomes a detail, and since detail engenders detail, everyone sets to finding detail in their surroundings; the house becomes a detail, details those gathered there, life a detail and . . . What horror! Art, a detail, itself full of amusing, succulent details.]

We should add that one of Piñera's central complaints in "El País del Arte"—which like his stories lacks references to specific places or individuals—is that artists and their so-called critics are too easily lured into the game of turning the creation and contemplation of art into exercises of adoration. Piñera argued that too frequently modern artists were more concerned with enrapturing their audiences than they were with the quality of their work. On the same token, he posited that the inhabitants of the imagined "País del Arte" were predisposed to turning even the most worthless works of art into objects of praise. In "El álbum," the behavior of the "artist" and her audience during the preposterous exhibitions suggests a similar notion. It seems that the corpulent landlady is able to enthrall the onlookers not because her photos are worthy of praise, but rather because the residents of the guesthouse are programmed to esteem anything that is presented as Art with a capital "A."

The narrator's automatic recognition of the album session's value as an artistic exercise and his carefree acceptance of the outrageous rules that govern it suggest a highly exaggerated parody of the ilk of modern artists that Piñera frequently ridiculed for adhering to established trends or ways of thinking instead of forging new ground. The narrator is a spineless conformist who allows others to distract him from his own priorities and values. Just moments after expressing his shock at the mere idea of the photo exhibition, for instance, he pays the insistent doorman an exorbitant price for the best seat. Moreover, instead of keeping his commitment with his blind employer, the narrator chooses to attend the album session. Ironically, he comes across as being blind himself when he happily admits that once other members of the audience managed to convince him of the great artistic value of what he originally considered a senseless event, he was happy to remain in the audience for over eight months.

The narrator's encounter with Minerva, his next-door neighbor, is illustrative of his lack of autonomy and his inability to think and act on his own. When she enters his room with her screaming child in her arms, the narrator immediately informs her that he must leave for his new job. She ignores his attempts to excuse himself and begins to recount the unsettling story of her life. The gutless narrator, however, cannot muster up the courage to leave: "Yo inicié una débil resistencia pero ella me empujó y acabó por sentarme" (70) (I began to resist weakly, but she pushed me until I sat in the chair [43]). As if to foreshadow his months-long attendance of the ludicrous album session, the narrator passively listens to Minerva's prattle—even after admitting that he does not understand her—for more than three hours.

The symbolic importance of Minerva should not go unnoticed. The air of bewilderment that characterizes the narrator's bizarre encounter with a woman whose name is universally associated with wisdom and art again suggests Piñera's parody of certain modes of artistic expression. To be sure, in much the same way that the narrator underscores his lack of understanding of the words of this Cuban version of the goddess of Art—"hablaba con ese lenguaje poco comprensible para mí" (68) (she was talking in this language that I found barely comprehensible)—Piñera often claimed that he did not comprehend the language that some of his literary cohorts employed in their writings. On another level, however, the narrator's puzzlement in the presence of Minerva can also be construed as an evocation by Piñera himself of his own impressionability as a young artist looking for meaning in the coded language of Art. Referring to his early years as an aspiring artist in Havana Piñera made the following observations, which reflect certain themes in his story:

> Era mi época en que creía ciegamente que para ser artista debemos estar rodeados de objetos de arte; y digo así objetos de arte, porque tal término responde punto por punto al lenguaje cifrado de nuestro tiempo en lo que respecta el Arte. . . . y al igual que uno que ha tomado un doble purga y siente la necesidad de defecar al instante, sentí yo que debía rodearme de objetos de arte. . . .
> No, nosotros [los artistas jóvenes] con verdadero instinto animal, nos habíamos replegado a la sombra de Minerva.[44]

> [It was the era in which I believed blindly that in order to be artists we should surround ourselves with objects of art; and I say objects of art because the term responds point by point to the coded language of our time in respect to Art. . . . and like one who has taken a double purgative and feels the urge to defecate immediately, I felt that I should surround myself with objects of art. . . .
> No, we [the young artists], with true animal instinct, had withdrawn to the shadows of Minerva.]

With its tangible air of absurdity and its gratuitous scatological imagery "El álbum" reflects both Piñera's deliberate efforts to forge a unique literary voice and to shock a literary community that he found stuffy and bookish. The narrator's bizarre encounter with the "mujer de piedra" (woman of stone)—a forty-year-old paralytic who is strapped to an inclined metal board—is illustrative of these qualities that dominate Piñera's writings from the early 1940s. Instead of expressing sympathy for the woman when she informs him that she is about to die, the narrator asks an impertinent question: "¿Y cómo hace usted para defecar?" (73) (And how do you defecate? [46])). The "mujer de piedra"—whose name reflects both her physical paralysis and her emotional coldness—is not in the least bit offended by the narrator's impertinence. She is happy to demonstrate how she takes care of her biological needs, and she is likewise delighted to explain why she is not afraid of being bit in the anus by an insect when the narrator suggests the possibility of such a scenario:

> "¡Alberto!"—se dirigió a uno de los criados—, "enséñele al señor la tapa . . ." Entonces el criado que respondía por Alberto se inclinó, descorrió dos pequeños pestillos de una tapa que caía justamente debajo del ano de la señora, y me explicó minuciosamente que, poniendo un recipiente, la señora

podía hacer con suma facilidad sus naturales necesidades. "¿Y no teme usted que algún insecto . . ."? dije yo con vivo interés. "Ninguno—¡no lo sentiría! A ver, Alberto, pellízqueme fuerte en cualquier parte." (73)

["Alberto"—she ordered one of her servants, "show the man the cap. . . ." The servant who responded to the name Alberto then bent over and drew back two small latches from a catch that opened just below the lady's anus, and explained in minute detail that by putting a receptacle there, the lady could perform her bodily functions with complete ease. "And don't you fear that some insect. . . ?" I asked with burning curiosity. "Not at all—I wouldn't feel it! To demonstrate, Alberto, pinch me hard anywhere you want."] (46)

Though this farcical exchange between the narrator and the paralytic woman is undeniably humorous, there is also something eerie, almost nightmarish about it. The narrator's obsessive interest in the woman's bowel movements gives us the feeling that he has entered a realm of absurdity, and that he has inexorably lost contact with the rationality and respectability that he expressed at the beginning of the story.

It is significant that the album session begins just as this discourse on feces comes to an end. In fact, as soon as he has finished describing his brief encounter with this freak of nature, the narrator notes with surprising poise—and as if it were a foregone conclusion—that by the appointed time, he was seated and eager for the session to begin. Incredibly, the narrator who had so energetically decried the idea of viewing the landlady's photos ends up spending the next eight months doing just that.

The narrator's descriptions of the tacky setting of the album session and the pompous commencement of the event are highly symbolic when viewed in light of Piñera's ongoing attempts to poke fun at the false pretensions that in his mind permeated contemporary attitudes about Art:

El comedor presentaba, como se dice, un "golpe de vista magnífico." . . . parecía un pequeño anfiteatro, cerrado al fondo por falsas columnas de cemento estucado que eran parte de la recargada ornamentación del comedor; de columna a columna corrían festones y hayas, hojas y frutas de piedra, todo pintado de un delicioso y ridículo color amarillo. En las cuatro paredes del comedor se veían cuadros colgados con los tradicionales temas de cenas y convites; otros representaban inmensos fruteros llenos de zapotes, piñas, mangos, y también frutas de otros países.[45] . . . Una gran lámpara, cuyos ocho brazos eran otros tantos tritones, colgaba del centro del comedor. Yo me había perdido en la contemplación de sus bronces (cagados de moscas) y de sus lágrimas (más cagadas todavía) cuando un silencio repentino me hizo bajar la vista. Este silencio lo había provocado la dama del álbum que acababa de hacer su aparición. La seguía un hombre de pequeña estatura y regordete que llevaba en sus brazos, como los sacerdotes llevan la Sagrada Forma en el cojín de terciopelo, un álbum inmenso de fotografías. (73–74)

[The dining room offered, as they say, a "magnificent view." . . . [It] looked like a small amphitheater lined in the back by fake stucco columns, part of the overwrought ornamentation of the dining room. Strung from column to column were garlands and beechnuts, leaves and fruits made of stone, all painted a delicious and ridiculous yellow. On the four dining room walls hung paintings with traditional themes of dinners and banquets; other paintings showed immense fruit bowls filled with sapota fruit, pineapples, mangoes, and fruits of other countries as well. . . . A great lamp with eight arms ending in as many tritons hung from the center of the dining room. I was lost in contemplation of its bronze arms (soiled with flies) and its even dirtier crystals, when a sudden hush made me lower my gaze. The hush had been caused by the appearance of the lady of the album. A chubby man of small stature followed her, carrying an immense photograph album in his arms the way priests carry the sacrament on a velvet cushion.] (47)

The "overwrought ornamentation" of this mock banquet hall, which the narrator ironically declares to be a magnificent setting for the album session, reflects in many ways the falsely pretentious, meaningless event that takes place in it. The fake stucco columns, for example, embody the notion of superficial magnificence since they are hollow adornments that support no weight. The intricate decorative molding, which is covered with what the narrator refers to as a "ridiculous" hue of yellow paint, and the ornate chandelier, whose arms and crystals are covered with dead flies and their droppings, likewise lend to the air of false ostentation that characterizes the album session.

This passage's intimation that things that aim to impress often lack substance, once again echoes a leitmotif of Piñera's early literary and cultural criticism: the contemporary tendency (in Cuba and throughout the Americas) to cheapen art by placing more importance on ornamental language than on meaning and substance. As he put it in an article written in Buenos Aires in 1946, "el americano se ve continuamente tentado por el demonio de la ornamentación. . . . El escritor persiste atado a una segunda naturaleza—ornamentación, fórmula formal—y el verdadero mundo de la realidad cada vez más se le escapa" (the American sees himself constantly being tempted by ornamentation. . . . The writer remains tied to a second nature—ornamentation, formal formula—and the true world of reality escapes him more and more).[46]

The corpulent landlady's pious entrance into the gaudy locale where she will exhibit her photographs serves to draw the reader's attention to another target of ridicule in "El álbum," that is, the mixing of art and religious adoration. The landlady is presented as a caricature of a revered church figurehead who enters her "temple of worship" in the midst of a solemn silence. At her side, her husband-turned-altar boy bears the large photo album on a velvet pillow as if it were a sacred artifact or the Body of Christ. For their part, the residents of the guesthouse revere the imposing woman, put great stake in her every word, and consider her photo exhibitions to be sacred events. In "El País del Arte" Piñera made the following remarks concerning the blending of artistic and religious sensibilities and the tendency to adore art without really understanding it.

> En la base de todo sentimiento religioso está la adoración, pero el arte no es adoración sino acto. ¿Cómo podría hablarse, pues, de la religión del arte? . . . La religión es un dios que exige más y más adoración; ahora bien, toda adoración es ciega, abismal y pasiva. Pero lo contrario del arte es ser lo menos adorable: allí donde se le erige un altar, donde se le rinde culto se presenta como todo menos como arte.[47]

> [At the foundation of all religious sentiment is adoration, yet art is not adoration but action. How can one talk, then, of the religion of art? . . . Religion is a god that requires more and more adoration; now then, all adoration is blind, abysmal, and passive. But the contrary of art is to be the least adorable: the place where an altar is erected, where homage is paid, shows itself to be anything but art.]

The type of blind exaltation of art that Piñera speaks of in his article is clearly parodied in the album session. Even though most of those present are too far away to see the photos—"sólo podían ver los huéspedes que estaban sentados en las dos primeras filas" (75) [the only ones who could see were those boarders seated in the first two rows [48])—, everyone marvels at their beauty and significance. Likewise, the notion of passive adoration is emphasized by the notable lack of action among the spectators who, throughout the eight-month album session, don't get up from their seats to take a closer look at the photos or even to take care of their bodily necessities.

In addition to parodying certain literary tendencies and intellectual mentalities, Piñera also pokes fun at various aspects of contemporary Cuban society in "El álbum." In light of the fact that Piñera lampooned marriage and societal attitudes toward matrimony in many of his writings, it is especially significant that the landlady focuses on photos of her wedding day during the eight-month exhibition. She speaks for weeks about the most inconsequential aspects of that supposedly grand event—the extravagant reception, the regalia of the guests, her intricately embroidered wedding gown, the countless gifts, and the rich ingredients of the wedding cake—but makes no mention of the wedding ceremony itself. The narrator's exaggerated excitement over the photos that he can barely see despite occupying one of the best seats— "Aquello sí constituía un espectáculo magnífico" (80) (That did indeed create a magnificent spectacle [54])—accentuates the mockery of the shallowness of modern sensibilities, and the propensity of individuals to place undue importance on things that don't matter.

Despite the dearth of specific references to Cuba, the social inequities and class divisions described in the story coincide with certain aspects of Cuban society in the early 1940s. For example, the narrator is careful to point out the disparities between the rich and poor tenants of the guesthouse several times in his account. He notes early in the story that the poorest tenants always took the worst seats during the album session in order to avoid upsetting the landlady and the wealthy boarders: "Claro que hubieran podido sentarse en cualquiera de ellos, pero el temor de provocar un escándalo que habría ofendido con toda seguridad a la dueña del álbum les hacia soportar esta suprema humillación que toda pobreza impone" (65). (Of course, they could have sat in any of the seats, but the fear of provoking a scandal—which surely would have offended the owner of the album—forced them to suffer this supreme humiliation that all poverty imposes [38].) This observation is in keeping with certain themes and ideas that recur frequently in Piñera's stories. In the first place, the passage reminds us that the poor and disenfranchised often suffer in silence since they fear that rebelling against the source of their oppression will bring unwanted consequences. Their compliance with the will of the wealthy residents calls attention to one of the central motifs in Piñera's early stories, that is, that poverty is a source of shame and suffering.

Later in the story the narrator recounts that because the rich and poor tenants were seated in different sections of the room, the former group could see the album while the latter could not. This comment suggests a critique of the illusory prosperity of 1940s Cuba, during which time the upper class benefited greatly from the country's economic growth while many in the middle and lower classes were adversely affected by rising housing prices and shortages of all kinds.

It is, of course, ironic that the narrator of "El álbum" alleges that everyone in the guesthouse, which can be construed as a highly exaggerated microcosm of Cuban society, was allegedly content despite the obvious inequities among them. He insists, for example, that "[l]a felicidad de aquella gente era absoluta y ni la más categórica reparación social los habría satisfecho tanto como los satisfacían las explicaciones de la dama" (77). (The happiness of those people was absolute, and not even the most categorical social restitution would have satisfied them as much as the lady's descriptions [51]). Moreover, the narrator's ironic declaration that all of the tenants in the guesthouse enjoyed listening to the landlady's senseless speeches and descriptions while sitting in their own feces can be read as a parody of the tendency among the powerful to engage in political rambling and to make idle promises, while paying little attention to transcendent issues like social and economic reform. If we do choose to see the sociopolitical commentary embedded in "El álbum," we must be careful to acknowledge that Piñera's criticism was not just aimed at the government, which he felt ignored the plight of the poor and disenfranchised, but also at the people themselves, embodied in the pathetically impressionable and passive narrator, for failing to do anything about it.

In this chapter we have examined what I consider to be a representative sample of the short stories that Piñera wrote during the early years of his literary career. As I suggested earlier in this chapter, of all the diverse terms that have been employed to categorize or elucidate these stories, "grotesque" and "absurd" seem to best embody the fundamentally paradoxical nature of the environments, situations, and characters that Piñera depicts in them. In Piñera's stories the grotesque manifests itself largely through contradictions in the text itself—between the ordinary and the bizarre, the familiar and the foreign, loftiness and vulgarity—but also through the diverse range of emotions that they provoke. When reading "La carne" or "La cena," for example, we are moved to laugh at the tales' strangely comical undertones at the same time that we intuit the ominous implications of the protagonists' circumstances. Correspondingly, the narrator/protagonist of "El álbum" leaves us unsure if we are supposed to be amused or repulsed by his merry admission of having defecated in his seat during the outlandish album session.

Piñera's early tales are especially significant because they attest to the fact that from the beginning of his literary career, his worldview reflected several key components and attitudes of absurdism, which he would later draw on in some of his greatest dramatic works. Several of the texts discussed in this chapter are illustrative, for example, of the futility of modern man's efforts to surmount the obstacles that make human existence a constant, meaningless struggle. The pervading air of nonsense, ambiguous mix of misfortune and preposterous comedy, and the fundamental incongruity between bizarre circumstances and the protagonists' responses to them are also signature elements of the literature of the absurd that can be seen in many of the tales that Piñera published in *Poesía y prosa* in 1944. In short, these early stories are filled with paradoxes that recall the "perpetual oscillations between the natural and the extraordinary, the individual and the universal, the tragic and the everyday, the absurd and the logical" that Albert Camus saw as trademarks of the absurd world.[48]

In closing, I deem it appropriate to explain why I have made it a point to call attention to the subtle sociopolitical undertones of these early stories. On the one hand, I have done so largely because much has been made of the Piñera's supposed tendency to avoid social and political issues in his writing. On the other, even though I agree to an extent with McQuade's opinion that it makes more sense to inscribe Piñera "in the broader context of world literature, than to ascribe his humour and his literary world-view to a position centered on and generated by a local, Cuban socio-political reality,"[49] I also feel that it is disingenuous to imply, as many critics have, that the stories that we have discussed are completely dislocated from a Cuban context. Despite the fact that they lack specific references to places, individuals, and historical circumstances, these singular tales are not without Cuban accents that serve to contextualize them. Their language is marked by idiomatic expressions and vocabulary that exude local color, for example, and the unique sense of humor that permeates them is clearly informed by the Cuban *choteo*.[50] But perhaps more importantly, many of the stories' central themes and motifs—poverty, hunger, frustration, mixed-up priorities, miscommunication—while clearly anchored in the universal aesthetic of the absurd, also echo certain aspects of Cuba's sociopolitical reality in the early 1940s.

Though one must be cautious not to take the following remarks too literally, Piñera's response to an interviewer who asked him if these early texts should be considered "Cuban stories" is as revealing as it is characteristically derisive:

> ¡Caramba! La pregunta se las trae. ¿Y qué pueden ser sino cubanos? No los ha escrito ni un francés ni un japonés, los ha escrito Virgilio Piñera, que según mis informes nació en la ciudad de Cárdenas . . . de padres cubanos y abuelos de lo mismo. Además están escritos en cubano, no en español, que es un idioma que me resulta extremadamente difícil de leer. Además de además, los temas son cubanos, unos encubiertos, otros descubiertos. ¿Quieres una justificación más científica? Pues ahí va: cuando estos cuentos fueron escritos, mi cuerpo se movía en lo cubano . . . en una palabra respiraba lo cubano por todos los poros. Un cuerpo que se alimenta con productos cubanos—tanto materiales como psíquicos—sólo puede expulsar residuos cubanos. Y digo expulsar y digo residuos porque la literatura no es otra cosa que una defecación de la materia transformada.[51]

[I'll be damned! That question is annoying. And what else can they be but Cuban? They weren't written by a Japanese or Frenchman, they were written by Virgilio Piñera, who according to my information was born in the city of Cárdenas . . . to Cuban parents and grandparents. Besides, they are written in Cuban, not in Spanish, which is a language that I find extremely difficult to read. In addition to besides, the themes are Cuban, some concealed, others exposed. Do you want a more scientific justification? Well, here it is: when these stories were written, my body moved about in things Cuban . . . in a word I breathed Cubanness through all of my pores. A body that feeds itself with Cuban products—both material and spiritual—can only expel Cuban waste products. I say expel and I say waste products because literature is nothing but a defecation of transformed material.]

5

Religion, Philosophy, and Sexuality in *La carne de René*

Let thy suffering increase, it is for thy good.
—Søren Kierkegaard, *The Gospel of Our Sufferings*[1]

He sido como un perro
sumiso a la voz del amo
¡Hop, Virgilio, Salta!

[I have been like a dog
submissive to its master's voice
Hop, Virgilio, Jump!]

—Virgilio Piñera, "Final"[2]

SHORTLY BEFORE THE PUBLICATION OF *LA CARNE DE RENÉ* IN NOVEMBER 1952,[3] Virgilio Piñera penned an emotional text that he presumably planned to read at a presentation of the novel in Buenos Aires. Piñera declared in this three-page, handwritten document that two years of virtually nonstop writing had left him physically and emotionally exhausted, and he presented a pathetic image of himself as a lonely, frustrated author living in exile in near anonymity:

La carne de René ha tenido la terrible virtud de dejar maltrecha la carne de Virgilio Piñera: maltrecha, y, además, plena de sobresalto, angustia y melancolía.

¿Puedo revelar ahora las patadas en el trasero, el furor de la humillación, la cara roja como un tomate por el latigazo recibido. . . ? Puedo describirme ahora con el rabo entre las piernas, huyendo de las furias del siglo? . . .

Estoy cansado, enfermo, asqueado. ~~Quién dijo que la literatura es~~ He escrito este libro con telas de mi propia carne: días enteros, meses, en fin dos años de manos a la obra, careciendo de lo más elemental, ~~rodeado de la estupidez de mis compatriotas~~ casi sumergido en la deletérea indiferencia de mis compatriotas, arrastrándome hasta Buenos Aires, . . . llevando por las aguas del destino ~~hacia aguas al fin de~~ a trabajar con otros compatriotas no menos odiosos que los dejados allá en Cuba . . . haciéndome el tonto con los tontos, el imbécil con los imbéciles.

¿Qué me puede importar nada después de haber atravesado esta selva? ¿El éxito del libro? Me carcajeo ante el éxito de La carne de René. ¿Traducido a idioma extranjero? Prosigo con convulsas carcajadas. ¿Dinero? Las carcajadas me ahogan.[4]

[*René's Flesh* has had the terrible capacity to leave Virgilio Piñera's flesh battered: battered and, moreover, full of fear, anguish, and melancholy.

Can I reveal the kicks in the bottom, the furor of humiliation, my face red like a tomato from the whip that it's received. . . ? Can I describe myself now with my tail between my legs, fleeing from the furies of the century? . . .

I'm tired, sick, disgusted. ~~Who said that literature is~~ I have written this novel with pieces of my own flesh: entire days, months, in short, two years hard at work, lacking the most elemental things, ~~surrounded by the stupidity of my compatriots~~ almost submerged in the deleterious indifference of my compatriots, dragging myself to Buenos Aires, . . . carried by the waters of destiny ~~toward waters at the end of~~ to work with other compatriots who are no less odious than those left behind in Cuba . . . playing the fool among fools, the imbecile among imbeciles.

What could be of any importance to me after having traversed this jungle? The success of my book? I roar with laughter at the idea of the success of *René's Flesh*. Translated to a foreign language? I continue to laugh convulsively. Money? The guffaws overwhelm me.]

Piñera's comments call attention to the fact that the initial years of his second period of exile in Argentina were marked by intense frustration and disappointment on a number of levels. In terms of his daily existence, Piñera detested his position at the Cuban consulate, and he struggled to get by on the minimal wages that he earned there. Given that Piñera wanted nothing more than to dedicate his life to his writing, the mind-numbing administrative tasks that filled his days must have seemed like an insufferable waste of time. To make matters worse Piñera, who always craved intellectual stimulation, could hardly bear his coworkers, whom he considered dimwitted, and who likely saw him as an eccentric outsider.

As far as his intellectual pursuits were concerned, Piñera felt disillusioned from the outset at what was to become a four-year stay in Buenos Aires. During his previous residence in the Argentine capital, the funds from a scholarship awarded to him by the Comisión Nacional de Cultura de Buenos Aires had afforded him the opportunity to dedicate virtually all of his time to intellectual pursuits while living in relative comfort. In 1946 and 1947 Piñera had kept very busy mixing with Argentine and foreign authors, working on the translation of *Ferdydurke*, soliciting collaborations for *Orígenes*, and dreaming up ways to agitate the Argentine intelligentsia with Witold Gombrowicz. But during his second period of self-imposed exile, Piñera had much less time and fewer opportunities to interact with literary circles or to cultivate his cultural interests. Moreover, his minimal salary made for an uncomfortable and precarious existence that added to his feelings of inadequacy and gloom.

In the midst of such frustrating circumstances, Piñera turned to his writing. For months on end he worked tirelessly on *La carne de René*, a work that he viewed as something of a testament to the many hardships he had undergone in his determined pursuit of a fulfilling career as a writer. Piñera's sardonic assessment of his novel's chances of success draw attention to his keen awareness that a contemporary Latin American audience would not embrace his novel's radically subversive subject matter. Sadly enough, his predictions about the fate of *La carne de René*, which he rightly considered his masterpiece, turned out to be prophetic. Much like the translation of *Ferdydurke*, which had received little attention upon its publication in Buenos Aires in 1947, *La carne de René* was largely ignored and failed to stir up the controversy that Piñera had envisioned.

Though Piñera often went to great pains to point out that his reputation and the success of his works would always take a backseat to his need to express himself honestly in his writings, he was deeply disappointed by the virtual silence that followed the publication of *La carne de René*. It is difficult to determine with any certainty how many copies of the novel were sold or who read it, but it was not reviewed in either *Orígenes* or *Sur*. This may be due to the fact that few members of the two intellectual circles read *La carne de René*, but it may also indicate that Piñera's Argentine and Cuban cohorts saw the novel for what it was—a radically subversive and controversial text that represented a clear affront to their aesthetic sensibilities—and thus chose to ignore it.

It is hardly surprising that the novel was not popular among the largely conservative reading public in 1950s Argentina and Cuba. Piñera's defiance of traditional values, his audacious denunciation of Christianity and Catholicism, and his treatment of taboo subjects such as homosexuality, sadomasochism, and cannibalism would surely have been too much for most contemporary readers to digest. Despite the fact that *La carne de René* was not widely read or discussed, mere awareness of its scandalous contents would have served to reinforce Piñera's ever-growing reputation as a provocateur who delighted in stirring up debates and shocking the intellectual establishment. We must recall that several of the works that Piñera published before his first novel had fueled controversy in Cuba. In the early 1940s, for example, Cintio Vitier and Gastón Baquero expressed their distaste for of *La isla en peso*, which they accused of intentionally distorting Cuban reality with its deeply pessimistic tones and syphilitic imagery. Likewise, from the pages of *Orígenes* Vitier had criticized the coarseness of some of the texts from *Poesía y prosa*. Several years later, after Piñera had returned from his two-year stint in Buenos Aires, a group of Havana theater critics denounced his masterful play *Electra Garrigó* for its irreverence and absurdity and condemned *La boda* and *Jesús* on similar grounds. The allegedly controversial nature of those earlier works, however, paled in comparison to the downright scandalous content of *La carne de René*. And though Piñera clearly understood that by publishing his novel he was putting his already tarnished reputation at risk, he also relished the opportunity to deliver another blow to those who had objected to his highly unorthodox literary sensibilities in the past.

Negating the Soul through Carnal Education

In an introductory essay to the English translation of Piñera's *Cuentos fríos* Guillermo Cabrera Infante quips that when he speaks of getting a kick out of reading the works of Virgilio Piñera, he is actually "talking of a true kick. A kick in the groin or in the stomach, but most of the time a kick in the soul where it hurts metaphysically and you bleed internally."[5] Though Cabrera Infante was specifically referring to Piñera's short stories, his observation seems equally applicable to the powerful impact that *La carne de René* tends to have on those who brave their way through its pages. Indeed, the novel's shocking corporeal imagery, gruesome violence, audacious eroticism, and derisive mockery of traditional Christian concepts and beliefs all serve to deliver the figurative "kick in the soul" that Cabrera Infante describes in his essay.

Through the disturbing experiences of the novel's young protagonist, Piñera challenges the reader of *La carne de René* to view human existence in a new light. Departing from his own conviction that the soul's actuality cannot be proven, for example, Piñera invites us to consider the possibility that the body, not the soul, serves as the driving force of human existence. One of the most salient aspects of *La carne de René* is its relentless parody of traditional Christian concepts regarding the body and the soul. The obsessive carnal imagery in the novel, for example, challenges the Christian notion that "the soul-spirit is good, immortal, involved in salvation" while "the body is evil, mortal, not involved in salvation."[6] Moreover, by presenting the human body as the lone driving force of human existence—a notion that Piñera may have borrowed from his readings of the materialist philosophies of the Marquis de Sade— Piñera at once negates the existence of the soul, and challenges the very concept of spirituality. As part of the novel's systematic derision of

Christianity and Catholicism, Piñera parodies everything from the rigorous practices of Jesuit educators, to the solemn rites of the sacraments and the celebration of the Eucharist, to the sacred images of Christ and the saints that adorn Christian places of worship.

It will be argued throughout this chapter that Piñera's blasphemous subject matter, and his bold treatment of myriad forbidden topics such as homosexuality and sadomasochism, not only reveal the influence of the writings of the Marquis de Sade, but also share with them a common goal: to provoke a conservative audience with disturbing ideas and highly unorthodox philosophies. It should be noted that in *La carne de René* Piñera does not reach the extremes of what one critic has appropriately referred to as Sade's "sacrilegious venom."[7] His novel does, nonetheless, bear the mark of the French author and philosopher, especially in terms of its mockery of mystic suffering and the Christian martyrs, its denial of the existence of the soul, and, perhaps most importantly, its daring exploration of eroticism and sexuality.

It is through René's bizarre education, first under the tutelage of his father and then at the Escuela del Dolor, that Piñera most directly challenges Christian dogma and traditional views on sexuality. When we first meet the young protagonist, he is waiting to purchase meat at a butcher shop, an activity that his father requires him to perform weekly as part of his so-called carnal education. This setting is highly symbolic of the tensions between carnality and spirituality that pervade the text, and it is a perfect backdrop for the introduction of René, whose journey of self-discovery will eventually lead him to realize that his own flesh is the driving force of his existence.

Though by the end of the novel René develops a fascination for all things carnal, at its outset he is repulsed by both meat and human flesh. Unlike the rest of the clients at the butcher shop, therefore, who are eager to purchase meat after a period of rationing, René is terrified by the huge chunks of beef, pork, and lamb that hang from meat hooks in the ceiling.

> René, que casi roza con su cara un cuarto de buey suspendido de un garfio, exhibe una palidez espantosa. Le horroriza cuanto sea carne descuartizada y palpitante . . . la vista de una res muerta le provoca arqueadas, después vómitos y termina por echarlo en la cama días enteros. (14)

> [René, whose face is practically rubbing up against a quarter ox suspended from a meat hook, displays a frightening pallor. Butchered, throbbing flesh

horrifies him . . . the sight of a dead steer provokes him to nausea, then vomiting, and finally leaves him bedridden for days on end.] (4)[8]

In the "Translator's Note" to his English translation of the novel, Mark Schafer observes that one of the central maxims in the novel is "that life is one big, existential slaughterhouse in which we are at once the butchers and the butchered" (xxi). He further points out that throughout the novel the ambivalence of the word "carne," which means both "meat" and "flesh" in Spanish, "constantly undermines any moral or conceptual boundaries the reader might draw between the characters and the physical continuum they share with the bloody side of beef" (xxi). The slaughtered meat hanging in the butcher shop, then, reminds René that his own flesh could suffer the same fate, and it therefore provokes feelings of horror and dismay. The nature of René's fear is captured in the words of the Irish painter Francis Bacon, whose grotesque images of fragmented bodies were popular during the 1940s and 1950s: "We are meat, we are potential carcasses. If I go into a butcher's shop I always think it surprising that I wasn't there instead of the animal."[9]

From the outset of the novel René is associated with the helpless, slaughtered carcasses in the butcher shop. For example, René's eccentric neighbor Dalia Pérez, who contemplates him from her place in the line at the butcher shop, envisions his flesh on the verge of annihilation.

> La señora Pérez la imaginaba herida por un cuchillo o perforada por una bala. . . . [E]xperimentó la desagradable y angustiosa sensación de que esa carne estaba a dos dedos de ser atropellada por un camión, que estaba intacta de puro milagro, que tan sólo faltaban unos minutos para que algo demoledor se le echara encima aniquilándola. (15)

> Mrs. Pérez imagined his flesh wounded by a knife or punctured by a bullet. . . . [S]he experienced the unpleasant sensation that it was mere inches from being crushed by a truck, that it was a sheer miracle it remained intact, that it would only be a few minutes before something demolishing fell on top of him, annihilating his flesh.] (5–6)

Dalia's haunting thoughts at once recall the image of the slaughtered animal carcasses in the butcher shop and foretell the fate of René's own flesh, which—like meat designated for human consumption—is also destined to be sacrificed for a greater cause.

Dalia's visualization of a force destroying René's body quickly materializes in the figure of René's tyrannical father, Ramón, who has mapped out a bizarre carnal apprenticeship for his son that will include physical violence much like that imagined by Dalia. Ramón plans to turn René into a purely physical being through corporeal suffering in order to prepare him for the leadership of the "Causa de la Carne Acosada" (The Cause of Pursued Flesh), a mysterious cult dedicated to physical torture and antispiritual teachings. As its future leader René will be required to disavow the traditional Christian notion that "If there is a physical body, there is also a spiritual body."[10] René's frequent visits to the butcher shop correspond to the initial stage of his education, which aims at once to familiarize him with images of brutalized flesh and to make him cognizant that his carnal existence is all that matters.

On the day before René's twentieth birthday—after years of sending him to the butcher shop—Ramón decides to advance his son's apprenticeship by forcing him to examine mutilated human flesh. As Ramón removes his clothing to reveal a prized collection of wounds, René is appalled by what he sees: a massive gash in his father's chest, a bruise on his leg, a huge scar from heel to toe on one of his feet, a collarbone transformed into a grotesque protuberance, and a grossly deformed abdomen. René's visceral reaction underscores the important role of the sense of sight as a trigger for sensations of horror. Throughout the novel the young protagonist will have many similar experiences when he is forced to contemplate shocking images that are meant to help him learn how to experience pain in his own flesh.

While Ramón shows off his mutilated body, he urges René to examine it very carefully in order to learn what he is supposed to emulate as future leader of the cult. Ramón knows, however, that his son will not believe in the value of his practice simply by seeing the cuts and sores, and he therefore exhorts René to touch them. In much the same way that Christ invited St. Thomas to touch his wounds as a means of dispelling his doubt—"Put your finger here and see my hands. Reach out your hand and put it in my side. Do not doubt, but believe"[11]—Ramón, who sees himself as the "Christ" figure of his own cult, seeks to convince his doubting son of the truth through sight and touch.

In his parodic refashioning of the encounter between Christ and St. Thomas, Piñera reveals a subversive homoerotic tension between René and his father, which resurfaces a number of times in the novel. The provocative image of René's fingers exploring the open sores suggests a symbolic act of sexual penetration, which fills Ramón with great excitement. "¡Vamos, ánimo! Me estás viendo como realmente soy. Pero hay más, esto no es todo . . ." (25) (Come on! Courage! You're seeing me as I really am. But there's more, this isn't all . . .) (15), he exclaims, as René touches him. When he removes his clothing in order to reveal more cuts and bruises, Ramón further charges the scene with erotic tension.

René is not convinced by his father's teachings on the advantages of mangled and tortured flesh. From the beginning he resists ideologies imposed on him by others, and when his father asks him if he would like to have a body like his, René insists that he hates wounds and prefers to keep his body intact. Ramón's angry reply underscores the bizarre tenets of the sadomasochistic, carnal cult: "¿Qué significa eso del cuerpo intacto? Entonces, si no lo quieres vulnerado, ¿a qué lo destinas? . . . ¿No amas la carne descuartizada?" (26). (What does that mean, your body whole? So, if you don't want it damaged, what are you keeping it for? . . . Don't you love butchered flesh? [16].)

Since "joining La Causa demands the recognition of the flesh as an instrument of torture and the willingness to self-inflict bodily wounds,"[12] Ramón is determined to demonstrate how his own dedication to self-mutilation has led him to his prestigious position as leader of this carnal cult. Ramón's dogged insistence that flesh is the driving force of existence challenges Christian notions concerning the preeminence of the soul. Moreover, his audacious carnal teachings echo many of the sermons and speeches of Sade's libertines who tried tirelessly to debunk Christian doctrines. In her groundbreaking critical evaluation of Sade's work, Simone de Beauvoir asserts, for example, that according to Sade "it is when the flesh is torn and bleeding that it is revealed most dramatically as flesh."[13] It is clear that this is a notion that Ramón wants to impart to his son.

It is especially noteworthy that Ramón asks his son if he loves mutilated flesh since such a notion underscores the resolutely antispiritual nature of his beliefs and of his corporeal sermonizing. The idea of "loving" human flesh also challenges Christian teachings on the subject, which tend to condemn those who place too much importance on the body. The book of Romans, for example, stipulates "if you live according to the flesh you will die; but if by the Spirit you put to death the deeds of the body, you will live."[14]

INSTRUMENTS OF CARNAL INSTRUCTION IN THE SCHOOL OF SUFFERING

Shortly after showing off his mutilated body, Ramón invites René into a room in the house that he has never been allowed to enter. It is in this secret space that Ramón has pledged to reveal the enigma of his cult to his son. Upon entering René is startled to find himself in what looks like an Inquisition-style torture chamber, complete with surgical instruments, a complicated series of ropes, pulleys and slings, an iron table, and oxyacetylene torches. A large oil painting on the wall especially catches René's attention. At first glance it appears to depict the martyrdom of St. Sebastian, but after careful scrutiny René notices that unlike the contemplative martyr riddled with the arrows of his enemies, this rendition of St. Sebastian sticks the arrows into his own body.

As he contemplates the painting more closely, René recognizes his own face in the perverted image of a young man enjoying self-inflicted pain. Again echoing Sade, who in "Dialogue Between a Priest and a Dying Man" derides the martyrs and insists that they are the weakest of all Christian arguments,[15] Piñera uses the painting of St. Sebastian to poke fun at the very notion of martyrdom. The disconcerting grin on the face of St. Sebastian/René, for example, makes sport of both the physical and spiritual components of Christian suffering. David Morris has pointed out that the typical image of St. Sebastian portrays an individual who "exists suspended between the world of the body, which he has not yet entirely abandoned, and the world of the spirit, which he has not yet entirely attained."[16] Ramon's painting, however, mocks these spiritual connotations of the image by depicting physical suffering as a source of masochistic pleasure. As we soon learn, the painting's function is didactic since Ramón hopes it will at once incite René to sacrifice his own body to the Cult of the Flesh and help him to appreciate the role that physical torture will play in his future.

When René questions why he is torturing himself in the painting, Ramón offers the following explanation: "¿Quién, en medio de tantas flechas, resistirá la tentación de clavarte una más?" (40) (Who, faced with so many arrows, could resist the temptation to stick one more into you? [30]). In this sense the painting clearly foreshadows René's carnal education in the Escuela del Dolor and his eventual capitulation to the dictates of his father's cult. Ramón's use of "clavar," which means "to nail," but also, "to fuck," in vulgar discourse, is especially loaded with meaning since, as Rafael L. Ramírez has noted, when a man is "clavado" his masculinity is challenged and devalued and he is placed "in the sphere of the feminine" and made equal "to a penetrated woman."[17] In this sense the phallic arrows foreshadow the erotic atmosphere of the all-male school where René and the other first-year students are forced to take part in sadomasochistic exercises with the older students and the instructors.

Ana García Chichester holds that the image of St. Sebastian "synthesizes the conflict René must resolve: to suffer in silence the purposeful and systematic torturing of his body for the service of La Causa (pain) or for the service of women (pleasure)."[18] However, Ramón's deliberate choice of a masochistic and homoerotic icon for the painting implicitly removes women and heterosexual pleasure as components of the future that he envisions for his son. Though René does indeed struggle to comprehend his feelings for Dalia Pérez, the painting itself simply serves to foreshadow René's eventual capitulation to his father's will.

Furthermore, René does not necessarily see Dalia Pérez as an embodiment of pleasure. In his mind, she, like Ramón and the officials in the Escuela del Dolor, is a force that seeks to dominate him and to rob him of his right to govern his own existence. Despite his best efforts, however, René is destined to be dominated by others. The painting of the martyr who accepts and enjoys pain is simply the first of many doubles that will be used as pedagogical tools to prepare René for an inexorably violent destiny.

René's formal carnal education takes place at the Escuela del Dolor—a dreadful institution that Arrufat correctly sees as a caricature of Catholic schools.[19] Through the Escuela del Dolor Piñera aggressively parodies Catholic educators' reputation for strictness: the students are subjected to brutal punishments, not for their unruly behavior or for academic deficiency, but rather for such "violations" as refusing to suffer in silence, or bursting out in tears when they are subjected to various forms of physical torture. The students live in rooms that the officials refer to as prison cells, they are shocked with electric currents, branded on the buttocks with hot irons, and forced to wear muzzles and gags in order to maintain silence.

At the Escuela del Dolor there is no intellectual or spiritual instruction. In fact, the common notion that the mind and soul are immaterial and separate from bodily existence is an object of scorn in the institution. By way of illustration, Sr. Mármolo, the school's headmaster, underscores his opinion that the body and the mind are essentially the same thing by complaining that René's capacity for thinking is inextricable from his flesh: "su carne no es del todo carne; todavía le baila por dentro el demonio del pensamiento" (his flesh isn't just flesh. The demon of thought still dances within it). Another of the school's officials backs up Mármolo's observation with an equally provocative remark: "Es una carne que permite pensamientos sobre si misma" (132). (It's flesh that permits itself to think about itself [123].)

This concept of flesh with thoughts echoes another Sadean notion, which is expressed by the libertine Delbene in *Justine*. As he puts it, "I am not aware of having a soul . . . it is the body which feels, which thinks, which judges, which suffers, which enjoys."[20] David Morris has pointed out that to Sade the body encompassed everything. In his opinion "The concept of the 'thinking body' is Sade's response to Cartesian dualism that rigorously divides material bodies from immaterial thoughts. In Sade's libertine system, body and mind are both equally material."[20a] In a similar manner Piñera denies the notion that mind and body are split. The leaders of the Escuela del Dolor, for example, argue that René's carnal education is important precisely because of the bond between psyche and flesh. Departing from this notion, the narrator makes a rather illuminating comment regarding Mármolo's concept of the spirit: "¿Qué cosa es eso del espíritu? . . . [S]i por el espíritu se entendía el cuerpo, entonces la escuela que él dirigía era altamente espiritual" (74). (What do you mean by spirit? . . . [I]f by spirit one understood the body, then the school he directed was highly spiritual [64–65].)

This attitude similarly echoes Delbene's negation of the spiritual side of human existence. Like Sade's libertine, who underscores the body's multifaceted role in human existence, the exclusive concern of the officials at the Escuela del Dolor is the body. Corporeal punishments are their key educational tools, and the only textbook that they use is referred to as "the book of the human body."

The school's mottoes—"Hay que sufrir para aprender" (You have to suffer to learn) and "Sufrir en silencio" (Suffer in silence)—call attention to its pedagogical focus, but they also serve to underscore another aspect of Piñera's parody of Christian doctrine. Like Christ, who "learned obedience through what he suffered,"[21] René is expected to accept suffering in order to be worthy of following in his father's footsteps. The Escuela del Dolor, then, plays with the Christian notion that suffering is essential if one wishes to attain grace with God. In this sense, too, Piñera seems to have borrowed a key theme from Sade, whose derisive mockery of Christianity aims to debunk Christian attitudes about redemptive suffering.[22] Like Sade, Piñera parodies Christian dogma by bringing René's lessons of suffering and obedience to a purely carnal level. According to the teachings of the institution's anti-Christian leaders, an individual's suffering is not valuable as a vehicle of spiritual development, but rather it serves only to cultivate the flesh and make it more resilient to pain.

This important aspect of Piñera's novel calls to mind another likely influence on its thought-provoking subject matter, that is, the writings of the Danish philosopher Søren Kierkegaard, whose works Piñera is said to have read assiduously.[23] In many of his writings on Christianity, Kierkegaard derides his contemporaries for seeing the Church as a place of comfort and pleasure. According to Kierkegaard's interpretation of the New Testament, true Christians were meant to obey God. As he saw it, such a goal could only be achieved through the acceptance and transcendence of a lifetime of suffering. In *The Gospel of Our Sufferings* (1847), Kierkegaard envisions human existence as a sort of "school of suffering" that, by teaching us to obey God and to let him command, makes us fit for eternal life. "And so the length of time at school is in direct proportion to the importance of what one is going to be," he argues. "If then the school of sufferings lasts a whole lifetime, it is the very evidence that this school must be fitting us for what is highest. . . . The school for life shows its results in time, but the lifelong school of suffering fits us for eternity."[24]

Piñera's Escuela del Dolor can be seen, then, as a sarcastic play on Kierkegaard's "school of suffering." Piñera's institution ridicules this notion that one must suffer in order to be considered worthy of a higher form of being. Against Kierkegaard's "school of suffering" that prepares the spirit for eternity, Piñera's pits the Escuela del Dolor, which is meant to prepare René's body for its role as leader of the Cause. René's horrible experiences seem to mock some of the ideas that the Danish philosopher discusses in his work. According to Kierkegaard, "the greater the suffering the nearer to perfection . . . on that way where man follows Christ, the height of suffering is the height of glory."[25] At the Escuela del Dolor, though, this notion of attaining inner, spiritual glory through suffering is turned topsy-turvy by carnal teachings that negate the spiritual component of suffering. There, suffering is seen as a purely physical phenomenon. The students are not supposed to transcend it like Christian mystics, but rather to let it dominate and control them.

As we have mentioned above, the strict and violent atmosphere at the Escuela del Dolor suggests a highly exaggerated mockery of an all-male Catholic school. More specifically, Piñera's target seems to have been Jesuit schools, which had a long tradition in Latin America of strict and austere educational methodologies. It should not go unnoticed that Cochón, the head "priest" of the school, had tried to become a member of the Jesuits. His radical interpretations of the Scriptures and Christian doctrine were too extreme, however, even for an order with a reputation for liberal thinking.[26] At the Escuela del Dolor Cochón is praised for having been expelled from the Church, and his so-called "espíritu de lo bajo" (102) (spirit of lowliness [93]), perfectly suits the school's carnal curriculum.

Cochón's anti-Catholic philosophies, which uphold the school's mission of negating the existence of the soul, are viewed as a form of revenge against the Church:

[S]u venganza contra ésta [la Iglesia Católica] fue algo que superó en crueldad a todas las crueldades intelectuales. Por ejemplo, interpretó la crucifixión de Cristo de acuerdo con el espíritu de la escuela. Así, decía . . . "Cristo no murió en la cruz por amor hacia los hombres. Ergo: Cristo murió en la cruz por amor hacia su propia carne." (102–3)

[H]is revenge [against the Catholic Church] was something that surpassed all intellectual cruelty in its cruelty. For example, he interpreted the crucifixion of Christ in the spirit of the school. This is how he told it: . . . "Christ didn't die on the cross for the love of men. *Ergo*: Christ died on the cross for the love of his own flesh."] (93–94)

Cochón's defiance of God also evokes the works of the Marquis de Sade, who exploited many of the arcane teachings of Christianity in his brutally anti-Christian writings. The Marquis was a declared atheist who, as David Coward puts it, saw God as "an irrelevant hypothesis" and Christianity as a foolish "moral system based on the supposed goodness of a non-existent being."[27] For Sade the very notion of blasphemy was an absurdity since utterances or actions against God could not be considered impious or irreverent if he didn't exist in the first place. Following the example of Sade, Piñera—who was known for his mistrust of Catholic doctrine, especially in regards to salvation and the existence of the soul[28]—challenges those who accept unprovable religious dogma by advocating atheism.

Like Sade, who swore that "The idea of God is the sole wrong for which I cannot forgive mankind,"[29] Cochón holds a similarly vehement grudge against God and the Church. Since the main aim of the Escuela del Dolor is to educate the students' bodies, it behooves the leaders to debunk any Christian ideology that contradicts their carnal philosophy. In his sermon Cochón challenges, for example, the idea that upon dying on the cross Christ "gave up his spirit."[30] He intimates that Christ was a masochist who died for the sake of experiencing pain in his own flesh.

It is worth noting here that Cochón's frequent use of the word "carne" in his venomous profanation of the crucified Christ is especially provocative when considered in light of the thematic intersections that exist between meat and crucifixion. In his study of several grotesque interpretations of the crucifixion by the Irish painter Francis Bacon, Wilson Yates points out that both meat and the crucifixion are symbols of the body as a dead object that has suffered greatly. He further notes that crucifixion is "a cultural reference that points to and pulls us into an encounter with the reality of suffering."[31] When René encounters the plaster image of himself nailed to the cross in the next chapter, then, he is implicitly brought into contact with an image that at once recalls the slaughtered carcasses in the butcher shop and the intense human suffering experienced by Christ.

Shortly after arriving at the Escuela del Dolor, René learns that the institution's pedagogical approach is very similar to his father's. For example, the school officials also make use of doubles in the form of grossly perverted parodies of religious icons in order to underscore one of the basic philosophies of the Cult of the Flesh: that pain and pleasure are intimately related to each other. The grotesque plaster sculpture that René finds in the bathtub of his private apartment is meant to express precisely this notion:

> Ante sus ojos estaba la consumada reproducción de sí mismo en el trance de la crucifixión.... [E]n vez de la patética y angustiada faz de Cristo, ésta de René, en yeso, se ofrecía, no caída sobre el pecho, sino muy erguida, y la boca mostraba la risa de la persona satisfecha. (67)

> [Before his eyes was a perfect reproduction of René himself in the moment of crucifixion.... [I]n place of Christ's face, full of pathos and anguish, René's face, sculpted in plaster, was held high rather than slumped against his chest and his mouth displayed the laughter of a contented man.] (57)

This profanation of the icon of Christ on the cross is illustrative of Piñera's propensity to mock all things sacred. The statue's contented grin implicitly makes sport of traditional icons of the suffering Christ, which are meant to inspire pity for a man who was subjected to unimaginable torture for the sake of the redemption of the human race. René's crucified double, whose contented face belies the obvious horror of being nailed to a cross is meant to demonstrate the notion that suffering is not simply a question of pain, but also of pleasure. Like the painting of St. Sebastian in Ramón's office, this sculpture is intended to help René learn how to experience in his own flesh the sentiments of his doubles, as Arrufat has correctly noted.[32]

The two images also remind René of a theory that his father and Mármolo both espouse, that is, that repetition works miracles. They believe that René will eventually understand and accept his destiny if they bombard him with images of suffering bodies. The sculpture of the smiling, crucified René also points to Piñera's parody of the passion of Christ, since René is destined to undergo his own passion of sorts. Later in the novel the narrator makes an explicit comparison between René's painful existence and Christ's passion when he remarks that René has just begun "una estación más de su *vía crucis* pro-carne" (223) (another station of his pro-meat *via crucis* [217]).

The Pedagogies of Masochism and Homoeroticism

Even before René arrives at the Escuela del Dolor, there are a number of indications that he is being trained to become a passive masochist in a homosocial world. Through his corporeal instruction, for example,

Ramón aims to teach René to experience sexual pleasure from the bodily injuries inflicted upon him by the leaders of the all-male flesh cult. The provocative images of René as a self-sacrificing St. Sebastian and a crucified Christ figure and the perverse exercises at the Escuela del Dolor are integral components of a program that aims to train young men to associate physical pain with sexual pleasure. According to Baumeister, masochists associate "sexual pleasure with one or more of the following three features: receiving pain; relinquishing control through bondage, rules, commands, or other means; and embarrassment and humiliation."[33] All of these are central to the pedagogical methods of the Escuela del Dolor.

On his first day at the institution René and his classmates take part in an exercise that underscores the role of submission and humiliation in their educational program. Within hours of their arrival, the new students are forced to remove their clothing. They are then corralled into a room where groups of naked upperclassmen inspect their flesh to make sure that it is suitable for the rigorous corporeal agenda of the school. In this explicitly homoerotic scene the second-year students arrive first, and with evident pleasure that contradicts the seemingly humiliating nature of their behavior, they smell the young men from head to toe:

> como perros de cacería, se lanzaron sobre los neófitos y empezaron a olisquearlos afanosamente. . . . [S]ólo tocaban con sus narices el cuerpo de los neófitos. . . . ¡Y cuánta precisión en los movimientos de esos "perros"! Se cruzaban unos con otros en busca de nuevas presas, se miraban comunicando sus impresiones olfativas. (72–73)

> [like hunting dogs [they] flung themselves at the neophytes and began sniffing them zealously. . . . [T]hey only touched the neophytes' bodies with their noses. . . . And what precision of movement these "dogs" displayed! They passed one another in search of new prey; they looked at each other, sharing their olfactory impressions.] (63)

It should not be overlooked that in popular discourse, the nose and penis have often been linked since they are both protuberances that discharge similar substances. Moreover, it is commonly quipped that the length of one is directly proportional to that of the other. It is significant, then, that so much emphasis is placed on the noses of the naked second-year students who ostensibly use them to examine the naked flesh of the neophytes.

This scene is also interesting in terms of its play on Freud's theory that the sense of smell often serves as a deterrent to sexual desire.[34] According to Freud, as humans began to assume an erect posture, the location of the nose changed dramatically in relation to the position of the genitals. For this reason humans, unlike dogs, evolved into creatures whose sexual desire is typically turned off by anal and genital odors.

In the bizarre scene in the novel, the adolescent boys implicitly challenge Freud's theory by showing such intense excitement when they smell their new classmates. It is especially significant that the boys are compared to dogs, and that their canine postures implicitly call attention to the position of their avidly sniffing noses in relation to the genitalia of the neophytes. Their behavior echoes the notion that masochists commonly behave like submissive dogs that bend to the will of their masters.

Once their task is done, the first group of students is herded to a corner and fifty third-year students are sent out to perform a similar inspection. Like their second-year counterparts, their behavior underscores the fact that they have been trained to act according to the will of their masters. They work with military precision, and they examine the unspoiled bodies of the new students with utmost seriousness. The narrator's description of the activity clearly implies its explicitly homoerotic nature.

> Entonces, con sus manos semejantes a tentáculos, empezaron a palpar el cuerpo de los neófitos. . . . Sin duda, experimentaban un enorme placer en ese tacto; se miraban unos a otros comunicándose sus impresiones, y esas miradas expresaban lo que podría hacerse con esos cuerpos aún intactos. Por fin dieron término a tan apasionada manipulación. . . . (73–74)

> [Then, with hands like tentacles, they began to probe the bodies of the neophytes. . . . Without a doubt, they were experiencing enormous pleasure in this contact; they looked at one another, sharing their impressions, and their glances expressed what could be done with these still-intact bodies. At last they put an end to such passionate handling. . . .] (64)

After being forced to endure this mortifying exercise René and the other neophytes are forced to don muzzles, which are meant to facilitate their compliance with the institution's creed of suffering in silence. The degrading process of fitting the students with what Mármolo calls their most important "school supply" emphasizes the muzzle's power to dehumanize the students:

> al alumno le había puesto un bozal, causando el efecto de un animal acorralado. Pronto se generalizó el paso de hombre al estado de bestia. A medida que los neófitos ban (*sic*) siendo embozalados el silencio se hacía opresivo.
> A René le llegó su turno. Entró en la oficina y vio a un tipo muy risueño.

... Le dijo a René que se acercara; mientras le ponía el bozal le dijo con suma cortesía: "No tema. Pronto se acostumbrará a llevarlo." (76–77)

[The student had been fit with a muzzle, making him look like a trapped animal. The passage of men into the condition of beasts was soon generalized. As the neophytes were muzzled, the silence became oppressive.
   It was René's turn. He entered and saw a very cheerful man. . . . He said with extreme courtesy: "Don't be afraid, you'll soon be used to wearing it."] (66)

The animal imagery stresses the loss of status that the muzzles represent, and suggests the students' conversion into subjects of the institution's will. Moreover, the loss of voice that the muzzles confer is highly symbolic since, as Elaine Scarry has noted, "ultimate domination requires that the prisoner's ground become increasingly physical and the torturer's increasingly verbal, that the prisoner become a colossal body with no voice."[35]

According to Roy Baumeister, "Masochism replaces identity with body."[36] Likewise, one of the central goals of the pedagogical program of the Escuela del Dolor is the destruction of the students' identities by turning them into beings who are ruled by physical instincts. By the time of their scheduled initiation ceremony, it seems that the students have lived up to the institution's exacting standards. Describing the students as they line up naked to be inducted into the Cult of the Flesh, the narrator observes that "Las carnes desnudas de los muchachos y la igualdad de sus actitudes hacía difícil su individualización" (135) (The naked flesh of the boys and their identical postures made it difficult to tell them apart [125]).

In addition to being compared to animals, the students are also referred to as "neófitos." This term is loaded with significance, especially in terms of Piñera's parody of Christian traditions and of the Catholic Church. The term comes from the Latin *neophytus* (newly planted), and in the primitive church it was used to refer either to a newly converted Christian or a person who had been baptized recently. Images of and references to baptism are quite frequent in the novel, and even René's name (in French *rené* means "reborn") calls attention to the importance of the leitmotif of rebirth in *La carne de René*. With this in mind, it should not go unnoticed that René's painful process of self-discovery ends in a figurative rebirth when he finally gives himself up to the homoerotic world of his father's cause. Furthermore, in the Catholic Church the term "neophyte" is sometimes used interchangeably with novice, an individual who is received into a particular religious order for a period of probation before a final taking of vows.

Like their counterparts in the Catholic Church, the young novices of the Iglesia del Cuerpo have to undergo a series of tests to prove that they are fit to serve as ministers in an exclusive cult that is dominated by males. Piñera's parody is especially striking in its sarcastic suggestion that the cult in the novel has much in common with Catholicism, which has a long history of depicting pain as a potential source of mystic pleasure and healing. The martyrs are fine examples of this notion, and it is not a coincidence that Piñera mentions so many of them in his novel: St. Sebastian, St. Catherine, St. Vitus, and, of course, Christ himself, whose suffering was meant to serve as a source of healing to all of humanity.

Through the exaggerated violence of the teachings of the Escuela del Dolor and the Iglesia del Cuerpo, Piñera pokes fun at what he saw as the archaic teachings of Christianity and the Catholic Church. He ridicules notions such as redemptive suffering and visionary pain in order to underscore his own religious skepticism. In Piñera's distorted world, the ideals of the Christian ascetics, "for whom humiliation of the flesh provided an indispensable avenue for a direct approach to God," are pitted against the far-fetched carnal philosophy of the leaders of the Escuela del Dolor, who see the purpose and value of pain in the opposite light. The former view physical suffering as spiritualized pain. For the ascetics pain and suffering are not so much meant to be endured but rather, as Morris puts it, they are vehicles of knowledge that offer "access to an otherwise inaccessible understanding." By suffering physically, the ascetic "employs the body in order to free [him/herself] from the body."[37] The members of the novel's flesh cult, on the other hand, seek out bodily suffering precisely to remind themselves of their fleshy existence. In other words, pain is meant to keep them chained to the body and to make them forget about everything else.

In order to underscore this point, the instructor of the "Course on Electricity" gives the following explanation before subjecting the students to his wicked form of shock therapy: "El *quid* de nuestro problema radica en el sufrimiento. . . . Nosotros no somos fakires que dominamos el dolor, es el dolor quien nos domina" (83). [The *quid* of our problem is rooted in suffering. . . . We aren't fakirs who master pain; it is pain that masters us [73].) This electric shock class, during which the students are shocked by currents of electricity that make their bodies shake uncontrollably, is a fine example of the institution's violent pedagogical methods. It is significant that the narrator compares the boys' jerking movements to St. Vitus's dance, a nervous disorder that causes violent, uncontrollable bodily shaking.[38] Indeed, the legend surrounding St. Vitus's life and his symbolic importance to the Church suggest that Piñera included his name in this passage for its highly symbolic nature.

Most importantly, St. Vitus is widely revered as the patron of dogs. This is a noteworthy detail since René and the other students wear muzzles and are called "perros" by the officials of the school. Furthermore, Vitus's legacy is reflected in several ways in René's own painful existence. According to Catholic tradition, during his adolescent years Vitus's pagan father, who was determined to make him denounce Christianity, subjected him to various forms of torture. As legend has it, Vitus was also tortured during his adulthood—supposedly by being submerged in a kettle of boiling oil—by the emperor Diocletian for refusing to renounce his Christian beliefs. Much like St. Vitus, then, René is victimized by his father and by higher authorities of the cult, who essentially force him to renounce a way of thinking that they do not espouse.

The electric shock treatment at the Escuela del Dolor aims to teach the students to disregard their way of thinking and to accept the teachings of the carnal priesthood; that is, to learn to enjoy pain like masochists. Through the school's perverse gospel of suffering in silence, Piñera implicitly challenges the Christian ideal of tight-lipped suffering as a means to gain grace with God. When the professor warns the neophytes that the gags are meant to prevent outbursts, he implies that vocal expressions of suffering constitute the failure of the exercise's key aim: "saber que se sufre, que los dolores son espantosos, que se está a dos dedos de pedir tregua y, sin embargo, no cejar, constituye el abc del sufriente" (85) (To know one is suffering, that the pain is awful, that one is that close to begging for mercy, and yet, not give in, constitutes the sufferer's *abc's* [74]). Once again the influence of Piñera's readings of Kierkegaard is evident in the ideological approach of the Escuela del Dolor. In a treatise on Christian suffering, the Danish philosopher offers the following advice for those who find it difficult to accept suffering as a necessary component of human existence:

> And if anybody wants to hear sighing and moaning and crying, he may hear it in plenty from those who suffer. . . . But to endure with tight lips, or perhaps even find joy in the bitterness of suffering—and not find it only in the hope that the suffering will come to an end in time—but to find it in the suffering, as when we say that sorrow is mixed with joy; this is something worth learning.[39]

The school's attitudes toward suffering in silence, however, invert the Christian ideal of tight-lipped pain. The muzzles that the students are forced to wear emphasize the fact that their silent suffering is imposed rather than voluntary or spiritual. When René bursts into tears during the exercise, the school officials are shocked by his implicit refusal to accept the pain, and he is stigmatized from that moment on as a rebel. As if being compared to a wayward Christian who has denied the spiritual teachings of Christ, the narrator remarks that "René se negó abiertamente a recibir el sagrado pan de la enseñanza" (96) (René had overtly refused to receive the holy bread of instruction [87]). To a certain extent, René's so-called rebelliousness and his refusal to suffer seem to parody another of Kierkegaard's lessons: "For flesh and blood it must be difficult to bear the light burden," he insists, "but if the light burden becomes hard to bear it is because of a rebellious spirit, that will not believe."[40]

Many of the incidents in the novel that pit the school's teachings against those of the Church draw attention to the homoerotic nature of René's carnal education. The most dramatic of these episodes takes place in the novel's seventh chapter. After several months at the Escuela del Dolor René has been marked as a rebel because of his refusal to embrace pain and to give up control of his body. It becomes increasingly apparent in this chapter, however, that René is also seen as a rebel because he refuses to be a passive object of the older men's sexual desire.

When Mármolo and Cochón are unable to persuade René to submit to their will, they lock him in his room and force him to listen for several days to a recording of Mármolo explaining the meaning and importance of the word "querer." The object of this exercise is to convince René, through repetition of the same message, to yield to their sexual desire: "¿Por qué no quiere?" (94) (*Why do you not want?* [85]), the voice on the recording asks, "*No, René, no piense; nunca piense; sólo quiera quiera, quiera . . .*" (94) ("No, René, don't think, don't ever think; just want, want, want . . ." [86]). Despite their tireless attempts to make René give in, the young protagonist refuses to yield control of his body to Cochón or any other school official. As the narrator puts it, René, "Le había dicho por lo claro que no estaba dispuesto a ceder su cuerpo para ese servicio del dolor, el cuerpo era propiedad sagrada de cada cual y nadie tenía derecho de profanarlo" (104) (He had told him straight out that he was not prepared to place his body in the service of pain, that one's body was one's sacred property and no one had the right to profane it [95]).

Since their ultimate goal is to turn the young neophytes into masochists who derive sexual pleasure from pain and humiliation, Cochón and Mármolo decide to resort to drastic measures with the rebellious René.

After assuring René that he will soon give in, Cochón pounces on him and vows to ignite his desire and to make him accept his passive role by licking his flesh: "Ahora soy un perro. Te voy a ablandar en menos de lo que canta un gallo. Si como Cochón no he logrado ablandarte, como perro mi lengua obrará el milagro" (106) (Now I'm a dog. I'm going to soften you up faster than you can say "cock-a-doodle-doo." If I haven't managed to soften you up as Swyne, as a dog my tongue will work miracles [97]). Cochón's choice of *ablandar* ("to soften" or "to tenderize"), a term that he repeats scores of times throughout the scene, suggests not just the notion of "softening" René's insubordinate attitude, but also of making him physically and sexually passive. To be sure, the suggestive language employed throughout this episode emphasizes its homoerotic undertone.

> Volvió a sacar la lengua y la emprendió con la nariz. A las dos o tres pasadas se fue hinchando y enrojeciendo. Cochón lamía de arriba a abajo, lo cual provocábale violentos estornudos a René y experimentando [*sic*] la extraña sensación de que la punta de su apéndice nasal le llegaba al techo. (106)

> [He stuck his tongue out again and started on René's nose. After two or three passes, his tongue began to swell and get redder. Swyne was licking from top to bottom, which made René sneeze violently and experience the peculiar sensation that the tip of his sinus cavity was touching the ceiling.] (97–98)

Though there is some truth to García Chichester's assertion that the homosexual world in Piñera's works is "latently, surreptitiously present,"[41] this scene is explicitly homoerotic, and Piñera clearly made no effort to mask it.

In the spirit of a Sadean libertine, Cochón forces René to take on a passive role in a process of sexual foreplay that is meant to prepare him to be "initiated" later by Mármolo. René's red, swollen "nose," which according to the narrator rises toward the ceiling as Cochón's tongue passes back and forth across it, is an unmistakable metaphor for the erect penis. Likewise, René's uncontrollable sneezes clearly suggest ejaculation. William Miller's observation about the relationship between the nose and the phallus supports this reading. "The penis," Miller notes, "was always thought to be a nether nose, the length of one supposedly corresponding to the length of the other, both spewing contaminating substances of similar consistency."[42]

Moments later Cochón begins to lick René's "ojo de Polifemo" (107) (Polyphemus's eye). Though he is ostensibly referring to René's right eye, which he licks avidly, we must keep in mind that the term *ojo* denotes both "eye" and "hole." Given the word's common usage in vulgar discourse, the narrator's use of it here is indeed quite suggestive. According to Fernando Valerio Holguín, for example, in Latin America the expressions "ojo del culo" and "ojo ciego" have come to denote the anus.[43] William Miller likewise points out that, in addition to being a contaminating orifice, the anus can also be seen as "the center, the eye" of the lower regions of the human body.[44] Piñera's reference to the mythic Cyclops, Polyphemus, whose only eye was pierced by Odysseus's hot dagger, then, also evokes an image of sexual penetration.

After an hour of licking René's body, Cochón poses a provocative question—"¿Dígame, ya está listo para que le sirvamos su carne al señor Mármolo?" (107) (Tell me, are you ready for us to serve your flesh to Mr. Marblo? [98])—which, given that the gratification of sexual desire has traditionally been seen as analogous to satisfaction of hunger, underscores the homoerotic nature of the episode.[45] René resists, however, and the headmaster's response to his continued recalcitrance is even more transparent than Cochón's sexually charged inference:

> Lo cargó como si fuera una pluma y lo acostó en la mesa.
> . . . .
> "Así que sigues sin querer . . ." y al mismo tiempo que le hablaba lo dejaba en cueros. "Pues, oye, vas a querer, y pronto." (111)

> [He picked René up as if he were light as a feather and laid him on the table.
> . . . .
> "So, you still don't want . . ." and as he spoke, he stripped René naked. "Well, listen to me: you're going to want, and soon."] (102)

Following his pledge to make René desire him, Mármolo and fifty of the students, most of whom are wearing only their underpants, form an entangled mess on the floor and begin to lick René. When they realize that licking will not do the job, Mármolo and Cochón decide to use alcohol to "tenderize" René's flesh and to minimize his sexual inhibitions.[46] After making René drink liquor, the school officials pour it over his naked body in an act of symbolic baptism:

> Alzó la botella por arriba de su cabeza y dejó caer la ginebra sobre el cuerpo de René.
> Cochón se acercó con otra botella.
> "Permita, Mármolo, permita que como Sumo Pontífice . . ."
> Y dejo caer un chorro de ginebra sobre la cara de René.
> "*In nomine Pater, Filius et Espiritu Marmolus* . . ." (117)

[He held the bottle high above his head and covered René's body with gin. Swyne came over with another bottle.
"Allow me, Marbolo. Allow me, as Supreme Pontiff . . ."
And he let a stream of gin fall on René's face.
"In nomine Pater, Filius et Espiritu Marmolus . . ."] (108)

This parody of the sacrament of baptism is notable both for its grotesque humor and its irreverence. Cochón, a vulgar priest of the flesh, is compared to the pope, while the vehemently sacrilegious Mármolo is equated to a divine spirit. At the same time the holy ritual that serves in traditional Christianity as a symbolic spiritual rebirth and remission of sin, is subverted in a vulgar exercise that suggests René's metaphorical homosexual reincarnation. Here, again, the reader should recall the symbolic importance of René's name, which in itself evokes the notion of rebirth. It is worth pointing out, too, that the liquor serves to accentuate the sexual perverseness of the scene and calls attention to Piñera's parody of the symbolic pureness of spiritual cleansing with holy water.

During this scene Mármolo implies repeatedly that René's flesh is no different than that of animals (117), a notion that recalls certain aspects of the materialist philosophy expressed in the works of Sade. According to Sade's worldview, Nature is completely indifferent to anything that "does not directly contribute to the renewal of the material universe." For that reason "whether we eat pork or human flesh is a matter of indifference [to the materialist], for both adequately sustain life."[47] Sade's cannibalistic fantasies may have served to inspire Piñera's own interest in the topic. On numerous occasions in the novel, the characters refer to the consumption of human flesh, such as when Cochón threatens to serve René's flesh to Mármolo in the passages cited above. Later when Cochón suggests that there is a difference between René's flesh and the meat that that they consume during the orgiastic licking scene, Mármolo retorts, "¡Pura causísitica, Cochón! Al final, todo es carne y nada más que carne" (118) (Pure casuistry, Swyne! In the end, everything is flesh and nothing but flesh [108]). This idea represents, of course, another strike against Christian dogma, which clearly distinguishes between human and animal flesh, and holds that the consumption of the former—unless done in extremis—is a mortal sin.

When the teachers and students become intoxicated, the scene takes on singularly nightmarish qualities that recall some of the orgy scenes in Sade's *The 120 Days of Sodom*, a book that Piñera surely knew well.[48] Mármolo's decision to bring copious amounts of alcohol and huge trays of meat into the room suggests another link with the works of Sade. As de Beauvoir has pointed out, Sade saw a "close bond between the food orgy and the erotic orgy."[49] To be sure, the Marquis himself insisted that "there is no passion more closely involved with lechery than drunkenness and gluttony."[50]

The orgiastic scene in which fifty half-naked men and boys eat, drink, and wallow in a fetid mix of meat, alcohol, and excrement is one that surely gives Sade a run for his money, as the following passage attests.

> Los muchachos que estaban sentados sobre la cómoda, le dejaron el sitio a las bandejas, pero como el espacio era reducido, puerco y morcillas se vinieron al suelo con estrépito. . . .
> . . . Los muchachos más próximos al puerco metieron sus manos, y arreglándose como podían empezaron a sacar postas de carne. La avidez era extraordinaria; había una especie de frenesí por querer meterse en la boca todas esas carnes al mismo tiempo. . . .
> Tragado y bocado; bocado y trago . . . Pero los cuerpos se defienden contra los excesos. Así pues, los muchachos empezaron a vomitar y a orinar, y todo eso se unió a la manteca derramada. . . . (118)

> [The boys seated on the bureau got off to make room for the trays, but since space was limited, pig and blood sausages tumbled to the floor with a deafening crash. . . .
> . . . The boys closest to the pig stuck their hands in and, accommodating themselves as best they could, began to pull off pieces of pork flesh. Their greed was extraordinary; they exhibited a certain fury, wanting to stuff all that meat into their mouths at once. . . .
> Gulp and mouthful, mouthful and gulp . . . But the body protects itself against excess. So the boys soon began to vomit and urinate, and it all mixed with the spilled fat. . . .] (108–9)

It would be difficult to find another scene in Piñera's works that more perfectly epitomizes his capacity to shock the reader. The scene is reminiscent of the words of one of the libertines in *The 120 Days of Sodom* who proclaims before an orgy that "everything shall be pell-mell, everyone shall be sprawled on the floor and, after the example of animals, shall change, shall commingle, entwine . . . The company shall give itself over to every excess and to every debauch."[51] The mixing of bodily waste into the fetid stew of human flesh and carnal dishes on the floor not only recalls Sade's coprophilia and his marked obsession with filth in general—"Nothing more logical than to adore degradation"—but also his tendency to extol humiliation and punishment as sources of sexual pleasure. As Curval puts it in *The 120 Days of Sodom*, "Who is unaware that even punishment produces enthusiasms, and have we not seen certain individuals' pricks stiffen into clubs at the same instant they find themselves publicly disgraced?"[52]

Much like Sade's grotesque intermingling of eroticism and filth, Piñera's introduction of human waste into the orgy surpasses the limits of comedy and farce. In this appalling scene Piñera bombards us with images that are difficult for even the most strong-stomached reader to digest. The vision of seminaked boys and their middle-aged professors licking each other, despite—or perhaps precisely because of—the grease, blood, and human waste that covers them, takes us beyond a simple homoerotic orgy and into the realm of lunacy, where everything seems to be hopelessly out of control.

The boys' doglike behavior points to the sadomasochistic undertones of the scene, as does the fact that Mármolo and Cochón become aroused by watching them degrade themselves. It is worth pointing out, furthermore, that getting on all fours and eating and drinking from the floor is a scenario that is often played out in the writings of the Marquis de Sade. It is quite telling that one of the scenes from *The 120 Days of Sodom* that Piñera selected for the first number of *Ciclón* finds Duclos recounting a time when she was forced to get on all fours and to eat and play like a dog in order to satisfy a libertine: "I had to obey. Still on all fours, I plunged my head into the trough. . . . And that was the critical instant for our libertine; the humiliation of a woman, the degradation to which he reduced her, wonderfully stimulated his spirits."[53]

Like Sadean libertines Mármolo and Cochón become aroused by watching the scantily clad boys lap the fetid mess off the floor. Forgetting about René, who refuses to submit, the two instructors undress each other and then demand that the other students disrobe and join in. Mármolo's words to one of the boys are among the most unambiguously homoerotic in the novel: "Usted mismo, usted, ¿qué hace que no me lame? ¿No ve que me endurezco? . . . No hay tiempo que perder. Ya lo ha dicho nuestro admirado predicador. Usted me lame y yo lo lamo . . ." (122). ("You. Yes, you. Why aren't you licking me? Don't you see that I'm getting hard? . . . There's no time to lose. Our admirable preacher has already said it. You lick me and I lick you . . ." [112].)

Such explicit, orgiastic scenes are fine examples of Piñera's singular approach to attacking human spirituality and his tendency to poke fun at the popular morality and the Catholic sensibilities of the time. Like Sade, who resolutely denied the existence of the soul and created a world in which everything was material,[54] Piñera presents the members of the Escuela del Dolor as pleasure-seeking libertines who are driven into frenzy by their carnal appetites and biological needs. In doing so the author implies that in his topsy-turvy world there is no place for the sacred or the divine.

A "Pro-carne" Sermon in the Church of the Body

In the eighth chapter René undergoes the final test of his carnal education at the Escuela del Dolor. The bizarre initiation ceremony resembles a bawdy parody of certain Catholic sacraments of initiation, such as confirmation and ordination. Here René once again proves to be a troublesome rebel when he refuses to give in to the leaders of the school. This at once disconcerting and comic ceremony takes place in a "chapel" whose farcical atmosphere pokes fun at a typical Christian house of worship:

> el golpe de vista que ofrecía "la iglesia del cuerpo" era el de una farsa colosal. . . . De sus paredes colgaban . . . tapices hechos con asuntos de torturas célebres y con la técnica de los dibujos animados. Tan cómicos resultaban que, como decía Cochón, curaban toda suerte de males . . . (133–34)

> [the sight offered by "the church of the body" was that of a colossal farce. . . . On its walls hung . . . tapestries woven with the subjects of celebrated cases of torture and employing the techniques of animated cartoons. The result was so comical that—as Swyne said—they would cure you of any malady . . .] (124)

In this passage Piñera parodies the Christian tradition of viewing icons of the saints and martyrs as symbolic embodiments of their subjects. The spiritual agony of the Christian martyrs is opposed to the purely physical pain of the caricatures, which implicitly pokes fun at the common Catholic belief that religious icons possess healing qualities. The notion that the icons in the Iglesia del Cuerpo have the power to heal since they inspire laughter reflects Piñera's own belief that comedy mitigates pain by providing a source of distraction and amusement.

As in a typical Christian place of worship, a crucified "Christ" hangs above the altar of the Iglesia del Cuerpo. This figure, however, is viewed as the Savior of the Flesh who, according to Cochón, died on the cross to save his own body (105). The icon's jovial grin—like that of the statue of the crucified René, the painting of St. Sebastian, and the tapestries of torture victims in the chapel—belies the body's apparent suffering by suggesting that pain is a laughing matter. As Cochón sees it, this modern, smiling Christ reflects the profane, godless spirit that dominates the mid-twentieth century. It is diametrically opposed to the typical Christian image, which he sees as archaic and meaningless to contemporary society. The narrator sums up Cochón's radical theory as follows:

> Sostenía que el Cristo, tal y como venía representándose desde siglos, era una rémora en época tan ajena a la piedad como la presente. Esa faz angustiada, esa cabeza cacída [*sic*] sobre el hombro, esas lágrimas y ese sudor de muerte resultaban ridículos a nuestro espíritu deportivo. Nuestra época huía a todo tren de la piedad. (103–4)

[He maintained that Christ as he has been represented for centuries was a hindrance in times so foreign to piety as the present. The anguished countenance, that head fallen on its shoulder, those tears, and that mortal sweat seemed ridiculous for our sporty spirit. Our age fled from piety at top speed.] (94–95)

During the initiation ceremony that takes place in this so-called modern church, the officials once again oppose their carnal view of humanity to the Christian belief that the soul is the driving force of existence. Against Jesus's proclamation that "It is the spirit that gives life; the flesh is useless,"[55] the ex-Catholic Cochón pits what he calls his "sermón pro-carne," which the narrator explains as follows:

Cochón les llevaba un punto de ventaja a los sacerdotes del alma. En tanto éstos debían predicar o insistir sobre la salvación del ama, Cochón se limitaba a cuestiones tan concretas como brazos, piernas, huesos, sangre . . . El individuo no tendría que operar con esa cosa huidiza, incorpórea y problemática que es el alma, ni tampoco preocuparse por su salvación. . . . En cuanto a la otra vida, a la de un más allá, no existe. (124–25)

[Swyne had one advantage over priests of the soul. While the latter have to preach or insist upon the salvation of the soul, Swyne limited himself to such concrete matters as arms, legs, bones, blood . . . The individual wouldn't have to deal with that elusive, incorporeal, and problematic thing that is the soul, nor worry about its salvation. . . . As for the next life—a life after death—there is none.] (116)

Cochón's corporeal view of humanity challenges traditional Christian beliefs concerning the nature of the body and the soul by negating immortality, resurrection, and the afterlife. Given that the leaders of the Iglesia del Cuerpo strive to disseminate their central precept that the body is all that matters, they are eager to dismiss any Christian concept that contradicts their pedagogical practices. In his sermons, then, Cochón essentially negates the notion that "If there is a physical body, there is also a spiritual body."[56]

Cochón's irreverent "sermón pro-carne" (pro-flesh sermon)—which he delivers with hands folded and eyes fixed upon the smiling, crucified "Christ"—is one of the high points of the novel's profanation of things sacred. In his sermon Cochón presents some of the novel's most daring ideas. For instance, he challenges the biblical teaching that "Not all flesh is alike, but there is one flesh for human beings, another for animals"[57] with his own conception of human materiality: "En el degolladero nuestra carne se empareja con la de las reses, le sirve de alimento al hombre"[58] (126) (In the slaughterhouse, our flesh is nothing more nor less than the flesh of cattle. It is food for people [117]). By placing humans on the same level as animals, Cochón posits the nonexistence of the soul and underscores the purely carnal nature of our being. Moreover, his apparent advocacy of cannibalism is especially significant when viewed in light of the novel's parody of Catholicism, given that in the Catholic tradition the consumption of human flesh is viewed as one of the most profane and morally reprehensible acts that a person can commit. Yet for Catholics the idea that cannibalism is a grave offense is complicated by the fact that through the eating of the Eucharist members of the cult perform "an act of symbolic cannibalism as a central rite of the religion."[59] This important ritual of the Catholic Mass is based on the words of Jesus himself who, before his death, insured his disciples that "Those that eat my flesh and drink my blood have eternal life . . . for my flesh is true food and my blood is true drink. Those who eat my flesh and drink my blood abide in me, and I in them."[60]

The parallel that Cochón draws between animal and human flesh is also important because it points to one of Piñera's favorite stylistic devices in the novel. The word "carne" is at once used as a metonym for the body and for the very essence of the individual. Cochón and the members of his cult believe that flesh is more than just part of our physical body. Indeed, in their view it is the essence of human existence.

After Cochón's sermon, the naked neophytes line up on all fours in front of the altar, where they will be branded in the buttocks by Sr. Mármolo. Mármolo's pompous entrance into the chapel is another comical example of Piñera's parody of the Catholic Church and its figureheads. Wearing a red cap that mimics those worn by popes and bishops and a bloodstained frock that recalls both a priest's vestments and a butcher's apron, Mármolo brandishes a red-hot metal branding rod (which the narrator compares to a bishop's scepter) as he marches down the aisle. Mármolo's exaggerated sense of self-importance and his obvious eagerness to brand the young students with the hot iron serve to underscore his sadistic inclinations. Indeed, his attitude brings to mind that sadism appeals especially to those "who desire to have their sense of self bolstered" and who see their erotic desires "as sacred, legitimate obligations."[61]

The branding ceremony also stands out for its subversively homoerotic atmosphere. The act of thrusting a hot metal rod into the students' buttocks, for example, has strong sexual undertones as the following passages indicate: "el neófito se paró y llegó junto a Mármolo, pero en vez de ponerse frente a éste le dio el trasero" (136) (the neophyte rose to his feet and went to Marblo's side, but instead of facing

Marblo, he showed him his behind) (127); "De su brasero sacó un hierro al rojo vivo y lo fue aproximando al juvenil trasero del neófito" (137) (He pulled a red-hot branding iron from the brazier and began to bring it close to the neophyte's youthful behind [127]); "¿Es que el trasero de René se ofrecería mansamente a la marca. . . ?" (138) (Would René's behind offer itself meekly to the branding iron. . . ? [129]).

When the headmaster finally gets to René, the narrator remarks suggestively that his state of excitement reached a climax. Upon seeing the young man's naked body, Mármolo grabs René by the behind and shouts out with excitement "Hundamos el hierro" (139) (We'll plunge in the iron [130]). René, however, violates the school's strict code of silent submission when he lets out a desperate cry and flees from his victimizer. Though René is supposedly kicked out of the school for his refusal to suffer in silence, it is clear that his expulsion is largely due to the fact that he is viewed as an unacceptable pupil since he spurns the school officials' attempts to turn him into a passive member of their homosocial cult.

The fact that René is punished for breaking the code of suffering in silence is crucial since it again points to Piñera's implicit mockery of Christian dogma. Though many Christian writers have extolled the values of tight-lipped suffering, Piñera's familiarity with the writings of Kierkegaard again points to a possible source of this theme in the novel. In the following passage, which bears certain similarities with the doctrine preached by the leaders of the Escuela del Dolor, Kierkegaard suggests that by refusing to see the purpose of suffering the individual risks his/her chances to attain glory with God:

> When . . . suffering so overwhelms a man that his reason will no longer cope with all his suffering because reason cannot comprehend what can be gained by suffering; when the sufferer cannot comprehend anything of this dark reckoning, neither the cause of his suffering, nor the intention in it, neither why he of all others should be thus oppressed, nor what purpose it holds of benefit to himself—and then, in his weakness feeling that he cannot throw off his suffering, rebels and throws off his faith, and will not believe that suffering gains him anything; why then it is certain that blessedness will not outweigh it, then it is quite left out of the man's account.
>
> But if the sufferer holds fast to what no doubt the mind cannot comprehend but to which faith clings—that suffering gains a surpassingly great, an eternal weight of glory.[62]

Through René's rebellion against imposed affliction that makes no sense to him, Piñera seems to call into question Christian concepts of suffering. To be sure, the author challenges the idea that in order to ascend to a higher level of being one needs to accept—with faith and silence—pain and punishment that have no obvious purpose.

It is worth adding here that René's rebellion against an institution that tirelessly attempts to "convert" him, suggests another aspect of Piñera's criticism of the Catholic Church, an institution with a long history of imposition and forced conversions in Latin America. Despite the fact that René does not want to accept the teachings of the Cult of the Flesh, its leaders continue to impose their beliefs and practices on him. Their ideological fervor makes it impossible for them to see the illegitimacy and dishonesty of a system that imposes beliefs and values upon those who do not want to accept them. To a certain extent the attitudes of Ramón and the officials at the school evoke the absurdity of forced conversion, since the imposition of a given ideology, tradition, or sexual persuasion rarely leads to genuine acceptance.

Debunking the Myth of the Latin American Macho

Throughout the novel the reader is given numerous indications that René does not lead a normal life and that he is not a typical Latin American adolescent male. In many ways the young protagonist can be viewed as an inversion of the stereotypical macho.

But before we discuss the specific case of René, it is important to emphasize that inversion is an important leitmotif in *La carne de René*. In Piñera's topsy-turvy world common images and notions are rendered unfamiliar and the so-called normal nature of things is constantly challenged. We have already seen, for example, how Piñera manipulates universally recognized religious icons in the novel as part of his parody of Christian theology and the Catholic Church. The mystic suffering of Christ and St. Sebastian, for example, is inverted in a painting and a sculpture that portray the two figures as masochists. Likewise, the biblical "Let there be light" is comically turned into "Let there be flesh" (¡Hágase la carne!), the Christian cult of the spirit is parodied by both Ramón's bizarre flesh cult and the Church of the Body, and the vulgar officials at the educational institution where René is sent by his father aim to fine-tune the students' bodies, but ignore the cultivation of mind and spirit.

It is hardly surprising, then, that Piñera approaches the idea of inversion from a sexual standpoint as well. The carnal teaching of Ramón and his all-male cult and the erotically charged atmosphere of the Escuela del Dolor clearly point to the novel's strong homoerotic subtext. Moreover, many of René's personal attributes serve to emphasize the notion that he is meant to represent an inversion of the traditional image of a twenty-year-old Latin American male. Those who know René tend to label him as different: "Decididamente René era un anormal, o si se cabe peor calificativo, un excéntrico. Eso es, estaba fuera de centro, siempre se empeñaba en girar en sentido contrario. . . ." (104). (René was decidedly abnormal, or, if a worse qualifier were possible, eccentric. That is, he was off-kilter, striving to swim against the tide. . . .)

Likewise, one of the few physical descriptions of the young protagonist underscores his stereotypically effeminate qualities: "cuerpo cultivado, piel intacta, uñas pulidas, cabellera abundante y rizada" (104) (cultivated body, intact skin, polished fingernails, abundant, curly hair [95]).

These descriptions of René are especially noteworthy when looked at in light of Ian Lumsden's assertion that in Cuba, machismo has tended to be more "socially punitive toward deviations from traditional male appearance and manners than toward homosexual behavior in itself."[63] In prerevolutionary Cuba, Lumsden adds, "males whose comportment appeared effeminate and deviated from stereotypical masculinity" were assumed to be homosexuals. "They were called *maricones*, a word also used to denote cowardice."[64] Like a *maricón*, then, René is presented throughout the novel as a so-called antithesis of masculinity and his precarious journey of self-discovery can be seen as something of a process of coming to terms with his sexual "difference."

Whereas the *machista* ideology stresses that a man should either be or act like an essentially sexual being, and should enjoy, declare, and brag about his sexuality,[65] René is presented as an asexual young man who dreads contact with women, who knows nothing about sex, and who blushes upon seeing naked images. It is crucial to point out that since René has never even seen the naked body of another young man, it goes without saying that he is not given to the common practice of comparing his sexual prowess, so to speak, with his buddies. Ramírez points out that the macho is an aggressive figure who "seduces, conquers . . . pursues,"[66] but René is seduced, conquered, and pursued by others. He is not aggressive, but rather flees from the people and the things that threaten him.

The constant comparisons between him and the perverted icon of St. Sebastian who delights in mutilating his own flesh are among the most obvious indicators that Piñera purposefully fashioned René as the antithesis of the stereotypical macho. When René asks why the figure in the painting—which bears his own face—is torturing himself with the phallic arrows, Ramón responds with an evocative comment: "Es una manera de invitar a los otros que te torturen. ¿Quién, en medio de tantas flechas, resistirá la tentación de clavarte una más?" (40) (It's a way of inviting others to torture you. Who, faced with so many arrows, could resist the temptation to stick one more into you? [30]). As we noted earlier in this chapter, the notion that the painting is supposed to make others want to stick arrows into René implicitly points to his father's wish to feminize him, to turn him into a vulnerable object of the sexual desire of other men. In the same manner, Ramón's "gift" to René for his twentieth birthday—he sticks his arm with a hypodermic needle—suggests René's loss of masculine power and symbolically turns him into a passive member of the homosocial world that his father controls.

René's encounter with the plaster statue of himself nailed to a cross also serves to reinforce the notion of his devalued masculinity and his implicit passivity. The comparison of René to the image of the crucified Christ is indeed provocative and highly symbolic. The grin on the plaster face, like that on the painted image of St. Sebastian, evokes the notion of masochistic homosexuality and it reminds René that he is expected to learn to enjoy the pain that will be inflicted upon him by the male leaders of the institution.

It is worth repeating that the image of St. Sebastian carries strong homosexual connotations in modern art and literature. According to Gregory Woods, "of all the figures of the Christian Pantheon, apart from Christ Himself, only Sebastian achieves the erotic status of so many boys and men in Greek myth." Woods adds that St. Sebastian's ambiguous reaction to his apparent suffering makes him an important symbol "of the male, homosexual masochist." Likewise, Woods has pointed out that Jesus "generally fails to make the grade of *machismo*."[67] He cites a "tradition of the androgynous Christ" with certain so-called feminine qualities—long hair, maternal love—and the periodic recurrence of the subject of Christ's homosexuality in texts by authors as diverse as Christopher Marlowe, the Marquis de Sade, and Frank O'Hara to underscore not just his nonmacho qualities but also his homoerotic potential in modern art and literature.[68] Piñera certainly took advantage of such traditions and themes in his irreverent manipulation of images of crucifixion in *La carne de René*.

Woods's comparison of St. Sebastian to the erotic images of boys and men of Greek myths is especially interesting given that René is seen by Dalia Pérez as a living incarnation of a Greek demigod. She is intensely attracted to René's physical qualities, and especially his fine skin and pretty face, which distinguish the young protagonist from the image of the powerful, sexually dominant macho.

In his classic essay on human sexuality Freud points out that "Among the Greeks, where the most virile men were found among inverts, it is quite obvious that it was not the masculine character of the boy, which kindled the love of man, but it was his physical resemblance to woman as well as his psychic qualities, such as shyness, demureness and need of instruction and help."[69] While Freud's observation might help explain why René is so desired by the exaggeratedly virile Mármolo—"[era] de una estatura fuera de lo común" (61) ([he was] of an unusual stature [52]), "las madres [estaban] particularmente excitadas por el prestigio físico de Mármolo" (128) (The mothers [were] particularly excited by Marblo's physical reputation [104])—it does little to clarify why Dalia Pérez finds him so attractive. However, as the novel progresses, it becomes increasingly clear that Dalia herself also represents an inversion of sorts. Indeed, if René can be viewed as the antithesis of the stereotype of the macho, Dalia, too, subverts the stereotypical image of the submissive and vulnerable Latin American woman.

The *machista* mentality presupposes that men are aggressive and that they demonstrate strength and invulnerability in the presence of women. René, however, is portrayed as vulnerable, weak, and sensitive. It is quite suggestive indeed that, upon seeing René at the butcher shop, Dalia immediately has visions of him being stabbed by a knife, pierced by bullets, and crushed by a heavy object. All of these violent images evoke the helplessness and passivity that characterize René's personality. The phallic image of the penetrating knife is especially intriguing since it foreshadows the arrows in the painting of St. Sebastian and the penetrating nails of the crucified image of René.

Dalia further reinforces the notion of René's vulnerability when she notes that it seems like René "está pidiendo protección contra las furias del mundo" (15) (is appealing for protection against the furies of the world [5]). Likewise, it is Dalia who calls attention to René's hypersensitivity, which is another alleged quality of the stereotypical *maricón*. She warns Ramón, for example, that René's nerves are very sensitive (29), and later when she seduces René, Dalia complains about his hysterical outbursts and she compares him to a timid damsel (158).

René's intense aversion to meat, which is widely held to inflame men's lustful passions, also suggests his cowardice and his fear of sexual contact. His chronic pallor, fainting spells, and fits of vomiting, which are all allegedly brought about by meat and the male-dominated worlds of the slaughterhouse and the butcher shop, are also stereotypically feminine symptoms. In terms of René's sexual experiences, the narrator clearly points out that, unlike the typical twenty-year-old male, "René sólo conocía su propia carne" (15–16) (René knew only his own flesh [6]).

Echoes of Kierkegaardian Seduction

René's relationship with Dalia Pérez, his eccentric neighbor who is secretly in love with him, is one of the most intriguing aspects of the novel. Dalia is not turned off by René's vulnerability and obvious lack of sexual prowess. In fact, she finds these qualities seductive and tempting: "carne tan 'expuesta' (así la calificaba) prometía goces insospechados" (15) (Flesh that "vulnerable" (as she called it) promised unsuspected delights [6]). From the beginning of the novel she is portrayed as a shrewd, calculating woman who is obsessed with the idea of introducing René into a realm of sexual pleasure. Dalia is bothered by Ramón's plans to teach René to derive pleasure from corporeal mutilation. She envisions and plans a different destiny for René's body, which involves heterosexual pleasure. According to her, René's flesh is suited for pleasure rather than pain.

Dalia tries to convince Ramón that his son's flesh will not flower (she uses the term "florecer")[70] unless it is subjected to the type of pleasure that only an erotic, heterosexual relationship can provide. Instead of seducing René with the arrows of the self-destructive St. Sebastian, as Ramón does, she prefers the seductive arrows of Cupid. Her aggressive seduction of René serves to further underscore how far the young protagonist strays from traditional notions of Latin American machismo. By appropriating both the lexicon and the behavior of the male seducer who sees the process of finding a sexual partner as a conquest, she symbolically turns René into a feminized subject of her quest.

Throughout Dalia's first attempt to seduce René, the young protagonist is horrified by his seductress's power over him. His head is filled with disturbing ideas and images that call attention to the reversal of traditional gender roles that takes place during their encounter: "Le asaltó la idea de que . . . Dalia le quemaría las plantas de los pies o lo clavaría a la pared con una flecha . . ." (49–50) (He was assaulted by the idea that . . . Dalia herself would burn the soles of his feet or would stick him to the wall with an arrow . . . [40]). René's vision of Dalia as the possessor of the phallic arrow suggests her assumption of the sexual power traditionally wielded by her male counterparts. Again the verb "clavar" is key to the double meaning of the passage since it implies not only violence and power, but also forcible insertion and sexual penetration.

Dalia's aggression and her perceived domination of her young object of desire challenge the myth of the vulnerable, submissive, and chaste Latin American woman. She is not the object of sexual pleasure, but rather the pursuer of it, and she turns her proclaimed goal of sexual conquest into a source of arousal: "la iniciación sexual de René la excitaba salvajemente" (51) (René's sexual initiation savagely excited her [41–42]). When Dalia manages to lure René into her realm at her dinner party in the fourth chapter, for example, she sees this successful completion of a stage in the seduction process as a major triumph, and she delights in showing off her trophy to her friends. It is significant that Dalia sees René as an object of desire precisely because she knows he is vulnerable, innocent, and inexperienced in matters of love. In this sense, her intense desire to initiate him sexually recalls the macho's alleged obsession with deflowering virgins.

According to Antón Arrufat, René is an anti–Don Juan, a seducer who "operates by inversion." He "conquers without proposing to do so. He is a seducer precisely because he does not wish to seduce."[71] Interesting as Arrufat's observation is, it is also somewhat misleading since the very notions of operation, conquering, and seduction suggest deliberate, purposeful action. René, however, is not an operator in any sense of the word. He does not conquer Dalia Pérez, for example. Indeed, she conquers him despite his desire to avoid her. Instead of acting or operating, René is acted and operated on, and he usually flees from whatever threatens him. It must be stressed that even though Dalia and others find his flesh and his countenance to be seductive, René does not seduce at all.

Arrufat sees René as the antithesis of the Kierkegaardian seducer. The Cuban author and critic defends this point by asserting that René is not calculating and reflexive like Johannes in *The Seducer's Diary*. Arrufat's theory that René "seduces by subtraction, by withdrawal"[72] is flawed, however, since to seduce by withdrawing would be to flee so as to encourage a pursuit. René somehow becomes an object of desire despite his efforts to flee from all forms of personal contact. While he does flee, then, he doesn't do so in order to entice others to come after him.

Arrufat is correct to point out, though, that René's ignorance of the art of gallantry pits him against the figure of Johannes. Indeed, if René is to be considered the anti–Don Juan, it should not be because his method of seduction is different, but rather because of his total ignorance about women and sexual pleasure. In matters of love and women René is like the fool that Johannes the seducer mocks: "anyone who, when he is twenty years old, does not understand that there is a categorical imperative — Enjoy — is a fool."[73]

To a certain extent, though, Kierkegaard's infamous seducer does seem to have influenced Piñera's development of the relationship between René and Dalia Pérez. René's fear of sexual contact suggests a sort of anti–Don Juan. But he is the inversion of Kierkegaard's seducer precisely because he is the one who is seduced, beguiled, and conquered. He is more like bashful Cordelia who is, according to Johannes's own words, "an isolated person." Johannes's observations on isolation are especially interesting when looked at in light of René's marked tendency to flee. "A man ought never to be [isolated]," he insists, "not even a young man, because, since his development depends essentially upon reflection, he must have contact with others."[74] Just as Cordelia's "womanliness will be matured"[75] through seduction, René also ends up learning more about his so-called manliness through his sexual contact with Dalia. All of this, of course, leads to an important aspect of the character of Dalia, which critics have ignored: that she is like a modern-day Doña Juana. She is the seducer, the manipulator, the reflexive conqueror.

Dalia's efforts to entice and then sexually initiate René are presented as parts of a carefully calculated, erotic agenda, which culminates when she forces herself on the young protagonist near the end of the novel. Like Johannes, who through seduction "conducts a perverse sort of educational experiment,"[76] Dalia sees herself as an educator—"maestra soy de la carne" (156) (teacher of the flesh I am [147])—who aims to teach the innocent René everything there is to know about the "powers of erotic love, its turbulent thoughts, its passion, what longing is."[77] Though Dalia seems to be in a rush to get René into bed, her aim to maximize pleasure is similar to that of Johannes who carefully lays out a plan to entrap his victim. Dalia's calculated plans to draw René into her realm and then to conquer him with erotic advances are especially evident during her dinner party in the fourth chapter, and in the moments preceding the violent scene of seduction and sexual conquest mentioned above.

It seems that Dalia invites René to her weekly get-together with the sole purpose of seducing him.[78] Her strategic plan of attack involves a carefully planned meal, alcohol, and a photo album of nude figures, all of which are meant to stimulate his passions. Dalia's calculated seduction of René is set into motion when she announces that the evening's dinner will consist of solely carnal dishes. Her deliberate selection of a variety of meats serves as an unmistakable allusion to her erotic scheming. Indeed, meat is widely reputed to be an aphrodisiac that, as Julia Twigg points out, "has been traditionally perceived as a stimulant, something that feeds the passions. . . . Reinforced by the language of carnality—flesh and fleshyness—meat has always been associated with the stimulation of lust."[79]

The first stage of Dalia's carefully laid out plan fails, however, when René reveals his anguish at the sight of so much meat. His horrified reaction to the meal ends up working to Dalia's advantage, though, since the guests become angry with René and decide to go home early, thus leaving René alone with Dalia. Furthermore, since René feels rejected, his weak emotional state gives him a reason to stay and to seek comfort while at the same time giving Dalia the perfect opportunity to manipulate and take advantage of him.

Under the guise of friendship Dalia begs René to stay, and then proceeds with her plan to seduce him. She turns off the lights, serves René a glass of cognac, and then pulls out a large book of nude anatomical paintings, which she hopes will excite him. Dalia's control over René is underscored when she ignores his obvious anxiety over the images in the album. Despite his protesting, she forces him to look at the nudes while she reclines seductively on the sofa. When René fails to take the hint, Dalia becomes more aggressive and appropriates the traditionally masculine role, forcing him onto the sofa and then lying down beside him.

Recalling the words of Johannes, who boasts "I am intoxicated with the thought that she is in my power . . . now she is going to learn what a powerful force erotic love is,"[80] Dalia is similarly affected by her power over René. As the narrator makes clear, Dalia takes great pleasure from her erotic conquest: "Este preludio a lo que ella imaginaba sería la iniciación sexual de René la excitaba salvajemente" (51) (The prelude to what she imagined would be René's sexual initiation savagely excited her [42]). Dalia's plans do not come to fruition, however, since in the midst of her excitement Ramón calls and demands that René return home.

René is sent the next day to the Escuela del Dolor, and therefore Dalia must wait until he is expelled from the school several months later for another chance to seduce him. It is significant that her second opportunity comes at the same time that the protagonist, liberated from the horrible institution, has decided to try to take control of his own life. "El quería independizarse," the narrator explains, "él ya tenía veinte años, y ya le eran suficientes como para que . . . él mandase en su carne" (142) (René wanted to become independent . . . he was now twenty, and that was old enough for him . . . to be giving his flesh orders [133–34]). In the midst of his musings René witnesses a murder on the street, and in his desperation he calls Dalia, hoping she will offer him a refuge in her house. The time that passes between the call and René's arrival affords Dalia the opportunity to plan her conquest.

Always a coldhearted, calculating seductress, Dalia makes no effort to comfort René, who arrives in tears. Rather she ridicules his supposed hypersensitivity and then gets to work on her plan to seduce him. The inversion of traditional gender roles is underscored through Dalia's exhibition of stereotypically masculine emotions—exaggerated insensitivity, aggressiveness, obsession with sexual conquest—as opposed to René's "feminine" vulnerability and hypersensitivity.

Dalia's behavior throughout the scene echoes Ramírez's definition of aggression as "cancellation of the other person's will."[81] To be sure, Dalia takes advantage of René's weak emotional state in her imposition of her erotic desire. Despite René's protests and his expressed desire to leave, for example, Dalia tries to entice him to stay by serving him meat and getting him drunk. Once René's ability to resist is weakened by his state of intoxication, Dalia follows through with a calculated plan, which ends in an episode that suggests sexual violation:

> Dalia lo miraba con profunda expectación. Se dijo que si no quería perder la presa tendría que poner en juego otros encantos. Sin duda el jovencito era de carne dura, y lo peor: era una carne que en seguida pedía tregua.
>
> . . . .
>
> En un segundo Dalia se hizo cargo de la situación. Si dejaba que René, con sus histerismos de doncella tímida se pusiera a gritar, todo estaba perdido. . . . Pero ella no se lo iba a permitir; por algo era supermaestra; ese mequetrefe no se saldría con la suya. Apretó aún más fuerte con brazos y piernas y, sin pérdida de tiempo, metió su lengua en la boca de René. Se estremeció su cuerpo, se arqueó un tanto y finalmente se "endureció." Dalia percibió que las carnes de René se iban endureciendo lentamente y que ya no era una masa desarticulada lo que estaba debajo de su cuerpo. Entonces retiró sus manos del cuello de su "víctima," apagó la lamparilla y empezó a quitarle el pijama. (158–59)

[Dalia watched him with profound anticipation. She said to herself that if she didn't wish to lose the prey, she'd have to bring other charms into play. Without a doubt, the young man was made of hard flesh, and what was worse, flesh that called for truce straightaway.

. . . .

Dalia grasped the situation in an instant. If she let René, with his blushing-maid hysterics, begin to shout, all would be lost. . . . But she wasn't going to let him. She wasn't a superteacher for nothing; that whippersnapper wouldn't have his way. With her arms and legs she squeezed him even harder, and without pausing for even a second, stuck her tongue into René's mouth. His body shuddered, he arched his back slightly, and finally "hardened up." Dalia perceived that René's flesh was slowly getting harder and that it was no longer a disarticulate mass lying under her body. So she withdrew her hands from around her "victim's" neck, turned off the lamp, and began to take off his pajamas.] (149–50)

During the sexual encounter, which is his first with a woman, René is overcome with thoughts of pain and submission, instead of excitement or pleasure. He imagines himself on the first day of classes, with a muzzle placed over his mouth and his body strapped to the electrically charged chair.

René's recollection of his disturbing experiences in the Escuela del Dolor while Dalia sexually dominates him underscores the violent nature of the episode. It is also significant that just before his aggressive sexual encounter with Dalia, René had made the following provocative observation: "¿Al final, qué diferencia había entre la horrible carne de Cochón lamiendo la endurecida de René y ésta perfumada de Dalia, en actitud de gladiadora que estudia el golpe definitivo a su adversario" (158) (In the end, what was the difference between Swyne's horrible flesh licking the hardened flesh of René and Dalia's perfumed flesh, with her semblance of a gladiator calculating the mortal blow to her adversary? [149]). Apparently cognizant of the fact that he is about to be conquered, so to speak, by Dalia, René does not put up a fight, but rather bears the episode in silence. In fact, his submission to Dalia is so complete that he lets her carry him to bed, where he wakes up the next morning feeling guilty and confused. The image of the gladiator is, of course, highly evocative since it suggests both Dalia's physical and sexual domination over René. In other words, she is the one who wields the weapon while René receives the penetrating blow. It is worth pointing out that Dalia's phallic sword and René's symbolic physical and sexual impotence materialize a few pages later in the figure of "Fifo" — Dalia's rubber dildo, which she significantly refers to as a double for René's penis.

René Comes Out of the Closet

René's sexual initiation with Dalia represents a turning point in his journey of self-discovery and sexual awakening. It is largely through this encounter that René becomes cognizant of the fact that too many individuals have dominated and victimized him. The forceful sexual encounter, the naked double of René in Dalia's bathtub, and the rubber dildo — a clear symbol of her appropriation of René's sexual autonomy — all point to the fact that Dalia, like Ramón and the officials of the Escuela del Dolor, has managed to usurp René's control over his body and his life.

Shortly after his disturbing encounter with Dalia, enemies of the cult assassinate René's father. René therefore seizes the rare opportunity to abandon the world dominated by the Cult of the Flesh and strives to work toward gaining control over his own destiny. René's vision of a future free of flesh-related worries, however, is soon shattered. Just when he begins to feel liberated from the grips of the cult, a chance encounter with Dalia's friend Powlavski leads him back into the organization. Powlavski lures René into the homosocial world of the cult by offering him a job with Bola de carne, a singular individual who, as Powlavski puts it, René must see to believe.

Given René's expressed desire to avoid all contact with the Cult of the Flesh, his enthrallment with Bola and his secret, carnal world seems inconsistent with his previous way of thinking. We must keep in mind, however, that René himself is also confused by his sudden change of heart. His inner struggle and confusion mirror the perplexity he had felt during his sexual encounters with Dalia Pérez. Indeed, by this point in the novel René begins to accept the fact that he is not like most other young men, and he therefore allows himself to be captivated by the homoerotic world that he earlier rejected.

When René enters the giant salon where the monstrous Bola awaits him, he is at once stupefied and fascinated by the shapeless mound of human flesh poised on top of a silver platter. The narrator's description of this hideous freak of nature, whose amorphous body is indeed more incredible than his name, is at once comical and disturbing: "No tenía brazos ni piernas; por efecto de la grasa el tórax y el abdomen se juntaban formando una especie de bola, aumentada por así decir por la cabeza, tan sumida en el pecho que parecía formar parte de éste" (213) (He had neither arms nor legs. The effect of his obesity was to join his thorax and abdomen, forming a sort of ball, enlarged one might say by his head, which was sunken into his chest to such an extent that it seemed to form part of this ball [205–6]). One critic has astutely noted that this description of Bola brings to mind "a grotesque caricature of a penis."[82] Bola's obvious similarity to a phallus is especially symbolic given that René feels an intense attraction to him and his world.

It is interesting that Bola, like the other adult male characters who are involved in the homoerotic culture of the cult, stands out for his physical deformity and difference. Like Cochón, a chunky, piglike homunculus; Mármolo, a bald and corpulent giant; and Ramón, whose body is grotesquely deformed by hundreds of self-inflicted wounds, Bola is also a sort of freak of nature. Like the other men, then, Bola's physical difference can be seen as an indicator of his sexual inversion. Bola's highly exaggerated sensibilities—in the space of just a few pages he sobs, pants, screams in high-pitched tones, and whimpers like a baby—and his lonely, closeted existence also suggest his homosexuality. The association of homosexuality with deformity and difference is an important motif in the novel. When René realizes that he is attracted to Bola and his secretive, lonely underworld, he implicitly accepts the fact that he, too, is different and will therefore never fit in to the so-called normal society.

Behind the walls of his opulent mansion Bola lives a secretive, libertinesque existence, which is underscored by his explicitly homoerotic relationship with a fifteen-year-old boy called "Príncipe" (Prince). Though the exact nature of their frequent encounters is never explained, Bola's description of them clearly indicates a strong sexual component. "Lo tengo en la habitación de al lado reponiéndose de la sesión. Te juro que me ha rejuvenecido lo menos veinte años" (213). (I have him in the next room, recovering from the session. I swear he's added at least twenty years to my life. [206]). When the naked Príncipe emerges minutes later, he responds to Bola's beckoning by leaping like a trained dog onto his mattress where he proceeds with a demonstration of his erotic talents. In his study of masochism, Baumeister asserts that masochists are often required to take part in belittling activities, and their implicit lowering of status is often reflected in their being made to act like dogs by responding to commands from their "masters" and performing tricks.[83] Príncipe's obvious enjoyment of this humiliating behavior and his symbolic degradation to the level of a domesticated pet call attention to the scene's masochistic undertones.

After witnessing this erotic encounter between Bola and Príncipe, René is invited to remove his clothing and to participate in the evening's so-called second act. René, who is moved by Bola's tenderness and sensitivity, is actually tempted to accept the invitation. His near submission to Bola's desires indicates that the encounter between the so-called King of the Flesh and Príncipe appeals to René's own erotic sensibilities. And even though René ultimately decides to leave Bola's mansion instead of giving himself over to him, his experience there signifies a watershed moment in his journey toward self-discovery.

Ana García Chichester has correctly pointed out that René's obvious fascination with Bola's world indicates an important step in his eventual acceptance of his own homosexuality. However, we are not meant to see René's acceptance of his homosexuality as "a personal triumph over the paternal tyranny that would have forced him in the direction of La Causa and the denial of pleasure."[84] Rather, it is made clear that by accepting his homosexuality René automatically assumes that he is destined to a life of loneliness, pain, and suffering. It is important to point out as well that Bola's libertine lifestyle does not induce René to turn away from his father's cult, as García Chichester suggests, but rather to accept the fact that as a homosexual man he has no other viable choice.

Indeed, immediately after his encounter with Bola and Príncipe, René concludes that he has no other option but to accept his role as leader of the Cult of the Flesh. At the opening of the final chapter he reports to the headquarters of the Cause. There he locks himself in a room and tries to come to terms with his difficult decision. Through his meditation he is struck by a realization that compels him to accept, for lack of other possibilities, the position vacated by his deceased father:

> Este enclaustramiento voluntario le hizo ver claramente su situación. El estaba hecho de carne. . . . Así pues, admitió que todo él era carne y tan sólo carne. No es que aceptara el sucio negocio de la Causa, ¿pero disponía de

otra cosa que no fuese su carne para oponerla como argumento convincente a los que se empeñaban en hacerle vivir la vida de la carne? (247–48)

[Voluntarily cloistering himself away allowed him to see his situation clearly. He was made of flesh. . . . So he admitted he was made of flesh and nothing but flesh. It's not that he accepted the dirty business of the Cause, but did he possess anything that wasn't flesh which he could use as a convincing argument against the people committed to having him lead the life of flesh?] (241)

René reports to the "Sede de la Carne Acosada" in the final scene of the novel, then, not because he wants to, but rather because he feels that it is necessary. By accepting what he clearly envisions as a painful destiny René is implicitly compared to a sort of Christ figure going through the preordained stages of his passion:

Clamó al cielo por un socorro salvador, pero el cielo permaneció destellante. Su comba no se abrió para dar paso al milagro. Entonces, René recurrió a sí mismo. Se contempló su cuerpo en la vana esperanza de poder ofrecérselo a Dalia, pero sólo carne de tortura halló su implorante mirada. (262)

[He appealed to the heavens for some saving grace but the heavens remained sparkling bright. Its bulge didn't burst to let the miracle through. Then René appealed to himself. He contemplated this body in the vain hope of being able to offer it to Dalia, but his imploring gaze found nothing but flesh for torture.] (255)

The parallel between René's circumstances and those of Christ are underscored not just by his pleas to the heavens before he turns himself in, but also by the decidedly biblical tone of the novel's final scene. At the headquarters of the Cult of the Flesh, one of the cult's members undresses René, weighs him, and nods his head with great satisfaction, suggesting that the youth's flesh is ready for its new role. As if to confirm that René's "Via Dolorosa" has come to an end, the narrator uses an expression that recalls the last words of Christ on the cross— "consumantum est"[85]—to explain to the reader how René gave up his own body for the Cause: "René no opuso resistencia. Ya todo estaba consumado" (263) (René offered no resistance. Everything had now been consummated [256]).

※

As we bring this chapter to a close, it is worth recalling part of the passage quoted at the beginning: *"La carne de René* ha tenido la terrible virtud de dejar maltrecha la carne de Virgilio Piñera" (*René's Flesh* has had the terrible capacity to leave Virgilio Piñera's flesh battered"). These words, spoken to a group of friends immediately after the publication of *La carne de René* seem, in retrospect, like a fitting prelude to a two-year period during which Piñera suffered from emotional crises that resulted in a lengthy literary hiatus. It was not until the advent of *Ciclón* in 1955 that he managed to regain his lost momentum. Through the pages of *Ciclón* Piñera took advantage of a new opportunity to communicate his controversial and uncompromising views by revisiting certain issues that he had explored in *La carne de René*. In the first two issues of the magazine, for example, he introduced translated passages from the Marquis de Sade's *The 120 Days of Sodom* by defending the French author's bold exploration of human sexuality. In his groundbreaking essay Piñera repeated an implicit message of his novel, that is, that sexuality is a major component of human existence that deserves to be studied and discussed openly and freely. It is important to further point out that the passages that Piñera chose to publish from Sade's singular text echoed the scandalous issues that he had dealt with in his novel, such as sadomasochism, homosexuality, eroticism, and the mockery of Christianity and Catholicism. In the same year, in another issue of *Ciclón*, Piñera echoed another major leitmotif from *La carne de René* in an article about the Cuban poet Emilio Ballagas. In that essay he brazenly derided Cuban attitudes toward homosexuals and defended homosexuality as a valid literary subject. His frank discussion of Ballagas's homosexual anguish is especially significant, not just because it mirrors René's painful efforts to come to terms with his own sexuality, but also Piñera's personal struggles as a homosexual in a *machista* society.

It is somewhat surprising, given the popularity among contemporary literary circles of so many of the themes and topics that Piñera examines in *La carne de René*—the human body, eroticism, sexual inversion, gender issues, machismo, spirituality—that this groundbreaking novel is still virtually unknown among experts of twentieth-century Latin American fiction. Despite its recent publication in Cuba and in Spain by major publishing houses,[86] *La carne de René* is read infrequently and very rarely studied. As is the case with so many of Piñera's best works—*Pequeñas maniobras* and *El no* immediately come to mind—only a small number of critical articles have been published on *La carne de René*. Though this might be largely due to the fact that Piñera himself was relatively unknown among critics of modern Latin American literature until quite recently, it is also likely that the novel's very uniqueness has ended up casting it into obscurity. *La carne de René* has been labeled "impossible to categorize," and "resistant to facile description." The Cuban author, Guillermo Cabrera Infante, who was one of a limited number of Piñera's contemporaries who read his works, has similarly contended that the novel is "far from any received notion of literature."[87] To be sure, it is hard to classify many of Piñera's works, and it is equally challenging to make sense of the contradictory or ambiguous notions and ideas that fill them. The bizarre world that Piñera presents in *La carne de René* is certainly a case in point. It is an ambiguous literary space that the reader may feel at once tempted to enter and to escape. It disgusts and attracts, bedazzles and horrifies, clarifies and confuses. And though the disturbing incidents of the novel at first seem absurd and entirely dislocated from our everyday existence, Piñera's disquieting universe is also shockingly realistic in its portrayal of the demons that haunt so many of the inhabitants of modern society. Perhaps the brief description of *La carne de René*—written by Piñera himself—that graced the front flap of the first edition of the novel puts it best: "Un brutal impacto de la realidad—de la dolorosa realidad contemporánea es esta novela: *LA CARNE DE RENÉ*, obra inesperada de un autor de Latinoamérica" [This novel is a brutal blow from reality—from our painful contemporary reality: *RENÉ'S FLESH*, an unexpected work from a Latin American author).

6
The Signs of Sebastián: Guilt and Sexual Frustration in *Pequeñas maniobras*

> At this moment, my weak soul stands in need of peace and philosophy: why do you now try to alarm it with your sophistry which will strike it with terror but not convert it, inflame it without making it better?
> —Marquis de Sade, "Dialogue Between a Priest and a Dying Man"[1]

VIRGILIO PIÑERA PENNED *PEQUEÑAS MANIOBRAS* IN BUENOS AIRES BEtween 1956–57. Though the setting for his second novel is clearly Havana, the work's specific historical context is somewhat ambiguous given that there is no mention of specific dates or names. Certain aspects of the text reflect, nonetheless, the increasingly oppressive social and political climate in Cuba during the tumultuous period that led to the triumph of the Revolution. Sebastián's fear of the government informers who have allegedly infiltrated the streets of Havana, and his periodic references to school strikes, social and political protests, and the subversive antigovernment plotting of a roommate who is eventually murdered, all reflect the repressive atmosphere in Cuba during the mid-1950s.

At the same time, though, it should be pointed out that political issues are given minimal importance in the novel. In fact, Sebastián, the thirty-year-old protagonist, clearly states that he is opposed to all forms of personal compromise and detests politics and social activism. He therefore limits himself to brief references to the circumstances in Cuba, which usually serve merely to emphasize his own disconnection from his country's sociopolitical reality. In this sense, Sebastián can be seen as a Cuban antihero and a sort of Latin American "everyman" whose struggle to make sense of his existence overshadows the importance of his country's revolutionary struggle.

Informed by the works of Albert Camus and his Latin American contemporaries such as Ernesto Sábato and Juan Carlos Onetti, Piñera largely based *Pequeñas maniobras* on the prevailing existentialist mode.

But as Seymour Menton has correctly observed, the Cuban author masterfully tempers the existentialist formula with certain techniques that make the novel unique among its contemporaries: "The picaresque job changes . . . help break the existentialist monotony. A few scenes of the absurd and conversations with the reader about the creative process also tend to inject some humor into the usually grim, lonely, and monotonous world of the existentialist hero with his traditional symbols of cats, flies, and nausea."[2]

When compared to Piñera's first novel, *Pequeñas maniobras* stands out as a radically different work. From a stylistic standpoint, for example, *Pequeñas maniobras* is better written and more clearly conceived. Unlike *La carne de René*, which is a somewhat clumsy novel that is often difficult to follow, *Pequeñas maniobras* flows very smoothly. Moreover, the intimate, confessional tone of the first-person narrator of *Pequeñas maniobras* sets it apart from its predecessor, whose third-person narrator recounts the novel's horrifying events with chilling matter-of-factness. *Pequeñas maniobras* also lacks the brutal violence and shocking imagery that make *La carne de René* Piñera's most daring and provocative work.

Despite the numerous differences between Piñera's first two novels, they do share certain thematic common ground. Like *La carne de René*, *Pequeñas maniobras* stands out for its portrayal of human existence as lonely, painful, and hopeless. Both protagonists are eccentric outcasts who are tormented by the constant efforts of others to impose their system of beliefs on them. To be sure, René's rebellion against the Cult of the Flesh bears something of a resemblance to Sebastián's resistance to Catholics and to the sacrament of confession, which the latter sees as obstacles to his personal freedom. While René defends himself against those who strive to control his body—"no estaba dispuesto a ceder su cuerpo para ese servicio del dolor . . . nadie tenía derecho de profanarlo" (104) (He was not prepared to place his body in the service of pain . . . no one had the right to profane it [95])—Sebastián puts up a similar fight against those who try to manipulate his mind: "Nadie tiene el derecho de turbar la paz de mi infierno"(41) (No one has the right to disturb the peace of my hell).[3]

The young male protagonists of both novels are similarly ill equipped to adjust to environments that they perceive as repressive and inhospitable. In both works Piñera indirectly criticizes problematic issues faced throughout Latin America: the exploitation of the weak and powerless, the innate cruelty of humankind, and the manipulative practices of powerful individuals and institutions. Neither of his two novels, however, can be classified as a political text. As we have already suggested, despite being written during a period of political struggle in Cuba, *Pequeñas maniobras* is by no means a revolutionary work. Sebastián is the antithesis of a revolutionary hero, a fact that is underscored by his resistance to all forms of commitment and his marked distaste for political protest. Throughout the novel Sebastián rejects the value of social-mindedness with categorical statements: "no me gusta comprometerme" (16) (I don't like to make commitments), "Nada de rebeldías . . . no firmaré ningún manifiesto" (29) (Nothing of rebellions . . . I won't sign any manifesto). Likewise, he ridicules individuals, like his friend Pablo, who possess strong political convictions.

Sebastián is a nonconfrontational loner, an antihero par excellence. Instead of seeking out excitement and adventure he lives vicariously through detective novels, gangster movies, and the memoirs of Casanova, his favorite literary character. As the following passage illustrates, Sebastián's boring, miserable, and ambitionless existence serves as an inverted version of the audacious exploits and amorous escapades of this legendary figure:

> me pasé la semana metido en mi azotea, en la cama, sin ánimo para nada, leyendo esas cosas que yo jamás haré, páginas que hablan de capitanes intrépidos, de audaces aventureros, de políticos de altura, de galanes irresistibles, de salvadores de almas . . . Aquí mi bajeza se empareja con su altura: no los tomo de modelo, sencillamente los contrapongo. (36)

> [I spent the week in my flat, in bed, with no energy for anything, reading about those things that I'll never do, pages that speak of intrepid captains, audacious adventurers, high-ranking politicians, irresistible gallants, saviors of souls . . . Here my lowliness pairs off with their loftiness: I don't take them as models, basically I set myself against them.]

Like René, Sebastián struggles to understand himself and the meaning of his existence. He longs for anonymity and solitude, and spends a good deal of his energy fleeing from family, friends, women, institutions, or anything else that threatens to take away his individuality. Both René and Sebastián eventually resign themselves to unhappy destinies that will bring them nowhere and will more than likely end in humiliation. It is worth pointing out that the thirty-year-old Sebastián's eccentric personality and physical appearance suggest a sort of model for a grown-up René. Much as the reader might expect René to turn out, Sebastián is a loner who has not managed to integrate himself into so-called normal society. Sebastián is small, weak, and cowardly. Despite his "cara seductora" (59) (seductive face)—a physical trait that he shares with René—he is anything but a seducer. Indeed, Sebastián fears sexual intimacy much like René does, and he therefore flees from those who desire him.

Sebastián is an anti-Casanova, the antithesis of the stereotypical

Latin American male. He is portrayed throughout the novel as an effeminate and sexually confused young man, and even his name conjures up the erotic image in *La carne de René* of the young martyr piercing himself with phallic arrows. Sebastián's repeated references to his submissiveness and passivity—"soy sumiso" (60) (I am submissive), "[soy] víctima propiciatoria" (130)[4] ([I am] a sacrificial victim)—certainly serve to reinforce this connection. In this regard, however, there is one important difference between René and Sebastián: while René at least tries to rebel against his father and the leaders of the Escuela del Dolor, Sebastián is a glutton for punishment who seems to be incapable of even attempting to liberate himself from the exploitative designs of others.

Catholic Guilt: To Confess or Not to Confess?

Like many first-person narratives, *Pequeñas maniobras* resembles a confession of sorts. Through his memoirs Sebastián acknowledges his flaws and attempts to explain the reasons behind his actions. His observations often suggest that he is deeply troubled by a sense of guilt and that he feels the need to atone for some secret transgression. But despite frequently coming across as a man with a contrite heart, Sebastián is vehemently opposed to the sacrament of confession, which he considers a grave threat to his individuality. Sebastián's categorical negation of confession early in the second chapter serves to forewarn the reader of the important role that the topic will play in his memoirs.

Antón Arrufat has observed that Virgilio Piñera was an assiduous reader of Kierkegaard and was especially fond of *The Concept of Anxiety*. Arrufat's observation is especially interesting in relation to *Pequeñas maniobras* since, to a certain extent, Sebastián's disproportionate dread of the confessional is reminiscent of what Kierkegaard called "inclosing reserve." According to the Danish philosopher, the "inclosed person" is afraid that a transgression that he hides within himself is "so terrible that he does not dare to utter it, not even to himself, because it is as though by the very utterance he commits a new sin or as though it would tempt him again."[5] Sebastián's nervousness, then, might stem from his conviction that by simply speaking of the source of his guilt he will be admitting a sin and his need to atone for it. Though Sebastián never explains exactly what he feels guilty about, we are lead to believe—through his own observations and those of Teresa and his other acquaintances—that his anxiety is a product of his homosexuality.

Sebastián's avoidance of confessing, answering questions, and providing information about himself, then, can be seen as a defense mechanism that allows him to hide his secret, which he feels entitled to keep to himself. In this sense Sebastián's extreme distaste for all forms of confession boils down to an issue of personal freedom. Since he strives to exist as an individual, unaffiliated with institutions, with others, and with God, he cannot bring himself to divulge so-called sins or personal information just because others want to make him do so. He abhors the idea of moral obligation, and since he sees confession as a Christian duty—as opposed to an act of individual will—he does not believe that revealing his innermost secrets to a priest would have the cathartic effect that confession is supposed to produce.

Sebastián is especially opposed to the idea of capitulating to the coaxing of moral or legal authority figures, and he therefore feels compelled to lie when he finds himself in such compromising situations. His refusal to answer questions truthfully when he is wrongfully arrested for the murder of his neighbor, Gustavo, who had been charged with crimes against the state, is illustrative of this point. Indeed, Sebastián is so opposed to being forced to impart personal information that he feels the urge to confess to the crime despite his obvious innocence: "Durante los interrogatorios en la cárcel maldije mil veces no ser el estrangulador. Al menos éste puede escoger entre confesar su crimen o callarlo; en cambio, yo no tengo derecho a dicha elección. Más indefenso que el propio asesino, me veía reducido a declarar que yo era el estrangulador" (48) (During the interrogations at the prison I cursed a thousand times the fact that I was not the strangler. At least he can choose between confessing his crime or keeping it secret; I on the other hand don't have the right to such a choice. More defenseless than the murderer himself, I found myself reduced to declaring that I was the strangler).

Shortly after he is released from prison Sebastián revisits the issue of forced confession in a revealing conversation with Teresa. It must not be overlooked that Teresa's job as an assistant to the attorney general frequently involves coercing people to confess their crimes. As their conversation suggests, Sebastián considers this to be the most dreadful aspect of his friend's profession:

—... ¿No te parece algo horrible que un ser humano se vea obligado a confesar lo que ha hecho?
—No vayas a creer; ellos confiesan porque ya han sido puestos en evidencia.
—Eso es lo que no entiendo. Si yo cometo un crimen, si la policía descubre que soy el asesino, ¿a qué entonces torturarme con la confesión?
. . . .
—Hay muchas que no confiesan su crimen.

—Sufren más que los otros. Les asquea la confesión.
—No lo creo, es una táctica. Les queda esa esperanza.
—Esa esperanza es cosa aparte. Todos la tenemos. Sentir que nos arrancan una confesión es algo más grave, es como la pérdida de un ser querido, Teresa, es tomar contacto con la muerte.
—¿No te parece que la confesión es un alivio?
—¿Cómo podría serlo? Nadie se confiesa voluntariamente. La confesión siempre es arrancada; por evidencia, por temor a la justicia, por temor a Dios. Confesarse es morir. (93–94)

[—... Doesn't it seem terrible to you that a human being feels obligated to confess what he has done?
—Don't go thinking that; they confess because they have been exposed.
—That's what I don't understand. If I commit a crime, if the police discover that I am the assassin, why torture myself with a confession?
. . . .
—There are many who don't confess their crimes.
—They suffer more than the rest. Confession disgusts them.
—I don't think so, it's a tactic. They still have hope.
—That hope is a separate matter. We all have it. To feel that a confession is wrested from us is something more serious, it's like the loss of a loved one, Teresa, it's like making contact with death.
—Don't you think confession is a relief?
—How could it be? Nobody confesses voluntarily. Confession is always wrested; by evidence, by fear of justice, by fear of God. To confess is to die.]

This provocative exchange raises a number of interesting issues. Most importantly, Sebastián makes clear that what he finds horrible is not so much the act of confessing, but rather the coercion that brings one to own up to his/her misdeeds. To underscore his aversion to forced confessions, he goes so far as to equate them with torture and death. Sebastián underscores his belief that confessions are typically products of manipulation and coercion—whether by police detectives or Catholic priests—and that they are therefore insincere and meaningless. His assertion that he suffers more than those who confess is intriguing since it implies that he believes that his own anguish is due in large part to his unwillingness to relieve his guilt by performing an official act of contrition.

Sebastián declares repeatedly that he will never confess and that the sacrament has no real meaning, but it is obvious that he is not entirely convinced that eluding the confessional is the best plan of action. He admits, for example, that he is afraid of the consequences of failing to atone properly for his sins, and during a poignant moment of self-examination, he asks himself a question that ends up tormenting him for years: "¿Morir confesado es mejor que morir inconfeso?"(26) (Is dying confessed better than dying without confessing?).[6] Sebastián's anxiety over the matter once again recalls the writings of Kierkegaard who warned about the dangers of evading acts of contrition:

> So wonderful a power is contrition ... that quite the most terrible of fates is to have eluded it altogether. There is much a man might wish to avoid in life. ... But if anybody would violently, defiantly, avoid contrition: ah, which were the most truly terrible thing to say: he did not succeed, or — he succeeded?[7]

To a certain extent, then, Sebastián's guilt-induced anxiety can be seen as more than a result of his sexual inversion. To be sure, his guilt is made more intense by those who try to make him believe that he will be damned because he refuses to repent for his supposed egregious transgression against Christian morality.

Carlos the seminarian, Padre José, and other church officials, for example, repeatedly chastise Sebastián for his rejection of the Church and of a Christian way of life. They sermonize him and contend that his soul is doomed. Because they refuse to leave him alone and let him live as he sees fit, Sebastián sees the Church and its representatives as manipulative and condescending. He disdains Catholics for fueling his feelings of anxiety, and he becomes convinced that much human suffering is due to the constant pressure from the Church's "moral police." In his mind, Carlos and Padre José are typical Catholic bullies who meddle in other people's business, pass judgment on them, and intimidate those who do not embrace their beliefs. Moreover, Sebastián despises, much like Kierkegaard did, the common conviction that being a Christian is like being part of a club. In other words, he detests the prevalent attitude among Christians that spiritual enlightenment can be achieved by blindly accepting religious dogma and the demands of priests.

Padre José, who comes to visit his brother and sister-in-law from his provincial parish in Camagüey, epitomizes this frame of mind that Sebastián despises so much. During his visit he aggressively attempts to coerce Elisa's brother Orlando to renounce his playboy lifestyle and to confess his sins, despite the latter's vehement resistance. Padre José's uninvited proselytizing provokes a nasty argument between him and Elisa, who tries to defend her brother. Padre José's condescending attitude toward "sinners" and his simplistic belief that Orlando can save his soul with a disingenuous confession fills Elisa with rage:

> —Nuestra misión en la tierra es salvar a los pecadores.
> —Me parece bien, pero si Orlando no quiere que tu los salves, ¿a qué tanta insistencia?
>   . . . . .

—El pecado está en la sangre del hombre.... Tu hermano Orlando es un soberbio.
—Admitido: Orlando es un soberbio, pero no pretende tu alma; en cambio, tú pasas por humilde y quieres el alma de mi hermano. No entiendo: la humildad que colecciona almas. ¡Nada menos que almas!
—Para llevarlas a la presencia de Dios.
—¿Por qué no te dedicas, de acuerdo con tu humildad, a coleccionar moscas muertas. (68–69)

[—Our mission on Earth is to save sinners.
—That's fine with me, but if Orlando doesn't want you to save him, why so much insistence?
. . . . . .
—Sin is in the blood of man.... Your brother Orlando is an arrogant man.
—Agreed: Orlando is an arrogant man, but he isn't after your soul; you, on the other hand, pass yourself off as humble and you want my brother's soul. I don't understand: humility that collects souls. Nothing less than souls.
—To take them to the presence of God.
—Why don't you, in accordance with your humility, devote yourself to collecting dead flies.]

Padre José's conviction that Orlando can only be saved if he confesses his sins to a priest again calls attention to Piñera's criticism of the propensity of Christians to believe that one must conform to the rules of the cult even if he/she does not truly understand or believe them. Padre José's attitude is typical of this problem since he places more importance on the act of confession itself than on faith and belief in God and his power to forgive. Like Kierkegaard, who insists that a relationship with God must be a matter of individuality and inwardness and ridicules the false notion that through conformity the individual can reach God, Piñera implicitly mocks Christians who consider themselves saved by virtue of their selective membership to the cult and their adherence to its rules.

In *The Concept of Anxiety* Kierkegaard also argues that guilt is the opposite of freedom, and therefore the two cannot exist together. According to him, even though freedom returns through repentance, one must truly understand his/her guilt in order to repent with sincerity: "Whoever learns to know his guilt only by analogy to judgments of the police court and the supreme court never really understands that he is guilty."[8] It seems that this is precisely the notion that Padre José fails to understand. He expects that his judgments are sufficient evidence for Orlando—and later Sebastián and Teresa—to be convinced that they are guilty sinners. In other words, according to Padre José's shallow way of thinking, one's own understanding and acceptance of his/her guilt is not an essential ingredient for a genuine confession.

The argument between Elisa and Padre José fills Sebastián with so much rage that he decides to write a blistering attack against the priest and his Church. It is important to point out, however, that he does not plan to share the document with Elisa or to send it to Padre José. Instead, he sees his emotionally charged text as a symbol of revenge and a symbolic vehicle of catharsis. He believes that by writing down his rage he can at once exact revenge and mitigate his anger:

> Cojo el lápiz, escribo de un tirón. Tengo que vengar a Elisa; el Padre José expiará su pureza. Pero es mi venganza, no la de ella. . . . Si las acciones de los hombres recaen sobre uno, si nos hieren, si nos desvelan, si las heridas de los demás nos hieren a su vez con igual furia, yo tengo el derecho de vengarlas. (79)

> [I pick up the pencil, I write without stopping. I have to avenge Elisa; Father José will expiate his pureness. But it's my vengeance, not hers. . . . If men's actions bear upon another, if they hurt us, if they keep us awake, if the injuries of others hurt us in turn with equal fury, I have the right to avenge them.]

Sebastián's comments underscore Piñera's implicit suggestion that through his writings he, too, aimed to exact revenge against what he saw as a major cause of his own pent-up anxiety and frustration, that is, the Catholic Church.

The provocative dialogue that Sebastián dreams up echoes Piñera's blatant mockery of Christianity and Catholicism in *La carne de René*. In much the same way that Cochón pronounces his vehement sermons in order to debunk Catholic teachings and to expose the hypocrisies of church leaders, Sebastián aims to call attention to the falseness of certain Catholic ideas and attitudes. In this regard, Sebastián's written text also recalls the anti-Christian venom of the writings of the Marquis de Sade. In many of his texts, and especially "Dialogue Between a Priest and a Dying Man"—with which Sebastián's fictional confession shares certain points in common—the Marquis de Sade casts his aspersions on the empty and meaningless rhetoric of the clergy. Like Sade's "Dialogue," Sebastián's short text presents an imagined exchange between a priest and a nonbeliever. In what amounts to an inverted confession, the "confessor," instead of avowing his sins, professes disbelief in God and hatred for the priest and his sermonizing:

> —. . . Ruega en cada momento por tu salvación.
> —No puede salvar mi alma quien primero la perdió. No te creo; tus palabras son consuelo de tontos.

6: THE SIGNS OF SEBASTIÁN

—Dios me cree. Adorémosle.
—No creo en la justicia divina.
—Blasfemas. Dios te lo tendrá en cuenta a la hora de tu muerte.
—¡Ya he blasfemado tanto! El odio se alimenta de blasfemias.
. . . .
—Arrepiéntete, estás a tiempo todavía.
—No he venido a arrepentirme. Eso no arreglaría nada. He venido a verter mi odio en tu oreja.
—Ese veneno llega a Dios hecho amor.
—Otra vez tus palabras que no dicen nada. . . .
—¡Cúmplase la voluntad de Dios!
—Es inútil, tienes el viejo vicio de tu raza. Te encantan las grandes frases. (81–82)

[—. . . Pray at every moment for your salvation.
—He who first ruined my soul cannot save it. I don't believe you; your words are consolation for fools.
— God believes me. Let us adore him.
—I don't believe in divine justice.
—You are blaspheming. God will bear it in mind at the hour of your death.
—I have already blasphemed so much. Hate feeds itself on blasphemy.
. . . .
—Repent, you still have time.
—I have not come to repent. That wouldn't resolve anything. I have come to spill my hate into your ear.
—That poison reaches God in the form of love.
—Once again your words mean nothing. . . .
—Carry out the will of God!
—It's useless, you have the old vice of your breed. You adore grandiose sayings.]

Echoing the ailing libertine in Sade's "Dialogue," Sebastián's fictional sinner turns a supposed confession into an opportunity to deride the priest and his Church. In both cases the nonbelievers invert the typical nature of the sacrament. Instead of asking for God's forgiveness, they put the priest on the defensive. Sade's libertine, for example, speaks of being "blinded by the absurdity of [Christian] doctrines," and insists that "I owe you not gratitude but hatred" for having "confused but not enlightened my mind."[9] The dying man chastises his confessor for his idle talk, "preconceived ideas," "fabricated reasons," and his supposed power to forgive through the agency of God. Moreover, he scoffs when the priest accuses him of blasphemy. In the same way, Sebastián's version of a nonpenitent sinner underscores the uselessness of confession for one who does not believe in God's unconditional love or his divine justice.

Despite the fact that Sebastián scorns the Christian sacrament of confession, he does seem to understand the potential healing powers of divulging personal "sins" and secrets. Later in his memoirs he likens himself to a storehouse full of damaged goods, and insinuates that he feels a need to free himself from accumulated guilt: "La mercancía que vendo está averiada; los granos están secos, la carne es dura, la sal se ha mojado . . . Sin embargo, tengo que salir de ella, darla por nada. Si no lo hiciera, muy pronto el repugnante hedor de lo podrido apestaría todo el almacén. Quedaré así limpio de culpa y mancha" (135). (The merchandise that I sell is spoiled; the grains are dry, the meat is tough, the salt has gotten wet . . . However, I have to get rid of it, give it away. If I failed to do it, very soon the repugnant stench of rottenness would stink up the storehouse. In this way I will be free of guilt and stain.)

Notwithstanding his apparent awareness of the need to unload his "spoiled merchandise," Sebastián avoids anything that even remotely resembles a form of confession. The mere idea of acknowledging love or friendship, or the possibility of having to discuss personal information with anyone makes Sebastián intensely queasy. He suffers from a sort of existential nausea that forces him to expend a remarkable amount of energy fleeing from situations that he thinks might entail commitment or personal compromise. Whenever he sees his friends approaching, he runs the other way to avoid having to speak to them. Likewise, if a landlord becomes inquisitive for any reason, he simply moves into a new apartment. When Carlos, a young seminarian, tries to convince him to speak with a local priest, Sebastián is so overwhelmed by anxiety that he decides to leave his home of fifteen years and move to a more remote area of Havana. He is so afraid to discuss personal issues that he even refuses to confide in Teresa, his occasional lover and only true friend. In short, Sebastián certainly manages to evade others and to keep his secrets safe within himself, but he ends up paying a high price for his tight-lipped existence.

Sebastián's fear of commitment makes it increasingly difficult for him to bear his intense loneliness and his pent-up anguish. As he bounces from one demeaning job to another—servant to his boss, street photographer, magazine salesman—Sebastián avoids confession but fails to alleviate his internal suffering, that is, until he finds a job as a night watchman at a spiritualist center. The name of the institution, "Centro Espiritista Paz y Concordancia" (Spiritualist Center of Peace and Harmony), is highly symbolic since it is there that Sebastián finally begins to feel at peace with himself and with his decision to guard his deepest secrets.

Given his tireless flight from the confessional and from Catholic priests and haughty Christian moralists, it is hardly surprising that Sebastián feels his first sense of relief in a place where alternative lifestyles are the norm. Though Sebastián does not share the philosophy of the Spiritualists with whom he lives, he is moved by the simplicity and the sincerity of their beliefs and he is delighted by the lack of pressure that they exert upon him. He is also pleased that his Spiritualist companions are, for the most part, of limited mental capacity because this makes him confident they will not treat him condescendingly like his Catholic acquaintances have.

Much like Sebastián himself, who feels shunned by a society of convention, the members of the Spiritualist cult are marginalized eccentrics and loners who have come to live in the center to avoid those who look down on them and their alternative lifestyles. In this sense, their communication with spirits and their ongoing dialogue with the great beyond are highly symbolic of their desire to escape from the anxieties and frustrations of life in a society in which they are seen by so many as moral degenerates who need to atone for the social "transgression" of going against the moral mainstream.

The final line in his memoirs—"'Paz y Concordancia,' ampárame, ampárame" (214) (Peace and Harmony, protect me, protect me)—underscores Sebastián's desire to escape from a world in which he feels compelled to atone not so much for a misdeed that he has committed, but rather a "sin" for which a morally righteous society holds him accountable. It is especially interesting how Sebastián admits that he had contemplated suicide as a way of escaping his guilt. His brief reference to suicide is significant for two reasons. On the one hand, it serves to further underscore his tendency toward self-deprecation since he claims that he does not deserve such a dramatic way out of life's problems: "Sebastián, no te pongas triste, acá tienes el remedio: métete un tiro en la cabeza. Pero es que no puedo, el tamaño de mi vida no estaría en proporción con el desmesuramiento de un suicidio.... Todo el mundo se reiría de tal acto" (213) (Sebastián, don't be sad, here's your remedy: put a bullet in your head. But I can't, the size of my life would not be in proportion to the enormity of suicide.... Everyone would laugh at such an act.)

On the other hand, Sebastián's decision not to commit suicide can also be interpreted as a definitive act of avoiding confession. In *The Myth of Sisyphus*, an essay that served as something of a model for Piñera's worldview, Albert Camus writes at length on the relationship between absurdity and suicide. According to the French author and philosopher, the central question of human existence is whether life is or is not worth living. Suicide, therefore, can be seen as a confession from an individual who has decided against the value of his/her existence. As Camus puts it, "Killing yourself amounts to a confession. It is confessing that life is too much for you or that you do not understand it."[10] Given Sebastián's professed fear of every other kind of confession, it follows logically that suicide is not a viable option for him to take. Moreover, since Sebastián goes to great lengths to avoid revealing even his most insignificant feelings to others, it comes as no surprise that he rejects the idea of implicitly admitting that his life is not worth living. Instead, he opts to continue to push ahead with his life of small and insignificant maneuvers and to keep his inner secrets to himself. Though Sebastián concludes his memoirs without having revealed the source of his obvious inner turmoil, a careful reading of the novel suggests that his guilty conscience is a product of his homosexuality.

Homosexual Shame and Atonement through Self-Denigration

In his controversial article "Ballagas en persona" (1955), Virgilio Piñera daringly explored the notion of homosexual anxiety and its frequent translation into moral guilt through his analysis of the poetry of his friend Emilio Ballagas. In the article, which caused something of a scandal in the Cuban intellectual community and especially among its Catholic contingent, Piñera defended homosexuality as a valid subject of literary and intellectual concern, and he implicitly denounced the predominant *machista* mentality in Cuba that more often than not forced homosexuals into painful silence. In a particularly revealing section of the article Piñera discussed the various ways that homosexuals viewed their sexuality. In his opinion, Ballagas opted to interpret his homosexuality as a sin that called for atonement:

> Para él su inversión equivalía al pecado original. Entonces . . . se dedicó con toda conciencia a ser ese personaje de una comedia de Terencio:[11] el que se atormenta a si mismo.
>
> Ahora bien, ¿cuál es el saldo de esto? Un sufrimiento perenne. No lo olvidemos: Ballagas se puso, per vita, un severo cilicio psíquico el cual le causaba atroces dolores psíquicos. . . . ¿Qué hace el pecador que quiere obtener el perdón de su Dios? No sólo darse golpes en el pecho, no sólo prosternarse en el templo. Hace algo más sólido: los expía. Ballagas entendía que él expiaba el suyo humillándose.[12]

> [To him, his inversion was equivalent to original sin. Therefore . . . he devoted himself conscientiously to being the character from a play by Terentius: the one who torments himself.
>
> Now then, what is the result of this? Perennial suffering. Let's not forget: Ballagas put on, for life, a stringent, psychic hair shirt, which caused him

atrocious spiritual pains. . . . What does a sinner who wants to obtain his God's pardon do? Not only beat his breast, not only lie prostrate in the temple. He does something more concrete: He expiates his sins. Ballagas understood that he expiated his by humiliating himself.]

Piñera's discussion of Ballagas's painful personal struggle with the moral guilt brought on by his "sin" was significant not just because it exposed Cuban prejudices and hypocrisies, but, perhaps more importantly, because it served to call attention to similar themes and issues in his own works. When examined in light of Piñera's compelling remarks about expiation of moral guilt through humiliation, for example, Sebastián's behavior in *Pequeñas maniobras* takes on added significance. Sebastián's marked tendency to degrade himself can also be interpreted as his method of atoning for what he secretly sees as his "transgression" against the moral mainstream.

Though Sebastián never discloses the source of his guilt in his memoirs, we are led to believe that his anxiety is caused largely by his closeted homosexuality. Sebastián's strong distaste for Catholic priests and the sacrament of confession, for instance, suggests that the "sin" that he ostensibly hides is one that he knows they would find particularly reprehensible. We must recall that despite the relative weakness of the spiritual authority of the Church in Cuba, conservative Catholic values have long been deeply rooted in the island's culture.[13] Since the condemnation of homosexuality is part and parcel of the Catholic tradition, Sebastián's pent-up anger toward Catholics is hardly surprising.

Sebastián's homosexuality is implied in a number of ways throughout the novel. First and foremost, his name immediately conjures up the image of the pale-skinned, hairless body of the young Christian martyr, which figures so prominently as a homoerotic icon in *La carne de René*. It is clear that Piñera chose the protagonist's name with one of Christianity's most erotically charged icons in mind. As if to dispel any doubts, a remark by one of Sebastián's acquaintances confirms the connection: "Pues usted es un santo. San Sebastián" (142) (So, you're a saint. Saint Sebastian).

Moreover, Sebastián's disinterest in sexual contact with women, which he reveals in his reflections on his troubled relationship with Teresa, also suggests that he is homosexual: "Para Teresa su amor no tiene barreras, para mí las tiene todas, la primera de ellas el amor mismo. No logro enamorarme, de Teresa ni de alguna otra mujer" (31–32) (For Teresa love has no boundaries, for me it has them all, the first of which is love itself. I can't fall in love, with Teresa or any other woman). For her part, Teresa, who is madly in love with Sebastián, is forced to concede that a happy relationship with him would be impossible since he is living what she calls "un terrible sueño de su propia negación" (97) (a terrible dream of his own denial). As we will discuss later in this chapter, Teresa is not angry with Sebastián after he calls off their planned wedding precisely because she realizes that for Sebastián marriage would have represented a denial of his sexuality.

Sebastián's homosexuality is also suggested through the derogatory comments of others and through his own blatant presentation of himself as a weak, submissive, and powerless man. As we noted in our discussion about René in chapter 5, *machista* attitudes throughout Latin America dictate that men are supposed to be assertive and sexually compulsive. Like René, Sebastián is presented as something of an inverted image of this stereotype. Teresa's boss, for instance, calls Sebastián "el *cobarde*, el indeciso, el vacilante" (99, italics are Piñera's) (the *coward*, the indecisive one, the faltering one], terms that clearly point to his departure from traditional images of manliness. The frequent use of "cobarde" to describe Sebastián evokes the most common pejorative name for a homosexual man, *maricón*, which is also used to denote cowardice.

Sebastián constantly reinforces our perception of him as a radical departure from the stereotypical Latin American male by degrading himself and emphasizing his decidedly nonmasculine personality traits: "no tengo valor" (53) (I'm worthless), "me faltan los pelos en el pecho, sin ellos no es posible afrontar las situaciones" (59) (I don't have hair on my chest, and without it it's impossible to face situations), "soy sumiso" (64) (I'm submissive).

Animals and insects play a particularly important role as symbols of Sebastián's low self-esteem and his marked tendency to humiliate himself. He compares himself to a slew of creatures throughout his memoirs—"mosca" (fly), "zángano" (drone), "bicho raro" (strange bug, but also "weirdo"), "animal indescriptible" (indescribable animal), "perro" (dog), "lagarto" (lizard), "ratón" (mouse)—, all of which denote undesirable qualities such as insignificance, submissiveness, cowardice, disgust, and defenselessness. In an attempt to describe his propensity to flee from people and from compromising situations, for example, Sebastián compares himself to a vulnerable fly that buzzes around to avoid being smashed: "Yo soy la mosca, yo sólo trato de escapar revoloteando de acá para allá sobre los manteles. Tarde o temprano me aplastarán de un puñetazo" (41) (I am the fly, I just try to escape flitting from here to there above the tablecloths. Sooner or later they'll smash me with a blow). It should be added that the image of a fly is also important because it suggests that Sebastián is convinced that others see him as an unwanted pest—an object of disgust and contempt.

Sebastián also frequently likens himself to a lizard, a lowly creature that evokes a number of negative aspects of his personality, such as his cowardice and his tendency to flee from compromising situations: "Si cada uno tiene el derecho de seleccionar su animal, yo ahora mismo escojo el lagarto. El tigre y el león acaban por ser matados, el lagarto tiene probabilidad de escapar" (29) (If each individual has the right to select his animal, I choose at this moment the lizard. The tiger and the lion end up being killed, but the lizard has the prospect of escaping). This is a very fitting comparison considering that Sebastián spends so much energy trying to run and hide from nearly everyone and everything. In this sense Piñera pits Sebastián against the supermacho Cuban revolutionary heroes who, by the mid-1950s, were risking their lives for their political convictions. According to Sebastián's decidedly craven worldview, bravery doesn't pay off since it exposes the individual to too many inherent dangers. Since revolutionaries—like lions and tigers—risk being hunted down by their foes, Sebastián prefers the escapist life of the inconspicuous antihero who is programmed to flee from peril. Sebastián does admit, however, that being weak and cowardly poses certain risks since at any moment he might be crushed. As he puts it, "yo estoy a la merced de los zapatos de la vida" (33) (I am at the mercy of the shoes of life).

Several critics have suggested that Sebastián, like a masochist, seeks out and enjoys humiliation. Méndez y Soto, for example, speaks of the strange pleasure that Sebastián derives from the "orgiastic rite" of his voluntary servitude, while Balderston and Valerio Holguín both argue that like the Christian martyr of the same name, whose image figures prominently in *La carne de René*, Sebastián seeks out humiliation and turns it into a source of erotic pleasure.[14] Notwithstanding certain similarities between the protagonists of Piñera's novels, this tendency to see Sebastián as a masochist and to compare him to the icon of the self-destructive St. Sebastian in *La carne de René* is risky. Most importantly, Sebastián's suffering in *Pequeñas maniobras* lacks the physical and sexual components that lend the strong masochistic undertones to *La carne de René*. Moreover, even though Sebastián seems to look for humiliation at times, he does not enjoy his suffering or his belittling experiences, but rather he sees them as necessary and deserved elements of his existence.

Sebastián's propensities to take jobs that make him feel worthless, and to resist improving his circumstances, exemplify this notion. Sebastián sees his woeful life as something of a penitence that requires him to fulfill certain obligations. He underscores this idea when he refers to his degrading job as a servant of the school director's wife: "merezco ser criado de semejante monstruo" (55) (I deserve to be the servant of such a monster). Teresa puts it best when she insists, after seeing Sebastián give in to so many unreasonable demands, that he leads his life as if it were a "penoso deber" (92) (painful obligation). Sebastián's position at the elementary school, where he has worked for several years, surely reaffirms this opinion. Despite the fact that he detests the schoolchildren—a problem that he blames on his own miserable childhood—and despises the job itself, he resigns himself to his unfulfilling daily routine. "Yo estoy resignado a malcomer, a enseñar a los niños . . . ni una queja sale de mis labios" (18). (I am resigned to eating poorly, to teaching the children . . . not a single complaint emerges from my lips.)

While working at the school Sebastián allows himself to be manipulated and used by his co-workers, the director, and his students. For example, when the director unjustly lowers the teachers' salaries, Sebastián is the only one who does not protest. His explanation of the motives behind his passivity calls attention to his tendency not just to humiliate himself, but to invite others to humiliate him: "Por fin nos rebajaron el sueldo. María, Inés y Julia han renunciado. . . . Yo me quedo, ahora más que nunca, tratando de pasar desapercibido, haciendo ver al director que no he participado en la protesta, que soy un fiel cumplidor de mi deber" (32) (At last they reduced our salary. María, Inés and Julia have resigned. . . . I'm staying, now more than ever, trying to go unnoticed, letting the director see that I didn't participate in the protest, that I am a faithful fulfiller of my obligations). Sebastián's passivity enrages the other teachers, who see him as a cowardly sycophant. He admits that they have the right to hate him, and even goes so far as to suggest that he deserves to die for his spinelessness. However, since currying the director's favor is the simplest solution, Sebastián is willing to accept their evil looks and disparaging remarks.

The director, for his part, knows that Sebastián is a coward who would rather be belittled than protest an injustice. He responds to Sebastián's docility, therefore, by exploiting him even further, as Sebastián explains several pages later.

> Así me dice, que soy un defensor de la institución . . . que de hoy en adelante soy un hijo y él es mi padre, y como consecuencia de todas estas loas me encarga la contabilidad de la escuela. . . . Un hombre de pelo en pecho, un ser a quien la sangre ardiera en las venas, ése que tiene la justicia social como primer mandamiento aplastaría a este director como se aplasta a una mosca. Yo no puedo, yo soy la mosca. (41)

> [So he tells me that I am a defender of the institution . . . that from this day forward I am a child and he is my father, and as a result of all of these praises he puts me in charge of the school's bookkeeping. . . . A man with hair on his chest, a being whose blood burns in his veins, he who holds social

justice as the first commandment would smash this director as one smashes a fly. I can't, I am the fly.]

In his self-deprecating comments, Sebastián makes use of two leitmotifs that he repeats throughout his memoirs as a means to emphasize his feelings of humiliation: "infantilization" and animalization.

The notion of "infantilization" is especially significant when looked at in light of Piñera's friendship and extensive literary collaboration with Witold Gombrowicz. In a brief comparative study on *Ferdydurke* and *Pequeñas maniobras*, Daniel Balderston correctly observes that both novels are centered on notions of humiliation. However, Balderston's insistence that Sebastián's humiliation is unlike Kowalski's because he is not treated like a child, but rather as an idiot, is somewhat misleading. While it is true that Sebastián's shame originates partly from the fact that many of his friends and acquaintances take him for a fool, it is inaccurate to suggest that they do not just as frequently treat him like a little boy.

While the subject of "infantilization" in *Pequeñas maniobras* does not take on the same level of importance that it does in *Ferdydurke*, it is, nonetheless, one of the text's central themes. Even a cursory reading of the novel reveals that Sebastián devotes an inordinate amount of space to musings on the notions of "niñez" (childhood) and "bajeza" (lowliness), both of which underscore his preoccupation with his own childishness. It is similarly evident that Sebastián sees himself and is frequently seen and dealt with by others as if he were a child. On several occasions in his memoirs Sebastián laments that despite his thirty years, he often feels as though he has regressed to his youth. For example, his peculiar relationship with Teresa—which seems more like one between mother and son—leads Sebastián to feel more like a baby than a man: "Una mujer se compone de tres cuartas partes de madre y una sola de mujer.... [D]oy la sensación de tres cuartas partes niño y una de hombre" (30) (A woman is made up of three parts mother and only one part woman.... I give the impression of three parts child and one part man). Likewise Sebastián's expressed fear of the bogeyman and his infantile responses to shame and intimidation underscore his childishness: "me siento humillado y reacciono como un niño" (37) (I feel humiliated and I react like a child); "Lloro como un niño" (50) (I cry like a child); "Tiemblo, me empequeñezco" (132) (I tremble, I belittle myself).

It is in his capacity as a schoolteacher that Sebastián most obviously displays his tendency to regress toward infancy. In the same way that the thirty-year-old narrator/protagonist of *Ferdydurke* is made to feel like a juvenile when he is forced to take part in the silly games of a bunch of cantankerous schoolboys, Sebastián feels belittled when he is surrounded by the youngsters in his classroom. "Me hacen muecas, me tiran bolitas de papel, algunos me desafían a pelearnos a la salida, en una palabra, me infantilizan" (42).[15] (They make faces at me, they throw paper balls at me, some challenge me to scuffle as we leave, in a word, they infantilize me.) It is certainly not a coincidence that Piñera uses the very word that plays such an important part in the Spanish-language translation of *Ferdydurke* to describe Sebastián's impressions of age regression.[16]

The intense humiliation that Sebastián experiences is due in large part to the fact that he is so frequently made to feel that those who deal with him are unable to see that he is a grown man and not a little tyke. In this sense the reader of *Pequeñas maniobras* can see the important thematic common ground that the novel shares with Gombrowicz's masterpiece. In both novels, as Balderston has pointed out, the school represents the locus of humiliation par excellence.[17] In the odd atmosphere of the classroom full of pupils less than half his age, Kowalski is dismayed when the children fail to treat him like the adult that he is: "Unos se propinaban palmaditas o papirotazos . . . otros aun se hacían monerías o zancadillas o piruetas y sus miradas atontadas o borreguiles o aguadas se posaban sobre mí sin descubrir mi treintena" (36).[18] (Some were energetically scrapping or exchanging blows . . . others were making faces at each other, or trying to trip each other up, or pushing each other about, and their stupefied, lifeless, sheeplike eyes rested on me without seeing that I was a man of thirty [28]).

The two protagonists' situations are certainly different: Kowalski is a student and Sebastián is a teacher. Nonetheless, they are both degraded and exploited by individuals who should show respect for them. While Kowalski's teachers treat him in the same way that they treat the young boys, Sebastián's students boss him around as if he were one of them. As a pedagogue Sebastián is an utter failure, not only because he founders in terms of academic instruction, but also because he fails to teach discipline and to inspire respect. Like a child himself he crumbles under the will of his mischievous students: "He ahí que yo no, sino ellos, ponen condiciones. . . . Pero no puedo oponerme a mi cobardía, a mis terrores, tengo que dejar que estos niños me impongan condiciones" (128) (Behold that not I, but they, impose conditions. . . . But I can't defy my cowardice, my terrors, I have to let these children impose conditions on me).

It is interesting to note that while both Sebastián and Kowalski bemoan the fact that their younger counterparts do not respect them, they are equally hard-pressed to find a way to escape from their humiliating circumstances. Kowalski and Sebastián are both overwhelmed by what

Gombrowicz termed "nopodermiento" (no-can-do-ment) and they resort to flight as one of few viable options for avoiding compromising circumstances. For instance, when he is unable to bear the humiliation in the schoolroom any longer, Kowalski concludes that running away is his only choice: "largarse ¿Adónde? ¿Cómo?—no lo sabía, pero sabía que debía huir" (55) (I must escape. How or where I had not the slightest idea, but it was clear that I must get out [48]). In a similar manner Sebastián often speaks of his "vida escapatoria" (36) (getaway life) and he insists near the end of the novel that his most typical mode of operation is avoiding commitments (197).

Sebastián's most frequent method of avoiding commitment is to skip from one job to another.[19] However, with each new position come new humiliations and degrading criticism. When he takes on a job as an encyclopedia salesman, his boss, Sr. Poggi, repeatedly chastises him for his ineptitude. But like many of those who interact with Sebastián, the elderly man sees Sebastián as nothing more than a helpless child who needs his assistance: "Sebastián, usted es un niño. Por ser un niño no le tomo en cuenta sus desaciertos" (170) (Sebastián, you are a child. Since you are a child I don't take your mistakes into account). Likewise, shortly after taking a job as a street photographer, Sebastián is chastised by his new boss for knowing absolutely nothing about taking pictures. True to form, Sebastián defends the opinion of his boss and admits that he is hopelessly inept in his new profession.

Sebastián's impulsive acceptance of the position as a servant in the school director's house underscores his powerlessness in many ways. There, he is constantly belittled and degraded by Elisa, the director's wife, who goes to great lengths to remind Sebastián that he is nothing but a servant. Likewise, Elisa's brother Orlando also makes Sebastián feel worthless by treating him like a ten-year-old boy. As Sebastián puts it, "tengo treinta años, pero él, con ese modo de mirarme, me saca veinte de arriba" (57) (I am thirty years old, but he, with that manner of staring at me, takes twenty away from me). It is interesting, though, that Sebastián declares on a number of occasions that he deserves his lowly position in society. He despises Elisa, for instance, but even his realization that she aspires to make him suffer does not push him to resist or rebel. Instead, he concedes that it is what he deserves. Even Sebastián's relationships with the other servants in the house intensify his sense of humiliation. For example, he allows himself to be bossed around by the house cook, Josefa, despite the fact that he technically occupies a higher social position than she does. "Parece que la condición humana exige que tengamos a alguien a nuestras plantas. Ella está a los pies de Elisa y parece justo que a su vez yo esté a los pies de ella" (60). (It seems like the human condition requires that we have someone at the soles of our feet. She is at Elisa's feet and it seems fair that at the same time I am at her feet.)

By making such remarks Sebastián insinuates that he accepts humiliation as a necessary and fair price to pay for being a cowardly outcast. By insisting that he deserves to be treated with contempt, Sebastián seems to admit his guilt and to suggest that he sees humiliation as a key component in a program of atonement. But Sebastián also sees his miserable existence on the margins of society as a means of escape from the pressures of the scrutinizing eyes of those intent on making him change his ways. As he puts it, "yo soy el amo de mi destino y un destino triste ayuda a escapar de las complicaciones" (61) (I am the master of my destiny and a sad destiny helps one to escape complications). Sebastián's claim that he is master of his existence is not convincing, however, given that he speaks frequently about the crucial role of fate in his life.[20] His ironic comment is significant, though, since it suggests that the only way to avoid the harassment and rejection that the disclosure of his secret would entail is to live a painful life in the closet. In his mind, anything—working as a servant, grading the exams of the director's students without pay, selling tacky encyclopedias, or even marrying a woman who he does not truly love—seems better than revealing his well-kept secret.

Marriage: An Imperfect Antidote to [Homo]sexual Frustration

Around the time that Virgilio Piñera began working on *Pequeñas maniobras*, he was involved in what was probably his only amorous relationship with a woman. Piñera had met Graziella Peyrou shortly after his arrival in Buenos Aires in 1946, and they eventually became very close friends. According to Alejandro Rússovich, Graziella was madly in love with the young Cuban author who, though flattered by her attention, did not feel the same magnitude of emotional and physical attraction to her.[21] In this sense, it is reasonable to presume that Piñera's relationship with Graziella served as a model for the frustrating romance between Sebastián and Teresa. One can imagine that, like the relationship between the young couple in *Pequeñas maniobras*, Piñera's romance with Graziella was a source of satisfaction but also of confusion and frustration.

Indeed, despite his affection for her, Piñera was apparently never in love with Graziella. In one of his most emotionally charged letters to Humberto Rodríguez Tomeu, in fact, Piñera insisted that he had never experienced true love:

Ya veo que estás "bien metido" en el amor. Dichoso tú que al menos lo has experimentado; para mi no haberlo sentido es un vieja nostalgia y hasta un castigo. Esa frase popular que dice que no ha vivido la vida quien no ha sentido el amor, me flagela cada día más.[22]

[I see that you are "deeply involved" in love. Lucky you, who have at least experienced it; for me not having felt it is an old nostalgia and even a punishment. That popular expression that says that he who has not loved has not lived, flagellates me more and more each day.]

In many ways Sebastián embodies the image of the frustrated lover that Piñera presents in his letter to Humberto. He is a lonely, sexually confused man for whom love and marriage are issues that provoke feelings of repression and anxiety. Throughout his memoirs Sebastián struggles to make sense of his feelings for Teresa, his middle-aged friend and occasional lover. Although he eventually proposes marriage to her, he is motivated by feelings of guilt and confusion to break off their engagement several days later.

As we have already suggested, in matters of love Sebastián has much in common with the young protagonist of *La carne de René*. Both he and René are described as having certain beguiling qualities, namely their seductive faces, yet they stand out for their decidedly nonalluring behavior and their avoidance of physical contact with women. Likewise, Dalia and Teresa desire sex, but the young male protagonists of the novels are afraid of it. Teresa is so frustrated by Sebastián's incapacity in matters of seduction that she sees him as the antithesis of a Don Juan figure (88).

Despite his anti–Don Juanesque qualities, Sebastián does share some of the typical personality traits that Søren Kierkegaard discusses in his writings on the aesthetic lifestyle. According to Kierkegaard the aesthete is moved by his life experiences to avoid pledges, promises, and compromise of any kind given that he firmly believes that commitment is never fulfilling. As Peter Vardy notes, however, "this lack of commitment results in emptiness and boredom."[23] Though Sebastián's aversion to marriage is largely due to his homosexuality, his obsession with avoiding all forms of commitment and personal compromise also seems to reflect Piñera's readings of Kierkegaard. Sebastián's solitary existence echoes in many ways the Danish philosopher's presentation of the aesthete's attitude toward commitment. According to the aesthete narrator of "The Rotation Method," for example,

> One must always take care not to enter into any relationship in which there is a possibility of many members. For this reason friendship is dangerous, to say nothing of marriage. Husband and wife are indeed said to become

one, but this is a very dark and mystic saying. When you are one of several, then you have lost your freedom . . . you cannot move aimlessly about the world.[24]

Sebastián's systematic avoidance of meaningful relationships and his inability to commit to Teresa reflect how his point of view overlaps with that of Kierkegaard's aesthete. One of Sebastián's most frequent utterances and a personal motto of sorts—"no me gusta comprometerme" (I don't like to make commitments)—underscores not just his innate reluctance to make friends, but also his natural predisposition to avoid entanglements of any kind. Since Teresa knows Sebastián well, his repeated pledges of love and devotion do not convince her. She is, in fact, always quick to point out the emptiness of his words. Even Sebastián's cautious proposal of marriage—"Teresa, ¿qué te parece si nos casamos?" (95) (Teresa, what do you think about us getting married?)—which he utters in the midst of an unrelated conversation, calls attention to the bankruptcy of his implied commitment.

Like so many relationships between men and women in Piñera's works, Sebastián's relationship with Teresa is anything but conventional, especially when considered in light of the *machista* mentality that has traditionally dominated male/female relationships in Cuba. In the first place, Sebastián is not physically attracted to Teresa in any way. His only description of her paints a portrait of a homely woman toward whom Sebastián feels indifferent: "Teresa, con sus cuarenta años, con sus pechos caídos, con sus labios exangües y con sus 'rosas marchitas'" (30) (Teresa, forty years old, with her fallen breasts, with her anemic lips, and with her "withered roses"). Moreover, though he admits to having made love to Teresa two times, Sebastián is always careful to point out that his carnal encounters with her have had nothing to do with his own sexual drive.

Sebastián's aversion to promises and personal commitment lends an air of futility to his dealings with Teresa, who holds on to hope despite the fact that she knows that he will never be hers. Despite certain similarities between Sebastián's worldview and that of the aesthete, however, the former has little in common with Don Juan or Kierkegaard's Johannes when it comes to seduction. Their denunciation of commitment is a sign of their pride and deceitfulness, while Sebastián's inability to commit to Teresa is a symptom of the guilt and anxiety brought on by his closeted homosexuality.

Teresa realizes that Sebastián's vain attempts to fall in love with her represent his denial of his true nature, and she is therefore not surprised when he calls off their engagement. In fact, she and Sebastián both know that their talk of matrimony is little more than a charade and that their marriage would represent for Sebastián little more than a capitulation to societal expectations. Since he knows he has not been honest in his dealings with Teresa, Sebastián is relieved once he calls off their wedding. It is important to note, though, that his sense of relief does not come from his abandonment of Teresa—he is deeply saddened by her disillusionment—but rather from his realization that he has escaped from what would have been an absurd destiny for a homosexual man:

> ¡Uf, escapé por un pelo! . . . Si me hubiera casado con Teresa, he aquí el tenor de mi diario: *Casados el veinte. Dicha eterna. Hemos recibido muchos regalos. La ceremonia religiosa estuvo muy lucida. Tenemos casa propia. Mi habilidad como contador me gana la estimación de mis superiores. Pronto tendremos un hijo. Compraremos un automóvil. Nuestra luna de miel es perfecta . . .* (123–24)
>
> [Phew, I made a narrow escape! . . . If I had married Teresa, this would have been the tenor of my daily life: *Married the twentieth. Eternal joy. We have received many gifts. The religious ceremony was quite splendid. We have our own house. My skill as a bookkeeper earns me the respect of my superiors. Soon we will have a child. We will buy an automobile. Our honeymoon is perfect . . .*]

To have followed through with his marriage would have obligated Sebastián to conform to a whole set of societal norms and values that he does not espouse. Like the narrator in Kierkegaard's "The Rotation Method," who insists that "marriage brings one into fatal contact with custom and tradition,"[25] Sebastián suggests that he, too, sees matrimony as a surrender of the individual to secular convention. But unlike Kierkegaard's unrepentant Johannes who sees getting out of a commitment as "a masterstroke,"[26] Sebastián is distraught by the loneliness that he feels obligated to bring upon himself and Teresa. As his reflections suggest, his decision to call off of the wedding is not a matter of deceitfulness, but rather of great courage. He points out, for example, that conforming to societal expectations would have been the happiest and perhaps the least complicated remedy for his personal anguish. Piñera implicitly suggests that many men like him would have chosen such a path, but Sebastián remains truthful to himself by taking the more painful but higher road. In doing so, he spares Teresa an imperfect and dishonest marriage of convenience.

Teresa, for her part, is not angry with Sebastián precisely because she understands that their marriage would have represented a denial of his homosexuality. In fact, she concedes that by accepting his offer she too was denying the truth: "*yo misma olvidé mis dudas, mis prevenciones, cómo no olvidarlas frente a un hombre puro, decidido, frente a un hombre que durante quince días vivió el hermoso y terrible sueño de su propia negación*" (97) (*I myself forgot my doubts, my precautions. How could I not have forgotten them in the presence of a pure, resolute man who for fifteen days lived the beautiful and terrible dream of his own denial*). Teresa's ardent defense of Sebastián in spite of her sadness not only underscores her respect for him and for his decision, it also signifies her implicit defense of his homosexuality. While others malign him for his cowardice, indecision, and deceitfulness, Teresa insists that they simply misunderstand him. Against her indignant aunt's declaration that Sebastián is falseness incarnate, for example, Teresa argues that *"El juego de Sebastián ha sido limpio, tan limpio como el del amante apasionado que llega hasta la real consumación del casamiento"* (96)[27] (*Sebastián's game has been honest, as honest as that of the passionate lover who makes it to the real consummation of marriage*).

Given the fact that the family was one of the most important institutions in prerevolutionary Cuba, it is important to call attention to Sebastián's decidedly unconventional relationship with his parents. The lack of communication among them and their inability to understand each other suggest the type of tension that often resulted when children deviated from the social and cultural mainstream or broke from the traditional family model. While his father remains tight-lipped about the upcoming wedding, Sebastián's mother warns Teresa to beware of her son, who she deems incapable of keeping his promise.

It is ironic that while the abandoned bride strives to have compassion for her confused ex-fiancée, Sebastián's mother is furious and deeply upset by the incident. But she is more concerned with her own image than with the reputations of either Teresa or her son. As Sebastián's comments make clear, his mother interprets the canceled wedding as an offense to her and to the family name: "Mamá tronó por todo lo alto. Me dijo que yo era el borrón de la familia, la oveja negra, que se avergonzaba de tener un hijo tan cobarde" (122) (Mother raged full blast. She told me that I was the stigma of the family, the black sheep, that she was ashamed to have such a cowardly son). The mother's self-centered reaction underscores Piñera's criticism of traditional societal norms and pressures that often lead individuals into getting married for the wrong reasons. Like Kierkegaard, who strongly rejected in many of his writings the common practice of seeing marriage as a social obligation or as a means to find one's identity, Piñera ridicules this type of social conformity. But Piñera also mocks the oppressive role that parents play when they reject their children for failing to live up to their expectations. This is a theme that Piñera developed much further in his masterful play *El no* (1965), which is discussed at length in the next chapter.

Sebastián feels intense guilt after calling off his engagement, not so much because he feels that what he did was wrong, but rather because his parents and other members of society have made him feel ashamed for being a nonconformist. "Según las leyes, según la sociedad merezco el castigo. No he tratado de eludirlo" (121). (According to the laws, according to society I deserve punishment. I haven't tried to elude it.) By not getting married, then, Sebastián has symbolically rejected the established mold for the family man—wife, children, new house, and respectable employment—and is therefore condemned by society.

It is worth pointing out here that Teresa and Sebastián are not the only frustrated lovers in *Pequeñas maniobras*. Their problematic relationship is one of several in the novel that point to Piñera's fascination with the topic. Elisa, for example, admits to having married her husband not out of love, but out of a desire to seek revenge against his brother, an aspiring Catholic priest who rejected her because of his love for God. As a result of her selfishness, Elisa is bound by the sacred vows of marriage to a man that she does not love. The story of Teresa's friend Julia, who was stood up by her fiancée Manuel on their wedding day, is also significant since it foreshadows Sebastián's decision to abandon Teresa hours before the wedding ceremony is supposed to take place.

Pequeñas maniobras is just one of many of Piñera's works in which love, marriage, and troubled relationships between men and women take on a central thematic importance. In the next chapter we will examine Piñera's unique treatment of heterosexual couples in three plays: *La boda*, *El no*, and *Dos viejos pánicos*. In each work the protagonists are forced to deal with problematic issues that underscore how relationships between men and women often belie the simplistic and ingenuous societal attitudes toward love and marriage. Sebastián and Teresa, Alberto and Flora, Laura and Vicente, and Tabo and Tota are all examples of what I have chosen to call the "odd couples" that populate Piñera's works. Though the specific circumstances of each couple are different, in one way or another all of them are doomed to failure by a combination of familial and societal pressures that have turned the powerful institution of the Cuban family into an imperfect measuring stick of normalcy.

7
Odd Couples: Frustrated Love and Imperfect Unions in Three Plays

¿Sabe lo que hace un hombre de verdad? Pues, se casa, ¿me entiende?, se-ca-sa . . .

[Do you know what a real man does? Well, he gets married. Do you understand me? He-gets-mar-ried . . .]
— Virgilio Piñera, *El no*[1]

Marriage brings one into fatal connection with custom and tradition, and traditions and customs are like the wind and weather, altogether incalculable.
— Søren Kierkegaard, "The Rotation Method"[2]

THOUGH IT IS NOT A CENTRAL AIM OF THE PRESENT STUDY TO ESTABlish concrete links between Virgilio Piñera's personal experiences and those of his literary characters, it would be disingenuous to claim that the author's life circumstances did not have some bearing on the disillusioned lovers, broken engagements, and problematic heterosexual relationships that fill his works. It is easy to understand why, as a homosexual man living in a *machista* society, Piñera felt compelled to challenge traditional societal attitudes about sexuality, family, and especially marriage, which had long been seen as something of a social obligation for "normal" men and women throughout Latin America. Such was the pressure to live up to the expectations of family, friends, and society as a whole that homosexuals were often pushed into marriages that further compounded their feelings of guilt and confusion.

Piñera departed from just such a scenario in his article "Ballagas en persona" (1955), which contains some of his most daring and enlightening social criticism. Piñera's discussion of Emilio Ballagas's moral struggle with his homosexuality was not simply meant to call attention to the intellectual community's denial of homosexuality as a valid literary topic. In the article Piñera also aimed to offer concrete proof that Cuban society was determined to mask difference and individuality under a veneer of normalcy. Moreover, he derided the social and cultural pressures and the "idiotic myths"[3] that he felt compelled so many individuals to act against their will in order to conform to the expectations of the moral mainstream. In many of his literary works from the 1950s and 1960s Piñera implicitly called attention to this social illness of sorts through the presentation of problem-ridden relationships between men and women who strive in vain to find happiness in a *machista* society that condemns difference and deviation from tradition.[4]

In this chapter we will concentrate on three of Piñera's dramatic works—*La boda* (1957), *El no* (1965), and *Dos viejos pánicos* (1968)—in which ill-fated or unconventional relationships between men and women serve as vehicles through which Piñera criticizes various aspects of Cuban and Latin American society. In *La boda*, written in Cuba in 1957, Piñera ridicules the superficiality of societal attitudes toward love, and he presents the Christian sacrament of marriage as a bankrupt institution whose deeper spiritual meaning has taken a backseat to meaningless conventions. In *El no*, a fiercely derisive work that mocks many levels of traditional Cuban society, Vicente and Emilia rebel against convention by refusing to get married. In the play love and marriage are once again shown to be complicated and problematic issues that belie the simplicity and ingenuousness of societal attitudes toward them. Tabo and Tota, the aging couple in *Dos viejos pánicos*, are unique among Piñera's protagonists because their marriage has lasted for many years. However, as we learn in this dramatic masterpiece, their matrimony is by no means "normal" since they are bound together by fear of persecution rather than by love.

La boda: Capital Defects, Irreconcilable Differences

Around the time he was completing *Pequeñas maniobras*, Virgilio Piñera began writing his play *La boda*, which premiered in Havana in February 1958. The title of the work may evoke images of love and conjugal union, but it is misleading since the wedding to which it eludes never occurs. It is hardly surprising, given the fact that successful marriages stand out for their absence in Piñera's literary production, that the action of this play ends up revolving around the cancellation of a wedding and the irreconcilable breakup of a young couple. Just as Sebastián and Teresa's wedding is called off on the day that it is set to take place, in *La boda* the plans of Flora and Alberto go awry just minutes before they are supposed to be joined in wedlock. The motives behind Flora's cancellation of her wedding ceremony, however, are radically different from those that move the sexually confused Sebastián to break his engagement with Teresa.

In the final moments before being married Flora discusses the upcoming ceremony with her maid of honor, Julia. When they hear Alberto and the best man, Luis, approaching the room where they are speaking, the two women decide to eavesdrop on the men's conversation. In the midst of an inappropriate discussion of Alberto's sexual exploits with Flora, Alberto asks Luis an intriguing question that sets the wedding-day debacle into motion: "¿Crees que a una persona que se quiera con toda el alma se le puede pasar por alto una falla capital?" (179) (Do you think that it is possible to overlook a capital defect of a person you love with all your soul?).[5] Luis naturally asks Alberto to give him a concrete example, after which the two engage in a shallow discussion about different types of physical and mental defects that might be grounds for terminating an amorous relationship. As they speak Luis, who is snooping around in Flora's dressing room, finds one of her brassieres hanging in the closet. Realizing that his friend has discovered evidence of the defect to which he had referred, Alberto confides in his friend that Flora has droopy breasts.

When Flora and Julia emerge from their hiding place Alberto, who correctly assumes that they have heard him, tries to excuse his blunder by suggesting that his conversation with Luis was nothing but harmless talk. It should be pointed out here that Alberto's foolish attitude is important in that it points to another issue that Piñera implicitly censures in the play, that is, the tendency of people to gossip and to say hurtful things about each other without properly considering the consequences. Flora is justifiably infuriated, and when the priest informs the couple that the ceremony is about to start she responds by calling off the wedding. Her blunt response typifies the air of absurdity that permeates so many of Piñera's plays: "no habrá boda porque hay tetas caídas" (195) (there will be no wedding because of droopy tits). Flora's comment suggests that she is not simply angered over Alberto's insensitive revelation of her secret, but rather she is dismayed that the physical defect that has already caused her so much grief has led Alberto to question his love and reconsider his plans to marry her.

The rest of the play is devoted to a series of highly contrived and ridiculous games dreamed up by Alberto, through which he hopes that he and his ex-fiancée can come up with a formal explanation for what has transpired. He and Flora go to great lengths to determine what exactly caused the breakup, but they seem uninterested in actually finding a solution to their problem. This of course suggests that neither one was fully committed to marriage in the first place. The absurdity of the situation lies in the fact that during the two days that they waste in meaningless communication and empty dialogue, neither Alberto nor Flora makes any effort to reconcile their differences or to proceed with their plans. Alberto even goes so far as to admit that the exercises are simply senseless formalities that he feels obligated to perform: "Explicaciones que no explican nada, explicaciones formales, explicaciones que se tienen entre gente bien nacida" (198). (Explanations that don't explain anything, formal explanations, explanations that are considered among well-bred people.)

It is important to stress that in her conversation with Julia at the beginning of the play, Flora alludes to her reticence about the upcoming ceremony, and she stresses her opposition to certain aspects of the institution of marriage. She suggests, for instance, that an overwhelming sense of social and cultural obligation has served to devalue the sacrament of matrimony:

> FLORA. (*Mirando a Julia a través del espejo.*) ¡Uf . . . Querida, hace un mes que andamos de acá para allá con los preparativos de esta boda. (*Pausa.*) Hay que darle por la vena del gusto a papá, a mamá, al cura que me bautizó, y que se cree con todos los derechos para casarme, a los amigos, que esperan una fiesta de las Mil y Una Noches. . . . [C]asarse es algo que la saca a una de quicio.
> JULIA. (*Riendo.*) Pero no casarse desquicia más. Hay que tener un status. (173–174)

> [FLORA. (*Looking at Julia in the mirror.*) Phew! . . . Darling, for a month we've been running here and there with the preparations for this wedding. (*Pause.*) I have to satisfy the tastes of my father, my mother, the priest who baptized me, who believes he is fully entitled to marry me, my friends, who expect a reception from *The 1,001 Arabian Nights*. . . . Getting married is something that gets on one's nerves.
> JULIA. (*Laughing.*) But not getting married is even more upsetting. One has to have status.]

Flora's sense of disillusionment is notable because it underscores, before the actual cancellation of the wedding, that she might already be predisposed to the idea of calling it off. Flora makes it clear that her marriage in the Church is meant to please everyone but herself. Most importantly, however, Flora forgoes her own desires—to get married in a ten-dollar dress by a justice of the peace, for instance—"para no dar un escándalo en la familia" (174) (so as not to raise a scandal in the family). In this sense, *La boda* is an important precursor to *El no*, in which Vicente and Emilia break with their family traditions by resolutely refusing to get married. In both works the formal ceremonies and fancy parties that the families, friends, and relatives long for never take place.

Flora's comments about her own wedding and Julia's insistence that marriage is necessary for social status underscore a notion that Piñera presents frequently in his works. Because of exaggerated familial and societal pressures that are part and parcel of upper-class life, marriage has lost its deeper, spiritual meaning. Little more than a watered-down formality, the religious wedding ceremony is overshadowed by secular expectations, such as the extravagant social event, which aim to impress everyone from family friends to the parish priest.

Piñera's attack on the superficiality of upper-class values also reveals itself in a number of more subtle ways in the play. The ridiculous discussions about personal imperfections and physical defects, for example, suggest his condemnation of a judgmental society that values perfection on the outside, but gives little importance to issues that really matter. While Flora detests herself because of her physical defect, Alberto sees her breasts as a possible obstacle to his conjugal happiness and his sexual satisfaction. The ultimate absurdity of the play, then, is that a pair of saggy breasts ends up ruining the lives of a perfectly happy couple.

The social criticism in *La boda* is stronger and more direct than in most of Piñera's previous works. In the play he denounces everything from the superficiality of upper-class social conventions, to the stereotypical lewdness of *machista* rhetoric, which is exemplified by Luis's obsession with Alberto's sexual escapades and their insensitive discussion of Flora's imperfect breasts. As mentioned above, Piñera also condemns the Cuban penchant for gossip and rumors, which end up stirring up harmful family and community scandals. The sardonic tone of the play gives the impression that Piñera wrote it with a sense of rage against the mediocrity and superficiality of Cuban society that had pushed him on more than one occasion to seek a more meaningful existence in Argentina.[6] A remark made by Julia at the end of act 1 is illustrative of the author's bitter criticism, and it can be read as a denunciation from Piñera himself of Cuban upper-class values: "gente rabiosa, mundo lleno de gente rabiosa, con espumarajos, con colmillos afilados, con paredes que oyen. . . . Tisquismiquis, sutilezas, susceptibilidades . . . ¡Qué asco!" (198) (rabid people, world full of rabid people, with froth at the mouth, with sharpened fangs, with walls that have ears. . . . Fussy details, subtleties, susceptibilities . . . How disgusting!).

The obsessive repetition of "tetas," which is uttered scores of times in the sixty-page play, and the frequent allusions to Flora's saggy breasts are, in their own right, further examples of Piñera's social and cultural criticism. Piñera was especially aggravated by the reactionary, repressive climate that dominated Cuba during the Batista years. He was well aware that the play would stir up quite a scandal among the prudish members of the Cuban public, and as he later admitted in "Piñera teatral," that is precisely what he intended. "Sabía que dotar Flora con un par de pechos caídos levantaría una ola de indignación, pero confieso que me encantan tales marejadas."[7] (I knew that endowing Flora with a pair of droopy breasts would bring forth a wave of indignation, but I confess that I love such stormy seas.) Shortly after the play's somewhat disastrous premiere in February 1958, Piñera delivered a conference entitled "¿Por dónde anda lo cubano en el teatro?" (Where is the Cubanness in Our Theater?) as part of a series of events planned for the Mes del teatro cubano. In his talk Piñera expressed his disillusionment with the exaggerated sense of modesty that made it difficult not just for Cuban audiences to attend and appreciate the play (many audience members reportedly plugged their ears during performances), but also for the actresses to perform it.

> Y hay más todavía: queda la moral, las buenas costumbres, el qué dirán. . . . Como todavía no se han desprendido de la crisálida hogareña tenemos un compuesto de actriz y niña de su casa, cómico a la vez que patético. Una actriz que no trabajará en cierta obra porque en ella se dice cierta palabra que ofende a sus oídos, que ofenderá a sus padres, y finalmente al barrio completo.[8]

> [And there's more still: there's morality, good habits, what people will say. . . . Since they still haven't freed themselves of the family chrysalis, we have a mix of actress and mama's girl, at once comical and pathetic. An actress who wouldn't work on a certain play because in it is uttered a certain word that offends her ears, will offend her parents, and finally the whole neighborhood.]

The efforts of a Catholic youth group who organized a boycott of the "morally offensive" play shortly after its first performance simply reaffirmed Piñera's conviction that his country had still not managed to break out of its cultural lethargy and social prudishness.

The laughable deposition that takes place at the end of *La boda* similarly pokes fun at the stupidity and shallowness of social conventions and formalities that end up making people betray their true feelings. Despite the fact that Alberto and Flora declare their love to each other in front of the notary public, for example, their warped sense of etiquette—that is, the belief that Alberto's faux pas constitutes an irreparable social blunder—is enough to convince them that they must officially undo their bond. The play ends, then, with what essentially amounts to be an inverted wedding, as Arrufat has correctly observed.[9]

Alberto and Flora, convinced that nothing can be done to salvage their ruined relationship, sign a contract that attests that their marriage did not take place.

Just before they sign the legal document that will make official their decision not to get married, Flora and Alberto each make a brief statement, in the presence of legal council, about the events of the past two days. The scene is among the play's most amusing:

> FLORA. Declaro que Alberto ha sido el causante directo de nuestro rompimiento. (*Pausa.*) Que ha hecho público un defecto mío. . . . Que por tal motivo, me negué a contraer sagrados vínculos. . . . Que como gente bien nacida que somos hemos procedido correctamente. Que no nos separamos enemigos, pero tampoco amigos. (*Pausa.*) Eso es todo. (237–38)
> . . . .
> ALBERTO. . . . Que suscribo en todo y por todo las declaraciones de la señora. Que añado: durante dos días hemos vivido una pesadilla con el fin único de que la verdad resplandezca en toda su gloria. Que no hay intensión sádica en nuestro comportamiento. Que no hemos tenido bodas pero hemos cumplido todas las formalidades. Que dichas formalidades son terribles pero las hemos afrontado serenamente. Por último, que estoy satisfecho del resultado.
> NOTARIO. ¿No olvida nada? Se lo pregunto porque los notarios también tenemos nuestros formalismos. (238–39)

> [FLORA. I declare that Alberto has been the direct cause of our breakup. (*Pause.*) That he has made public a defect of mine. . . . That for that reason, I refused holy matrimony. . . . That as the well-bred people that we are we have proceeded correctly. That we don't separate as enemies, but not as friends either. (*Pause.*) That is all.
> . . . .
> ALBERTO. . . . That I endorse wholly and completely the declarations of the lady. That I add: for two days we have lived a nightmare with the sole intention that the truth shine in all its glory. That there is no sadistic intent in our behavior. That we haven't had a wedding, but we have carried out all the formalities. That such formalities are terrible but we have confronted them serenely. Lastly, I am satisfied with the result.
> NOTARIO. You haven't forgotten anything? I ask you because we notaries also have our formalities.]

This exchange epitomizes Piñera's criticism of social conventions in the play. Flora and Alberto, who do everything according to the rules of their social class, share much in common with the notary public, who also acts strictly according to the book. The couple's supposed belief that they have acted properly and according to established rules of social decorum serves to make their breakup seem even more ludicrous than it did up to this point.

As is so typical in Piñera's theater, the final declarations of Flora and Alberto, which are meant to clarify their feelings and explain their motives, end up shedding little light on the bizarre circumstances of the play. Their statements simply call attention to the fact that in a society in which individuals place more importance on the expectations of others than on their own opinions and feelings, human existence ends up taking on an air of absurdity and senselessness.

EL NO: DEFYING REVOLUTIONARY MORALITY AND SOCIAL CONVENTION

The broken engagements and canceled weddings in *Pequeñas maniobras* and *La boda* are similar in that they call attention to the tendency of Piñera's protagonists to resist commitments. In both works Piñera pokes fun at the institution of marriage not just by presenting wedding-day fiascos, but also by calling into question the traditional family and societal values that have turned the sacrament of matrimony into a social obligation. This is one of the main issues that Piñera criticizes in *El no* (1965), a play that shares much thematic common ground with *La boda*.

But in *El no* Piñera takes the notions of familial obligation and societal expectations to a new level by suggesting that marriage in contemporary Cuba has been turned into an indicator of one's adherence to revolutionary ideology and morality. Emilia and Vicente's refusal to get married is seen by their parents and other members of their community as an unequivocal sign of their eccentricity and political nonconformity. The numerous derogatory names—"monstruo" (monster), "maricón" (faggot), "enfermo" (sick), "momia" (mummy), "raros" (weirdoes), "tortolitos absurdos" (absurd little lovebirds), "idiotas" (idiots), "anormales" (oddballs)—that others call them serve to underscore their supposed deviation from the mainstream.

Vicente's interpretation of the couple's precarious situation is especially enlightening, since it reflects the vulnerability and tension that many so-called nonconformists in Cuba must have felt when faced with the political and social upheaval brought by the Revolution. As he puts it early in the first act of the play, "En ese mundo de los otros que se empeñan en que seamos como ellos, son tus padres los más peligrosos" (31).[10] (In this world of others who insist that we be like them, your parents are the most dangerous.)

Vicente sees Laura and Pedro as the couple's most dangerous adversaries for a number of reasons. First, and most importantly, because they have witnessed the couple's unconventional and unproductive lifestyle, and could therefore eventually turn them in to the authorities. Laura and Pedro also seem dangerous to Vicente because they so blatantly demonstrate that they are not interested in understanding why the young lovers feel and act the way they do. Pedro's reaction to Vicente's supposedly untraditional love for Emilia—"No lo comprendo ni quiero comprenderlo" (53) (I don't understand it, and I don't want to understand it)—parodies the intolerance, narrow-mindedness, and moralistic rigidity common in Cuba after the triumph of the Revolution.

There are many nonconformists in Piñera's works, but as Arrufat correctly points out, Emilia and Vicente are the renegades par excellence.[11] Any discussion of *El no* must take into account the political atmosphere in Cuba during the mid-1960s. During this crucial stage in the revolution, unqualified commitment was expected of all Cuban citizens. Those who opposed the regime or who said "no," so to speak, to revolutionary ideology or to its political goals and causes ran the risk of being arrested and imprisoned. In 1965, the year during which Piñera wrote *El no*, Fidel Castro himself acknowledged that the Cuban government held some 20,000 political prisoners who had been accused of various "crimes" against the Revolution. The increasingly oppressive atmosphere of postrevolutionary Cuba made many citizens feel compelled to "prove" their revolutionary fervor whenever possible, even if this meant betraying their true feelings. Vicente and Emilia represent the relatively small number of individuals who refused to give in to the pressure to conform.

By 1965 Virgilio Piñera had gone from an enthusiastic and active supporter of the Revolution who enjoyed considerable recognition for his literary achievements, to a disillusioned critic who was seen by government officials as a troublesome homosexual and nonconformist. We should recall that in 1961 Piñera had been arrested for his supposed violation of revolutionary morality, and that shortly thereafter *Lunes de Revolución* was closed down, largely because it was considered a haven for eccentrics and homosexuals. Another blow came in 1964 when Piñera was demoted from his prestigious position as director of Ediciones R to a lackluster and decidedly less visible position as assistant editor and translator for the Imprenta Nacional.

The increasingly repressive atmosphere that pervaded Cuba in the early 1960s undoubtedly served as the motivating factor behind Piñera's play, which reflects in many ways the puritanical rigidity of a period during which the revolutionary government committed itself to "sanitizing the environment politically and socially."[12] These were frightening times for those Cubans whose personal or political convictions did not firmly comply with those espoused by the Revolution. The stifling political atmosphere was especially unfavorable for homosexuals like Piñera who often feared that at any time they could be arrested by officials and sent to prison. To be sure, as Piñera began his fall from grace, he grew increasingly afraid of being accused of living a life outside of the law by the ever-vigilant members of the Comités para la Defensa de la Revolución (Committees for the Defense of the Revolution) (CDR).

In *El no*, Vicente seems to be possessed by a similar fear of being arrested and sent to prison for his nonconformity. He implies on a number of occasions, for example, that his relationship with Emilia might be considered by their fellow citizens to be a violation of the law. "[Vivimos] al margen de la ley" (36) (We live outside of the law), he explains to her on one occasion. During the tense final act of the play, during which Emilia and Vicente are put on trial by their neighbors, the *viejo* who holds that Vicente is a moral degenerate because of his supposed violation of social norms, makes a comment that underscores the validity of Vicente's fears of being accused of a crime. After accusing Vicente of being a homosexual he adds, "si un juez lo coge a usted por su cuenta lo manda directo a la cárcel" (106) (if a judge gets you on his own account, he'll send you directly to prison).

But Vicente, who can be seen as something of a reflection of Piñera himself, is a rebel who refuses to give in to the demands of others or to espouse ideologies that go against his own way of thinking. While Piñera often said "no," even when saying "yes" would have made his life easier—"Había otros caminos más fáciles . . . en que sólo con decir 'Sí' mi vida material cambiaría de noche a la mañana. Pero yo siempre dije 'No.'"[13] (There were other easier roads . . . on which, simply by saying "Yes" my material existence would have changed from night to day. But I always said "No.")—Vicente similarly sees negation as a means to reaffirm his personal convictions, as the following remark suggests: "el único modo que tenía de afirmar mis principios era diciendo no" (111) (the only way had to affirm my principles was saying no). Likewise, Vicente's testy response to his neighbors, who tirelessly try to convince him to marry Emilia, is also illustrative of his tendency to defy those who question his nontraditional lifestyle: "Pero es que ya ustedes han ido más allá de todo límite. Me niego a proseguir con esta farsa. No contestaré a una pregunta más, ni proporcionaré más información" (106). (But now you've gone beyond all limits. I refuse to go on with this farce. I won't answer another question, and I won't provide more information.)

Emilia is also moved by a rebellious spirit to refute the charges that are brought against her and Vicente. To the *viejo*'s shallow, unfounded allegations of monstrosities and moral violations, for example, Emilia retorts with her own accusations against him: "Habla de monstruosidades y no ve la suya, es decir, la suya de acusador público" (110). (You speak of monstrosities and you don't see your own, that is, yours as a public accuser.) Emilia's response to the charges brought against the young couple is illustrative of the author's condemnation of the frequent violation of privacy and the abuses of individual rights that became increasingly common in the mid-1960s. The constant surveillance of the civilian population by organizations such as the CDR created an atmosphere of suspicion, and during those years individuals were frequently accused by their neighbors and other "concerned" community members of infractions that they did not commit.

In many ways Vicente and Emilia epitomize the type of individuals who presented a problem for the revolutionary government, which expected total commitment and condemned dissent. From the outset, the two are shown to be insubordinates who steadfastly adhere to their own way of thinking and acting. Vicente's call for rebellion against Emilia's repressive parents, for example, symbolizes a revolt against similar tactics by the government, which strove to make Cuban citizens act according to established norms and to adhere to its ideals.

The couple's negation of marriage parallels their political rebellion. Throughout the play battle terms are used to underscore the idea that they see their unconventional behavior as a way to fight back, not only against the intolerance of their family, friends, and community, but also against the government's moral and political inflexibility. As Emilia puts it, "No nos queda otro remedio que luchar" (34) (We are left with no other option but to fight). Vicente, for his part, holds a similar opinion, as his response suggests: "empezamos una larga guerra. . . . Tenemos al tiempo por aliado" (34–35) (we begin a long war. . . . We have time on our side). Vicente's implication that as younger members of the community he and Emilia will likely outlive their oppressors is, of course, ironic when one considers the fact that the government that Piñera was implicitly criticizing would end up far outliving him and many other members of his generation.

It should not go unnoticed that both Vicente and Emilia are accused several times in the play—either directly or indirectly—of being homosexuals. Emilia's parents and the watchful neighbors see their ambiguous sexuality and their apparent disinterest in physical contact as signs of their moral deviance and abnormality. In his book *Machos, Maricones, and Gays: Cuba and Homosexuality,* Ian Lumsden points out that the persecution of Cuban homosexuals in the mid-1960s was not so much due to their sexual orientation, but rather to the perception that they were nonconformists who "refused to endorse the political dogmas of the regime with appropriate enthusiasm."[14] Since their behavior was deemed suspicious or questionable by the authorities or the leaders of the CDR, such individuals were often accused of leading nonproductive lives during a time in which productivity was imperative.

Interestingly enough, Emilia and Vicente are also vilified throughout the work for choosing to lead stagnant lives. They spend most of their time together knitting and reading, activities that others see as self-serving, individualistic, and nonproductive. The couple's excessive fondness of pursuing such pastimes while sitting in their favorite armchairs—Emilia goes so far as to claim that there is nothing that she enjoys doing more—is interpreted by Emilia's parents as an unhealthy obsession and as a sign of their sexual indifference.

Emilia's constant knitting is especially symbolic. Arrufat suggests, for instance, that Emilia can be seen as an inversion of Penelope, the wife of Odysseus, who knitted tirelessly while waiting for her wandering husband to return and save her from the countless suitors who assumed that Odysseus had died. It should be pointed out, though, that both Emilia and Penelope's constant knitting serves to buy them time and to aid them in avoiding pressures from the outside. Penelope, as a pretext to avoid her suitors, declares that she will not marry until she has finished knitting a shroud for her husband. She then plays a trick on her suitors by unknitting at night what she has knitted by day, hoping to drag on her activity indefinitely. Like Penelope's activity, then, Emilia's constant knitting and unknitting—"Teje . . . y también desteje" (62) (She knits . . . and she also unknits)—can be interpreted not just as an unproductive pastime, but also as a symbol of her avoidance of commitment.[15]

Vicente's sedentary existence infuriates Emilia's mother, who complains that he has done little more than read and write for twenty years. Vicente and Emilia are indeed unproductive individuals, but it seems that the attitudes of the rest of the characters actually serve to provoke their passivity. The more that others try to force them to change, the more resolute the two become in their rebellion of inactivity. According to Antón Arrufat, the power of the couple lies in their passivity.[16] That is, they provoke the anger of others not so much by what they do, but rather by what they don't do. Arrufat's observation is especially important if we take into account that a static routine like that of Vicente and Emilia would have met with disapproval in postrevolutionary Cuba, and particularly in the mid-1960s. Cuban citizens were expected to be selfless contributors to the Revolution's ideals and active participants in its campaigns.

Productivity was of the essence during those times of political, economic, and social changes when Cuba was working to establish a new-found sense of nationhood, and government officials held that antisocials and separatists needed to be reformed in order to see things the "right" way. Fidel Castro's words to prisoners at a camp on the Isle of Pines in 1965 epitomize the government's opinion on such matters. "You have to adapt yourselves to reality. You were thinking in a way different from ours, you were thinking different things, and time will tell who is right." Castro went on to declare that imprisonment and rehabilitation through work and education were "a way out of the situation" since "men who improve themselves . . . are going to be treated with great respect."[17]

The ongoing attack on Vicente's scholarly pursuits is also notable because it reflects well the growing anti-intellectual atmosphere that led to a number of unsettling incidents in 1965. In that year, for example, Ernesto "Che" Guevara publicly announced his conviction that many Cuban writers and intellectuals were not genuine revolutionaries. Likewise, José Lezama Lima's novel, *Paradiso*, which contained explicitly homoerotic scenes, stirred up the ire of government officials, who considered it an affront to revolutionary morality,[18] and many educational institutions such as the University of Havana were purged.[19] Moreover, large numbers of writers, artists, and intellectuals were sent to organized camps.

The Cuban government had begun to organize the infamous Unidades Militares para la Ayuda de Producción (UMAP) in the final months of 1964 with the expressed purpose of rehabilitating those citizens who the government felt were not contributing adequately to the country's political and social aims. Homosexuals and other "nonconformists" who were among the most vulnerable targets of the government campaign to politically and socially sanitize the country were often "potential, rather than overt, opponents of the regime."[20] Many sent to the camps were writers and intellectuals, and therefore Virgilio Piñera feared that at any moment he could be taken in by government authorities. The oppressive atmosphere of *El no*, then, reflects the growing sense of paranoia among certain factions of the population that resulted from the formation of these internment camps.

As we have already mentioned, even before the institution of the UMAP the Cuban government had set up efficient organizations such as the CDR whose members were empowered to report and to prevent behavior and activities that seemed antisocial, unconventional, or antiproductive. The committees, which were organized in neighborhoods and workplaces, clearly served as a model for the group of watchful neighbors who, in the fifth act, judge Vicente and Emilia for their "crimes" against social and moral codes. The attitude of the leader of the group is illustrative of the political and social attitudes that instilled fear in many of those who had fallen out of government favor: "Nosotros, como vecinos de este barrio, tenemos todo el derecho a poner las cosas en claro. . . . Sólo somos simples ciudadanos, que escandalizados por el caso de ustedes, nos hemos constituido en tribunal para juzgarlos y aplicarles sanciones morales" (107). (We, as neighbors of this district, are entitled to make things clear. . . . We are just simple citizens who, scandalized by your case, have come together as a tribunal to judge you and apply moral sanctions.)

Emilia and Vicente are essentially turned into criminals by the neighborhood vigilantes who call them names—"los acusados" (the accused), "los criminales" (the criminals), "los cómplices" (the accomplices)—that underscore their supposed culpability. According to the *vieja* the couple should be punished for their refusal to get married since their decision represents a rejection of one of Cuba's most hallowed institutions: the family. In this sense, Emilia and Vicente's nonproductivity takes on a whole new meaning since by not getting married they implicitly forgo their role as parents. As Hernández Busto correctly suggests in his excellent introduction to *El no*, the myth of the Cuban family accounts for much of the repressive and asphyxiating atmosphere in the play.[21] First Pedro and Laura, and then the anonymous men and women in the final act, condemn Vicente and Emilia for their negation of family tradition.

Pedro and Laura's distress over their daughter's rejection of matrimony is largely caused by their fear that the family line will terminate when they pass away. They both dream of grandchildren, but Pedro is particularly unshakable in his conviction that Emilia must fulfill her familial "obligation" to produce offspring. Even after Pedro's death, Emilia is overwhelmed by a sense of obligation to her father largely because Laura essentially tries to convince her that his soul will not rest until she has a child.

Difference is a Disease

Frequently in *El no* Vicente and Emilia's alleged moral deviance is equated to mental and physical illness. This aspect of the play is especially important since during the early years of the Revolution the term *enfermos* was often used to single out those whose appearance or lifestyle deviated from traditional expressions of machismo.[22] Vicente and Emilia are often characterized as sick individuals, it is thus significant that Emilia's father is a doctor and that one of the two stage settings of the play is his consulting room. As a man trained to remedy the maladies of his patients, Pedro is especially determined to diagnose and cure what he sees as Vicente's sexual "sickness."

According to Pedro's professional medical opinion, Vicente has given him every reason to suspect that he is a homosexual. In this regard, the opening scene of the second act is especially notable. When the curtain rises Pedro is consulting a young patient who has come to seek a treatment for a malady that Pedro diagnoses as psychological impotence. The young man is troubled because he is supposed to be married in a few months, and he therefore fears that he will be unable to consummate his matrimony:

> PEDRO. Le digo y le repito que en el estado en que usted se encuentra, su matrimonio sería un completo fracaso. . . . Si su inhibición sexual no ha desaparecido con el plan que le he puesto, entonces habrá que acudir a un psiquiatra. Fisiológicamente hablando es usted como cualquier hombre normal, sus órganos genitales están en perfecto estado. . . .
> PACIENTE. ¿Y sería un tratamiento muy largo, doctor? Tengo el compromiso con mi novia y con la familia de casarme este año. . . .
> PEDRO. En esta vida nada se puede dar por seguro, pero sus posibilidades de curación por el psicoanálisis son muchas. (49–50)

> [PEDRO. I'll tell you once and I'll tell you again, in the state that you are in, your matrimony would be a complete failure. . . . If your sexual inhibition doesn't disappear with the course of treatment that I have prescribed to you, then you'll have to call on a psychiatrist. Physiologically speaking you are like any normal man, your genital organs are in perfect shape. . . .
> PATIENT. And will it be a long treatment, doctor? I have a commitment with my fiancée and the family to get married this year. . . .
> PEDRO. In this life nothing is certain, but your chances of a cure through psychoanalysis are high.]

The suggestive dialogue between Pedro and his concerned patient can be seen as a parody of socialist ideologies that emphasized, with decidedly *machista* rhetoric, the importance of masculinity and the "rehabilitation" of sexual degenerates. This was, after all, the era of undying commitment to the formation the the Cuban "new man." As Marvin Leiner points out, such an individual was not only supposed to be "a person of high morals" but also "a strong and virile revolutionary," in contrast to the "'weak' homosexual."[23]

Certain elements of the conversation between Pedro and his patient suggest that the young man's real problem is his sexual inversion. According to Lumsden, most Cuban doctors and psychiatrists of the time considered homosexuality to be a sign of a mental disorder that required treatment.[24] Since a homosexual would have been considered by many experts to be physiologically "normal" but mentally unsound, this patient's inability to have intercourse with his fiancée can be interpreted as a symptom of a psychological "disease." In other words, Pedro interprets the patient's inability to achieve an erection in the presence of his betrothed as an unequivocal sign of both his sexual indifference toward women and his homosexuality.

The young man's insinuation that he, like Vicente and Emilia, is being pressured by others to get married within a certain time frame is also quite significant since it inspires Pedro to issue an ultimatum to Vicente just moments after the patient leaves his office: either he marries Emilia before the end of the year or Pedro will take his daughter away from him. Moreover, the patient's condition also inspires Pedro to address the subject of psychological impotence with Vicente, whose apparent disinterest in sex has led Pedro to suspect that he might suffer from a similar problem.

Pedro's manner of bringing up the issue calls attention to Piñera's implicit criticism of typical *machista* attitudes about women and sex in Cuba. When Vicente asks Pedro what is wrong with the young patient, Pedro offers the following response: "le pasa lo peor que puede ocurrirle a un hombre: hace seis meses que no puede acostarse con una mujer" (51). (He's experiencing the worst thing that can happen to a man: for six months he has not been able to sleep with a woman.) Pedro's comment is typical of a mentality that gives an exaggerated importance to sexual intercourse. According to his way of seeing things, any self-respecting man would not be able to tolerate a heterosexual relationship without lovemaking. It is this line of thinking, then, that leads him to assume that Vicente is a homosexual.

Such a possibility fills Pedro with fury, not only because he cannot tolerate homosexuality, but also because he is convinced that Vicente's alleged moral degeneration has infected his daughter. At the end of the second act Pedro finally decides to confront Vicente with his suspicions. What begins as a series of pointed questions concerning Vicente's sexuality—"¿Eres impotente?" (54) (Are you impotent?); "¿Estás seguro de ser un hombre en todo el sentido de la palabra?" (55) (Are you sure you are a man in every sense of the word?); "¿Estás seguro de que te gustan las mujeres?" (56) (Are you sure that you like women?)—turns into a blistering personal attack. When Vicente tries to evade the issue by insisting that he is the happiest man in the world, Pedro explodes with anger. His furious response, which brings on the heart attack that kills him, is surely one of the most politically and emotionally charged moments in Piñera's theater:

PEDRO. (*Gritando*) ¡Maricón! Eso eres, un maricón. (*Le va arriba y lo abofetea.*) Le has hecho creer a Emilia que el amor es pasar el tiempo sentado en un sillón; le has hecho creer que esa boca es sólo para hablar y comer; que esas manos (*las señala*) no han sido hechas para tocarla a ella, que eso que Dios te dio (*le señala el sexo*) es tan sólo un adorno. (*Pausa*.) ¡Pues se acabó! ¿Lo oyes? ¡Se acabó! Ahora mismo te vas. (*Gritando*.) ¡Fuera de aquí, fuera! (*Se desploma en la butaca y se aprieta el pecho con ambas manos*.) (60)

PEDRO. (*Screaming*.) Faggot! That's what you are, a faggot. (*He sets upon him and slaps him*.) You have made Emilia believe that love is spending time sitting in an armchair; that those hands (*he points to them*) weren't made to touch her, that that thing that God gave you (*he points to his sexual organ*) is merely an adornment. (*Pause*.) Well, it's over! Do you hear? It's over! Leave, right now. (*Screaming*.) Get out of here, out! (*He collapses in the armchair and grasps his chest with both hands*.)]

When we consider the fact that *El no* was written in the midst of a period during which so many homosexuals were, in a manner of speaking, systematically "booted out" of society by being carted off to the UMAP or publicly maligned by government leaders, Pedro's condemnation of Vicente is loaded with symbolism. Most importantly, the oppressive atmosphere of the scene underscores Piñera's own sense of insecurity during those trying times when homosexuality was seen as a problem that needed to be stamped out. But Pedro's tirade also suggests the author's criticism of the prevailing belief that homosexuals were infecting Cuban society and that they needed to be either reformed or removed.

Through this and other similar scenes in *El no*, Piñera derided prevalent attitudes in Cuba that homosexuals and other "eccentric" individuals were incapable of being true revolutionaries. In 1965, Fidel Castro himself declared in an interview with Lee Lockwood that the government "would never come to believe that a homosexual could embody the conditions and requirements of conduct that would enable us to consider him a true Revolutionary, a true Communist militant."[25] Likewise, the attitude of the Cuban writer Samuel Feijoó was typical of that of many Cubans who felt that the revolution was essentially a masculine undertaking and therefore unsuited for homosexuals. In an editorial in the Cuban daily *El Mundo* in April 1965 Feijoó insisted that "No homosexual represents the Revolution, which is a matter for men; of fists and not of feathers; of courage, not trembling."[26] In *El no* Pedro's sudden death, which is brought about by his anger and his intense homophobia represents a form of poetic justice, and Piñera's message rings clear: hatred and intolerance eventually lead to one's downfall.

The typical *machista* devaluation of women is also a target of censure in the play. Pedro's patronizing conviction that Vicente's homosexuality has turned his daughter into something of an asexual dimwit who is incapable of figuring things out for herself is certainly illustrative of this point. In addition to seeing Emilia as an object that he controls, Pedro clearly implies that Emilia is helpless without the guidance of a "real man" and that her supposedly innate submissiveness has made her easy to manipulate and beguile.

Piñera is careful to intimate that men are not totally to blame for the *machista* mentality that tends to devalue femininity in Cuba. Indeed, the attitudes of the women in the play serve to perpetuate many of the damaging stereotypes that he condemns. According to Laura's way of seeing things, for instance, marriage is precisely what legitimates a woman's role in society. "Una mujer no es una mujer hasta no estar debajo de un hombre" (66) (A woman is not a woman until she is under the control of a man), she tells her husband. Likewise, the *vieja* also perpetuates the image of the submissive, compliant woman.

> VIEJA. . . . (*Avanza hacia Emilia.*) Usted es algo peor que una mujer mala; por lo menos la mujer mala dice "sí" y ya sabe lo que hace, se acuesta, ¿me entiende?, se acuesta. Pero usted dice "no," usted ni se acuesta ni tiene hijos. (*Pausa.*) (108)
>
> [OLD LADY. . . . (*She advances toward Emilia.*) You are worse than a whore; at least the whore says "yes" and you already know what she does, she has sex, do you understand?, she has sex. But you say "no," you don't have sex or have children. (*Pause.*)]

Once again we see here how traditional values are often governed by contradictory standards. According to the *vieja*'s skewed way of seeing things, Emilia is worse than a whore since she has spent her whole life saying no to men and refusing to submit to them.

Emilia's parents and the group of neighbors reflect in many ways the stringent ideological framework of the Cuban government during the early years of the Revolution, and their narrow-minded and inconsistent convictions imbue the work with its asphyxiating quality. The final scene of the play, during which the hombre announces the group's intention to force Vicente and Emilia to change their ways, is important in terms of Piñera's criticism of such attitudes. The authoritarian approach of the neighborhood group parodies that of the Cuban government and official organizations such as the CDR whose determination to "clean up" Cuban society created an oppressive atmosphere that filled supposed nonconformists with paranoia.

> HOMBRE: . . . Y vamos a ver si ustedes o nosotros tenemos la última palabra. En adelante vendremos a esta misma hora a decirles a ustedes dos: "Emilia y Vicente, es hora de casarse. Manos a la obra."
> . . . .

Volveremos mañana a la misma hora. Y seguiremos volviendo hasta que ustedes digan Sí.
EMILA Y VICENTE. ¡NO!
HOMBRE. (*Caminando hacia la puerta*.) Decir no ahora, es fácil; veremos dentro de un mes. (*Pausa*.) Además; a medida que la negativa se multiplique, haremos más extensas las visitas. Llegaremos a pasar las noches con ustedes, y es probable, de ustedes depende, que nos instalemos definitivamente en esta casa. (*Sale, seguido por el auditorio*.) (121–22)

[MAN. . . . And we'll see if you or we have the last word. From now on we will come at this very hour and say to the two of you: "Emilia and Vicente, it's time to get married. Get to work!"
. . . .
We will come tomorrow at the same time. And we will keep coming until you say "yes."
EMILIA and VICENTE. NO!
MAN. (*Walking toward the door*.) Saying no now is easy; a month from now, we'll see. (*Pause*.) Furthermore, as the refusals multiply, we will make more extensive visits. We will end up spending the night with you, and it is likely, it depends on you two, that we will settle down definitively in this house. (*He leaves, followed by the audience*.)]

It is significant that at the end of the play a private, family matter has become an issue of public concern. Whereas Pedro and Laura's resolve to convince their daughter to get married is at least comprehensible when considered in light of the strong tradition of the Cuban family, the persistence of the neighbors seems absurd, and is symbolic of the individual's loss of autonomy in a totalitarian state.

Vicente and Emilia's decision to commit suicide by asphyxiation is highly symbolic, since by doing so they effectively defeat their oppressors at their own suffocating game. Like so many frustrated lovers in the annals of world literature, Emilia and Vicente end up with the sweetest revenge against those who have tried so hard to impose their will upon them: they take their own lives before their enemies can. The couple's suicide is especially significant because it implies that death is the only feasible way out of certain types of oppression, a theme that is developed much further in Piñera's next great play, *Dos viejos pánicos* (1968).

Vicente and Emilia are convinced that the ever-increasing vigilance from those who are opposed to their unconventional lifestyle will make their existence unbearable. Therefore, always the rebels, they choose to determine their own fates instead of allowing others to continue to judge and manipulate them. Their defiance is emblematic of Piñera's own refusal to embrace the Cuban government's ever-increasing ideological and moral rigidity. *El no* represents Piñera's rejection of the stifling social, cultural, and political environment in Cuba, but it is also a testament to his fear of the regime's growing control over individual behavior. As the play suggests, by the time Piñera wrote it, escaping from the ever-watchful eye of officialdom had become quite difficult.

It is not surprising that the play was not published during Piñera's lifetime. Its condemnation of the intolerance and oppression in Cuba would have met with government disapproval and would likely have caused further problems for Piñera, whose own situation was quickly deteriorating. Incredibly, though, three years after writing *El no* Piñera managed to publish, thanks to an international jury, a dramatic work whose denunciation of certain aspects of life in contemporary Cuba eventually lead to an official ban of his writings. While it is true that in *Dos viejos pánicos* Piñera treats universal themes such as fear and death, he ties them to his own life circumstances and to those of many other Cuban intellectuals who also felt a sense of panic and paranoia in the midst of a system that dramatically increased its control over them.

Dos viejos pánicos: A Personal Testament of Fear

After a visit with Virgilio Piñera in Cuba in 1967, the Spanish writer Juan Goytisolo remarked that "signs of a life of panic and distress were quite visible" in the Cuban author, who he said looked and acted like a man on the run.[27] By the time of Goytisolo's visit Piñera had become increasingly afraid of becoming a victim of one of the frequent government roundups of homosexuals and other supposed nonconformists who were being imprisoned or sent to camps around the island to be reformed through work and education. Piñera's fears were actually quite well founded since he was by that time viewed by the government as a troublemaker and a defiant provocateur. His influence in the Cuban cultural scene had been greatly limited by the mid-1960s and his publications had become less frequent. Because his activities and writings were being scrutinized more carefully, for example, in 1967 copies of his novel *Presiones y diamantes* were confiscated by government authorities when it was brought to their attention that the name of the novel's "protagonist," Delphi, a once precious diamond that had lost its value, could be read as a play on the name "Fidel."

It may seem inconceivable that, despite Piñera's status as persona non grata, his play *Dos viejos pánicos* was awarded the prestigious Casa de las Américas Prize in 1968. It is important to point out, however, as Mario Novoa has observed, that the award had nothing to do with government flexibility or freedom of expression in Cuba.[28] Rather, *Dos viejos pánicos* won the award largely because four of the five members of the jury for the drama prize that year were foreign supporters of the Revolution who chose to interpret the work from a universal perspective and therefore failed to see many of the play's implicit denunciations of specific circumstances in Cuba.[29] In his assessment of the play, which was printed on the dust jacket of the Cuban edition, the Uruguayan Hiber Conteris underscored the play's great literary merit by comparing it to the works of Eugene Ionesco, Samuel Beckett, Edward Albee, and Harold Pinter. He stressed, among other things, the play's skillful treatment of important universal themes such as "the myth of the eternal return," "the terror of senility," or the plight of a lost generation "that can't find a way to recuperate its sense of history."

Notwithstanding the jury's positive appraisal of the play and their opinion that its aging, panicky protagonists represented a fitting contrast to the invigorating atmosphere of revolutionary Cuba, *Dos viejos pánicos* ended up causing problems for Piñera. Shortly after its publication the play was deemed counterrevolutionary, and despite its great international success (or perhaps precisely because of it), its performance was forbidden in Havana during Piñera's lifetime.[30] In fact, the play did not premiere in Cuba until 1990. However, the international attention that the play received represented a rare victory for the author whose literary voice would soon be officially silenced by the Cuban government.

In addition to being Piñera's best-known play, *Dos viejos pánicos* is also one of his finest. It is important to point out that while it can be seen as a work patterned after the European theater of the absurd, as many critics have noted, it is not simply a play about the illogical and purposeless nature of human existence. Indeed, so much attention has been paid to the play's treatment of universal themes—"man's lonely, confined existence, his alienation and non-communication with his fellow men," "man's dependence on games," and "the anguish and helplessness of modern man in attempting to impose a rational order upon an incomprehensible world," for example—that its intimate relationship to Piñera's own circumstance and to the increasingly repressive climate in revolutionary Cuba have often been cast into the shadows.[31]

As much as *Dos viejos pánicos* expresses many of the main themes and concerns of the theater of the absurd, it is also a very personal work that deals with a number of uniquely Cuban circumstances. The *planilla* (questionnaire), for instance, whose invasive and ludicrous personal questions fill the two protagonists with fear, has been offered by many as an example of the play's absurdity. However, members of the CDR and other government organizations, which aimed to obtain intimate personal information from suspected nonconformists or counterrevolutionaries, handed out similar questionnaires and surveys in large numbers. Many of the forms asked questions of a similar ilk of those on the *planilla* in the play, and they often exposed the oppressive measures taken by the government to control the activities of Cuban citizens.

❧

Dos viejos pánicos fits well into the present chapter's discussion of the unconventional relationships in Virgilio Piñera's works. The play's aging protagonists, Tabo and Tota, are among the most intriguing of Piñera's creations, and their singular relationship stands out even among those that we have analyzed thus far. Tabo and Tota are both sixty years old, but their crotchety behavior and their physical frailty make them seem much older. Their present state offers a marked contrast to their youthful years when the two were carefree and sexually liberated individuals. As we learn early in the play, Tota was once an attractive, sexually desirable prostitute, while Tabo worked as a flashy pimp who was known by his street name, "El Lindo" (Mr. Good-Looking). In their advanced age, however, only memories remain of those happier times. They both suffer from numerous physical infirmities and live in constant fear. One of the most significant details that we learn about their relationship is that their decision to wed during middle age was not motivated by love, but rather by fear that their unconventional lifestyles might lead to problems with government authorities.

In this regard, *Dos viejos pánicos* deals with issues that were relevant during the mid-1960s in postrevolutionary Cuba. Despite many critics' suggestions that the play is typical of the theater of the absurd for its exploration of universal themes such as fear and death, Tabo and Tota's unique relationship and the paranoia that binds them can also be tied directly to a Cuban reality. As Marvin Leiner has pointed out, one of the Revolution's principal goals was to rid Havana of decadence and immorality. As the Cuban government began to embrace Marxism-Leninism, which has a long history of promoting puritanism and social rigidity, "Not only was the corruption of prostitution condemned," but also notions of sexual freedom or relationships that "endangered the traditional family."[32] Tabo and Tota's claim that they married out of fear is plausible, then, given that pimps and prostitutes were typically seen as nonconformists who required reeducation or rehabilitation in order to fit into Cuba's evolving socialist society.

At the beginning of the second act of the play Tabo and Tota are confronted with a concrete manifestation of the increasing government involvement in the private affairs of the citizenry. The *planilla* that they are required to fill out reflects the government's concerted efforts to reform certain members of the population. The first reference to the anxiety that the document has instilled in the distressed protagonists comes when Tabo blames his wife's aggravated bowels on her fear of answering the questions on the form:

> TABO. ... ¿Cuántas veces has ido hoy al inodoro?
> TOTA. ¡No me digas nada! ¡Ocho! Parece que el pescado de ayer me cayó mal.
> TABO. ¿El pescado...? Diría más bien que lo que te ha caído mal es la Planilla.... Mañana viene el hombre de la planilla y eso te tiene del coro al caño ... (43–44)[33]

> [TABO. ... How many times have you gone to the toilet today?
> TOTA. Don't even mention it! Eight! It seems that yesterday's fish disagreed with me.
> TABO. The fish...? I would say, rather, that what disagreed with you was the questionnaire.... Tomorrow the man with the questionnaire is coming and he has you on edge ...]

Though Tabo's comments are laced with the grotesque humor found in so many of Piñera's works, intestinal distress is a common indication of emotional anguish. Incidentally, Tabo's fear is also represented in part by his own inability to control his bodily functions, as Tota points out: "Al menos, yo todavía no me orino, pero tú, un reguero, viejito, un reguero ..." (31–32) (At least I still don't wet myself, but you, a mess, old man, a mess...). While it is true that Tabo's prostate problem can also be seen as sign of his old age, his habit of wetting himself, much like Tota's intestinal discord, is an unmistakable sign of his constant state of panic.

The *planilla* is especially important in that it calls attention to the intensifying government awareness of the individual's private existence in the 1960s. Tabo and Tota realize, for example, after reading the five questions on the document, that the officials—like the neighbors in *El no*—know almost everything about their past and present lives together. Furthermore, they suspect that their marriage has not served to free them from the prying eyes of the authorities, but rather to arouse their suspicion:

> TABO. ... [E]sa planilla se las trae ... ¿La has leído?
> TOTA. Mil veces y cada vez que vuelvo a leerla me da más miedo.
> . . . .
> TABO. (*Lee*.) La primera [pregunta] dice así: "Si no se hubiera casado con el hombre que se casó, ¿con cuál le hubiera gustado casarse?"
> TOTA. ¿Tú crees que esa pregunta tiene filo?
> TABO. ¡Vaya si lo tiene! Esa gente de la oficina de preguntas sabe mucho; para mí es que ellos conocen nuestro caso. (44–45)

[TABO. . . . That questionnaire is really tricky . . . Have you read it?
TOTA. A thousand times, and every time I reread it, it scares me more.
. . . .
TABO. (*Reads*.) The first [question] reads as follows: "If you hadn't married the man you married, with whom would you have liked to get married?"
TOTA. Do you think that's a trick question?
TABO. Of course it is! Those people at the office of questions know a lot; to me it seems like they know our case.]

After reading the first question Tabo fears that the administrators of the forms (in Cuba in the 1960s such questionnaires were usually handled by the CDR) have figured out that the couple's matrimony is simply a guise intended to save them from suspicion and from the possible consequences of their past behavior. The second question, which asks if the couple has married out of fear, confirms the couple's concern that they have not fooled the officials, and its frightening accuracy leads Tabo to conclude that those who formulated the questions already know the answers: "contestan por ti. . . . Ya te dije que la respuesta de cada pregunta está en la pregunta siguiente" (46–47)[34] (they answer for you. . . . I already told you that the response to each question is in the following question).

Tabo's observation is noteworthy because it reminds us that, on the one hand, in a totalitarian system individual freedoms and opinions are displaced by those of the state. On the other hand, given that only certain answers to official interrogation are acceptable, such systems effectively turn people into liars and deceivers. As Tota puts it, "El miedo ayuda a mentir. . . . ¡Qué par de mentirosos somos!" (36) (Fear helps you lie. . . . What a pair of liars we are!). Despite her acknowledgment that lying is at times necessary, however, Tota also emphasizes that she and Tabo need to be truthful to each other when they are alone. Tota's attitude underscores her perception of a need for at least some measure of sincerity in a society in which lying has become a way of life for those who live in fear of being accused of wrongdoing. In Tabo and Tota's case, marriage itself becomes a form of deception since they hope it will minimize the likelihood of being punished.

It is interesting to point out that while in *El no* Vicente and Emilia choose to be true to their desires by defying authority through their rejection of matrimony, Tabo and Tota choose to take a very different route. In both cases, however, the couples end up being defeated by the oppressive tactics of their adversaries. The invasive interrogation from the representatives of officialdom underscores how rigid expectations lead to the destruction of individuality. Vicente and Emilia, for example, are grilled in person about their unconventional engagement by an organized group of neighbors who expect them to change their ways, while Tabo and Tota are forced to explain and justify their relationship in writing on an official government document.

The fear and paranoia that are brought on by invasive questioning and similar violations of individual privacy are emphasized in both plays by a tangibly stifling atmosphere and by explicit references to suffocation. In *El no*, the stuffy space of Emilia's home—there is no mention of doors or windows—provides an atmosphere of enclosure and stagnation, and the couple's suicide by asphyxiation also adds to the suffocating air that permeates the play. The environment of *Dos viejos pánicos* is also stifling. The only tangible contact that Tabo and Tota have with an external reality is the *planilla*, which is itself a major contributor to the play's asphyxiating atmosphere. Moreover, though Tabo and Tota don't actually commit suicide like Vicente and Emilia do, they temporarily escape from their overwhelming fear through violent games during which they pretend to strangle and smother each other with pillows.

The rationale behind their singular games is that by feigning death they can at least temporarily free themselves from their frightful reality and from the possible repercussions of their allegedly morally reprehensible activities as pimp and prostitute. But Tabo and Tota see other advantages to being "dead." They can, for example, say and do whatever they want without fearing punishment. Their games, however, are an imperfect antidote to their lives of panic since by taking part in them they merely change the perspective from which they dwell on their fear. Interestingly, while they often pretend to kill each other by strangulation and suffocation, Tabo and Tota resort to a similar tactic to "kill" their fear. Despite their best efforts, however, their greatest enemy actually ends up smothering them:

> TOTA. Figúrate tú . . . Si te cuento el cuento del hombre que se murió de miedo te cagas en los pantalones; cuando tratas de matar tu miedo, él te mete más miedo en el cuerpo . . .
> . . . .
> Convéncete: nunca lograremos matarlo. . . . Total, nos agitamos, perdemos el resuello, me expongo a morir asfixiada, el azúcar me sube, a ti la presión te sofoca, la respiración te falta, y él cada vez más vivo. (54–55)

> [TOTA. Just imagine . . . If I tell you the story of the man who died of fear you'll shit your pants; when you try to kill your fear, it puts more fear in your body . . .
> . . . .
> Convince yourself: we'll never manage to kill it. . . . In short, we get worked up, we lose our breath, I run the risk of dying of asphyxiation,

my blood sugar runs high, your blood pressure suffocates you, you get short of breath, and it is more alive with each turn.]

Tota's conviction that it will be impossible to kill their fear echoes Vicente's declaration that he and Emilia will never manage to escape the prying eyes of their neighbors. In both plays an air of futility characterizes the protagonists' efforts to combat the forces that try to make them change. At the same time, however, the two couples are surprisingly persistent in their fights.

With characteristic perseverance Tota, despite her doubts, agrees to join Tabo in an elaborate game during which they will assail an imaginary personification of their fear. In the elaborate exorcism they pretend to tie the "victim" to a bed, after which Tabo smashes a pillow against the imaginary figure's face. At the same time Tota, making believe that she is the incarnation of fear, gasps for breath and cries out for mercy. However, just when Tabo declares that they have succeeded, a cone of light appears on the stage and begins to skip around it. Tabo and Tota recognize the light as another manifestation of their fear. In a state of panic they try to grab it and then attempt to smother it with the pillow. But, as if to indicate that fear has total control over them, the beam splits and focuses on their chests. Tabo suggests that they snuff out the beams by embracing each other, but the lights, mirroring the protagonists' growing fright, simply increase in size and eventually cover the protagonists and their surroundings. Terrified, Tabo and Tota can do little but admit their powerlessness against their omnipresent yet elusive adversary:

> TOTA. El miedo es así; tú lo ves por aquí y aparece por allá, tú lo quieres coger y se va entre las manos, tu lo quieres matar y él te mata.
> TABO. Y se va haciendo más grande, más grande . . .
> TOTA. Más grande, más grande.
> TABO. Y se infla.
> TOTA. Y se agiganta.
> TABO. Y engorda.
> TOTA. Y asfixia.
> TABO. Y ahoga.
> TOTA. Y sofoca.
> TABO Y TOTA. Y mata. (64–65)

> [TOTA. That's how fear is; you see it here and it appears over there, you want to snatch it and it escapes from your hands, you want to kill it and it kills you.
> TABO. And it keeps getting bigger, and bigger . . .
> TOTA. Bigger and bigger.

TABO. And it inflates.
TOTA. And it becomes huge.
TABO. And it gets fat.
TOTA. And it asphyxiates.
TABO. And it smothers.
TOTA. And it suffocates.
TABO Y TOTA. And it kills.]

As they speak the cone of light grows steadily, so that by the time they shout together it covers the entire stage. Once again, fear gets the best of them, and it becomes painfully clear that further attempts to evade or capture it will also be futile. As their words suggests, Tabo and Tota come to realize that their games and mutual exorcisms have only served to make their fear more powerful. Severino João Albuquerque is correct to point out that of the two Tota is particularly aware of the importance of game playing as a strategy of avoiding fear.[35] However, Tota is also more realistic than her husband and she is thus more inclined to acknowledge that their games will not change things for the better. While Tabo expects the games to help diminish their fear, for example, Tota is careful to remind him that he is dreaming: "¿Y tú crees que podemos decir: miedo, vete y el miedo se va?" (66) (And you think that we can say: fear, go, and fear will leave?).

Likewise, after playing another game the following evening, during which they pretend to regress to infancy, Tota once again cuts the game short by literally shoving her husband back into reality:

TOTA. Vuelve a tu materia. Mírate: hueso y pellejo. (*Con ternura.*) Vamos, Tabito, acuéstate. (*Lo lleva a la cama, lo acuesta, le canta.*) Duérmete cretino, duérmete mi horror, duérmete pedazo de mi corazón. (*Tarareando va a su cama, se acuesta.*) (75–76)

[TOTA. Return to your senses. Look at yourself: skin and bones. (*Tenderly.*) Come on, Tabo, go to bed. (*She takes him to bed, she lays him down, she sings to him.*) Go to sleep fool, go to sleep my dread, go to sleep piece of my heart. (*Humming she goes to bed, she lays down.*)]

Conjugal Aggression, Mutual Dependence

Tota's tenderness in the scene cited above is something of an anomaly in a play in which aggression and violence are the norms. Throughout the play Tabo and Tota's interaction is marked by their tendency to assail each other with verbal insults, emotional abuse, and threats of physical violence. At the same time, however, they both admit in their own way that they are mutually dependent on each other for survival. Their conflictive behavior can be explained by the fact that years of paranoia and panic have made them increasingly tense, and their claustrophobic existence has turned them both into victims of their partner's pent-up anxieties. When looked at in the context of their stressful existence Tabo and Tota's antagonistic relationship is actually quite believable.

Tota inflicts emotional distress on her husband in a number of ways, but she is especially fond of calling attention to his fragile state of health and threatening to make him look at himself in a mirror. These tactics are particularly effective since Tabo, who spends much of his time dreaming of his youthful vigor as a handsome pimp, is deeply distressed by his rapid physical decline. Tabo's favorite pastime—cutting out figures of youths from magazines and tearing them up or burning them— symbolizes his unwillingness to accept his aging. When the play opens Tabo, who is cutting out figures, refuses to play a game with Tota. Piqued by her husband's defiant attitude, Tota instinctively resorts to verbal abuse to convince him to take part in the game. "Tabo, dos infartos, un principio de hemiplejía, un edema pulmonar, sesenta años. Todo eso deja huellas. (*Pausa.*) Vamos a jugar" (13). (Tabo, two heart attacks, early stage of stroke, pulmonary edema, sixty years old. All of that leaves its mark. (*Pause.*) Let's play.)

Tota's cruel verbal attack is meant to remind Tabo of his physical decadence and to scare him into taking part in the game. But Tabo does not give in easily. He continues to cut out the figures from the magazine until Tota pulls out a mirror and thrusts it in his face:

TABO. ¿Qué quieres ahora?
TOTA. Que te mires en el espejo.
. . . .
TABO. Estoy muy viejo para mirarme, me da miedo. Tú sabes que cuando me conociste me decían El Lindo. Y ahora, Tota, ahora . . .
TOTA. Déjate de sentimentalismos baratos; ahora eres horroroso y si no juegas al juego te obligaré a mirarte en el espejo. (18–19)

[TABO. What do you want now?
TOTA. That you look at yourself in the mirror.
. . . .
TABO. I'm too old to look at myself, it scares me. You know that when you met me they called me Mr. Good-Looking. And now, Tota, now . . .
TOTA. Enough of the cheap sentimentalism; now you're horrendous and if you don't play the game I'll make you look at yourself in the mirror.]

Tabo's fear of his own reflection is highly symbolic as it underscores his unwillingness to accept the fact that he is closer to death than he wants to be. At the same time, Tabo's intense anxiety over his rapid aging and his conflictive attitude toward youth—embodied in his destruction of photos of children and his constant recollection of his youthful days as a handsome pimp—suggest his reluctance to accept his present reality.

When Tota finally pulls her husband's hands away from his eyes and forces him to look at his reflection, Tabo responds with verbal threats that mirror his wife's aggression: "Puta vieja, te voy a estrangular" (20) (Old whore, I'm going to strangle you). Upon hearing the word "puta" Tota is not so much insulted, however, as she is overwhelmed by nostalgia since it makes her recall her days as a prostitute when she was young and sexually desirable. Unlike her husband, however, Tota does not deny her state of physical decline. Rather she cleverly turns it into a sort of weapon of provocation. Since she is not afraid to acknowledge bodily ailments, for example, she makes light of them in order to underscore the fact that her husband is worse off then she is.

Tota is usually the aggressor in the couple's altercations, but Tabo does manage to exploit his wife's soft spots on occasion. In the second act, for example, Tabo employs his wife's tactic of bringing up a subject that he dreads. He frightens Tota by reminding her that she must hand in her *planilla* to the authorities or risk certain punishment (48). In the same way that Tabo sees a concrete manifestation of his anxiety in the mirror, Tota's deepest fears are reflected in the *planilla*. While Tabo dreads looking at his physical reflection, then, Tota is loath to acknowledge the sheet of paper that contains so many of her most intimate secrets. Tabo's deliberate attempts to both provoke and trivialize Tota's fear of the *planilla* and the *planillero* serve to stir up her anger. With characteristic fury Tota resorts to slander, intimidation, and physical violence—much as Tabo had done when forced to look at the mirror—to insure that her husband doesn't actually follow through with his plans to make her confront the government representative. The situation spins out of control as they bandy insults and threats:

> TOTA. . . . Así que redactando planillas para meterme miedo. Pues voy a hacértelas comer. . . . ¡Hijo de perra!
> TABO. (*Forcejea.*) Puta mala, puta vieja, te voy a estrangular. (*Le echa las manos al cuello.*) . . . Así que me rompo la cabeza descifrando tu planilla y me pagas con esto. Eres peor que una rata de cloaca. Pero te voy a estrangular. (*Le aprieta el cuello.*) . . .
> TOTA. (*Echa las manos al cuello de Tabo.*) ¡Hipócrita! Lo que tu quieres es que me muera de verdad. ¡Imbécil! . . . (49)

> [TOTA. . . . So you're drawing up questionnaires to fill me with fear. Well, I'm going to make you eat them. . . . Son of a bitch!

TABO. (*He struggles with her.*) Nasty bitch, old whore, I'm going to strangle you. (*He puts his hands around her neck.*) . . . So it is that I rack my brains deciphering your questionnaire and you pay me with this. You are worse than a sewer rat. I tell you, I'm going to strangle you. (*He squeezes her neck.*) . . .
TOTA. (*She puts her hands around Tabo's neck.*) Hypocrite! You really do want me to die. Imbecile! . . .]

The frequent altercations between Tabo and Tota are not simply meant to represent conjugal discord. They also serve to reflect the fact that their lives are controlled by the fear and anxiety that keep them constantly on edge. Moreover, their most heated disputes arise when one or the other is being coerced to do something that he/she does not want to do. Tota's declaration of a cruel and manipulative ultimatum — play my way or pay the consequences — when Tabo refuses to take part in her game is illustrative of this point. When Tota resists filling out the *planilla*, Tabo threatens her in a similar manner by reminding her that if she doesn't do as she is told, she will have to settle the score with the *planillero* himself.

On a symbolic level, the couple's reliance on such threats is especially reminiscent of the typical approach of totalitarian regimes, which tend to be most oppressive for those citizens who resist taking part in the game, so to speak. This notion of conformity through game playing is a central leitmotif of Heberto Padilla's infamous book, *Fuera del juego*, also published in 1968. The title poem of that text was condemned by the government for suggesting that those who don't follow all of the rules of the "game" in a totalitarian regime end up becoming enemies of the state.

Notwithstanding the play's violent atmosphere and the protagonists' aggressive treatment of one another, Tabo and Tota are both plainly aware that their companionship is indispensable to their survival. Even in their violent interactions the couple's mutual dependence is apparent. If for nothing else, Tabo and Tota need each other to carry out their death games and their complicated exorcisms of fear, without which their existence would be unbearable. And even though their companionship is imperfect, it sets them apart from so many of Piñera's characters who face and suffer their fears and anxieties by themselves.

Together Tabo and Tota pretend to kill each other, but they can't bear the notion of living alone. Tota's reaction when Tabo suggests that she is trying to kill him by showing him the mirror underscores this idea: "Claro que no quiero que Tabo se muera, si se muera, Tota se queda sola, y sola se aburre" (14) (Of course I don't want Tabo to die, if he dies, Tota will be alone, and she'll get bored alone). Correspondingly, when Tabo plays dead in order to repay his wife for making him look in the mirror, Tota is stricken with dread at the thought of being left alone (29). Tabo is also well aware that his life would mean nothing without Tota. In a rare moment of tenderness, he expresses his appreciation for his longtime companion: "Mi Tota, mi Totica, qué hubiera sido mi vida sin ti?" (50) (My Tota, my Totica, what would my life have been like without you?). Moreover, Tabo's fear and paranoia have led him to see his wife as a guardian of sorts. One night before they go to bed, for example, Tabo implores Tota not to leave him alone in the dark, and he begs her to promise that they will no longer have to endure their fear.

Tabo dreads being left alone in the dark because he is so afraid that he will never wake up if he falls asleep, and it is therefore especially significant that the final dialogue of the play takes place just as Tabo and Tota are turning in for the evening:

> TABO. Tota, ¿qué vamos a comer mañana?
> TOTA. Carne con miedo, mi amor, carne con miedo.
> TABO. ¿Otra vez? Ya no la resisto.
> TOTA. ¿No la resistes, de verdad que no? Pues, entonces comeremos miedo con carne. (*Pausa.*) Y ahora, duerme, mi amor. Hasta mañana.
> TABO. Hasta mañana. (*Pausa.*) Tota . . .
> TOTA. ¿Qué?
> TABO. ¿Mañana será otro día?
> TOTA. Sí, Tabo, otro día, otro día más . . .
> TABO. (*Suspira.*) Otro día más . . .
> TOTA. Y otra noche más . . .
> . . . .
> TABO. Y otra noche y otro día más . . .
> TOTA. Y otro día y otra noche más . . . (76)

> [TABO. Tota, what are we going to eat tomorrow?
> TOTA. Meat with fear my love, meat with fear.
> TABO. Again? I can't stand it anymore.
> TOTA. You can't stand it, really? Well, then, we'll eat fear with meat (*Pause.*) And now, sleep my love. See you tomorrow . . .
> TABO. See you tomorrow. (*Pause.*) Tota . . .
> TOTA. What?
> TABO. Will tomorrow be another day?
> TOTA. Yes, Tabo, another day, another day . . .
> TABO. (*Sighs.*) Another day . . .
> TOTA. And another night . . .
> . . . .
> TABO. And another night and another day . . .
> TOTA. And another day and another night . . .]

The couple's uncharacteristically tender exchange underscores the bond that unites two individuals who married not out of love, but out of need. Their final dialogue is especially significant in that it offers a notable contrast to their constant bickering and aggressive physical interplay. Like a frightened child Tabo, in particular, demonstrates his dependence on his wife. His naive questions underscore his longing for an added sense of security, which, given the couples' total isolation from the outside world, can only be afforded by her. Despite her best efforts to pacify her husband before he falls asleep, however, Tota's answers simply call attention to their bleak circumstances. The concluding lines of the play are largely pessimistic in that they suggest with an overwhelming air of resignation that things will never get better. It is clear, however, that at least Tabo and Tota will be together as they while away the monotonous and meaningless days and nights that lay before them.

In conclusion, the three plays studied in this chapter attest to the fact that the few heterosexual couples that populate Piñera's works are plagued with problems and destined to meet with an unhappy end. In many of his works Piñera used relationships between men and women as a means to convey his views of matrimony as a cheapened convention that had lost its spiritual meaning or as a social imperative that pressured men and women to wed for the wrong reasons. The wedding-day fiascos, canceled ceremonies, and unconventional, tension-filled relationships in *La boda*, *El no*, and *Dos viejos pánicos* also call attention to Piñera's desire to debunk traditional Cuban attitudes on sexuality, family, and marriage and to criticize the ideological rigidity that emerged in Cuba after the triumph of the Revolution.

In *La boda* Flora calls off her wedding to Alberto after overhearing him converse with the best man about her saggy breasts. The couple's ridiculous preoccupation with explaining the precise cause and nature of Alberto's blunder—instead of working toward resolving their differences and proceeding with their wedding ceremony—reflects the superficiality of their love. The sacrament of matrimony itself is presented as a senseless sacrament that has lost its spiritual meaning. In the play Piñera ridicules a number of issues related to love and marriage, from the *machista* devaluation of women to the shallowness of bourgeois values and social conventions, which lead people into hastily made commitments that they can't keep.

In *El no* Emilia and Vicente rebel against the conception of matrimony as a societal and familial obligation by refusing to get married. Because of their unconventional relationship they are maligned by their parents and by members of their community, who see them as nonconformist oddballs. The pressure from outside becomes so overwhelming that Laura and Vicente decide to commit suicide in order to defy the societal demands that they do not agree with. *El no* is one of Piñera's most politically charged works, and in it he parodies the moralistic rigidity of the revolutionary government and the ideological homogeneity that it demanded.

Tabo and Tota, the aging couple in *Dos viejos pánicos*, represent an anomaly in Piñera's literary production in that they have been married for twenty years. Their relationship, however, is problematic and anything but conventional. As we learn early in the play the two were moved by fear of official retribution to retire from their prosperous careers as pimp and prostitute. Upon realizing that their sexually liberated lifestyles no longer had a place in their morally rigid society and could therefore bring them unwanted troubles, Tabo and Tota decided to wed at the relatively advanced age of forty. Their marriage out of fear is emblematic of a growing sense of paranoia in Cuba in the 1960s, which often led individuals to speak and act insincerely in order to avoid suspicion and punishment.

Epilogue: The Death and Resurrection of an Iconoclast

Como he sido iconoclasta
me niego a que me hagan estatua;
si en la vida he sido carne
en la muerte no quiero ser mármol

[Since I've been an iconoclast
I refuse to let them make a statue of me;
if in life I have been flesh
in death I don't want to be marble]

—Virgilio Piñera, "Testamento"[1]

Aunque generalmente los escritores sólo mueren dos veces, primero cuando dejan de escribir, luego cuando abandonan este mundo (no tenemos noticias de que habiten en otro), también en este sentido Virgilio fue diferente.

[Though writers generally die only twice, first when they stop writing, and then when they abandon this world (we don't have news that they're inhabiting another one), in this sense Virgilio was also different.]

—Reinaldo Arenas, "La isla en peso con todas sus cucarachas"[2]

VIRGILIO PIÑERA'S DEATH ON OCTOBER 19, 1979, HAS BEEN THE SUBJECT of much speculation and has been turned into the stuff of legends by two of Cuba's most important literary figures. In an oft-cited article written in 1983, Reinaldo Arenas surmised, for example, that his friend and mentor died at the hands of members of the Seguridad del Estado, who had been known to harass the author in his later years.[3] Likewise, in his best-selling autobiography, *Antes que anochezca*, Arenas dismisses the official cause of death, a massive heart attack, and speculates that Piñera was snuffed out by government officials.

In a similar but somewhat less dramatic fashion, Guillermo Cabrera Infante observes in his essay "The Death of Virgilio" that Piñera's death of a heart attack seemed improbable for a man who was very lean (he erroneously claims that Piñera was a vegetarian) and had quit smoking years earlier. Though he does not go so far as to suggest that Cuban officials actually killed Virgilio Piñera, Cabrera Infante posits that the fear that the authorities had instilled in him during his final years was the ultimate cause of his untimely demise. "I'm afraid that fear killed him," Cabrera Infante alleges. "He was not a paranoid but he lived in Paranoia, a police state."[4]

In an interview in 1969 Piñera made a rather telling remark that reflected his fear of living under an increasingly repressive regime, and foreshadowed the dismal personal circumstances that he endured during the last decade of his life: "El peor de todos los miedos es el miedo de la vida misma. Es tan traumatizante que cambia al ser en pura cosa."[5] (The worst of all fears is the fear of life itself. It is so traumatizing that it turns a person into a sheer thing.) Though Piñera was ostensibly referring to the recent premier in Colombia of *Dos viejos pánicos*, the fact that the observation was made just before he virtually disappeared from the public eye in Cuba suggests that Piñera knew what was coming.

It is by now widely known that Virgilio Piñera spent his final years immersed in an anxiety-ridden period of official silence that he and a few of his friends often referred to as their "civil death" or "living death."[6] In a 1975 letter to Humberto Rodríguez Tomeu, Piñera summed up this notion of a so-called living death in the same pessimistic tone that dominates his correspondence from his later years: "estoy limitado a lo que se llama 'vida vegetativa' . . . En el famoso verso atribuído [*sic*] a Santa Teresa he definido lo que me resta de la vida: Vivo sin vivir en mi, y tan hondo abismo espero, que muero porque muero."[7] (I'm reduced to what they call "vegetative state" . . . In the famous verse attributed to Saint Teresa I have found the definition of the rest of my life: I live without feeling alive inside, and expect such a deep abyss that I die because I die.) In the span of just a couple of years in the 1960s Piñera had gone from an enthusiastic and active supporter of the Revolution who enjoyed wide recognition as a major writer and dramatist to a social pariah who was seen by the government as a provocative individualist and an author of counterrevolutionary works.

As we discussed in the first part of this book, Piñera's problems with the Cuban authorities and his gradual decline into oblivion began in 1961, when the author was just beginning to achieve the fame and recognition that had evaded him for so long. Several inauspicious events of that fateful year set into motion a downward spiral that would eventually bring the author from the climax of success and happiness to despair and near total obscurity.

In June 1961, during the now legendary series of meetings between government officials and Cuban intellectuals, which were brought to a close with Fidel Castro's infamous "Words to the Intellectuals," Virgilio Piñera stood up and expressed his fear in front of the crowd of intimidated writers and artists.[8] Though Piñera allegedly admitted to not knowing the exact cause of his fear, he clearly suspected by then that his own circumstances were likely to worsen considerably. Just four months after Castro's speech, Piñera was arrested for his supposed violation of revolutionary morality (he was accused of being a pederast), and shortly thereafter *Lunes de Revolución*, to which he had contributed scores of articles, editorials, and translations, was closed down in part because it was considered to be a haven for eccentrics and homosexuals. In subsequent years Piñera would undergo one disillusion after another; from missed opportunities to see the premieres of his plays abroad, to ill-fated translation deals for his major works, to his demotion from his prestigious position as director of Ediciones R to a lackluster and decidedly less visible position as assistant editor and translator for a Cuban publishing house. Sadly, most of Piñera's misfortunes during this trying era of his life were, at least to some extent, results of the government's mounting efforts to silence his voice and limit his influence among Cuba's increasingly restricted cultural circles.

A derisorily terse obituary published in the Havana newspaper *La Nación* on October 20, 1979, the day after Piñera's death, claimed that the author had been considered an enemy of the revolution since the publication in 1967 of his novel *Presiones y diamantes*, which government officials banned when attention was called to its supposed counterrevolutionary undertones. But it is clear that Piñera's pitiful fall from grace began long before the inauspicious banning of his third novel. After 1967, however, Piñera's situation began to deteriorate more rapidly. In 1968 his play *Dos viejos pánicos* was awarded the prestigious Casa de Las Américas Prize, which immediately turned it into the subject of international critical acclaim. But the play was deemed counterrevolutionary, and subsequently banned from the Cuban stage. It was not performed in Cuba until 1990.

In 1971 all of Piñera's works were officially censored in Cuba, a move that Arenas has referred to as the assassination of Piñera the writer.[9] Virgilio's books were pulled from bookstore and library shelves, his plays were no longer performed, he was not allowed to publish essays, reviews, and editorials in Cuban newspapers or literary journals, his name ceased to appear in literary dictionaries and anthologies, and he and his writings became forbidden subjects at literary conferences and in university classrooms.[10]

Despite the ban on his works and his official status as persona non grata, however, Piñera wrote tirelessly during the final years of his life. During the 1970s he penned numerous short stories, worked on several plays, and composed scores of poems, hoping against hope that they would be published in his native land during his lifetime. That, of course, did not happen. In fact, after the 1969 publication of Piñera's collected poetry, *La vida entera*, no book of his was published in Cuba for nearly two decades. Virgilio Piñera's death as an author, then, did not come about with his passing in 1979, but rather with an imposed silence that effectively ended a literary career and erased Piñera's name from the Cuban collective consciousness.

In an essay written shortly after Virgilio's death, Guillermo Cabrera Infante, who by that time had been living in exile in London for many years, insisted that despite the prohibition of Piñera's works in Cuba, his legacy would live on forever. He admitted, however, that he feared for the future of his vastly unique oeuvre:

> I am truly worried about what happens to his body of work. I know that he will soon be out of print in Cuba and never be printed again. What was left unpublished remained for a while in his furnished flat . . . All the papers found there—Virgilio's last literary will and theatrical testament—will be put in a cardboard box and buried in one of the secret sections in the basement of the State Security Building.[11]

Though Cabrera Infante's observations had something of a prophetic quality about them—Piñera's works did go out of print, for example, and government agents confiscated many of his papers—they thankfully turned out to be overly pessimistic. The official ban of Piñera's writings in Cuba was eventually lifted, and most of the papers and manuscripts that Cuban security agents had appropriated in 1979 were returned in due course to members of Piñera's family. The author and his works, after years in obscurity, were poised to emerge from the darkness.

The resurrection of the writer Virgilio Piñera was heralded in the first half of the 1980s by the appearance in Spain of several of his works— *Cuentos* (1983), *La carne de René* (1985), *Pequeñas maniobras / Presiones y diamantes* (1986)—which were published in Madrid by Ediciones Alfaguara.

But a real rebirth of one of twentieth-century Cuba's greatest literary figures could only take place in his homeland. Finally in 1987, eight years after Piñera's death and nearly two decades after the last publication of one of his books in Cuba, two new collections of short stories, *Muecas para escribientes* and *Un fogonzao*, were published in Havana. The following year, thanks to the work of Piñera's longtime friend Antón Arrufat, who painstakingly corrected and revised scores of original manuscripts, *Una broma colosal*, a book of poems that Piñera had composed during the final decade of his life, appeared in Havana bookstores.

By the summer of 1990, when an issue of *Unión*, a leading Cuban literary journal under the auspices of the Unión de Escritores y Artistas de Cuba (UNEAC), was dedicated to the long-forgotten author, Piñera's resurrection seemed to have turned into a conscientious undertaking. The brief essay that introduced the feature on Piñera began with the following comments that at once tacitly acknowledged the need to introduce the great Cuban author to a readership that had been denied access to his writings or forced to read them in secret, and attested to the fact that Piñera was back on the Cuban literary scene and there to stay.

> Virgilio Piñera tal vez sea entre nosotros el autor más ignorado, célebre y olvidado. Recientemente las editoriales Unión y Letras Cubanas han publicado títulos suyos donde se recogen cuentos y poemas que fueron hallados entre la papelería que el escritor dejó . . . a la hora de su muerte. Toda una generación de jóvenes lectores, preocupados por lo cubano en la literatura, buscan el teatro, los cuentos, las novelas, la poesía la labor crítica de este hombre.[12]

> [Virgilio Piñera is, perhaps, the most obscure, celebrated, and forgotten author among us. Recently the publishing houses Unión and Letras Cubanas have published books of his that collect stories and poems, which were found in the papers that the author left behind . . . at the time of his death. An entire generation of young readers, concerned with the Cuban elements in our literature, search for the theater, stories, novels poetry, and critical writing of this man.]

The decision of the official journal of the UNEAC, a government-sponsored organization that had denied membership to Piñera in his later years, to fill more than sixty pages with a variety of largely unpublished texts by Piñera (excerpts from his autobiography, poems, letters, essays) and numerous critical appraisals of his writings by prominent Cuban authors, clearly indicated that a concerted effort was being made in Cuba to resuscitate Piñera from his many years of silence and oblivion.

Signs of Piñera's definitive reemergence in his homeland continued to appear throughout the 1990s. The Cuban theater critic Rine Leal, for example, edited and published *Teatro inconcluso* (Unfinished Theater) in 1990, a compilation of seven dramatic works that Piñera had left unfinished and scattered among the eighteen boxes of manuscripts, notebooks, letters, and clippings that were found in his apartment after his death. Piñera also left behind three completed, full-length plays—*El no*,

Una caja de zapatos vacía (*An Empty Shoebox*), and *La niñita querida* (The Beloved Little Girl) — which were published, along with two shorter pieces, in 1993 under the title *Teatro inédito* (Unpublished Theater). In the same year a colloquium dedicated to Piñera and his works was organized in his hometown of Camagüey, and in 1995, forty-three years after its original publication in Buenos Aires, the first Cuban edition of Piñera's masterful first novel, *La carne de René*, hit the shelves of Havana bookstores. The edition of several thousand copies sold out within weeks, and it continues to be a highly sought-after title among the stalls of the daily book fair in Havana's Plaza de Armas. The first comprehensive collection of Piñera's poetry, *La isla en peso: Obra poética* (1998), was similarly popular among a new generation of readers who had finally come to see Virgilio for what he really was: a master of Cuban letters and a major player in their country's literary and intellectual history.

In the opening years of the twenty-first century Piñera's fame has continued to grow. His works are being reedited by major publishing houses in Cuba, Spain, and Latin America, more translations have been done of his major works, and scholarly studies of his writings have begun to appear with increasing frequency. In Havana, for example, two prize-winning studies of Piñera and his work have been published since the start of the new millennium. Likewise, the publication in Puerto Rico of *Virgilio Piñera: La memoria del cuerpo* (2002), a five-hundred-page compilation of essays by more than thirty critics from Cuba, Latin America, and the United States, has served to call attention to Piñera's ever-growing international stature as a major figure of twentieth-century Cuban and Latin American letters.

It seems fair to say that Piñera's audience is much larger and more diverse today than it ever was during his lifetime. More people are reading and studying his stories, novels, and poems, and his dramatic works continue to be staged in Cuba, Latin America, the United States, and Europe. But as I bring this study to a close, I cannot help but wonder how Virgilio Piñera's fate would have been different if he had taken Carlos Franqui's advice not to return to Cuba when the two met in Paris in 1964. According to Cabrera Infante, when Franqui suggested the idea of another period of exile to Virgilio, the latter "insisted that he wanted to go back to Cuba, that it didn't matter to him what could happen to him, that he could stand confinement, prison, the concentration camp — but not being far from Havana."[13] Cabrera Infante adds that the idea of permanent exile in a cold climate must have seemed like a rather unpalatable option for Piñera, who had spent so many years in Buenos Aires.

It is important to point out, though, that Virgilio had expressed to Cabrera Infante himself his great interest in serving as a cultural attaché in a European country, and he had, in fact, applied for such a position in Bern, Switzerland, the previous year. When he was rejected for the post in Bern, he suggested the possibility of taking Cabrera Infante's position in Brussels if the author of *Tres tristes tigres* were to be moved elsewhere. "Parece que mi nominación para Berna no se dará" (It seems that my nomination for the post in Bern won't happen), Piñera wrote in a letter to Cabrera Infante in 1963. "Pero si consiguieras el traslado para París, Roma o Londres, entonces aceptaría Bruselas."[14] (But if you consider the transfer to Paris, Rome, or London, then I would accept Brussels.) Several weeks later, Piñera expressed in another letter his dismay that the Cuban writer César Leante had been designated as the cultural attaché in Paris, suggesting that he had hoped to be assigned to the recently vacated post: "te hago enterado . . . de la designación de Leante como A. C. en París. ¡Chúpate esa! Casi no cabe en la boca . . . Je suis tombé des nuages. C'est a voir . . . , mon cher."[15] (I'm letting you know . . . about the designation of Leante as C. A. in Paris. Put that in your pipe and smoke it! It practically doesn't fit in your mouth . . . I've fallen from the clouds. We'll have to see. . . , my dear.)

It should be further pointed out, as I discussed in chapter 3, that Piñera explained in a letter to Humberto written from Madrid that he felt compelled to return to Cuba for two reasons. On the one hand, his sister Luisa had written him a letter in which she begged him to come back to help sort out problems with their ailing father. Piñera may have been pulled back to Cuba, then, more by a sense of familial obligation than by a lack of desire to stay in Europe. On the other hand, Piñera feared that if he opted for political exile—either in Europe or Argentina—he risked losing the translation deals that he had been working on in Europe for nearly two months. Since most of the major publishers there supported the revolution, he was convinced that they would have disapproved of such a decision.

During his trip to Europe in 1964 Piñera brokered a translation agreement and received an $800 advance from the prestigious Italian publisher Feltrinelli Editore for *Cuentos fríos*, *La carne de René*, *Teatro completo*, and *Pequeñas maniobras*. Likewise, through a connection with the Spanish author Juan Goytisolo, Piñera had begun negotiations with Éditions Gallimard and Éditions du Seuil for the publication rights to *Cuentos fríos* and *Pequeñas maniobras*. What is more, during his stay in Milan, an agent of the New York publishers Alfred A. Knopf, which by that time had published many translations by major Latin American writers, contacted Piñera through Feltrinelli, and expressed interest in having several of his books translated into English.[16]

Piñera was surely mindful of the fact that getting his books translated into major European languages would have represented a breakthrough in his career and would have likely done much to strengthen his reputation as a significant player in the world literary scene. But the mere possibility of seeing them published in English must have been especially exciting. It seems that when Piñera returned to Cuba in December 1964 he was relatively confident that his translations would go ahead as planned. However, once back on the island, following up on his translation deals became increasingly difficult, and most of them were either delayed several years or fell through altogether. Likewise, the options of going into exile or seeking an appointment as Cuban cultural attaché in a European country also became increasingly unrealistic as Piñera's personal circumstances deteriorated. Yet Virgilio Piñera surely could not have imagined upon his return in 1964 that he would never leave Cuba again.

With the passing of the years Piñera became something of a prisoner in his homeland given that his activities were tightly controlled and he was prohibited from leaving the country. The eerily prophetic line from "La isla en peso"—"Nadie puede salir, nadie puede salir!" (No one can escape, no one can escape!)—became a reality. I often ponder Piñera's precarious circumstance during his final years, and I imagine how things would have turned out had he gone into exile or sought political asylum when he had the chance. I wonder, for example, if such a move really would have ruined his translation arrangements, as he feared. If not, I cannot help but speculate how the translation of his most important works into French, Italian, and especially into English in the mid-1960s, when Latin American literature was raising eyebrows around the world, would have changed his status among world literary figures. If we consider how the 1962 English-language translation of *Ficciones* turned Borges, who was virtually unknown in this country until then, into an instant phenomenon in the United States and Britain, it seems quite possible that the appearance of Piñera's works in English in the 1960s could have had similar career-altering consequences for the Cuban author.

But even more importantly, I ask myself how the course of Latin American letters, indeed of world literature, might have been more profoundly altered by this great Cuban author if, on the one hand, his works—and especially his stories and plays—had been widely available in several European languages, and if, on the other, he had not spent his final years in almost total isolation and silence. But, to borrow the final line of one of Piñera's best-known stories, "it would be petty to ask any more such inopportune questions,"[17] since what really matters is not what could have been, but rather what will become of Piñera and his legacy in the twenty-first century.

Notes

Introduction

1. Virgilio Piñera, "Cada cosa en su lugar," *Lunes de Revolución*, 14 December 1959, 11.
2. Anonymous, "Virgilio, tal cual," *Unión* 3.10 (1990): 21.
3. Virgilio Piñera, *Cuentos completos* (Madrid: Alfaguara, 1999).
4. Enrico Mario Santí, "Carne y papel: El fantasma de Virgilio," *Vuelta* 18.208 (1994): 59.
5. Piñera, "Cada cosa en su lugar," 11.
6. Virgilio Piñera, "Las plumas respetuosas," *Revolución*, 13 July 1959, 17.

Chapter 1. Living on the Margins

1. Virgilio Piñera, "Piñera Teatral," in *Teatro completo* (Havana: Ediciones R, 1960), 28. All translations in this chapter are my own, unless otherwise noted.
2. Virgilio Piñera, "La vida, tal cual," *Unión* 3.10 (1990): 23.
3. Roberto Pérez León, *Virgilio Piñera: Vitalidad de una paradoja* (Caracas: CELCIT, 2002), 155. This study includes lengthy, previously unpublished sections of Piñera's autobiography. Portions of Piñera's memoirs have been published in several sources. See the section titled "Published Autobiography Fragments" in the bibliography.
4. Quoted in Pérez Leon, *Vitalidad*, 159.
5. Piñera disavowed *Clamor en el penal* and another early play, *En esa helada zona* [*In That Frozen Zone*] (1943), shortly after writing them. Neither play has been published, but the original manuscript of *Clamor en el penal* was photo-reproduced for a special number of *Albur* (3.5: [1990]: 86–124), which includes several of Piñera's unpublished manuscripts.
6. The text of Piñera's application is reproduced in *Unión* 3.10 (1990): 74.
7. Piñera, "Las plumas," 17.
8. Virgilio Piñera, "Mis 25 años de vida literaria," *Revolución*, 3 February 1961, 3.
9. Virgilio Piñera, "Terribilia Meditans I," *Poeta* 1 (1942): 1.
10. Lezama's responses to the survey questions are reprinted in *José Lezama Lima: Imágen y posibilidad*, ed. Ciro Bianchi Ross (Havana: Letras Cubanas, 1981), 66–71.
11. Arcadio Díaz Quiñones, *Cintio Vitier: La memoria integradora* (San Juan: Sin Nombre, 1987), 92–93. Italics in the original.
12. Alessandra Riccio, "La revista *Orígenes* y otras revistas lezamianas," *Annali* 25.1 (1983): 343.
13. For a complete history of *Verbum* and Lezama's subsequent editorial endeavors see Alessandra Riccio's excellent article "La revista *Orígenes* y otras revistas lezamia-

nas," and Marcelo Uribe's introduction to *Orígenes: Revista de arte y literatura: Edición Facsimilar*, ix–lxx (Madrid: Ediciones Turner, 1989).

14. Piñera, "Cada cosa," 11.

15. Virgilio Piñera, "Cartas a José Lezama Lima," in *Fascinación de la memoria: Textos inéditos de José Lezama Lima*, ed. Iván González Cruz (Havana: Letras Cubanas, 1993), 268–69.

16. Ben A. Heller, *Assimilation/Generation/Resurrection: Contrapuntal Readings in the Poetry of José Lezama Lima* (Lewisburg, Pa.: Bucknell Univ. Press, 1997), 32.

17. Ibid., 33.

18. For details on Vitier's conversion to Catholicism, see Enrique Saínz, *La obra poética de Cintio Vitier* (Havana: Unión, 1998), 56, 70, 156; Enrico Mario Santí, "Entrevista con el grupo Orígenes," in *Coloquio internacional sobre la obra de José Lezama Lima*, vol. 2, *Prosa* (Madrid: Fundamentos, 1984), 173; Díaz Quiñones, *Cintio Vitier*, 106.

19. Teresa Cristófani Barreto, Pablo Gianera, and Daniel Samoilovich, "Dossier de Virgilio Piñera: Cronología," *Diario de Poesía* 51 (Spring 1999): 11.

20. It is worth noting that in the second paragraph of the letter Piñera was clearly referring to Gaztelu when he made reference to "the serpent" whose advice (that is, to choose Gaztelu as codirector of *Espuela*) Lezama had foolishly taken. If we take into consideration this image of Gaztelu as a serpent, a subsequent comment in the letter— "son los triunfos de la serpiente de última hora: del maiqueo a la moda" [they are the triumphs of the eleventh hour serpent: of the fashionable Manichaean]—strongly implies that Gaztelu is the so-called Manichaean.

21. According to my reading, Piñera is referring here to Lezama, Mariano Rodríguez, and Gaztelu, respectively.

22. Piñera, "Cartas a José Lezama Lima," 29 May 1941, 270.

23. Heller, *Assimilation*, 33.

24. It should also be noted that in many of his works—*Electra Garrigó* (1941), "El País del Arte" (1947), *Jesús* (1948), *La carne de René* (1952), and *Pequeñas maniobras* (1963), for example—Piñera explicitly ridiculed and poked fun at Catholicism and Christianity.

25. Marcelo Uribe, introduction to *Orígenes*, xx.

26. Piñera, "Cartas a José Lezama Lima," 29 May 1941, 269–70. This is an obvious allusion to Lezama's asthma, which caused him to breathe heavily. Lezama's labored breathing is clearly audible in the extant recordings of his poetry readings. See, for example, the following cassette: *José Lezama Lima: La muerte de Narciso*, Palabra de Nuestra América, Casa de las Américas, 1996.

27. José Prats Sariol refers to a deep wound, inflicted by Piñera, that led to the demise of *Espuela de Plata* in 1942. He further suggests that the same wound reopened in 1953, and thus played an important role in the downfall of the *Orígenes* group. Prats Sariol accuses Piñera of "belligerence," "acidity," "malevolence," and "virulence," but he fails to spell out his alleged central role in the demise of the two journals. While it can be argued that Piñera's provocations in 1941 were at least partially responsible for the demise of *Espuela*, it is not clear at all that his "belligerence and virulence" were to blame for the schism between Lezama and Rodríguez Feo in 1953–54. See José Prats Sariol, "La revista *Orígenes*," in *Coloquio Internacional sobre la obra de José Lezama Lima*, vol. 1, *Poesía* (Madrid: Fundamentos, 1984), 41, 52.

28. Uribe, introduction to *Orígenes*, xx.

29. The inaugural number of *Clavileño* lists the following individuals as members of its editorial board: Gastón Baquero, Cintio Vitier, Emilio Ballagas, Eliseo Diego, Justo Rodríguez Santos, Luis Ortega Sierra, Fina García Marruz, Bella García Marruz, and Ernesto González Puig. The title of the journal refers to the wooden horse upon which

Don Quixote and Sancho Panza take a fantastic flight through the air in Cervantes's masterpiece. The last two issues combined numbers 4/5 and 6/7.

30. Riccio, "La revista *Orígenes*," 347.

31. Piñera, "Las plumas respetuosas," 17.

32. Piñera, "Mis 25 años," 3.

33. Jorge Mañach, "Carta a Virgilio Piñera (21 December 1942)," reprinted in *La Gaceta de Cuba* 39.5 (2001): 3.

34. Piñera, "Cartas de Virgilio," 27 December 1942, 4.

35. Piñera, "Cartas a José Lezama Lima," no date, 273.

36. By 1943 Piñera had established himself as a major player in Cuba's intellectual scene. He had contributed poems and essays to several literary journals and published two slim volumes of poetry, a short story, and a pamphlet on the works of the great Cuban painter René Portocarrero. In the early 1940s Piñera began to dedicate more time and effort to drama and fiction, genres that would soon overshadow his poetic production. In 1941 he began work on *Electra Garrigó*, a groundbreaking play and a masterpiece of Cuban and Latin American drama. Piñera's first story, "El conflicto" [The Conflict], was published in March 1942 by Ediciones Espuela de Plata.

37. Virgilio Piñera, *La isla en peso: Obra poética* (Barcelona: Tusquets, 2000), 37. All quotations of Piñera's poetry are from this edition.

38. Ibid., 42.

39. It seems that Piñera's aspirations to live in exile may have been at least in part precipitated by his tensions with Lezama and the *Espuela de Plata* group. A comment made in a letter to Piñera (dated 5 November 1941) from the Spanish intellectual and philosopher María Zambrano suggests that Virgilio had written of his plans to move to Buenos Aires shortly after the notorious confrontation of May 1941: "Comprendo, sí, que quiera ir a la Argentina. Es ancha y hoy por hoy tiene vida intelectual" [Yes, I understand that you want to go to Argentina. It is open-minded and at the present has intellectual life]. See María Zambrano, "Carta a Virgilio Piñera (5 November 1941)." Reprinted in *albur* 3.5 (1990): 160.

40. The following verses typify the lexical coarseness of the poem that allegedly provoked the indignation of certain Cuban intellectuals: "los once mulatos fálicos murieron a la orilla de la playa" [the eleven phallic mulattos died at the edge of the beach], 38; "al compás de los himnos las doncellas agitan diestramente / los falos de los hombres" [to the rhythm of the hymns the maidens dexterously rub / the men's phalluses], 39; "la eterna historia de la cínica sonrisa del europeo / llegado para apretar las tetas de mi madre" [the eternal history of the cynical smile of the European / who has come to squeeze my mother's tits], 42; "el mediodía orinando hacia arriba, / orinando en el sentido inverso de la gran orinada / de Gargantúa en las torres de Notre Dame" [midday urinating upwards, / urinating in the opposite direction of the great urination / of Gargantua in the towers of Notre Dame], 47–48; "Una noche interrumpida por el europeo, / el inevitable personaje de paso que deja su cagada ilustre" [A night interrupted by the European / the inevitable celebrity who drops by and leaves his illustrious shit], 48.

41. Piñera, "Cada cosa," 12.

42. Piñera, quoted in Enrique Saínz, *La obra poética de Cintio Vitier* (Havana: Unión, 1998), 35.

43. Both letters have been reproduced in *La Gaceta de Cuba* 39.5 (2001): 5–6.

44. Article reprinted in Gastón Baquero, *Ensayos*, ed. Alfonso Ortega Carmona and Alfredo Pérez Alencart, (Salamanca: Fundación Central Hispano, 1995), 308–9.

45. Cintio Vitier, *Diez poetas cubanos* (Havana: Orígenes, 1948), 79.

46. Vitier's harshest appraisal of *La isla en peso* and its author appeared a decade later

in *Lo cubano en la poesía* (Havana: Universidad Central de las Villas, 1958), a collection of essays that Vitier had written for a poetry seminar that he conducted at the Havana Lyceum from October to December 1957. By the time Vitier penned the essays that make up this massive tome he and Piñera had had numerous literary spats and their relationship had become downright hostile. In a laughably brief section on Piñera's contribution to Cuban verse (just over four pages in the 500-page book), Vitier took his characteristically harsh appraisals of *La isla en peso* to a new level: "[convierte] a Cuba . . . en una caótica, telúrica y atroz Antilla cualquiera. . . . La vieja mirada de autoexotismo, regresiva siempre en nuestra poesía, prolifera aquí con el apoyo de un resentimiento cultural que no existió nunca en las dignas y libres trasmutaciones de lo cubano. Trópico de inocencia pervertida, *huit clos* insular radicalmente agnóstico, tierra sin infierno ni paraíso, en el sitio de la cultura se entronizan los rituales mágicos, y en lugar del conocimiento, el acto sexual. Pero ni siquiera los valores de la carnalidad sobreviven, porque los copuladores son imagines vacías, contornos de sombras" (407). [It turns Cuba . . . into any old chaotic, telluric, and atrocious Antillean island. . . . The old look of auto-exoticism, always regressive in our poetry, proliferates here with the backing of a cultural resentment that never existed in the dignified and free transmutations of what is Cuban. Tropics of perverted innocence, radically agnostic, insular *huit clos*, land without hell or heaven, in place of culture magic rituals are exalted, and in place of knowledge, the sexual act. But not even the values of carnality survive, because the copulaters are empty images, outlines of shadows.]

47. Rafael Rojas, "*Orígenes* and the Poetics of History," *New Centennial Review* 2.2 (2002): 177.
48. Guy Pérez Cisneros, "Presencia de 8 pintores," *Verbum* 1.1 (1937): 56–57.
49. Ibid., 60.
50. Ibid., 62.
51. Rojas, "*Orígenes*," 178.
52. Jorge Mañach, "Carta a José Lezama Lima (18 April 1938)," in *Fascinación de la memoria: Textos inéditos de José Lezama Lima*, ed. Iván González Cruz, (Havana: Letras Cubanas, 1993), 290.
53. Cintio Vitier, "El PEN Club y *Los diez poetas cubanos*," *Orígenes* 5.19 (1948): 42. In an essay written more than forty years later Vitier underscored with apparent pride the marginality of *Orígenes* by pointing out that one of the defining characteristics of the group was its deliberate separation not only from what he referred to as "las superficiales cabriolas del efímero y desvaído vanguardismo cubano" [the superficial pirouettes of the ephemeral and ill-defined Cuban avant-garde], but also from the so-called pure and social poetry that emerged from the impulse of the *Revista de Avance* generation. See Cintio Vitier, "La aventura de Orígenes," in *Para llegar a Orígenes* (Havana: Letras Cubanas, 1994), 66.
54. Lezama's letter to Mañach is reprinted in José Lezama Lima, *Imagen y posibilidad*, ed. Ciro Bianchi Ross (Havana: Letras Cubanas, 1981), 186. Mañach's letter originally appeared in *Bohemia* (39 [25 September 1949]: 37), and Lezama's response was published in the following issue of the same magazine (40 [2 October 1949]). See also the following texts related to the clash between the two groups: Jorge Mañach, "Reacciones a un diálogo literario (Algo más sobre poesía vieja y nueva)," *Bohemia* 42 (16 October 1949), and Cintio Vitier, "Jorge Mañach y nuestra poesía," *Diario de la Marina* (26 and 30 October 1949).
55. Lezama Lima, *Imagen*, 188–89.
56. Piñera, "Cartas de Virgilio," 19 March 1945, 6.
57. The editorial board of the first four issues included Lezama, José Rodríguez Feo, Mariano Rodríguez, and Alfredo Lozano. As of spring 1945, Lezama and Rodríguez Feo are listed as the journal's sole editors.

58. Piñera, "Cartas de Virgilio," 19 March 1945, 7.
59. Uribe, introduction to *Orígenes*, xxix.
60. In the essay Piñera specifically makes reference to *The Metamorphosis* (1915), which later served as a model for one of his best short stories, "Cómo viví y cómo morí" [How I Lived and How I Died] (1956), which was published in *Cuentos Fríos*.
61. Piñera's story "Unos cuantos niños" [A Few Children] (1957) is a case in point. The protagonist, much like the narrator of Swift's "A Modest Proposal," goes to great lengths to explain the benefits of eating babies.
62. Teresa Cristófani Barreto, *A libélula, a pitonisa: Revolução, homossexualismo e literatura em Virgílio Piñera* (São Paulo: Iluminuras, 1996), 120.
63. Cintio Vitier, "Virgilio Piñera: *Poesía y Prosa*, La Habana, 1944," *Orígenes* 2.5 (1945): 47.
64. Ibid., 49.
65. Ibid., 50.
66. Virgilio Piñera, "Aviso a los conformistas," *Revolución*, 22 September 1959, 2.
67. Many critics have pointed out that Piñera was not the only non-Catholic member of *Orígenes*. Indeed, Lorenzo García Vega was also an atheist, but he was nearly fifteen years younger than Piñera and did not become involved with the group until shortly before the latter left for Argentina. García Vega also became one of the most assiduous contributors to *Orígenes*, whereas Piñera's involvement in the journal was always quite limited. Moreover, though Cintio Vitier and Fina García Marruz did not convert to Catholicism until 1953, Vitier himself noted in a 1979 interview that from the beginning the Christian members of the group felt united by a common sense of religiosity. For a discussion of *Orígenes* and Catholicism see Enrico Mario Santí, "Entrevista," 172–73.

CHAPTER 2. FROM THE OUTSIDE LOOKING IN

1. Virgilio Piñera, "Las plumas respetuosas," *Revolución*, 13 July 1959, 17.
2. Advice from Witold Gombrowicz to Piñera concerning their need to avoid bowing to the influence of the members of the *Sur* group in Buenos Aires. Reprinted in Piñera's article "Gombrowicz en Argentina," *Cuadernos* 45 (1960): 61.
3. Piñera, "La vida, tal cual," *Unión* 3.10 (1990): 31.
4. Ibid., 25.
5. Piñera, "Poema para la poesía" [Poem for Poetry], *Papeles de Buenos Aires* (August 1944): 12.
6. Piñera, "Gombrowicz en Argentina," 61.
7. Humberto Rodríguez Tomeu, "'Épater le bourgeois': Piñera y Gombrowicz en Argentina," trans. Ernesto Hernández Bustos, *Biblioteca de México* 22 (July–August 1994): 44.
8. Piñera, "Gombrowicz por él mismo," in *Poesía y crítica*, by Piñera, ed. Antón Arrufat (México: Consejo Nacional para la Cultura y las Artes, 1994), 255–56.
9. Ibid., 243–44.
10. Ibid., 256.
11. See Enrico Mario Santí, "Carne y papel," 60.
12. Emir Rodríguez Monegal, *Jorge Luis Borges: A Literary Biography* (New York: Dutton, 1978), 236.
13. Ibid., 399.
14. Julio Cortázar, "Casa tomada," *Los Anales de Buenos Aires* 1.11 (1946): 13–18.
15. "El muñeco" was eventually published in Argentina in *Cuentos fríos* (1956) after Perón was deposed by a military coup.

16. The year 1946 was full of major professional and personal difficulties for Borges, as James Woodall points out in *Borges: A Life* (New York: Basic Books, 1996), 156. Just months after Perón's inauguration, Borges, who was an outspoken opponent of Perón, was fired from his job at the Miguel Cané Library, where he had worked since 1937. Though opinions among critics are mixed, Borges himself was convinced that his subsequent demotion to a post as a poultry and rabbit inspector at the Buenos Aires Municipal Market was arranged by Perón himself.

17. Woodall, *Borges: A Life*, 146.

18. Piñera, "Cartas a José Lezama Lima," 28 August 1946, 277.

19. Piñera, "Notas sobre literatura argentina de hoy," *Anales de Buenos Aires* 2.12 (1947): 52.

20. Ibid., 53.

21. Ibid., 55.

22. Piñera, "Cartas a José Lezama Lima," 28 August 1946, 276.

23. Piñera, "La vida, tal cual," 34.

24. It is interesting to note that in the final lines of "Razón que sea," the brief introductory editorial to the first number of *Espuela de Plata*, Lezama concluded with the following words: "Prepara la sopa, mientras tanto voy a pintar un ángel más." [Prepare the soup, meanwhile I'm going to paint another angel.] See *Espuela de Plata* A (August–September 1939): 1.

25. Rodríguez Tomeu, "Épater," 45.

26. Roberto Pérez León, who found a copy of "Aurora" among Piñera's papers, has convincingly laid to rest the theory that Piñera was not involved in the composition of the pamphlet. See his article "*Aurora y Victrola*," *Biblioteca de México* 22 (July–August 1994): 48.

27. Enrique Larreta (1873–1961), Argentine prose writer and dramatist. His masterpiece, *La gloria de don Ramiro* [*The Glory of Don Ramiro*] (1908), is widely considered to be one of the most outstanding and authentic novels of Spanish American *modernismo*; Arturo Capdevila (1889–1967), Argentine novelist, essayist, poet, and member of the *posmodernista* group. Capdevila allegedly criticized the translation of *Ferdydurke*.

28. Witold Gombrowicz, "Aurora: Revista de la Resistencia" (Buenos Aires: n.p., 1946), 1. Self-published pamphlet.

29. Piñera, "Gombrowicz por él mismo," 249–50.

30. Gombrowicz, quoted in Ernesto Hernández Bustos, "Los reyes del Rex: Piñera and Gombrowicz en Buenos Aires," *Biblioteca de México* 22 (July–August 1994): 43.

31. Gombrowicz, "Aurora," 3. Italics in the original.

32. Ibid.

33. Doris Meyer, *Victoria Ocampo: Against the Wind and the Tide* (New York: Braziller, 1979), 52.

34. Ibid., 51.

35. Gombrowicz, "Aurora," 3.

36. Rodríguez Monegal, *Jorge Luis Borges*, 236.

37. Borges, quoted in Rodríguez Monegal, *Jorge Luis Borges*, 236–37.

38. Rodríguez Tomeu, "Épater," 44.

39. Virgilio Piñera, "Victrola: Revista de la insistencia" (Buenos Aires: n.p., 1946), 1. Self-published pamphlet.

40. Ibid., 3.

41. In a letter to Lezama from November 1947, Piñera underscored his antagonism of the Argentine intelligentsia with apparent pride: "Te incluyo esas dos revistas, ataques a Sur y su grupo, a los poetas, a los connaisseurs, a los muy cultos, etc. Estamos dando la batalla." [I enclose these two reviews, attacks on Sur and its group, on poets,

on connoisseurs, on the very cultured, etc. We're waging war.] From Piñera, "Cartas a José Lezama Lima," 280.

42. Virgilio Piñera, "El país del Arte," *Orígenes* 4.16 (1947): 36.

43. Ibid.

44. Witold Gombrowicz, *Ferdydurke*, trans. Virgilio Piñera et al. (Buenos Aires: Argos, 1947), 83–84. All Spanish-language quotes are from this edition.

45. Gombrowicz, *Ferdydurke*, 2nd ed., trans. Eric Mosbacher (New York: Grove, 1961), 76–77. All English-language translations are from this edition.

46. Piñera, "El país del Arte," 37.

47. Virgilio Piñera, "El escritor Virgilio narra sus impresiones." Interview with Ernesto Ardura, *El mundo* [Havana], 1 February 1948, 12.

48. José Rodríguez Feo, *Mi correspondencia con Lezama Lima* (México: Era, 1991), 130.

49. Ibid.

50. Virgilio Piñera, "¡Ojo con el Crítico . . . !" *Prometeo* (November 1948): 3.

51. Piñera wrote most of his editorials in *Revolución* under the pseudonym "El Escriba," and he therefore often referred to himself in the third person. Items marked with an asterisk (*) in the bibliography are signed with Piñera's pen name.

52. Virgilio Piñera, "Un crítico que se las trae," *Revolución*, 13 August 1959, 9.

53. Carlos Espinosa-Domínguez, "El poder mágico de los bifes: La estancia argentina de Virgilio Piñera," *Cuadernos Hispanoamericanos* 471 (1989): 81.

54. *La carne de René* was Piñera's first published novel, but in 1946 he had already completed *El banalizador*, a novel that remains unpublished but is preserved among Piñera's papers. In December 1946 Piñera mentioned the novel in a letter to Lezama, and noted that it would be published in May 1947 by Editorial Argos. See "Cartas a José Lezama," 22 December 1946, 279.

55. In 1948 Piñera made several vain attempts to secure a teaching position at Columbia University in New York for the 1948–49 academic year. When his efforts failed, he decided that returning to Argentina was his only viable option. See Euginio Florit, "Carta a Virgilio Piñera (13 July 1948)," reprinted in *Albur* 3.5 (1990): 141.

56. Virgilio Piñera, "Cuba y la literatura," *Ciclón* 1.2 (1955): 51.

57. The original manuscript, which is discussed further in chapter 5, can be consulted in the Virgilio Piñera Collection in the Department of Rare Books and Manuscripts at Princeton University. See the bibliography for a complete listing. In an interview with Alejandro Rússovich, Pablo Gianera, who is careful to note the Cuban author's propensity to exaggerate the truth, notes that Piñera often mentioned his various sexual encounters in Buenos Aires. See Rússovich, "Piñera en persona," *Diario de Poesía* 51 (Spring 1999): 22.

58. *La carne de René* (Havana: Unión, 1995). The Havana edition is based on the second, revised edition of the novel (Madrid: Alfaguara, 1985), which Piñera worked on throughout the 1970s after a French publisher expressed interest in the novel.

59. Gombrowicz quoted in Carlos Espinosa-Domínguez, "Virgilio Piñera en persona," *Quimera* 98 (1989): 42.

60. The text of this anonymous review can be found in Barreto et al., 18.

61. Pérez León, *Vitalidad*, 171.

62. It is important to note that there are various contradictory accounts of the dispute. According to Rodríguez Feo, for example, Lezama had the article by Jiménez months before the former left for Spain but never consulted him about including it in *Orígenes*. Lezama, for his part, claimed in a letter to Jiménez written in April 1954 that Rodríguez Feo had indeed seen the article in question. See Pérez León, *Tiempo*, 72–73 and 143, respectively.

63. See Jorge Guillén, "Que van a dar en la mar," 58–61, and Luis Cernuda, "Retrato de poeta," 41–43. Both texts appear in *Orígenes* 10.33 (1953).

64. Juan Ramón Jiménez, "Crítica paralela," *Orígenes* 10.34 (1953): 4.

65. Ibid., 4–5.

66. Ibid., 9.

67. According to Lezama's own account, the following individuals pledged to stay with the original *Orígenes*: Ángel Gaztelu, Fina García Marruz, Cintio Vitier, Eliseo Diego, Lorenzo García Vega, Julián Orbón, and Octavio Smith. (See letter from Lezama to Juan Ramón Jiménez in Pérez León, *Tiempo*, 143.)

68. See the testimony of Mariano Rodríguez (80), José Antonio Portuondo (88), and Antón Arrufat (93) in Pérez León, *Tiempo de Ciclón*.

69. Efraín Rodríguez Santana, "Árbol bien plantado y suelto frente al cielo: La presencia de José Rodríguez Feo en *Orígenes*," *Unión* 7.18 (1995): 30.

70. See Pérez León, *Tiempo de Ciclón*, 204n82.

71. In a 1945 letter to Lezama Piñera used the term "ukases" to refer to Lezama's control over the editorial decisions at *Orígenes*. The same term, though spelled differently, is used in the editorial in *Ciclón*. "Como siempre ocurre" was one of Piñera's favorite catchphrases, which he used in many texts. See, for example, "La carne," "La cena," "En el insomnio."

72. José Rodríguez Feo and Virgilio Piñera, "Borrón y cuenta nueva," *Ciclón* 1.1 (1955): n. pag.

73. David Coward, ed., trans., introduction to *The Misfortunes of Virtue and Other Early Tales*, by the Marquis de Sade, 14th ed. (Oxford: Oxford Univ. Press, 1992), xxviii.

74. Sade's works were the subject of legal debate in France as late as 1957. In that year the critic Jean-Jacques Pauvert was prosecuted for editing a scholarly edition of the French author's collected works. As David Coward points out, it was not until 1983 that editions of Sade's works were officially allowed to be sold in England, and "publishers and booksellers continue to tread warily." See Coward, *The Misfortunes of Virtue*, xxv.

75. See David Coward, introduction, xxi–xxv.

76. Virgilio Piñera, in the introduction to "*Las 120 jornadas de Sodoma*, por el Marqués de Sade," *Ciclón* 1.1 (1955): 35.

77. Ibid.

78. Marquis de Sade, "Las 120 jornadas de Sodoma" (Introducción y discurso del Duque), trans. Humberto Rodríguez Tomeu, *Ciclón* 1.1 (1955): 40–41.

79. Marquis de Sade, *The 120 days of Sodom and Other Writings*, trans. Austryn Wainhouse and Richard Seaver (New York: Grove, 1999), 252–53.

80. Enrico Mario Santí, "Entrevista con el grupo Orígenes," in *Coloquio internacional sobre la obra de José Lezama Lima*, vol. 2, *Prosa* (Madrid: Fundamentos, 1984), 173.

81. Virgilio Piñera, "Cartas entre Virgilio Piñera y José Rodríguez Feo," reprinted in Pérez León, ed., *Tiempo*, 11 April 1955, 170.

82. It is important to recall that Piñera was living with Rodríguez Tomeu while he was working on his translation of Sade's book. He was surely involved at least tangentially in the project, and it left its mark on much of his subsequent writing.

83. Piñera, "Ballagas en persona," 41.

84. See Cintio Vitier, "La poesía de Emilio Ballagas," in *Obra poética de Emilio Ballagas*, ed. Vitier (Havana: Ucar, García y Cía, 1955), v–xli.

85. Piñera, "Ballagas en persona," 42. Italics in the original.

86. Ibid.

87. Santí, "Carne y papel," 61.

88. Piñera, "Ballagas en persona," 44.

89. Piñera met Julio Cortázar during a visit to Paris in July 1954. See "Letters to Humberto," 28 January 1963.

90. Bianco has incorrectly stated that he first met Piñera in 1956 (see Espinosa-Domínguez, "Virgilio Piñera en persona," 40).

91. José Bianco, "Piñera narrador," introduction to *El que vino a salvarme*, by Virgilio Piñera (Buenos Aires: Sudamericana, 1970).

92. Piñera's correspondence with Rodríguez Feo has been published in various sources. For complete information, see the section titled "Correspondence" in the bibliography.

93. Piñera, "Cartas entre," 25 March 1955, 168.

94. Ibid., 6 February 1956, 177.

95. Piñera, "Cartas a José Rodríguez Feo," 16 November 1955, reprinted in *La Gaceta de Cuba* 37.5 (1999): 3; Raymond Queneau (1903–76), French novelist, poet, comic, and critic. Queneau's article "Filósofos y vagos" [Philosophers and Lazy Men] appeared in *Ciclón* 1.4 (1955): 3–9; Robert Merle (1908–2004), eclectic French writer and scholar. A fragment from his critical study *Oscar Wilde ou la destineé de l'homosexuel* [*Oscar Wilde or the Destiny of the Homosexual*] (Paris: Gallimard, 1955) was translated by Julia Rodríguez Tomeu for the section "Revaluaciones" in *Ciclón* 1.3 (1955): 188–89; Julien Torma (1902–33), French essayist and critic. His essay "Euforismos," trans. Álvaro Rodríguez, appeared in *Ciclón* 1.6 (1955): 30–36; H. A. Murena (1924–75), Argentine essayist and critic.

96. Piñera, "Cartas entre," 16 March 1955, 166.

97. Woodall, *Borges: A Life*, 177.

98. Piñera, "Cartas entre," 16 March 1955, 165–66.

99. Ibid., 4 March 1955, 164–65.

100. In June Piñera returned to Cuba for a lengthy visit that had been paid for by Rodríguez Feo. He spent much of his time there working on future issues of *Ciclón* and writing his play *Los siervos*. Pepe had financed his return largely because he needed assistance in the organization of a publishing house that would be run under the auspices of the journal. The project fell through by the end of 1955.

101. Piñera, "Cartas entre," 3 January 1956, 173.

102. Ibid., 3 January 1956, 173.

103. Piñera, "Cartas entre," 9 January 1956, 174.

104. James Irby, quoted in Woodall, *Borges: A Life*, 197.

105. José Bianco, quoted in Rodríguez Monegal, *Jorge Luis Borges*, 285.

106. Piñera, "Cartas entre," 5 January 1956, 174.

107. Jorge Luis Borges, "Nota de un mal lector," *Ciclón* 2.1 (1956): 28.

108. Ibid., 28.

109. The military general and political moderate Eduardo Lonardi became president in September 1955 after Perón, who had been given an ultimatum to either leave the country or risk civil war, fled Argentina. The zealously anti-Peronist military grew impatient with Lonardi's conciliatory policies and his avoidance of vindictive measures against their foes. The severe measures that the military called for were not met, however, and they therefore deposed Lonardi and replaced him with General Pedro Aramburu in November 1955. See Skidmore and Smith, 92.

110. Piñera, "Cartas a José Rodríguez Feo," 16 November 1955, 3.

111. Ibid., 24 August 1956, 3.

112. When Rodríguez Feo announced the suspension of *Ciclón* in June 1957, the third number of the magazine for that year was already well under way. Likewise, the fourth number, which was to be dedicated to the German philosopher Martin Heidegger (1889–1976), was also in preparation.

113. *Electra*, under the direction of Francisco Morín, opened on Valentine's Day in the Teatro Prometeo and ran for several weeks. It was not a resounding success like it would be after the triumph of the Revolution, but it received more favorable criticism than it had after its ill-fated premiere in 1948. *Los siervos* premiered in the Teatro el Sótano in February 1958. The play was directed by Juan Guerra.

114. Espinosa-Domínguez, "El poder," 87.

115. Virgilio Piñera, "¿Por dónde anda lo cubano en el teatro?" *Lunes de Revolución*, 3 April 1961, 30.

116. Rine Leal, ed., "Piñera inconcluso," in *Teatro inconcluso*, by Virgilio Piñera (Havana: Unión, 1990), 9.

117. Piñera never submitted the novel to the Losada competition. In fact he continued to work on *Presiones y diamantes* until mid-1961. In 1964 he submitted the completed text to a contest run by the Spanish publisher Seix Barral. As he expressed in a letter to Humberto Rodríguez Tomeu, he had little confidence that the novel would win: "En Madrid presenté al concurso de la editorial Seix Barral (Premio Biblioteca Breve) mi novela Presiones y Diamantes. . . . No tengo grandes esperanzas." [In Madrid I submitted my novel Presiones y diamantes to the Editorial Seix Barral (Biblioteca Breve Prize) competition. . . . I don't have high hopes.] See "Letters to Humberto," 10 December 1964.

118. Piñera, "Cartas a José Rodríguez Feo," 22 April 1958, 5.

119. Ibid.

120. Piñera, "Cartas de Virgilio," 11 June 1958, 7.

Chapter 3. Disillusion to Revolution

1. Virgilio Piñera, "Letters to Antón Arrufat," 4 September 1958, in Antón Arrufat Collection, Manuscripts Division, Department of Rare Books and Special Collections, Princeton University Firestone Library.

2. Fidel Castro, "Palabras a los intelectuales" (30 June 1961), in *Política cultural de la Revolución Cubana: Documentos*, ed. Joaquín G. Santana, 5–47. Havana: Ciencias Sociales, 1977.

3. During the final months of 1958 Piñera also spent much of his time as a contributor and assistant editor for a Cuban magazine *Carteles*. The job was very unsatisfying for the number of reasons. In a letter to Humberto Rodríguez Tomeu, Piñera noted that he could hardly bear his co-workers, and he refered to his boss, Guillermo Cabrera Infante, as "la cumbre de vulgaridad, de suficiencia idiota" [the epitome of vulgarity, of idiotic self-importance]. In the same letter he complained that the pay was barely enough to make ends meet ("Cartas de Virgilio," 10 November 1958, 8).

4. Piñera, "Cartas de Virgilio," 11 June 1958, 7.

5. See Mariano Rodríguez's testimony in Pérez León, *Tiempo de Ciclón*, 80.

6. Piñera, "La inundación," *Ciclón* 4.1 (1959): 13.

7. Ibid., 14.

8. Raymond D. Souza, *Guillermo Cabrera Infante: Two Islands, Two Worlds* (Austin: Univ. of Texas Press, 1996), 37.

9. Antón Arrufat, "Un poco de Piñera," introduction to *Cuentos completos*, by Virgilio Piñera (Madrid: Alfaguara, 1999), 15. By January 1960 *Lunes*' circulation topped 100,000. See the editorial "Un saludo a voces" in *Lunes* (4 January 1960): 2. According to William Luis's "Exhuming *Lunes de Revolución*" (*New Centennial Review*, 2.2 [2002]: 254), by late 1961 its circulation was nearly 250,000, a figure that exceeded comparable pub-

lications such as the *New York Times Review of Books*. By the same date *Revolución* had a circulation of about 500,000.

10. See the section titled "Critical Essays, Editorials, Book Reviews" in the bibliography for a complete list of Piñera's publications in *Revolución* and *Lunes*. Pablo Armando Fernández, codirector of *Lunes*, insists that Piñera was made to use the pseudonym by Carlos Franqui, who was allegedly moved both by sexual prejudices and his concern about Piñera's numerous enemies in the literary community. Fernández cites Franqui's "obvious" homophobia in the film *Conducta impropia* as proof of his claim (see Espinosa-Domínguez, "Virgilio Piñera en persona," 43). But given the fact that everyone knew that the articles were written by Piñera, it seems that using a pseudonym would have done little to protect the newspaper from Piñera's detractors. It is interesting to add that Piñera's articles in *Lunes*, a literary supplement that was considered by many to be a haven for homosexuals, were almost always signed with his own name.

11. Piñera, "Nubes amenazadoras," *Revolución*, 15 January 1959, 4.
12. Ibid.
13. Piñera, "Balance cultural de seis meses," *Revolución*, 31 August 1959, 18.
14. Piñera, "El Teatro Nacional funciona," *Revolución*, 19 April 1960, 2.
15. Piñera, "Balance cultural," 18.
16. Piñera, "El arte hecho Revolución, la Revolución hecha arte," *Revolución*, 5 November 1959, 2.
17. Ibid., 2.
18. Piñera, "Espejismo de revistas," *Revolución*, 20 June 1959, 2.
19. Piñera, "La nueva revista cubana," *Revolución*, 27 June 1959, 2.
20. See, for example, "El baquerismo literario," 27 July 1959, 21–23, and "Un ataque que honra: La 'Marina' vs. 'Lunes'" [An Attack that Honors: '[Diario de] la Marina' vs. 'Lunes'], 12 May 1960, 2.
21. Piñera, "Las plumas," 17.
22. Padilla was not the only one to challenge "Veinte años atrás," as Piñera himself pointed out a week later in an editorial entitled "Más Miscelánea."
23. Heberto Padilla, "La poesía en su lugar," *Lunes de Revolución*, 7 December 1959, 5.
24. Piñera, "Cada cosa," 11.
25. Ibid.
26. Ibid. In the same article Piñera described Cintio Vitier as a "sempiterna ovejita" [perpetual little lamb].
27. See, for example, Raimundo Fernández Bonilla, "Respuesta al Escriba" [Response to the Scribe], *Revolución*, 29 September 1959: 2; Odilio González, "Todo al revés: Carta abierta a Guillermo Cabrera Infante" [Everything Mixed Up (Open Letter to Guillermo Cabrera Infante)], *Lunes de Revolución*, 19 October 1959, 5; and Imeldo Álvarez-García, "Carta a *Revolución*" [Letter to *Revolución*], *Revolución*, 28 September 1960, 2.
28. Piñera, "Mis 25 años," 8.
29. More than seventy-five letters that Piñera wrote to Humbeto Rodríguez Tomeu between 1959–78 can be consulted in the Virgilio Piñera Collection at the Princeton University Firestone Library, Manuscripts Division, Department of Rare Books and Special Collections. Hereafter, letters from this collection will be referenced as "Letters to Humberto." See the bibliography under "Correspondence" for complete information.
30. Piñera, "Letters to Humberto," 7 June 1961.
31. See "Letters to Humberto," 6 March 1961. Piñera's letters to Humberto chroni-

cle the frustrating publication history of *Teatro completo*, which at one point Piñera referred to as "el parto de los montes" [a real anticlimax] (ibid., 18 January 1961).

32. Piñera, "Letters to Humberto," 18 March 1960.
33. Ibid.
34. Ibid., 29 June 1960.
35. Barreto et al., "Dossier," 27.
36. In February 1960 a Soviet trade delegation came to Havana, and shortly thereafter another delegation visited Cuba from East Germany. The following month Castro signed a trade agreement with Poland and officially resumed diplomatic relations with the Soviets. See Louis A. Pérez Jr., *Cuba: Between Reform and Revolution*, 2nd ed. (Oxford: Oxford Univ. Press, 1995), 325.
37. See Hugh Thomas, *Cuba: The Pursuit of Freedom* (New York: Harper and Row, 1971), 1460; and Jan Rogozinski, *A Brief History of the Caribbean*, rev. ed. (New York: Facts on File, 2000), 236.
38. Lee Lockwood, *Castro's Cuba, Cuba's Fidel*, exp. ed. (Boulder, Colo.: Westwood, 1990), 247.
39. Ibid., 231.
40. Pérez, *Cuba*, 324.
41. Carlos Franqui, *Family Portrait with Fidel*, trans. Alfred MacAdam, (New York: Random House, 1981), 130.
42. Piñera, "Letters to Humberto," 29 April 1961.
43. Ibid., 23 February 1961.
44. I was fortunate to have the opportunity to view *P.M.* at a rare public showing of the film, which was attended by Orlando Jiménez Leal, in Washinton, D.C., in 1997.
45. Michael Chanan, *The Cuban Image* (Bloomington: Univ. of Indiana Press, 1985), 150.
46. Guillermo Cabrera Infante, *Mea Cuba*, trans. Guillermo Cabrera Infante and Kenneth Hall (New York: Farrar, 1994), 52.
47. See William Luis, "Exhuming," 263–66, for more details on the incidents surrounding the banning of *P.M.*
48. Souza, *Guillermo Cabrera Infante*, 39–40.
49. Cabrera Infante, *Mea Cuba*, 68. Matías Montes Huidobro relates a similar version of the events, though he insists that it was Castro himself who invited the authors and intellectuals to speak. See *Persona, vida y máscara en el teatro cubano* (Miami: Universal, 1973), 433.
50. Piñera, "Mis 25 años," 3.
51. Fidel Castro, "Palabras a los intelectuales," 9.
52. Ibid., 11.
53. Ibid., 17.
54. Rogozinski, *A Brief History*, 239.
55. Piñera, "Literatura y Revolución," *Revolución*, 18 June 1959, 2.
56. Piñera, "Un ataque que honra," 2.
57. Ian Lumsden, *Machos, Maricones, and Gays: Cuba and Homosexuality* (Philadelphia: Temple Univ. Press, 1996), 59.
58. Marvin Leiner, *Sexual Politics in Cuba: Machismo, Homosexuality and AIDS* (Boulder, Colo.: Westview, 1994), 25.
59. Franqui, *Family Portrait*, 139.
60. Piñera, "Letters to Humberto," 23 October 1961.
61. Ibid., 15 February 1962.
62. See the bibliography under "Translations by Virgilio Piñera" for a list of Piñera's translations for the Editorial Nacional.

63. Piñera, *Teatro completo*, 30.
64. Piñera, "Letters to Humberto," 13 December 1962.
65. Ibid., 28 January 1963.
66. Nicolás Guillén was the director of the UNEAC at the time.
67. Piñera, "Letters to Humberto," 2 October 1963.
68. Most of the arrangements that Piñera made in Europe eventually fell through. To the best of my knowledge, more than twenty years passed before any of his works were published in Italy. Translation arrangements with Alfred A. Knopf in New York also failed to materialize.
69. In *Mea Cuba* Cabrera Infante erroneously cites 1965 as the date of the meeting. Piñera had returned to Cuba by December 1964.
70. Cabrera Infante, *Mea Cuba*, 355–56.
71. Piñera, "Letters to Humberto," 26 October 1964.
72. Leiner, *Sexual Politics*, 28.
73. Juan Goytisolo, *Realms of Strife: The Memoirs of Juan Goytisolo, 1957–1982*, trans. Peter Bush (San Francisco: North Point, 1990), 141–42.
74. The following passages taken from "Letters to Humberto" encapsulate Piñera's increasingly pessimistic morale in the mid-1960s: "Bueno, con estos 51, que Dios mediante cumpliré en agosto, casi no tengo ánimos para nada.... Soy como un caballo que aun con algunas fuerzas para seguir tirando del carro, se niega a la marcha." [Well, with these 51 years, that with God's help I will attain in August, I barely have energy for anything.... I'm like a horse that with some strength left to keep pulling the cart, refuses to keep going.] (16 July 1963); "Ahora me he dado por llorar, y me pongo como idiota." [Now I am given to crying, and I turn into an idiot.] (2 October 1963); "te confieso que me cuesta trabajo escribirte. Ya he perdido las esperanzas de reunirnos, entonces me digo: para qué seguir escribiendo. Achaca todo esto a la depresión que experimento. No olvides que este año cumplo 53 ... todo lo que hago es resistir, y nada más." [I confess that it takes great effort for me to write to you. I have already lost the hope of reuniting, and I say to myself: why keep writing. Blame all this on the depression that I am going through. Don't forget that this year I turn 53 ... all that I do is struggle, nothing more.] (8 May 1965); "Todas las ilusiones, los proyectos, los planes han desaparecido y sólo quedan los días, los días y tan sólo eso." [All the illusions, the projects, the plans have disappeared, and all that remains are the days, the days and only that.] (10 August 1965); "Pues aquí estoy más viejo y más triste, y cada vez más estupefacto con todo lo vivido." [Well, here I am older and sadder, and ever more astonished with all I have endured.] (18 July 1967).
75. Lumsden, *Machos*, 65.
76. *Dos viejos pánicos* premiered in Bogotá in 1969 to rave reviews. In 1970 it opened in Mexico City and Madrid and met with similar success.
77. The jury was made up of three Cuban authors—José Lezama Lima, José Zacarías Tallet, and Manuel Díaz Mártinez—and two foreigners, J. M. Cohen (Great Britain) and César Calvo (Peru).
78. Cohen's observations appear in his introduction to *Sent off the Field*, by Heberto Padilla (London: Andre Deutch, 1972), 12.
79. Cohen, *Sent off the Field*, 13.
80. "An Open Letter to Fidel Castro," in *The New York Times Review of Books* 16.8 (May 1971), 1. Text accessed via the Internet March 15, 2005 at http://www.nybooks.com/articles/10580.
81. Maurice Halperin, "Culture and the Revolution," in *The New Cuba: Paradoxes and Potentials*, ed. Ronald Radosh (New York: Morrow, 1976), 207.
82. Ibid., 209.

83. Fidel Castro, "At the Closing of the First National Congress on Education and Culture," *Granma* (English-language ed.), 9 May 1971, 8.

84. "Declaration by the First National Congress on Education and Culture," *Granma* (English language ed.), 9 May 1971, 5.

85. Reinaldo Arenas, "La isla en peso con todas sus cucarachas," *Mariel* 2 (1983): 22.

86. See Arrufat's article, "La muerte en vida," for a fascinating discussion of Piñera's participation in these secret meetings throughout the 1970s.

87. According to Arrufat, after years of silence between the two men Piñera, moved by his reading of *Paradiso*, called Lezama to discuss his impressions of the great novel. From that day on they were back on friendly terms. See Pérez León, *Tiempo*, 95.

88. Reinaldo Arenas, *Antes que anochezca* (Barcelona: Tusquets, 1992), 112.

89. In *Los años de Orígenes* (Caracas: Monte Ávila, 1979), Lorenzo García Vega pointed out that Lezama had purposely chosen to publish the least controversial pages of *Paradiso* in *Orígenes* (See *Orígenes*, 6.22 [1949]: 16–23; 6.23 [1949]: 18–26; 9.31 [1952]: 47–62; 9.32 [1952]: 75–97; 12.39 [1955]: 33–55). He added that Lezama was well aware that publishing what the former refers to as "los capítulos más escabrosos" [the most scabrous chapters], would have scandalized the more conservative members of the group. García Vega also notes, as many critics have, that Lezama waited until after his mother died to publish the novel (see *Los años*, 69). It is also worth adding that in a 1979 interview with Enrico Mario Santí, Cintio Vitier deliberately distanced himself from Lezama's novel. When asked to what extent *Paradiso* and its sequel, *Opiano Licario*, reflected the endeavor of *Orígenes*, Vitier offered the following answer: "Yo creo que . . . son libros estrictamente personales. A mi juicio, no representan un resultado de la gestión de *Orígenes*" [I believe that . . . they are strictly personal books. In my judgment, they do not represent a result of the endeavor of *Orígenes*]. See Santí, "Entrevista," 185.

90. Piñera, *La isla en peso: Obra poética*, 214.

91. Piñera, "Letters to Humberto," 15 November 1976.

92. Arrufat, "Un poco," 21–22.

93. Piñera, "Cartas de Virgilio," 5 July 1976, 9.

94. Barreto et al., "Dossier," 35.

95. Heberto Padilla, "Virgilio Piñera, el invisible," *Linden Lane Magazine* 4 (1982): 18.

96. Guillermo Cabrera Infante, "The Death of Virgilio," in the introduction to *Cold Tales*, by Virgilio Piñera, trans. Mark Schafer (New York: Eridanos, 1988), xiii–xiv.

97. See Reinaldo Arenas, "La isla en peso con todas sus cucarachas," and *Antes que anochezca*, 293–96.

98. *Granma*, 20 October 1979, 5.

99. Barreto et al., "Dossier," 35.

CHAPTER 4. TALES OF ABSURD HOPE

1. Albert Camus, *The Myth of Sisyphus and Other Essays*, transl. Justin O'Brien (New York: Vintage, 1983), 103.

2. Witold Gombrowicz quoted in Carlos Espinosa-Domínguez, "Virgilio Piñera en persona," 42.

3. The only English-language collection of Piñera's short fiction, *Cold Tales*, includes forty-three of the nearly one hundred stories that Piñera wrote between 1942 and 1979. Since the publication of *Cold Tales*, additional stories by Piñera have appeared

in anthologies in the United States. The recent Spanish edition of Piñera's *Cuentos completos* (Madrid: Alfaguara, 1999) consists of seventy-three stories, some of which were found among Piñera's papers. Well over a dozen of Piñera's stories have still not been published in any language. See the bibliography for a complete list of short story collections and translations.

4. See Frank McQuade, "Making Sense Out of Nonsense: Virgilio Piñera and the Short Story of the Absurd," in *After Cervantes: A Celebration of 75 Years of Iberian Studies at Leeds*, ed. John Macklin (Leeds: Trinity and All Saints, 1993); Read Grant Gilgen, "Virgilio Piñera and the Short Story of the Absurd," *Hispania* 63 (1980): 348–55; Carlos Narváez, "Lo fantástico en cuatro cuentos de Virgilio Piñera," *Románica* 13 (1976): 77–86; Ewald Weizdörfer, "El unicornio de Virgilio Piñera: Lo neofantástico cortazariano en algunos cuentos del autor cubano," *Letras del Deusto* 20.46 (1990): 151–64; Ana García Chichester, "Metamorphosis in Two Short Stories of the Fantastic by Virgilio Piñera and Felisberto Hernández," *Studies in Short Fiction* 31.3 (1994): 385–95; and Dolores M. Koch, "Virgilio Piñera y el neo-barroco," *Hispanérica* 13.37 (1984): 81–86. Three of Piñera's stories were published under the general title "Goyesques" in *Les Temps Modernes* 13.140 (1957): 619–23.

5. It is not my intention to take up such a task, but I find it fitting to point out here some of the common themes and narrative techniques that have led more than one critic to refer to Piñera as the "Kafka of the Caribbean." In terms of their general worldviews, for example, both authors tended to focus on the problematic existence of modern man. Indeed, many of their works depict marginalized, anxiety-ridden characters who are inexorably trapped in a universe governed by absurdity and paradox. The narrative techniques employed by Piñera also reveal at times his debt to Kafka. Like the Czech author, Piñera was a master of relating bizarre situations with incongruous coldness and surprising lucidity. Frank McQuade has pointed out that Kafka's influence is also apparent in Piñera's tendency to write pithy tales (several of his stories are less than a page in length), to depict nightmarish settings and circumstances, and to present outlandish resolutions to terrifying predicaments. See "Making Sense," 212. José Bianco, one of Piñera's most astute critics, downplayed Kafka's influence on Piñera by calling attention to the fact that the sarcastic, capricious humor that permeates Piñera's work sets it apart from the more austere tone of Kafka's writing. See Bianco, "Piñera narrador," 17. Piñera's essay "El secreto de Kafka" (1945) is especially enlightening in terms of his own perception of the common ground that he shared with the Czech author. Though Piñera implicitly acknowledges his profound respect for Kafka and his writing, he also intimates that his debt to him is less a product of direct influence than of a common quest for new modes of expression and an affinity for what Piñera called "la sorpresa literaria" [literary surprise].

6. For comparisons to Cortázar see Weitzdörfer, "El unicornio"; Gilgen "Virgilio Piñera"; and Antonio Fernández-Ferrer, "El 'disparate claro' en Cortázar y Piñera," *Revista Iberoamericana* 58.159 (1992): 423–36. The following two works examine Piñera's connections with Hernández: García Chichester, "Metamorphosis," and Reinaldo Laddaga, *Literaturas indigentes y placeres bajos: Felisberto Hernández, Virgilio Piñera, Juan Rodolfo Wilcock* (Buenos Aires: Beatriz Viterbo, 2000).

7. Cabrera Infante, "The Death of Virgilio," xiv.

8. Piñera, "Piñera teatral," in *Teatro Completo*, by Piñera, 8–9. (Havana: Ediciones R, 1960) 8–9.

9. See Gilgen, "Virgilio Piñera"; López-Ramírez, "Virgilio Piñera y el compromiso del absurdo," *Areito* 9.34 (1983): 38–40"; Carmen L. Torres, *La cuentística de Virgilio Piñera: Estrategias humorísticas* (Madrid: Pliegos, 1989); McQuade, "Making Sense"; and García Chichester, "Codifying Homosexuality as Grotesque: The Writings of Virgilio

Piñera," in *Bodies and Biases: Sexualities in Hispanic Cultures and Literature*, ed. David William Foster and Roberto Reis, 294–315 (Minneapolis: Univ. of Minnesota Press, 1996), respectively.

10. Bruce Murphy, ed., *Benét's Reader's Encyclopedia*, 4th ed. (New York: HarperCollins, 1996), 4.

11. For in-depth discussion of Piñera's contribution to the theater of the absurd see the articles by Woodyard, Quackenbush, Palls, Martin, and Jérez-Farrán in the bibliography.

12. Kayser, *The Grotesque in Art and Literature*, trans. Ulrich Weisstein (Bloomington: Indiana Univ. Press, 1963), 37.

13. Yates, "An Introduction to the Grotesque: Theoretical and Theological Considerations," in *The Grotesque in Art and Literature: Theological Reflections*, ed. James Luther Adams and Wilson Yates (Grand Rapids, Mich.: Eerdmans, 1997), 2.

14. Morris, *The Culture of Pain* (Berkeley: Univ. of California Press, 1991), 81 and 92.

15. The title of this story, like that of Piñera's novel *La carne de René* (1952), calls attention to the author's clever exploitation of the ambiguous nature of the term "carne," which in Spanish means both "meat" (the flesh of animals as used for food) and "flesh" (the substance of animal or human bodies consisting of muscles and fat).

16. Virgilio Piñera, "La carne," in *Cuentos completos* (Madrid: Alfaguara, 1999). All Spanish-language quotes from Piñera's stories in this chapter are from this edition and are cited parenthetically in the text.

17. Virgilio Piñera, "Meat," in *Cold Tales*, trans. Mark Schafer (Hygiene, Colo.: Eridanos, 1987). Unless otherwise noted, all English-language quotes from Piñera's stories in this chapter are from this edition and are cited parenthetically in the text.

18. Nick Fiddes, *Meat: A Natural Symbol* (London: Routledge, 1991), 14–15, and Julia Twigg, "Vegetarianism and the Meanings of Meat," in *The Sociology of Food and Eating*, ed. Anne Murcott (Croft, England: Gower, 1983), 21.

19. R. Hart Phillips, *Cuba Island of Paradox* (New York: McDowell, n.d.), 213. In his landmark work *Cuba: The Pursuit of Freedom*, Hugh Thomas (735) also makes reference to the frequent beef shortages in Cuba throughout the early 1940s. Under Batista Cuba underwent what many experts have described as an illusory period of economic prosperity, which was largely due to unprecedented sugar sales to the United States during the early war years. Louis A. Pérez has pointed out that despite the fact that many Cubans prospered during the early 1940s, the war was actually a mixed blessing for the country. While certain sectors of society flourished (mainly the large cities), others languished. Shortages of all kinds were frequent, food prices increased dramatically, and the cost of living nearly doubled (see *Cuba*, 283–85).

20. Pérez León, *Vitalidad*, 108.

21. Piñera, "Notas sobre la vieja y la nueva generación," *La Gaceta de Cuba* 1.2 (1962): 2.

22. Carmen Torres-Robles, "Grotesque Humor in Virgilio Piñera's Short Stories," *Humor: International Journal of Humor Research* 5.4 (1992): 409.

23. In his recent study of cannibalism, Lewis Petronovich has pointed out that when sources of animal protein have been exhausted, starving individuals typically turn first to "organic material that is usually not eaten," and then to human flesh. See *The Cannibal Within* (New York: Aldine de Gruyter, 2000), 177.

24. Ansaldo's decision to consume his own flesh in order to avoid starvation may not be as absurd as it seems. Pitirim A. Sorokin (*Hunger as a Factor in Human Affairs* [Gainesville: Univ. Press of Florida, 1975], 102–3) has shown in his study of the effects of hunger on human behavior, that when individuals perceive starvation as a possibility

they often do things they would never have dreamed of doing when satiating their appetite was not their foremost concern. Though Piñera clearly overstates this point in his story, the villagers' unanimous decision to eat themselves effectively underscores how hunger drastically changes individual and group mentalities and leads people to go to drastic lengths to fill their empty bellies. The numerous reports of cannibalism in the Ukraine in the 1920s (see Sorokin, 111–12), in German prison camps in the early 1940s, and in Stalingrad in 1941 and 1942 where bodies were found without appendages and heads, and often with the brains and organs scooped out (see Petronovich, *The Cannibal Within*, 193–94) are illustrative of this point.

25. Torres-Robles, "Grotesque Humor," 409.
26. Camus, *The Myth of Sisyphus*, 125.
27. Morris, *The Culture of Pain*, 93.
28. Ibid., 92.
29. Fiddes, *Meat*, 89.
30. Gilgen, "Virgilio Piñera," 348.
31. This pathetic image of ten men living together in a tiny room suggests the infamous slums that surrounded the outskirts of Havana. Louis Pérez's description of these urban ghettos offers a tangible portrait of the squalid living conditions that Piñera implicitly denounces in his story: "The neighborhoods . . . were crowded with tens of thousands of poor, unemployed, and unemployable, living in squalor and destitution, eight to a room in hovels of tin sheeting and cardboard without sanitary facilities, garbage collection, sidewalks, or street lighting, and increasingly without hope. Many wandered about aimlessly, without work and some without motivation, many crippled, maimed, and ill, living off public welfare and private charity." See *Cuba*, 304.
32. Translations of "La cena" are my own. To the best of my knowledge, this story has not been published in English translation.
33. Piñera, "Piñera teatral," 10–11.
34. The narrator's precise descriptions of the sounds, though clearly exaggerated, are reminiscent of a common side effect of intense hunger. According to Petronovich, in cases of semistarvation, "the sensory mechanisms of individuals are extraordinarily well-maintained, with hearing even more acute than normal." See *The Cannibal Within*, 15.
35. Julio Matas, "Infiernos fríos de Virgilio Piñera," *Linden Lane Magazine* 4.2 (1985): 23.
36. Torres-Robles, "Grotesque Humor," 414.
37. Marta Morello-Frosch, "La anatomía: Mundo fantástico de Virgilio Piñera," *Hispamérica* 7.23–24 (1979): 26. My translation.
38. Teresa Cristófani Barreto, "Los cuentos fríos de Virgilio Piñera," *Hispámerica* 24.71 (1995): 28. My translation.
39. Gilgen, "Virgilio Piñera," 352.
40. Piñera, "Terribilia Meditans . . . II," n.p.
41. Balderston, "Lo grotesco en Piñera: Lectura de 'El álbum,'" *Texto Crítico* 12.34–35 (1986): 174.
42. In many ways, "El álbum" serves as an important precursor to Piñera's second novel *Pequeñas maniobras*. In both texts the protagonists are unable to keep their commitments, and they end up being controlled and manipulated by everyone else. Furthermore, in both texts Piñera offers animated caricatures of the many guesthouses in which he lived.
43. John R. Clark, *The Modern Satiric Grotesque* (Lexington: Univ. Press of Kentucky, 1991), 117.
44. Piñera, quoted in Pérez León, *Vitalidad*, 62–63.

45. Though it is true that Piñera's stories tend to lack specific Cuban referents, the implicit suggestion that sapota fruit (which is indigenous to Cuba and other tropical regions of the Americas), pineapples, and mangoes are native fruits clearly points to Cuba as the likely setting for the story. I should add here that the narrator indirectly suggests that his account has a contemporary setting when he mentions that the fifty-year-old landlady's wedding took place in 1914.

46. Piñera, "Nota sobre," 52–53.
47. Ibid., "El País del Arte," 36.
48. Camus, *The Myth of Sisyphus*, 126.
49. McQuade, "Making Sense," 218.
50. For a discussion on the Cuban *choteo* in Piñera's short fiction, see chapter 4 in Torres, *La cuentística de Virgilio Piñera*.
51. Piñera quoted in Pérez León, *Vitalidad*, 109.

Chapter 5. Religion, Philosophy, and Sexuality

1. Søren Kierkegaard, *The Gospel of Our Sufferings* [1847], trans. A. S. Aldsworth and W. S. Ferrie (Grand Rapids, Mich.: Eerdman's, 1964), 36.
2. Virgilio Piñera, "Final," in *La isla en peso: Obra poética* (Barcelona: Tusquets, 2000), 158.
3. In the mid-1970s Piñera began a revision of the original edition of *La carne de René* (Buenos Aires: Siglo Veinte, 1952), which was eventually published in Spain several years after his death (Madrid: Alfaguara, 1985), and then later in Cuba (Havana: Unión, 1995). The two versions of the novel reveal numerous differences in style and content. In 2000 a new edition of *La carne de René* was published in Spain (Barcelona: Tusquets, 2000). This edition was revised and corrected by Antón Arrufat, who eliminated many redundant passages and polished Piñera's somewhat awkward style.
4. The complete text can be found in the "Virgilio Piñera Collection," box 1, Folder 10, Manuscripts Division, Department of Rare Books and Special Collections, Princeton University Library.
5. Cabrera Infante, "The Death of Virgilio," xiv.
6. C. R. Taber, "Soul, Spirit," in *The Perennial Dictionary of World Religions*, ed. Keith Crim (New York: Harper and Row, 1989), 702.
7. Coward, *The Misfortunes of Virtue*, xxxvi.
8. All citations in Spanish are from *La carne de René* (Madrid: Alfaguara, 1985), which Piñera considered to be the definitive edition of the novel. The English-language translations come from the following edition: *René's Flesh*, trans. Mark Schafer (New York: Marsilio, 1995). All quotes cited in this chapter by parenthetical page numbers refer to these two editions.
9. Francis Bacon quoted in Yates, "Francis Bacon," 183.
10. 1 Corinthians 15:44. All biblical citations are from *The HarperCollins Study Bible* (*New Revised Standard Version*), ed. Wayne A. Meeks (New York: HarperCollins, 1989).
11. John 20:27.
12. García Chichester, "Codifying," 303.
13. Simone de Beauvoir, "Must We Burn Sade?" [1955], trans. Annette Michelson, in *The 120 Days of Sodom and Other Writings*, ed. and trans. Austryn Wainhouse and Richard Seaver (New York: Grove, 1999), 22–23.
14. Romans 8:13.
15. Marquis de Sade, "Dialogue Between a Priest and a Dying Man," in *The Misfor-

tunes of Virtue and Other Early Tales, 14th ed., ed. and trans. David Coward (Oxford: Oxford Univ. Press, 1992), 156.

16. Morris, *The Culture of Pain*, 127.
17. Rafael L. Ramírez, *What it Means to Be a Man: Reflections on Puerto Rican Masculinity*, trans. Rosa E. Casper (New Brunswick, N.J.: Rutgers Univ. Press, 1999), 51.
18. García Chichester, "Codifying," 304.
19. Arrufat, foreword, in *Rene's Flesh*, xvi.
20. Sade quoted in Morris, *The Culture of Pain*, 232.
20a. Morris, Ibid, 234.
21. Hebrews 5:8.
22. Morris, *The Culture of Pain*, 330.
23. See Antón Arrufat, "Un poco de Piñera," 22.
24. Kierkegaard, *Gospel*, 61.
25. Ibid., 23.
26. Cochón's name, which means "swine" in French, is highly symbolic since the pig has long been associated with the type of "low" discourse that Cochón is praised for. Stallybrass and White explain, for example, that the pig's ambivalence places it at the "intersection of a number of important cultural and symbolic thresholds." See Peter Stallybrass and Allon White, *The Politics and Poetics of Transgression* (Ithaca: Cornell Univ. Press, 1986), 44–45. The pig is an intermediate beast, both wild and tame, whose habits tend to cause disgust. Like the ambivalent pig, Cochón combines both human and animal qualities. In the bizarre licking scene in the novel's seventh chapter, for example, Cochón's likeness to a swine is underscored as he wallows with Mármolo and fifty young students in feces and urine while they eat food from a floor that has been contaminated with their own bodily waste.
27. Morris, *The Culture of Pain*, xxxii.
28. See Reinaldo Arenas, *Antes que anochezca* (Barcelona: Tusquets, 1992), 105; Arrufat, foreword, xv; and Cabrera Infante, *Mea Cuba*, 332.
29. Sade quoted in Beauvoir, "Must We Burn Sade?" 41.
30. John 19:30.
31. Yates, "Francis Bacon," 182–83.
32. Arrufat, foreword, xv.
33. Roy F. Baumeister, *Masochism and the Self* (Hillsdale, N.J.: Erlbaum, 1989), 3.
34. For more discussion on Freud's theory, see William Ian Miller, *The Anatomy of Disgust* (Cambridge: Harvard Univ. Press, 1997), 70–74.
35. Elaine Scarry, *The Body in Pain* (New York: Oxford Univ. Press, 1985), 57.
36. Baumeister, *Masochism*, 30–31.
37. Morris, *The Culture of Pain*, 132 and 135.
38. The name of the disease is said to come from the similarities between the violent seizures of epileptics and the fanatical dancing performed by devotees in front of the shrine of St. Vitus.
39. Kierkegaard, *Gospel*, 29.
40. Ibid., 44.
41. García Chichester, "Piñera," 324.
42. Miller, *Anatomy*, 94.
43. Fernando Valerio Holguín, *Poética de la frialdad: La narrativa de Virgilio Piñera* (Lanham, Md.: Univ. Press of America, 1997), 107.
44. Miller, *Anatomy*, 101.
45. See Sigmund Freud, "Three Contributions to the Theory of Sex," in *The Basic Writings of Sigmund Freud* (New York: Modern Library, 1995), 531–32.
46. Those who aim to take control of René's flesh often use alcohol to facilitate their

goals. Alcoholic beverages are served at every meal in the Escuela del Dolor, and Mármolo invites René to a drink when he comes to his office. Likewise, Dalia Pérez also serves alcohol to René when she wants to seduce him since she assumes that it will make him more passive.

47. Coward, *The Misfortunes of Virtue*, xxxii–xxxiii.

48. The reader should recall that while Piñera lived with Humberto Rodríguez Tomeu in Buenos Aires, the latter was working on a translation of Sade's text. Several passages of *The 120 Days of Sodom* were published in the first two issues of *Ciclón* in 1955.

49. Beauvoir, "Must We Burn Sade?" 26.

50. Sade quoted in Beauvoir, 26.

51. Sade, *120 Days of Sodom*, 246.

52. Ibid., 495.

53. Ibid., 552.

54. Morris, *The Culture of Pain*, 232.

55. John 6:63.

56. 1 Cor. 15:44.

57. 1 Cor. 15:39.

58. Piñera repeats this notion in his disturbing story "Hay muertos que no hacen ruido" (1975) [There Are Dead Men Who Don't Make Noise]: "sería buen negocio poner una carnicería para vender carne de gente muerta. Después de todo, es tan carne como la de vaca" [it would be a good business to set up a butcher shop to sell dead people. After all, it's meat just like that of cows]. See *Muecas para escribientes* (Madrid: Alfaguara, 1990), 236.

59. Eli Sagan, *Cannibalism: Human Aggression and Cultural Form* (Santa Fe, Tex.: Fish Drum, 1993), 63.

60. John 6:54–56.

61. Baumeister, *Masochism*, 180.

62. Kierkegaard, *Gospel*, 119–20.

63. Lumsden, *Machos*, 29. Though the term "machismo" was not popularized until the 1950s, as Ramírez points out, the concepts of patriarchal sexism that it represents have a long tradition throughout Latin America (see *Puerto Rican Masculinity*, 7). Lumsden underscores this fact in the second chapter of his book, and he demonstrates that the attitudes typical of the *machista* ideology were deeply ingrained in the fabric of Cuban society long before the triumph of the Revolution in 1959.

64. Lumsden, *Machos*, 29–30.

65. Ramírez, *What it Means to Be a Man*, 44.

66. Ibid., 45.

67. Gregory Woods, *Articulate Flesh* (New Haven: Yale University Press, 1987), 28–29, 46.

68. Ibid., 46.

69. Freud, "Three Contributions," 528.

70. Given that her name comes from a variety of flower, Dalia's frequent use of the term "florecer" is especially significant.

71. Arrufat, foreword, in *Rene's Flesh*, xiii–xiv.

72. Ibid., xiv.

73. Søren Kierkegaard, *Stages on Life's Way* [1845], ed. and trans. Howard V. Hong and Edna H. Hong (Princeton: Princeton Univ. Press, 1988), 72.

74. Søren Kierkegaard, *The Seducer's Diary* [1843], ed. and trans. Howard V. Hong and Edna H. Hong (Princeton: Princeton Univ. Press, 1997), 54.

75. Ibid., 118.

76. Ibid., from the foreword by John Updike, xiii.
77. Kierkegaard, *Diary*, 115.
78. Piñera added this scene when he revised *La carne de René* in the early 1970s.
79. Twigg, "Vegetarianism," 23–24.
80. Kierkegaard, *Diary*, 105,
81. Rodríguez, *What it Means to Be a Man*, 73.
82. García Chichester, "Codifying," 304.
83. Baumeister, *Masochism*, 158–59.
84. García Chichester, "Codifying," 305.
85. John 19:30.
86. See note 3 of this chapter.
87. The first two citations are taken from the dust jacket of the first edition of the English-language translation of *La carne de René*. Cabrera Infante's quote appears on the back cover of a later edition of the same translation: *René's Flesh*, trans. Mark Schafer (New York: Marsilio, 1995).

Chapter 6. The Signs of Sebastian

1. Sade, "Dialogue," 152–53.
2. Seymour Menton, *Prose Fiction of the Cuban Revolution* (Austin: Univ. of Texas Press, 1975), 15.
3. All quotes in Spanish are from the following edition: *Pequeñas maniobras/Presiones y diamantes* (Madrid: Alfaguara, 1986). Parenthetical citations within the text are from this Spanish edition. Translations are my own.
4. René is also categorized as a "víctima propiciatoria" (see *La carne de René*, 14).
5. Søren Kierkegaard, *The Concept of Anxiety* [1844], ed. and transl. Reider Thomte and Albert B. Anderson (Princeton: Princeton Univ. Press, 1980), 128.
6. Though Sebastián is ostensibly referring here to confession in the religious sense, it is worth pointing out that the term "inconfeso" is commonly used to describe a closeted homosexual.
7. Søren Kierkegaard, *Purify Your Hearts* [1843], transl. A. S. Aldsworth and W. S. Ferrie (London: C. W. Daniel, n.d.), 28.
8. Kierkegaard, *Concept of Anxiety*, 161.
9. Sade, "Dialogue," 150 and 152.
10. Camus, *Myth of Sisyphus*, 5.
11. Piñera is referring here to Publius Terentius Afer (185?–159 BC), a comic playwright of ancient Rome.
12. Piñera, "Ballagas en persona," 45.
13. Lumsden, *Machos*, 45.
14. See E. Méndez y Soto, "Piñera y el tema del absurdo," *Cuadernos Hispanoamericanos* 299 (May 1975): 451; Daniel Balderston, "Estética de la deformación en Gombrowicz and Piñera," *Explicación de Textos Literarios* 19.2 (1990–91): 6; and Fernando Valerio Holguín, *Poética de la frialdad: La narrativa de Virgilio Piñera* (Lanham, Md.: Univ. Press of America, 1997), 43–56.
15. Sebastián's frequent references to the funny faces that his students make recall the bizarre "juego de las muecas" [the game of grimaces] that Kowalski is compelled to arbitrate in the third chapter of *Ferdydurke*.
16. The first Spanish language edition of *Ferdydurke* is preceded by a short text— "Nota sobre la traducción" [Note on the Translation]—written by Gombrowicz, Piñera, and other members of the translation team. In it they explain their reasons for

having used so many invented Spanish words in the translation. "Importa decir que dichas palabras no son, en ningún caso, soluciones verbales o puro juego conceptual; todas ellas son "llaves" en la narración. Por ejemplo, la palabra "culeíto" (y sus casi infinitas variantes) constituye, por así decir, la simbólica del problema capital en *Ferdydurke*—esto es: la infantilización" (18). [It is important to note that such words are not, in any case, verbal solutions or a pure conceptual game; all of them are "keys" in the narration. For example, the word "culeíto" (and its almost infinite variations) constitutes, to put it as such, the word that symbolizes the central problem of *Ferdydurke*—that is: infantilization.] I should add that in the English-language translation "backside" is used where "culeíto" appears in the Spanish-language edition.

17. Balderston, "Estética," 5. The Escuela del Dolor in *La carne de René* is also a place in which humiliation and shame are of central importance.

18. Parenthetical page numbers following Spanish quotations are from *Ferdydurke*, transl. Gombrowicz, Virgilio Piñera, et al. (Buenos Aires: Argos, 1947). The parenthetical page numbers following English translations refer to the following edition: *Ferdydurke*, 2nd ed. trans. Eric Mosbacher (New York: Grove, 1967).

19. Largely because of Sebastián's propensity to change jobs, *Pequeñas maniobras* has been compared to the picaresque tradition. Méndez y Soto (452), for example, insists that by the end of the novel Sebastián has become a "pícaro redomado" [an out-and-out picaro]. It is important to point out, though, that Sebastián lacks the rogue element and the innate ability to outwit his various employers that picaresque antiheroes so often possess. Indeed, one of Sebastián's most distinguishing characteristics is his tendency to be taken advantage of and made into a fool by others. To a certain extent, then, Piñera's novel can be seen as a refashioning of the genre since the "pícaro" is not the one who manipulates, but the one who is manipulated by others.

20. "[Teresa] es mi amistad de azar" [Teresa is my friend by fate]; "Yo lo confío todo al azar" (33) [I trust everything to fate]; "¿Dónde caeré? Es como una ruleta donde todo está regido por el azar. . . . Tengo que aceptar el 'número' que me ha tocado en suerte" (135). [Where will I end up? It is like a game of roulette in which everything is governed by fate. . . . I have to accept the "number" that has fallen to me by luck.]

21. Rússovich, "Piñera en persona," 23.

22. Piñera, "Letters to Humberto," 16 July 1963.

23. Peter Vardy, *Kierkegaard* (Liguori, Mo.: Triumph, 1996), 40.

24. Kierkegaard "The Rotation Method," in *A Kierkegaard Reader*, ed. Roger Poole and Henrik Stangerup (London: Fourth Estate, 1989), 48–49.

25. Ibid., 49.

26. Kierkegaard, *Diary*, 93.

27. These passages, which come from Teresa's interior monologues in the fourth chapter, are in italics in the original text.

Chapter 7. Odd Couples

1. Virgilio Piñera, *El no* (México: Vuelta, 1994), 101.
2. Kierkegaard, "The Rotation Method," 49.
3. Piñera, "Ballagas en persona," 41.
4. It is interesting to point out that many of Piñera's stories from the same period are populated with disillusioned heterosexual couples. The narrator of the short story "Amores de vista" (1962) [Look of Love] is something of a Piñeran archetype in terms of his loneliness and intense sexual frustration. In a confessional tone that echoes that of Sebastián in *Pequeñas maniobras*, he frankly admits he is incapable of having a fulfilling

relationship with a woman: "Es lamentable, pero no me queda otro remedio que confesarme derrotado: ninguna mujer me ha querido" (*Cuentos Completos*, 161). [It's a pity, but I must admit defeat: no woman has loved me] (*Cold Tales*, 233). Another text, "Unión indestructible" [Indestructible Union] (1962) offers a fine example of Piñera's tendency to suggest that heterosexual couples are doomed to suffering and misfortune. In that story the despondent male narrator begins by calling attention to the pathetic state of his marriage. He explains, however, that he has come up with an incredible solution that will insure a future of togetherness. He and his estranged lover will submerge themselves in thick tar and then embrace under the hot sun until they are literally inseparable. The implicit suggestion of both of these stories—that happy, lasting love between men and women is nearly impossible—is one that reverberates throughout Piñera's oeuvre.

5. Quotations of *La boda* in Spanish will be referenced in the text by parenthetical abbreviations and page numbers, and come from the following edition: *La boda* in *Teatro completo* (Havana: Ediciones R, 1960), 171–242. All translations of Piñera's plays in this chapter are my own.

6. Piñera wrote *La boda* during a long visit to Havana that lasted from October 1956–March 1958.

7. Piñera, "Piñera teatral," 25.

8. Piñera, "¿Por dónde anda lo cubano en el teatro?" *Lunes de Revolución*, 3 April 1961, 30.

9. Arrufat, "Virgilio Piñera y la escritura de la negación," *Unión* 7.19 (1995): 57.

10. Quotations from *El no* will be referenced in the text by parenthetical page numbers, which refer to the following edition: Virgilio Piñera, *El no* (México: Vuelta, 1994).

11. Arrufat, "Negación," 56.

12. Lumsden, *Machos*, 68.

13. Piñera, "Mis 25 años," 3.

14. Lumsden, *Machos*, 72.

15. Emilia's knitting is especially unproductive because she ends up stashing her creations in wardrobe drawers without putting them to use.

16. Arrufat, "Negación," 57.

17. Fidel Castro quoted in Lee Lockwood, *Castro's Cuba, Cuba's Fidel*, exp. ed. (Boulder, Colo.: Westwood, 1990), 258–59.

18. Lezama, a known homosexual, married María Luisa Bautista in the final months of 1964. It is plausible that the marriage of Piñera's longtime friend served as an inspiration for his play, which he began in January 1965. Piñera commented on the wedding in a letter to Humberto written shortly after the event: "Y ahora te diré que Lezama se casó. Con una prima María Luisa Bautista, de 48 años. Boda notarial y religiosa y luna de miel en el hotel Riviera." [Now I'll tell you that Lezama got married. To a cousin, María Luisa Bautista, 48 years old. Notarial and religious wedding and honeymoon at the Hotel Rivera.] See "Letters to Humberto," 10 December 1964.

19. Lourdes Casal, "Cultural Policy and Writers in Cuba," in *The Cuba Reader*, ed. Philip Brenner et al. (New York: Grove, 1989), 508.

20. Thomas, *Cuba*, 1461.

21. Ernesto Hernández Busto, "Una tragedia en el trópico," introduction to *El no*, by Virgilio Piñera (Mexico: Vuelta, 1994), 14–18.

22. Lumsden, *Machos*, 60.

23. Leiner, *Sexual Politics*, 34.

24. Lumsden, *Machos*, 65.

25. Lockwood, *Castro's Cuba*, 107.

26. Samuel Feijoó, quoted in Leiner, *Sexual Politics*, 25.

27. Juan Goytisolo, *Realms of Strife: The Memoirs of Juan Goytisolo, 1957–1982*, trans. Peter Bush (San Francisco: North Point, 1990), 141.

28. Mario Novoa, "Virgilio Piñera: Premio al pánico," *Exilio*, Winter–Spring 1971, 137.

29. The jury was made up of the following individuals: Max Aub (Mexico), Hiber Conteris (Uruguay), Manuel Galich (Guatemala), José Celso Martínez Correa (Brazil), and Vicente Revuelta (Cuba).

30. By early 1969 *Dos viejos pánicos* had been performed in Medellín, Bogotá, Santiago de Chile, Caracas, and Madrid. Arrangements were being made for performances of the play in Buenos Aires (where it was first performed on 28 March 1970), Berlin, and Lisbon.

31. Eleanor Jean Martin, "*Dos viejos pánicos* by Virgilio Piñera: A Political Interpretation of the Cuban Theater of the Absurd," *Revista/Review Interamericana* 9.1 (1979): 51; L. Howard Quackenbush, "The Legacy of Albee's *Who's Afraid of Virginia Woolf?* in the Spanish American Absurdist Theatre," *Revista/Review Interamericana* 9.1 (1979): 61; and George W. Woodyard, "The Theatre of the Absurd in Spanish America," *Comparative Drama* 3.3 (1969): 186, respectively. For a detailed discussion on Piñera and the theater of the absurd, see these and the articles by Palls and Jérez-Farrán mentioned in the bibliography.

32. Leiner, *Sexual Politics*, 25.

33. Quotations from *Dos viejos pánicos* will be referenced in the text by parenthetical page numbers, which refer to the Cuban edition: *Dos viejos pánicos* (Havana: Casa de las Americas, 1968).

34. Matías Montes Huidobro has made the astute observation that the questions on the *planilla* are reminiscent of the oratory style of Fidel Castro, who frequently fills his speeches with questions whose answers are either implicit or provided by Castro himself. See *Persona, vida y máscara en el teatro cubano* (Miami: Universal, 1973), 435. The text of "Palabras a los intellectuales" (1961) is illustrative of this point. According to my count, in that speech there are nearly one hundred questions, most of which are answered by others that follow.

35. Severino João Albuquerque, *Violent Acts: A Study of Contemporary Latin American Theatre* (Detroit: Wayne State Univ. Press, 1991), 256.

Epilogue

1. Virgilio Piñera, "Testamento," in *La isla en peso: Obra poética* (Barcelona: Tusquets, 2000), 140.

2. Arenas, "La isla," 22.

3. Ibid., 23.

4. Cabrera Infante, "The Death of Virgilio," xiv.

5. Piñera quoted in Pedro Pérez Sarduy, "Virgilio Piñera y los dos viejos," *La Gaceta de Cuba* 6.63 (1968): 3.

6. For an interesting account of Piñera's activities during the 1970s, see Antón Arrufat's article, "La muerte en vida," *Diario de poesía* [Buenos Aires] 51 (Spring 1999): 28.

7. Piñera, "Letters to Humberto," 28 May 1975.

8. See Cabrera Infante, *Mea Cuba*, 68.

9. Arenas, "La isla," 22.

10. Antón Arrufat, "La muerte en vida," 28.

11. Cabrera Infante, *Mea Cuba*, 84.

12. Anonymous, "Virgilio, tal cual," 21.
13. Cabrera Infante, *Mea Cuba*, 356.
14. Piñera, "Letters to Guillermo," 31 January 1963.
15. Ibid., 14 March 1963.
16. For more information regarding Piñera's translation deals, see the following "Letters to Humberto": 18 September 1964; 26 October 1964; 10 December 1964.
17. Piñera, "Meat," 12.

Bibliography

Works by Virgilio Piñera

Poetry

Piñera, Virgilio. "El grito mudo." In *La poesía cubana en 1936*, edited by Juan Ramón Jiménez, 211–12. Havana: Institución Hispanocubana de la Cultura, 1937.

———. "Amor." *Espuela de Plata* B (October–November 1939): 13.

———. "Poesía," "La hoja," "Espada," "Composición No. 1," "Composición No. 2," "La gracia," "Tránsito de la rosa," "Nacimiento del mar," "Estaciones de los cuatro elementos." *Espuela de Plata* C–D (December 1939–January–March 1940): 22–24.

———. "Aire," "Fuego." *Grafos* 8.86 (1940): n. pag.

———. *Las Furias*. Havana: Ediciones Espuela de Plata, 1941.

———. "Invención," "Ícaro y el sol." *Espuela de Plata* G (February 1941): 20–21.

———. "Sonetos oscuros." *Clavileño* 1.1 (August 1942): n. pag.

———. "Seca lamentación." *Clavileño* 1.4–5 (November–December 1942): 13.

———. "La destrucción del Danzante." *Clavileño* 1.6–7 (January–February 1942): 3–5.

———. "Elegie Lente." *Poeta* 1 (November 1942): 4.

———. "Los desastres." *Poeta* 2 (May 1943): 8.

———. *La isla en peso*. Havana: n.p., 1943.

———. "Poema para la poesía." *Papeles de Buenos Aires* (August 1944): 12.

———. *Poesía y prosa*. Havana: Serafín García, 1944. Contains eight poems and fourteen stories.

———. "Paso de caballo," "Tesis del gabinete azul," "Secreto del espía." *Orígenes* 2.5 (1945): 31–33.

———. "El delirante," "Un hombre es así," "Yo estallo," "Un bomboleo frenético." *Casa de las Américas* 1.4 (1961): 2–5.

———. "Los muertos de la patria." *Lunes de Revolución*, 16 May 1961, 33.

———. "Mientras moría." *Unión* 2.3 (1964): 37.

———. "El gato tuerto," "Solicitud de canonización de Rosa Cagí," "Cuando vengan a buscarme," "Cirugía plástica," "María Viván." *La Gaceta de Cuba* 6.57 (1967): 16.

———. *La vida entera*. Havana: Unión, 1969.

———. *Una broma colosal*. Havana: Unión, 1988.

———. "¿No es por esas ventanas . . . ?" "Las plañideras," "El fondo" [1955]. *Biblioteca de México* 22 (July–August 1994): 2.

———. *La isla en peso: Obra poética*. Havana: Unión, 1998.

———. "Dos o tres elegancias," "Santadiabla Juana," "La contemplativa dama," "La melancólica dama," "La última hada," "Jardines, rosas y margaritas del Japón." *Encuentro de la Cultura Cubana* [Madrid] 14 (1999): 5–10.

———. "Invitación al suicidio," "El empacho de Aquile . . . ," "Única canción de sal," "La baldada de ti," "Casi fuga," "Finos fantasmas sueñan de neblina," "La gracia," "Amor," "De la persona," "Fuga a cuatro voces," "Canción del sueño," "Muchacho azul," "El poema de la perfecta soledad." *Letras Cubanas* 5.15 (1999): 234–53.

———. *La isla en peso: Obra poética*. Barcelona: Tusquets, 2000. Page references are to this edition.

Short Stories

———. *El conflicto*. Havana: Ediciones Espuela de Plata, 1942.

———. *Poesía y prosa*. Havana: Serafín García, 1944.

———. "En el insomnio." *Anales de Buenos Aires* 1.10 (1946): 18.

———. "El señor ministro." *Anales de Buenos Aires* 2.15–16 (1947): 20–22.

———. "El enemigo." *Sur* 236 (1955): 52–57.

———. "El gran Baro." *Ciclón* 1.1 (1955): 4–8.

———. "La carne," "La caída," "El infierno." *Sur* 242 (1956): 17–22.

———. *Cuentos fríos*. Buenos Aires: Losada, 1956.

———. "El muñeco." *Ciclón* 2.2 (1956): 9–30.

———. "¡Elíjanme!" *Carteles* [Havana] 12 May 1957, 64–67.

———. "Grafomanía," "Una desnudez salvadora," "Natación," "Un parto insospechado," "La montaña." *Ciclón* 3.1 (1957): 3–5.

———. "La gran escalera del palacio legislativo." *Sur* 251 (1958): 25–27.

———. "Una mujer con importancia." *Carteles*, 8 June 1958, 74–76.

———. "Unos cuantos niños." *Casa de las Américas* 1.1 (1960): 6–10.

———. "Alegato contra la bañadera desemportada," "Amores de vista," "Unión indestructible," "Oficio de tinieblas." *Unión* 1.1 (1962): 22–26.

———. "El caramelo." *Unión* 1.3 (1962): 18–38.

———. "Un fantasma a posteriori." *La Gaceta de Cuba* 2.16 (1963): 2.

———. *Cuentos*. Havana: Unión, 1964.

———. "La rebelión de los enfermos." *Unión* 4.1 (1965): 55–66.

———. "Belisario." *La Gaceta de Cuba* 6.62 (1967): 15.

———. "El que vino a salvarme." In *Narrativa cubana de la Revolución*, edited by José Manuel Caballero Bonald, 69–74. Madrid: Alianza, 1968.

———. *El que vino a salvarme*. Buenos Aires: Sudamericana, 1970.

———. *Cuentos*. Madrid: Alfaguara, 1983. Contains same stories as *El que vino a salvarme*.

———. "Tadeo." *Revolución y Cultura*, April 1984, 60–63.

———. "Concilio y discurso," [1950]. *Letras Cubanas* 2.5 (1987): 79–89.

———. "El crecimiento del Señor Madrigal" [1979]. *La Gaceta de Cuba* 26.1 (1987): 18–19.

———. *Muecas para escribientes*. Havana: Letras Cubanas, 1987. Contains twelve previously unpublished stories.

———. *Un fogonazo*. Havana: Letras Cubanas, 1987. Contains eleven previously unpublished stories.

———. *Muecas para escribientes*. Madrid: Alfaguara, 1990. Also includes the stories from *Un fogonazo*.

———. *Algunas verdades sospechosas*. Havana: April, 1992.

———. *El viaje* ("Le voyage," "The Trip"). Havana: Unión, 1992.

———. "Otra vez Luis Catorce." *Revolución y Cultura*, June–August 1992, 51–52.

———. *Cuentos de la risa del horror*. Bogotá: Norma, 1994.

———. *Muecas para escribientes*. Mexico City: Editorial Diana, 1995.

———. *Cuentos completos*. Madrid: Alfaguara, 1999.

———. *Cuentos completos*. Havana: Ediciones Ateneo, 2000.

Dramatic Works

———. *Clamor en el penal* [1937]. *Albur* 3.5 (1990): 86–124.

———. "*Clamor en el penal*. Cuadro I." *Baraguá* [Havana] 1–3 (1937): 6, 10.

———. *Falsa alarma*. *Orígenes* 6.21 (1949): 29–35 and 6.22 (1949): 35–41.

———. *Jesús*, Comedia dramática en tres actos (Acto I). *Prometeo* [Havana], June 1951, 26–32.

———. *Jesús* (Acto II). *Prometeo*, October 1951, 26–35.

———. *Jesús* (Acto III). *Prometeo*, July 1952, 17–24.

———. *Los siervos*. *Ciclón* 1.6 (1955): 9–29.

———. "*Aire frío*, Cuadro I." *Lunes de Revolución*, 30 March 1959, 6–10.

———. "*Aire frío*, Cuadro II." *Lunes de Revolución*, 11 May 1959, 10–15.

———. "*Aire frío*, Cuadro III." *Lunes de Revolución*, 25 May 1959, 11.

———. *Aire frío*. Havana: Pagrán, 1959.

———. "El flaco y el gordo." *Lunes de Revolución*, 7 September 1959, 11–16.

———. "La sorpresa." *Lunes de Revolución*, 17 June 1960, 9–11.

———. *Teatro completo*. Havana: Ediciones R, 1960. Includes *Electra Garrigó*, *Jesús*, *Falsa alarma*, *La boda*, *El flaco y el gordo*, *Aire frío*, *El filántropo*.

———. "El álbum" [1961]. *Conjunto* 61–62 (1984): 61–70.

———. *Siempre se olvida algo*. *La Gaceta de Cuba* 3.34 (1964): 4–9.

———. *El no* [1965]. México: Vuelta, 1994.

———. "La niñita querida." [1966] *Tablas* 3 (1992): 1–16.

———. *Dos viejos pánicos*. Havana: Casa de las Américas, 1968.

———. *Dos viejos pánicos*. Buenos Aires: Centro Editor de América Latina, 1968.

———. *Una caja de zapatos vacía* [1968]. Luis F. González-Cruz, ed. Miami: Universal, 1986.

———. "Estudio en blanco y negro." In *Teatro breve hispanoamericano contemporáneo*, edited by Carlos Solórzano, 169–81. Madrid: Aguilar, 1970.

———. "Un arropamiento sartorial en la caverna platónica" [1971]. *Escandalar* 5.1–2 (1982): 181–85.

———. *Las escapatorias de Laura y Oscar*. *Primer acto*, September–October 1988, n. pag.

———. *Aire frío*. Madrid: Publicaciones de la Asociación de Directores de Escena, 1990.

———. *Teatro inconcluso* (*Las siameses, El viaje, Milanés, El ring, Pompas de jabón, Inerrmes, ¿Un pico, o una pala?*). Edited by Rine Leal. Havana: Unión, 1990.

———. *Teatro Inédito* (*El no, Niñita querida, Una caja de zapatos vacía, Ejercicio de estilo, Tema: Nacimiento de palabras, El trac*). Havana: Letras Cubanas, 1993.

———. *Teatro completo*. Havana: Letras Cubanas, 2002.

Novels

———. *La carne de René*. Buenos Aires: Siglo Veinte, 1952.

———. *Pequeñas maniobras*. Havana: Ediciones R, 1963.

———. *Presiones y diamantes*. Havana: Unión, 1967.

———. *La carne de René*. Rev. ed. Madrid: Alfaguara, 1985.

———. *Pequeñas maniobras/Presiones y diamantes*. Madrid: Alfaguara, 1986.

———. *La carne de René*. Havana: Unión, 1995. This first Cuban edition of the novel is based on the Alfaguara edition.

———. *La carne de René*. Rev. ed. Barcelona: Tusquets, 2000. This edition incorporates extensive new revisions to the 1995 Cuban edition.

Critical Essays, Editorials, Book Reviews

All entries followed by an asterisk (*) are signed "El Escriba."

———. "Poesía y crimen." *Espuela de Plata* E–F (April–July 1940): 20–22.

———. "Plástica de la expresión poética ovidiana." *Grafos* 3.80–82 (1940): n. pag.

———. "Dos poetas, dos poemas, dos modos de poesía." *Espuela de Plata* H (August 1941): 16–19.

———. "De la contemplación." *Clavileño* 1.3 (October 1942): n. pag.

———. "Terribilia Meditans I." *Poeta* 1 (1942): 1.

———. "Erística sobre Valéry." *Poeta* 1 (1942): 7.

———. "Terribilia Meditans II." *Poeta* 2 (1943): 1.

———. "Notas sobre una exposición." *Hoy* [Havana] 7.62 (1944): 3.

———. "Samuel Feijóo. *Camarada celeste*. Poemas. La Habana 1944." *Orígenes* 2:5 (1945): 50–51.

———. "El secreto de Kafka." *Orígenes* 2.8 (1945): 42–45.

———. "*Extrañeza de estar*: Poemas de Cintio Vitier." *Magazine de Hoy*, 29 July 1945, 4–5, 8.

———. "Victrola: Revista de la insistencia." Buenos Aires: n.p., 1946. Self-published pamphlet.

———. "Los valores más jóvenes de la literatura cubana." *La Nación* [Buenos Aires], 22 December 1946, sec. 2: 2.

———. "El País del Arte." *Orígenes* 4.16 (1947): 34–38.

———. "Notas sobre literatura argentina de hoy." *Anales de Buenos Aires* 2.12 (1947): 52–56. Also published in *Orígenes* 4.13 (1947): 40–45.

———. "Witold Gombrowicz: *Ferdydurke*." *Realidad* [Buenos Aires] 1.3 (1947): 469–70.

———. "André Gide: *La sinfonía pastoral*." *Realidad* 1.4 (1947): 124–26.

———. "¿¿¿Teatro???" *Prometeo*, April–May 1948, 27.

———. "¡Ojo con el Crítico . . . !" *Prometeo*, November 1948, 2–4.
———. "Posición actual de las letras americanas." *Hoy* 16.63 (1948): n. pag.
———. "*El hoyo*, Cuentos de Humberto Rodríguez Tomeu." *Mensuario del arte, literatura, historia y crítica* [Havana] 5 (1950): 15.
———. "Gertrudiz Gómez de Avellaneda: Revisión de su poesía." *Revista de la Universidad de Habana* 100–3 (1952): 7–38.
———. "*Las 120 jornadas de Sodoma*, por el Marqués de Sade." *Ciclón* 1.1 (1955): 35.
———. "Cuba y la literatura." *Ciclón* 1.2 (1955): 51–55.
———. "Un experimento feliz." *Ciclón* 1.4 (1955): 59–60.
———. "Ballagas en persona." *Ciclón* 1.5 (1955): 41–50.
———. "*El amor original*, por José A. Baragaño." *Ciclón* 1.6 (1955): 41–50.
———. "*El pensamiento cuativo*, por Czeslaw Milosz." *Ciclón* 2.4 (1956): 64–66.
———. "*Fin de semana*, por Juan Goyanarte." *El Hogar* [Buenos Aires], 17 February 1956, n. pag.
———. *La cifra*, por Alexandre Arnoux." *El Hogar*, 13 April 1956, n. pag.
———. "Enredos habaneros." *Carteles*, 25 November 1956, 62–64, 67.
———. "Un testigo implacable." *Ciclón* 3.2 (1957): 63–64.
———. "Giselda Zani: *Por vínculos sutiles*." *Sur* 253 (1958): 95–96.
———. "Silvina Ocampo y su perro mágico: *No sólo el perro es mágico*." *Sur* 253 (1958): 108–9.
———. "La inundación." *Ciclón* 4.1 (1959): 10–14.
———. "El caso Lolita." *Sur* 260 (1959): 72.
———. "Nubes amenazadoras." *Revolución* [Havana], 15 January 1959, 4.
———. "Alfred Jarry o un 'joven airado' de 1896." *Nueva Revista Cubana* 1.2 (1959): 156–62.
———. "La reforma literaria." *Revolución*, 12 June 1959, 2.
———. "¿Casal o Martí?" *Revolución*, 16 June 1959, 2.
———. "Literatura y Revolución." *Revolución*, 18 June 1959, 2.
———. "Espejismo de revistas." *Revolución*, 20 June 1959, 2.
———. "Teatro y traductores. . . ." *Revolución*, 22 June 1959, 15.
———. "La Nueva Revista Cubana." *Revolución*, 27 June 1959, 2.
———. "Agregados culturales y desaguisados culturales." *Revolución*, 30 June 1959, 2.
———. "Las plumas respetuosas." *Revolución*, 13 July 1959, 17.*
———. "Visita a la Biblioteca Nacional." *Revolución*, 22 July 1959, 2.
———. "El baquerismo literario." *Revolución*, 27 July 1959, 21–23.*
———. "Hablemos de excesos." *Revolución*, 31 July 1959, 7.*
———. "Algo pasa con los escritores (I)." *Revolución*, 4 August 1959, 2.*
———. "Algo pasa con los escritores (II)." *Revolución*, 10 August 1959, 17–18.*
———. "Un crítico que se las trae." *Revolución*, 13 August 1959, 9.*
———. "Un libro bueno y malo." *Revolución*, 21 August 1959, 2.*
———. "Balance cultural de seis meses." *Revolución*, 31 August 1959, 18.*
———. "Permanencia de Ballagas." *Lunes de Revolución*, 14 September 1959, 3–5.
———. "¡Cuán gritan esos malditos!" *Revolución*, 4 September 1959, 2.*
———. "Exhortación a Rodríguez Feo." *Revolución*, 9 September 1959, 2.*

———. "Aviso a los conformistas." *Revolución*, 22 September 1959, 2.*
———. "Libros a granel." *Revolución*, 26 September 1959, 2.*
———. "Miscelánea." *Revolución*, 5 October 1959, 18.*
———. "Unas cuantas cervezas." *Lunes de Revolución*, 5 October 1959, 5–6.
———. "Veinte años atrás." *Revolución*, 9 October 1959, 2.*
———. "Más miscelánea." *Revolución*, 16 October 1959, 2.*
———. "Declaraciones de los escritores cubanos." *Revolución*, 25 October 1959, 2.
———. "Por más novelas cubanas." *Revolución*, 29 October 1959, 2.*
———. "Llamamiento a los escritores." *Revolución*, 23 October 1959, 19.*
———. "La Revolución se fortalece." *Lunes de Revolución*, 2 November 1959, 15.
———. "El arte hecho Revolución, la Revolución hecha arte." *Revolución*, 5 November 1959, 2.*
———. "La historia de la Revolución." *Revolución*, 11 November 1959, 2.*
———. "Cambio de frente político." *Revolución*, 24 November 1959, 2.*
———. "Aviso a los escritores." *Revolución*, 10 December 1959, 2.*
———. "Un asalto frustrado." *Lunes de Revolución*, 14 December 1959, 15.
———. "Cada cosa en su lugar." *Lunes de Revolución*, 14 December 1959, 11–12.
———. "Once consejos para un turista ávido." *Lunes de Revolución*, 21 December 1959, 20–21.
———. "En la muerte de Albert Camus." *Lunes de Revolución*, 18 January 1960, 7.*
———. "Pasado y presente de nuestra cultura." *Lunes de Revolución*, 18 January 1960, 10–13.
———. "Un jurado internacional de escritores." *Lunes de Revolución*, 25 January 1960, 2–4.
———. "Milicia de trabajadores intelectuales." *Revolución*, 29 January 1960, 2.*
———. "Después de la novela social." *Revolución*, 5 February 1960, 2.*
———. "Post-concurso." *Revolución*, 12 February 1960, 2.*
———. "Miscelánea." *Revolución*, 19 February 1960, 2.*
———. "Dos libros de cuentos." *Lunes de Revolución*, 22 February 1960, 15–16.
———. "Votos y vates." *Lunes de Revolución*, 15 February 1960, 9.
———. "Infierno inesperado." *Lunes de Revolución*, 14 March 1960, 15.
———. "Diálogo imaginario [con Jean Paul Sartre]." *Lunes de Revolución*, 21 March 1960, 38–40.
———. "Piñera teatral." *Lunes de Revolución*, 28 March 1960, 10–11.
———. "Piñera teatral." *Lunes de Revolución*, 4 April 1960, 18–19.
———. "Una verdadera historia de la literatura cubana." *Revolución*, 8 April 1960, 2.*
———. "El Teatro Nacional funciona." *Revolución*, 19 April 1960, 2.*
———. "Concierto malogrado." *Revolución*, 22 April 1960, 2.*
———. "Espíritu de las milicias." *Lunes de Revolución*, 1 May 1960, 35–39.
———. "Un libro de Bioy." *Lunes de Revolución*, 9 May 1960, 13.
———. "Un ataque que honra: La 'Marina' vs. 'Lunes.'" *Revolución*, 12 May 1960, 2.*
———. "Poemas de Fernando Pazos." *Lunes de Revolución*, 30 May 1960, 15–17.
———. "A partir de cero." *Lunes de Revolución*, 6 June 1960, 2–3.

———. "¿Qué libros trataría Ud. de salvar? —Una encuesta de *Lunes*." *Lunes de Revolución*, 20 June 1960, 6.
———. "Señales de los tiempos." *Revolución*, 18 June 1960, 2.*
———. "26 de julio de 1960." *Revolución*, 18 July 1960, 17.
———. "Un testimonio del primero de mayo." *Casa de las Américas* 1.1 (1960): 32–33.
———. "¿Ya leyó el Quijote?" *Lunes de Revolución*, 8 August 1960, 7–8.
———. "A partir de cero." *Lunes de Revolución*, 8 August 1960, 18.
———. "A partir de cero." *Lunes de Revolución*, 29 August 1960, 28.
———. "Extracción de guano de murciélago en Cubitas." *Revolución*, 12 September 1960, 21.
———. "Retrato del tiempo." *Lunes de Revolución*, 12 September 1960, 27.
———. "La nueva imagen del escritor cubano." *Revolución*, 13 September 1960, 2.
———. "Presentación." *Lunes de Revolución*, 19 September 1960, 2–3.
———. "Una vuelta lograda." *Revolución*, 8 October 1960, 2
———. "Árboles sin raíces." *Revolución*, 22 October 1960, 3.
———. "Las artes: La poesía." *Lunes de Revolución*, 28 November 1960, 28–29.
———. "La nueva literatura." *Lunes de Revolución*, 5 December 1960, 2–3.
———. "Sentido de navidad." *Revolución*, 23 December 1960, 3.
———. "Una lección de amor." *Lunes de Revolución*, 26 December 1960, 9.
———. "*Lunes* conversa con Pablo Neruda." *Lunes de Revolución*, 26 December 1960, 38–44.
———. "Gombrowicz en Argentina." *Cuadernos* [Paris] 45 (1960): 60–62.
———. "Piñera Teatral." In *Teatro completo*, by Piñera, 7–30. Havana: Ediciones R, 1960.
———. "1960 reseña de la poesía." *Lunes de Revolución*, 9 January 1961, 19–20.
———. "Del cuaderno de anotaciones de Antón Chekhov." *Lunes de Revolución*, 16 January 1961, 4–7.
———. "Martínez Villena y la poesía." *Lunes de Revolución*, 23 January 1961, 30–31.
———. "Un arma directa y dirigida." *Revolución*, 27 January 1961, 3.
———. "Mis 25 años de vida literaria." *Revolución*, 3 February 1961, 3.
———. "A partir de cero." *Lunes de Revolución*, 13 February 1961, 2.
———. "Tiempo destrozado." *Lunes de Revolución*, 27 February 1961, 28–29.
———. "A partir de cero." *Lunes de Revolución*, 6 March 1961, 21–23.
———. "Barro y viento." *Lunes de Revolución*, 13 March 1961, 26.
———. "A partir de cero." *Lunes de Revolución*, 13 March 1961, 6–15.
———. "Lunes conversa con autores, directores y críticos sobre el teatro cubano." *Lunes de Revolución*, 3 April 1961, 3–7.
———. "¿Por dónde anda lo cubano en el teatro?" *Lunes de Revolución*, 3 April 1961, 28–30.
———. "Conversatorio con el poeta turco Nazim Hikmet." *Lunes de Revolución*, 11 June 1961, 2–6.
———. "Un congreso de escritores y artistas." *Lunes de Revolución*, 12 June 1961, 15.
———. "Fragmento de un prólogo." *Lunes de Revolución*, 25 September 1961, 7–8.
———. "Los diez mejores libros cubanos." *Lunes de Revolución*, 9 October 1961, 4–7.

———. "La conspiración (Fragmento de la novel inédita, *Presiones y diamantes*)." *Lunes de Revolución*, 23 October 1961, 16–20.
———. "Edmundo Desnoes: *No hay problema*." *Casa de las Américas* 2.9 (1961): 160–61.
———. "Notas sobre la vieja y la nueva generación." *La Gaceta de Cuba* 1.2 (1962): 2–3.
———. "Apuntes sobre la poesía de Heberto Padilla." *La Gaceta de Cuba* 1.6–7 (1962): 14.
———. "El caso Baragaño." *La Gaceta de Cuba* 1.6–7 (1962): 21.
———. "Rogelio Llopis: *La guerra y los basiliscos*." *Unión* 2.5–6 (1963): 124–26.
———. "Tres en uno a una." *La Gaceta de Cuba* 2.15 (1963): 11–12.
———. "Morín sigue teniendo demonio." *La Gaceta de Cuba* 2.25 (1963): 14–15.
———. "El teatro actual." *Casa de las Américas* 4.22–23 (1964): 95–107.
———. "Evora: Nietas y abuelas." *La Gaceta de Cuba* 3.37 (1964): 22.
———. "Final del repaso." *Unión* 4.3 (1965): 145–49.
———. "[José Triana] *Noche de los asesinos*." *La Gaceta de Cuba* 4.47 (1965): 25.
———. "[Miguel Collazo] *El libro fantástico de Oaj*." *Unión* 5.3 (1966): 185–87.
———. "Notas sobre el teatro cubano." *Unión* 6.2 (1967): 130–42.
———. "Mitificación de Santiago de Cuba." *Unión* 6.3 (1967): 136–39.
———. "Gombrowicz por él mismo." *Unión* 7.1 (1968): 115–26. Reprinted in *Poesía y crítica*, 243–56. See entry below.
———. "Su vida fue un continuo galopar." *Unión* 6.4 (1969): 180–81.
———. "Artaud, fundador de una nueva vanguardia." Introduction to *El teatro y su doble* by Antonin Artaud, edited and translated by Virgilio Piñera, Enrique Alonso, Francisco Abelenda, vii–xvii. Havana: Instituto del Libro, 1969.
———. "Contra y por la palabra." *La Gaceta de Cuba* 8.80 (1970): 8.
———. *Poesía y crítica*. Edited by Antón Arrufat. México: Consejo Nacional para la Cultura y las Artes, 1994. Includes 27 critical essays previously published in various newspapers and literary reviews

Interviews

———. "El escritor Virgilio narra sus impresiones." Interview with Ernesto Ardura. *El mundo* [Havana], 1 February 1948, 12.
———. "El flaco y el gordo." Interview with Rine Leal. *Lunes de Revolución*, 7 September 1959, 10–11.
———. "Habla Virgilio Piñera: Usted me hace una lectura bien excepcional." Interview with Mariano Rodríguez Herrera. *Bohemia*, 6 September 1963.
———. "Diálogo con Virgilio Piñera." Interview with Luis Agüero. *Bohemia*, 28 August 1964, 23.
———. "Cosas de un Virgilio." Interview with Leonel López Nusa. *El Mundo*, 16 April 1968, 2.
———. "*Dos viejos pánicos* en Colombia." *Cunjunto* 3.7 (1971): 69–71.

Correspondence

———. "Letters to Antón Arrufat." November 1955–October 1959. Antón Arrufat Collection, CO737. Box 1, Folder 16. Manuscript, Division, Department of Rare Books and Special Collections, Princeton University Library.

———. "Letters to Humberto Rodríguez Tomeu." June 1959–November 1976. Virgilio Piñera Collection, CO749. Box 1, Folder 11. Manuscripts Division, Department of Rare Books and Special Collections, Princeton University Library.

———. "Letters to Guillermo Cabrera Infante." November 1962–June 1966. Guillermo Cabrera Infante Collection, CO272. Box 1, Folder 17. Manuscripts Division, Department of Rare Books and Special Collections, Princeton University Library.

———. "Cartas a José Lezama Lima." In *Fascinación de la memoria: Textos inéditos de José Lezama Lima*, edited by Iván González Cruz, 263–84. Havana: Letras Cubanas, 1993.

———. "Cartas entre Virgilio Piñera y José Rodríguez Feo." In *Tiempo de Ciclón*, edited by Roberto Pérez León, 163–82. Havana: Unión, 1995.

———. "Cartas a José Rodríguez Feo." *La Gaceta de Cuba* 37.5 (1999): 3–7.

———. "Cartas de Virgilio Piñera a Jorge Mañach, Gastón Baquero, Editores de *Orígenes*, José Lezama Lima, Julia Rodríguez Tomeu, Humberto Rodríguez Tomeu." *La Gaceta de Cuba* 39.5 (2001): 3–9.

Published Autobiography Fragments

———. "Empiezo a vivir . . . De mi autobiografía, *La vida, tal cual.*" *Lunes de Revolución*, 27 March 1961, 44–47.

———. "La vida, tal cual." *Unión* 3.10 (1990): 22–36.

———. "Muchas veces me he preguntado." *La Gaceta de Cuba* 28.3 (1990): 31.

———. "Autobiografía." *El Público* 78 (May–June 1990): 108–15.

———. "Mis memorias (fragmentos)." *Albur* 3.5 (1990): 147–56.

———. "Autobiografía." *Magazine Dominical El Espectador*, 20 September 1992, 6–9.

———. "Memoria de Buenos Aires." *Biblioteca de México* 22 (July–August 1994): 50–51.

———. "La vida entera." *Diario de poesía* [Buenos Aires] 51 (Spring 1999): 8–9.

Translations of Piñera's Works

———. "La viande," "L'insomnie," "Histoire de boiteux." Translated by Felix Gattengo. *Les Temps Modernes* 13.140 (1957): 619–23.

———. *The Serfs*. Translated by Gregory Rabassa. *Odyssey Review* 2.4 (1962): 183–214.

———. "The Great Baro." Translated by Alan Osborne. *Odyssey Review* 2.4 (1962): 214–23.

———. "Le balcon." Translated by Milene Polis. *L'Arc*, Autumn 1963, 50–56.

———. "Le philanthrope." Translated by Robert Marrast. *Les Temps Modernes* 19.207–8 (1963): 448–65.

———. "The Dragée." In *Writers of the New Cuba*, edited and translated by J. M. Cohen, 60–85. Baltimore: Penguin, 1967.

———. "The Philanthropist." In *Cuban Short Stories: 59/66*, 19–32. Havana: Book Institute, 1967.

———. "De la bière a gogo," "La chute." Translated by Marie-Françoise Rosset. *Les Lettres Nouvelles*, December 1967–January 1968, 62–68.

———. "Quand ils viendront me chercher," "Damande de canonisation de Rosa Gagi," "Chirurgie esthétique," "Maria Vivan." Translated by Raphaël Sorin. *Les Lettres Nouvelles*, December 1967–January 1968, 69–73.

———. *Contes froids*. Translated by Françoise-Marie Rosset. Paris: Denoël, 1971.

———. *Mici manevre*. Translated by Valeriu Mihaila. Bucharest: Editura Univers, 1972.

———. "San balcone." Translated by Roberto Lupo. *Pianeta* 48 (1972): 117–23.

———. "Die Hochzeit." In *Wie ich zuhaus einmarschiert bin*, edited and translated by Karl August Horst and Peter Schultze-Kraft, 35–36. Frankfurt: Fischer Taschenbuch Verlag, 1973.

———. "Hell," "On Insomnia," "The Journey," "The Wedding," "The Acteon Case." Translated by David Pritchard. *Fiction* 6.3 (1981): 41–47.

———. "Meat." Translated by Jess Grant. Santa Cruz: Pooder Press, 1984. Private publication.

———. "Belisario." In *Cuba: Nouvelles et contes d' aujourd'hui*, translated by Liliane Hasson, 191–94. Paris: L'Hartmattan, 1985.

———. *Cold Air*. Translated by María Irene Fornes. New York: Theatre Communications Group, 1985.

———. "Augenliebe." In *Der Frauenheld: Geschichten Liebe aus Lateinamerika*, translated by Michi Starusfeld, 244–45. Frankfurt: Suhrkamp Verlag, 1986.

———. *Cold Tales*. Translated by Mark Schafer. Hygiene, Colo.: Eridanos, 1987.

———. *Nouveaux contes froids*. Translated by Liliane Hasson. Paris: Du Seuil, 1988.

———. *La carne de René*. Edited and translated by Giancarlo Depretis. Turin, Italy: Il Quadrante, 1988.

———. *Contos frios seguidos de outros contos*. Translated by Teresa Cristófani Barreto. São Paulo: Iluminuras, 1989.

———. *René's Flesh*. Translated by Mark Schafer. Boston: Eridanos, 1989.

———. *A carne de René*. Translated by Eric Nepomuceno. São Paulo: Editora Siciliano, 1990.

———. *Kleine Manöver*. Translated by Wilfried Böhringer. Frankfurt: Suhrkamp Verlag, 1990.

———. "A Conciliar Discourse." In *The Voice of the Turtle: An Anthology of Cuban Stories*, translated by Peter Bush, 87–102. New York: Grove, 1997.

———. *An Empty Shoebox*. In *Three Masterpieces of Cuban Literature*, edited and translated by Luis F. González Cruz, 191–246. Los Angeles: Green Integer, 2000.

Translations by Virgilio Piñera

Allais, Alphonse. "Tres cuentos de Alphonse Allais." Translated by Virgilio Piñera. *Lunes de Revolución*, 21 September 1959.

———. "Pobre Cesarine." Translated by Virgilio Piñera. *Unión* 5.4 (1966): 116–21.

Apollinaire, Guillaume. "Pablo Picasso." Translated by Virgilio Piñera. *Lunes de Revolución*, 6 November 1961, 24.

Artaud, Antonin. *El teatro y su doble*. Translated by Virgilio Piñera, Enrique Alonso, and Francisco Abelenda. Havana: Instituto del Libro, 1969.

Bastide, Roger. "El mito del África negra." Translated by Virgilio Piñera. *Lunes de Revolución*, 30 April 1959, 7–10.

Brouté, Jacques. *Rara la máquina*. Translated by Virgilio Piñera. Havana: Talleres Graphis, 1960.

Can, Huy. "Ofrenda." Translated by Virgilio Piñera. *Lunes de Revolución*, 31 July 1961, 26.

———. "Caminando por la tierra de nuestros antipasados." Translated by Virgilio Piñera. *Unión* 6.1 (1967): 28–30.

Cesaire, Aime. "Conquista del alba." Translated by Virgilio Piñera. *Poeta* 2 (1943): 4–6.

Che-Lan-Vien. "La llamada Morrison." Translated by Virgilio Piñera. *Unión* 6.1 (1967): 33–34.

Cong Hoan, Nguyen. *Las pantuflas del venerable jefe del distrito*. Translated by Virgilio Piñera. Havana: Editorial Nacional de Cuba, 1962.

Depestre, René. "35 años de la vida revolucionaria del Vietnam." Translated by Virgilio Piñera. *Lunes de Revolución*, 31 July 1961, 10–12.

———. *Mineral negro*. Translated by Virgilio Piñera. Havana: Ediciones R, 1962.

———. "El que no tiene de congo . . ." Translated by Virgilio Piñera. *Unión* 4.2 (1965): 66–78.

Dinh Ti, Nguyen. "El canto del marinero vienamita." Translated by Virgilio Piñera. *Lunes de Revolución*, 31 July 1961, 32.

El Relojero de Dien Bien Phu. Edited and translated by Virgilio Piñera. Havana: Editorial Arte y Literatura, 1975.

Escarpit, Robert. *Sociología de la literatura*. Translated by Virgilio Piñera. Havana: Instituto del Libro, 1970.

Farinelli, Arturo. *El romanticismo en Alemania*. Translated by Virgilio Piñera and Carlos Coldaroli. Buenos Aires: Argos, 1948.

Forets, Louis René. "Una memoria demencial." Translated by Virgilio Piñera. *Unión* 9.3 (1970): 152–70.

Giano, Jean. *Juan azul*. Translated by Virgilio Piñera and Humberto Rodríguez Tomeu. Buenos Aires: Argos, 1947.

Gombrowicz, Witold. *Ferdydurke*. Translated by Gombrowicz, Virgilio Piñera et al. Buenos Aires: Argos, 1947.

———. "El banquete." Translated by Virgilio Piñera. *El escarabajo de oro* [Buenos Aires] 39 (1969): 4–6.

Hanh, Te. "El pozo a la entrada de a aldea." Translated by Virgilio Piñera. *Unión* 6.1 (1967): 33–34.

Ho Chi Minh. "El poeta." Translated by Virgilio Piñera. *Lunes de Revolución*, 13 April 1960, 2–4.

———. "Poemas." Translated by Virgilio Piñera. *Lunes de Revolución*, 31 July 1961, 13.

Harding, Bertita. *Gloria perenne: Vida de Dusey d'Annunzio*. Translated by Virgilio Piñera. Buenos Aires: Hachette, 1951.

Jaloux, Edmund. *Edgar Poe y las mujeres*. Translated by Virgilio Piñera and Humberto Rodríguez Tomeu. Buenos Aires: Argos, 1947.

Lanoux, Armand. "Encuentro con Salvador Dalí." Translated by Virgilio Piñera. *Ciclón* 1.6 (1955): 51–58.

Lefebvre, Henri. "La política marxista." Translated by Virgilio Piñera. *Lunes de Revolución*, 30 April 1959, 2–4.

Lopes, Henre. *Tribálicas*. Translated by Virgilio Piñera. Havana: Editorial Arte y Literatura, 1974.

Lun-Tron-Lu. "La muchacha del río Gianh." Translated by Virgilio Piñera. *Unión* 6.1 (1967): 36–40.

Madách, Imre. *La tragedia del hombre*. Translated by Virgilio Piñera. Havana: Editorial Arte y Literatura, 1978.

Musil, Robert. "El mirlo." Translated by Virgilio Piñera. *Unión* 5.1 (1966): 103–18.

Ngoc, Nguyen. *Noup, héroe de la montaña*. Translated by Virgilio Piñera. Havana: Editorial Nacional de Cuba, 1961.

Ousmane, Sembene. *Los trozos de madera de Dios*. Translated by Virgilio Piñera. Havana: Editorial Arte y Literatura, 1975.

Oyono, Ferdinand. *Camino de Europa*. Translated by Virgilio Piñera. Havana: Editorial Arte y Literatura, 1975.

Paulhan, Jean. "Las causas célebres." Translated by Virgilio Piñera. *La Gaceta de Cuba* 9.84 (1970): 21.

Peyrefitte, Roger. "Las llaves de San Pedro." Translated by Virgilio Piñera. *Ciclón* 1.6 (1955): 57–62.

Price-Mars, Jean. *Así habló el tío*. Translated by Virgilio Piñera. Havana: Casa de las Américas, 1968.

Proust, Marcel. *Un amor de swan*. Translated by Virgilio Piñera. Havana: Editorial Nacional de Cuba, 1964.

Rimbaud, Arthur. "El barco ebrio." In *Poesía francesa: Mallarmé, Rimbaud, Valery*, translated by Virgilio Piñera, 160–70. Havana: Editorial Nacional de Cuba, 1966.

Sartre, Jean Paul. *Tintoretto, el secuestrado de Venecia*. Translated by Virgilio Piñera. Havana: Instituto del Libro, 1969.

Schulz, Bruno. "La visitación." Translated by Virgilio Piñera. *Lunes de Revolución*, 23 October 1961, 30–31.

Schwob, Marcel. "Asesinos." Translated by Virgilio Piñera. *Bohemia* 35.52 (1970): 26–27.

Teatro Africano, Antología. Translated by Virgilio Piñera. Havana: Editorial Arte y Literatura, 1975.

Trung Thanh, Ngu Yen. "En la selva." Translated by Virgilio Piñera. *Unión* 6.1 (1967): 54–75.

Valéry, Paul. "El amateur de poemas." Translated by Virgilio Piñera. *Poeta* 1 (1942): 6.

WORKS ABOUT VIRGILIO PIÑERA

Books

Abreu, Alberto. *Virgilio Piñera: Un hombre, una isla*. Havana: Unión, 2002.

Aguilú de Murphy, Raquel. *Los textos dramáticos de Virgilio Piñera y el teatro del absurdo*. Madrid: Pliegos, 1989.

Arrufat, Antón. *Virgilio Piñera: Entre él y yo*. Havana: Unión, 1994.

Barreto, Teresa Cristófani. *A libélula, a pitonisa: Revolução, homossexualismo e literatura em Virgilio Piñera*. São Paulo: Iluminuras, 1996.

Espinosa, Carlos. *Virgilio Piñera en persona*. Havana: Unión, 2003.

Garrandés, Alberto. *La poética del límite: Sobre la cuentística de Virgilio Piñera*. Havana: Letras Cubanas, 1993.

Laddaga, Reinaldo. *Literaturas indigentes y placeres bajos: Felisberto Hernández, Virgilio Piñera, Juan Rudolfo Wilcock*. Buenos Aires: Beatriz Viterbo, 2000.

Molinero, Rita, ed. *Virgilio Piñera: La memoria del cuerpo*. San Juan: Plaza Mayor, 2002.

Pérez León, Roberto. *Virgilio Piñera: Vitalidad de una paradoja.* Caracas: CELCIT, 2002.

Saínz, Enrique. *La poesía de Virgilio Piñera: Ensayo de aproximación.* Havana: Letras Cubanas, 2001.

Torres, Carmen L. *La cuentística de Virgilio Piñera: Estrategias humorísticas.* Madrid: Pliegos, 1989.

Valerio Holguín, Fernando. *Poética de la frialdad: La narrativa de Virgilio Piñera.* Lanham, Md.: Univ. Press of America, 1997.

Selected Articles and Reviews

Anonymous. "Efectuado el sepelio del escritor Virgilio Piñera." *Granma*, 20 October 1979, 5.

Anonymous. "Virgilio, tal cual." *Unión* 3.10 (1990): 21.

Arenas, Reinaldo. "La isla en peso con todas sus cucarachas." *Mariel* 2 (1983): 20–24.

Arrufat, Antón. "La carne de Virgilio," *Unión* 3.10 (1990): 44–47.

———. Foreword to *René's Flesh*, by Virgilio Piñera, ix–xxii. Translated by Mark Schafer. New York: Eridanos, 1989.

———. "La muerte en vida." *Diario de poesía* 51 (Spring 1999): 28.

———. "Notas prologales." In *La isla en peso: Obra poética*, by Virgilio Piñera, 9–16. Barcelona: Tusquets, 2000.

———. "Un poco de Piñera." Introduction to *Cuentos completos*, by Virgilio Piñera, 11–31. Madrid: Alfaguara, 1999.

———. "Virgilio Piñera o los riesgos de la imaginación." *Unión* 2.1 (1987): 145–50.

———. "Virgilio Piñera y la escritura de la negación." *Unión* 7.19 (1995): 54–59.

Balderston, Daniel. "Estética de la deformación en Gombrowicz and Piñera." *Explicación de Textos Literarios* 19.2 (1990–91): 1–7

———. "Lo grotesco en Piñera: Lectura de 'El álbum.'" *Texto Crítico* 12.34–35 (1986): 174–78.

Barreto, Teresa Cristófani. "Los cuentos fríos de Virgilio Piñera." *Hispámerica* 24.71 (1995): 23–33.

———, Pablo Gianera, and Daniel Samoilovich. "Dossier de Virgilio Piñera: Cronología." *Diario de Poesía* 51 (Spring 1999): 10–12, 14, 17–18, 21, 24, 27–9, 31.

Bianco, José. "Piñera narrador." Introduction to *El que vino a salvarme*, by Virgilio Piñera, 7–19. Buenos Aires: Sudamericana, 1970.

Cabrera Infante, Guillermo. "The Death of Virgilio." Introduction to *Cold Tales*, by Virgilio Piñera, translated by Mark Schafer. New York: Eridanos, 1988.

Camps, David. *"Dos viejos pánicos* producen pánico." *La Gaceta de Cuba* 6.64 (1968): 13.

Espinosa-Domínguez, Carlos. "El poder mágico de los bifes: La estancia argentina de Virgilio Piñera." *Cuadernos Hispanoamericanos* 471 (1989): 73–88.

———, ed. "Virgilio Piñera en persona." *Quimera* 98 (1989): 38–47.

Fernández-Ferrer, Antonio. "El 'disparate claro' en Cortázar y Piñera." *Revista Iberoamericana* 58.159 (1992): 423–36.

García Chichester, Ana. "Codifying Homosexuality as Grotesque: The Writings of Virgilio Piñera." In *Bodies and Biases: Sexualities in Hispanic Cultures and Literature*, edited by David William Foster and Roberto Reis, 294–315. Minneapolis: Univ. of Minnesota Press, 1996.

———. "Metamorphosis in Two Short Stories of the Fantastic by Virgilio Piñera and Felisberto Hernández." *Studies in Short Fiction* 31.3 (1994): 385–95.

———. "Piñera, Virgilio." In *Latin American Writers on Gay and Lesbian Themes*, edited by David William Foster, 322–26. Westport, Conn.: Greenwood, 1994.

———. "Superando el caos: Estado actual de la crítica sobre la narrativa de Virgilio Piñera." *Revista Interamericana de Bibliografía* 42.1 (1992): 132–47.

Gilgen, Read Grant. "Virgilio Piñera and the Short Story of the Absurd." *Hispania* 63 (1980): 348–55.

González-Cruz, Luis F. "Piñera Llera, Virgilio." In *Dictionary of Twentieth-Century Literature*, edited by Julio A. Martínez, 631–70. Westport, Conn.: Greenwood, 1990.

———. "Virgilio Piñera y el teatro del absurdo en Cuba." *Mester* 5.1 (1974): 52–58.

Hernández Busto, Ernesto. "Los reyes del Rex: Piñera and Gombrowicz en Buenos Aires." *Biblioteca de México* 22 (July–August 1994): 42–43.

———. "Una tragedia en el trópico." Introduction to *El no*, by Virgilio Piñera, 7–25. Mexico: Vuelta, 1994.

Ibieta, Gabriella. "Funciones del doble en la narrativa de Virgilio Piñera." *Revista Iberoamericana* 56.152–53 (1990): 975–91.

Jérez-Farrán, Carlos. "Un análisis diferenciador del teatro de Virgilio Piñera: El teatro satírico burlesco y el teatro absurdista." *Latin American Theatre Review* 22.2 (1989): 59–71.

Koch, Dolores M. "Virgilio Piñera y el neo-barroco." *Hispamérica* 13.37 (1984): 81–86.

———. "Virgilio Piñera, cuentista." *Linden Lane Magazine* 4 (1982): 14–15.

———. "Virgilio Piñera: Short-Fiction Writer." *Folio* 16 (1984): 80–88.

Leal, Rine. "Piñera inconcluso." In *Teatro inconcluso* by Virgilio Piñera, 7–42. Havana: Unión, 1990.

Llopis, Rogelio. "*Pequeñas maniobras* de Virgilio Piñera." *Casa de las Américas* 4.24 (1970): 106–7.

López-Ramirez, Tomás. "Virgilio Piñera." In *Spanish American Authors: The Twentieth Century*, edited by Ángel Flores. New York: H. W. Wilson, 1992.

———. "Virgilio Piñera y el compromiso del absurdo." *Areito* 9.34 (1983): 38–40.

———. "Virgilio Piñera: Las ceremonias de la negación." *Cupey* 1.2 (1984): 81–91.

Martin, Eleanor Jean. "*Dos viejos pánicos* by Virgilio Piñera: A Political Interpretation of the Cuban Theater of the Absurd." *Revista/Review Interamericana* 9.1 (1979): 50–57.

Matas, Julio. "Infiernos fríos de Virgilio Piñera." *Linden Lane Magazine* 4.2 (1985): 22–24.

———. "Vuelta a *Electra Garrigó* de Virgilio Piñera." *Latin American Theatre Review* 22.2 (1989): 73–80.

McQuade, Frank. "Making Sense out of Nonsense: Virgilio Piñera and the Short Story of the Absurd." In *After Cervantes: A Celebration of 75 Years of Iberian Studies at Leeds*, edited by John Macklin, 203–22. Leeds: Trinity and All Saints, 1993.

———. "Virgilio Piñera." In *Encyclopedia of Latin American Literature*, edited by Verity Smith, 363–64. Chicago: Fitzroy Dearborn, 1997.

Méndez y Soto, E. "Piñera y el tema del absurdo." *Cuadernos Hispanoamericanos* 299 (May 1975): 448–53.

Morello-Frosch, Marta. "La anatomía: Mundo fantástico de Virgilio Piñera." *Hispamérica* 7.23–24 (1979): 19–34.

Narváez, Carlos. "Lo fantástico en cuatro cuentos de Virgilio Piñcra." *Románica* 13 (1976): 77–86.
Novoa, Mario E. "Virgilio Piñera: Premio al pánico." *Exilio* Winter-Spring 1971, 127–41.
Padilla, Heberto. "Virgilio Piñera, el invisible." *Linden Lane Magazine* 4 (1982): 16–18.
Palls, Terry. "The Theatre of the Absurd in Cuba after 1959." *Latin American Literary Review* 4.6 (1975): 67–72
Pérez León, Roberto. "*Aurora y Victrola*." *Biblioteca de México* 22 (July–August 1994): 48–49.
———. "Con el peso de una isla de jardines invisibles." *Unión* 3.10 (1990): 37–43.
Pérez Sarduy, Pedro. "Virgilio Piñera y los dos viejos." *La Gaceta de Cuba* 6.63 (1968): 3.
Quackenbush, L. Howard. "The Legacy of Albee's *Who's Afraid of Virginia Woolf?* in the Spanish American Absurdist Theatre." *Revista/Review Interamericana* 9.1 (1979): 57–71.
Quiroga, José. "Fleshing Out Virgilio Piñera from the Cuban Closet." In *¿Entiendes?: Queer Readings, Hispanic Writings*, edited by Emile Bergman and Paul Julian Smith, 169–79. Durham, N.C.: Duke Univ. Press, 1994.
Rodríguez Feo, José. "Una alegoría de la carne." *Ciclón* 1.1 (1955): 43.
Rodríguez Tomeu, Humberto. "'Épater le bourgeois': Piñera y Gombrowicz en Argentina." Translated by Ernesto Hernández Busto. *Biblioteca de México*. 22 (July–August 1994): 44–45.
Rússovich, Alejandro. "Piñera en persona." Interview with Pablo Gianara. *Diario de Poesía* 51 (Spring 1999): 22–23.
Santí, Enrico Mario. "Carne y papel: El fantasma de Virgilio." *Vuelta* 18.208 (1994): 59–63.
Schafer, Mark, trans. "Translator's Note." In *René's Flesh*, by Virgilio Piñera, xxi–xxii. Boston: Eridanos, 1989.
Schóo, Ernesto. "Virgilio Piñera, *Cuentos fríos*." *Sur* 245 (1957): 110–15.
Torres-Robles, Carmen. "Grotesque Humor in Virgilio Piñera's Short Stories." *Humor: International Journal of Humor Research* 5.4 (1992): 397–422.
Vitier, Cintio. "Virgilio Piñera: *Poesía y Prosa*, La Habana, 1944." *Orígenes* 2.5 (1945): 47–50.
Weizdörfer, Ewald. "El unicornio de Virgilio Piñera: Lo neofantástico cortazariano en algunos cuentos del autor cubano." *Letras del Deusto* 20.46 (1990): 151–64.
Woodyard, George W. "The Theatre of the Absurd in Spanish America." *Comparative Drama* 3.3 (1969): 183–91.
Zalacaín, Daniel. "*Falsa alarma*: Vanguardia del absurdo." *Romance Notes* 21.1 (1980): 28–32.

General Bibliography

Albuquerque, Severino João. *Violent Acts: A Study of Contemporary Latin American Theatre*. Detroit: Wayne State Univ. Press, 1991.
Álvarez-García, Imeldo. "Carta a *Revolución*." *Revolución*, 28 September 1960, 2.

"An Open Letter to Fidel Castro." *The New York Times Review of Books*, 15 March 2005, 16.8 (May 1971). <http://www.nybooks.com/articles/10580>

Arenas, Reinaldo. *Antes que anochezca*. Barcelona: Tusquets, 1992.

Arens, W. *The Man-Eating Myth: Anthropology and Anthropophagy*. Oxford: Oxford Univ. Press, 1979.

Bakhtin, Mikhail. *Rabelais and His World*. Translated by Hélène Iswolsky. Bloomington: Indiana Univ. Press, 1984.

Baquero, Gastón. "Tendencias actuales de nuestra literatura." In *Ensayos*, by Gastón Baquero, edited by Alfonso Ortega Carmona and Afredo Pérez, 307–10. Salamanca: Fundación Central Hispano, 1995.

Baumeister, Roy F. *Masochism and the Self*. Hillsdale, N.J.: Erlbaum, 1989.

Beauvoir, Simone de. "Must We Burn Sade?" [1955]. Translated by Annette Michelson. In *The 120 Days of Sodom and Other Writings*, by the Marquis de Sade, edited and translated by Austryn Wainhouse and Richard Seaver, 3–64. New York: Grove, 1999.

Bianchi Ross, Ciro, ed. *José Lezama Lima: Imágen y posibilidad*. Havana: Letras Cubanas, 1981.

Borges, Jorge Luis. "Nota de un mal lector." *Ciclón* 2.1 (1956): 28.

———. *Obra poética*. Buenos Aires. Emecé, 1977.

Cabrera Infante, Guillermo. *Mea Cuba*. Translated by Guillermo Cabrera Infante and Kenneth Hall. New York: Farrar, 1994.

Camus, Albert. *The Myth of Sisyphus and Other Essays*. Justin O'Brien, trans. New York: Vintage, 1983.

Casal, Lourdes, ed. *El Caso Padilla: Literatura y Revolución en Cuba*. Miami: Universal, 1971.

———. "Cultural Policy and Writers in Cuba." In *The Cuba Reader*, edited by Philip Brenner et al., 506–13. New York: Grove, 1989.

Castro, Fidel. "At the Closing of the First National Congress on Education and Culture." *Granma* (English-language ed.), 9 May 1971, 7–9.

———. "En la clausura del Primer Congreso Nacional de Educación y Cultura." In *Discursos: Fidel Castro*. Vol. 1. Edited by Dagmara González de Mendoza et al. Havana: Ciencias Sociales, 1975.

———. "Palabras a los intelectuales" [30 June 1961]. In *Política cultural de la Revolución Cubana: Documentos*, edited by Juaquín G. Santana, 5–47. Havana: Ciencias Sociales, 1977.

Cernuda, Luis. "Retrato de poeta." *Orígenes* 10.33 (1953): 41–43.

Chanan, Michael. *The Cuban Image*. Bloomington: Univ. of Indiana Press, 1985.

Clark, John R. *The Modern Satiric Grotesque*. Lexington: Univ. Press of Kentucky, 1991.

Cohen, J. M., trans. Introduction to *Sent off the Field*, by Heberto Padilla. London: Andre Deutch, 1972.

Cortázar, Julio. "Casa tomada." *Anales de Buenos Aires* 1.11 (1946): 13–18.

Coward, David, ed. and trans. Introduction to *The Misfortunes of Virtue and Other Early Tales*, by the Marquis de Sade, vii–xxxviii. 14th ed. Oxford: Oxford Univ. Press, 1992.

"Declaración del Primer Congreso Nacional de Educación y Cultura." *Granma* [Havana], 1 May 1971, 2–4.

"Declaration by the First National Congress on Education and Culture." *Granma* (English language ed.), 9 May 1971, 3–6.

Díaz Quiñones, Arcadio. *Cintio Vitier: La memoria integradora*. San Juan: Sin Nombre, 1987.

Fernández Bonilla, Raimundo. "Respuesta al Escriba." *Revolución*, 29 September 1959, 2.

Fiddes, Nick. *Meat: A Natural Symbol*. London: Routledge, 1991.

Florit, Eugenio. "Carta a Virgilio Piñera (13 July 1948)." Reprinted in *Albur* 3.5 (1990): 141.

Franqui, Carlos. *Family Portrait with Fidel*. Translated by Alfred MacAdam. New York: Random House, 1981.

Freud, Sigmund. "Three Contributions to the Theory of Sex." In *The Basic Writings of Sigmund Freud*, edited and translated by A. A. Brill, 521–97. New York: Modern Library, 1995.

García Vega, Lorenzo. *Los años de Orígenes*. Caracas: Monte Ávila, 1979.

Gellman, Irwin F. *Roosevelt and Batista: Good Neighbor Diplomacy in Cuba, 1933–1945*. Albuquerque: Univ. of New Mexico Press, 1973.

Gombrowicz, Witold. "Aurora: Revista de la Resistencia." Buenos Aires: n.p., 1946. Self-published pamphlet.

———. "Contra los poetas." *Ciclón* 1.5 (1955): 9–16.

———. *Ferdydurke*. Translated by Gombrowicz, Virgilio Piñera et al. Buenos Aires: Argos, 1947.

———. *Ferdydurke* 2nd Ed. Translated by Eric Mosbacher. New York: Grove, 1967.

———. "Prefacio para la edición castellana." Preface to *Ferdydurke*, by Gombrowicz, 7–15. Buenos Aires: Argos, 1947.

González Cruz, Iván, ed. *Fascinación de la memoria: Textos inéditos de José Lezama Lima*. Havana: Letras Cubanas, 1993.

González, Odilio. "Todo al revés: Carta abierta a Guillermo Cabrera Infante." *Lunes de Revolución*, 19 October 1959, 5–6.

Goytisolo, Juan. *Realms of Strife: The Memoirs of Juan Goytisolo, 1957–1982*. Translated by Peter Bush. San Francisco: North Point, 1990.

Guillén, Jorge. "Que van a dar en la mar." *Orígenes* 10.33 (1953): 58–61.

Halperin, Maurice. "Culture and the Revolution." In *The New Cuba: Paradoxes and Potentials*, edited by Ronald Radosh, 190–210. New York: Morrow, 1976.

Heller, Ben A. *Assimilation/Generation/Resurrection: Contrapuntal Readings in the Poetry of José Lezama Lima*. Lewisburg, Pa.: Bucknell Univ. Press, 1997.

Jiménez, Juan Ramón. "Crítica paralela." *Orígenes* 10.34 (1953): 3–14.

Kayser, Wolfgang. *The Grotesque in Art and Literature*. Translated by Ulrich Weisstein. Bloomington: Indiana Univ. Press, 1963.

Kierkegarrd, Søren. *The Concept of Anxiety* [1844]. Edited and translated by Reider Thomte and Albert B. Anderson. Princeton: Princeton Univ. Press, 1980.

———. *The Gospel of Our Sufferings* [1847]. Translated by A. S. Aldsworth and W. S. Ferrie. Grand Rapids, Mich.: Eerdman's, 1964.

———. *Purify Your Hearts* [1843]. Translated by A. S. Aldsworth and W. S. Ferrie. London: C. W. Daniel, n.d.

———. "The Rotation Method." In *A Kierkegaard Reader*, edited by Roger Poole and Henrik Stangerup, 37–52. London: Fourth Estate, 1989.

———. *The Seducer's Diary* [1843]. Edited and translated by Howard V. Hong and Edna H. Hong. Princeton: Princeton Univ. Press, 1997.

———. *Stages on Life's Way* [1845]. Edited and translated by Howard V. Hong and Edna H. Hong. Princeton: Princeton Univ. Press, 1988.

Klossowski, Pierre. "Nature as Destructive Principle." Translated by Joseph H. McMahon. In *The 120 Days of Sodom and Other Writings*, edited and translated by Austryn Wainhouse and Richard Seaver, 65–86. 14th ed. New York: Grove, 1999.

Leiner, Marvin. *Sexual Politics in Cuba: Machismo, Homosexuality and AIDS*. Boulder, Color.: Westview, 1994.

Lezama Lima, José. "Carta a Juan Ramón Jiménez (22 April 1954)." In *Tiempo de Ciclón*, edited by Roberto Pérez León, 143–44. Havana: Unión, 1995.

———. "Respuesta y nuevas interrogaciones: Carta abierta a Jorge Mañach." In *Imagen y posibilidad*, edited by Ciro Bianchi Ross. Havana: Letras Cubanas, 1981.

Lockwood, Lee. *Castro's Cuba, Cuba's Fidel*. Exp. ed. Boulder, Colo.: Westwood, 1990.

Luis, William. "Exhuming *Lunes de Revolución*." *New Centennial Review* 2.2 (2002): 253–83.

Lumsden, Ian. *Machos, Maricones, and Gays: Cuba and Homosexuality*. Philadelphia: Temple Univ. Press, 1996.

Mañach, Jorge. "Carta a José Lezama Lima (18 April 1938)." In *Fascinación de la memoria: Textos inéditos de José Lezama Lima*, edited by Iván González Cruz, 290–91. Havana: Letras Cubanas, 1993.

———. "Carta a Virgilio Piñera (21 December 1942)." Reprinted in *La Gaceta de Cuba* 39.5 (2001): 3.

———. "El arcano de cierta poesía nueva: Carta abierta a José Lezama Lima." *Bohemia* 39 (25 September 1949): 37.

———. "Reaccinnes a un diálogo (Algo más sobre poesía vieja y nueva." *Bohemia* (16 October 1949): n. pag.

Menton, Seymour. *Prose Fiction of the Cuban Revolution*. Austin: Univ. of Texas Press, 1975.

Meyer, Doris. *Victoria Ocampo: Against the Wind and the Tide*. New York: Braziller, 1979.

Miller, William Ian. *The Anatomy of Disgust*. Cambridge: Harvard Univ. Press, 1997.

Montes Huidobro, Matías. *Persona, vida y máscara en el teatro cubano*. Miami: Universal, 1973.

Morris, David. *The Culture of Pain*. Berkeley: Univ. of California Press, 1991.

Murphy, Bruce, ed. *Benet's Reader's Encyclopedia*. 4th ed. New York: Harper Collins, 1996.

Padilla, Heberto. *Fuera del juego* [1968]. Commemorative ed. Miami: Universal, 1998.

———. "La poesía en su lugar." *Lunes de Revolución*, 7 December 1959, 5–6.

Pérez, Louis A., Jr. *Cuba: Between Reform and Revolution*. 2nd ed. Oxford: Oxford Univ. Press, 1995.

Pérez Cisneros, Guy. "Presencia de 8 pintores." *Verbum* 1.1 (1937): 56–67.

Pérez León, Roberto, ed. *Tiempo de Ciclón*. Havana: Unión, 1995.

Petronovich, Lewis. *The Cannibal Within*. New York: Aldine de Gruyter, 2000.

Phillips, R. Hart. *Cuba Island of Paradox*. New York: McDowell, n.d.

Prats Sariol, José. "La revista *Orígenes*." In *Coloquio Internacional sobre la obra de José Lezama Lima*. Vol. 1, *Poesía*, 37–57. Madrid: Fundamentos, 1984.

Ramírez, Rafael L. *What it Means to Be a Man: Reflections on Puerto Rican Masculinity.* Translated by Rosa E. Casper. New Brunswick, N.J.: Rutgers Univ. Press, 1999.

Riccio, Alessandra. "La revista *Orígenes* y otras revistas lezamianas." *Annali* 25.1 (1983): 343–89.

Rodríguez Feo, José. *Mi correspondencia con Lezama Lima.* México: Era, 1991.

———, and Virgilio Piñera. "Borrón y cuenta nueva." *Ciclón* 1.1 (1955): n. pag.

Rodríguez Monegal, Emir. *Jorge Luis Borges: A Literary Biography.* New York: Dutton, 1978.

Rodríguez Santana, Efraín. "Árbol bien plantado y suelto frente al cielo: La presencia de José Rodríguez Feo en *Orígenes.*" *Unión* 7.18 (1995): 25–31.

Rogozinski, Jan. *A Brief History of the Caribbean.* Rev. ed. New York: Facts on File, 2000.

Rojas, Rafael. "*Orígenes* and the Poetics of History." *New Centennial Review* 2.2 (2002): 151–85.

Sade, Marquis de. "Dialogue Between a Priest and a Dying Man." In *The Misfortunes of Virtue and Other Early Tales,* edited and translated by David Coward, 149–60. 14th ed. Oxford: Oxford Univ. Press, 1992.

———. "Las 120 jornadas de Sodoma" (Introducción y discurso del Duque). Translated by Humberto Rodríguez Tomeu. *Ciclón* 1.1 (1955): 36–41.

———. *The 120 days of Sodom and Other Writings.* 14th ed. Translated by Austryn Wainhouse and Richard Seaver. New York: Grove, 1999.

Sagan, Eli. *Cannibalism: Human Aggression and Cultural Form.* Santa Fe, Tex.: Fish Drum, 1993.

Saínz, Enrique. *La obra poética de Cintio Vitier.* Havana: Unión, 1998.

Santí, Enrico Mario. "Entrevista con el grupo Orígenes." In *Coloquio internacional sobre la obra de José Lezama Lima.* Vol. 2, *Prosa,* 157–89. Madrid: Fundamentos, 1984.

Sartore, Ricardo. *Humans Eating Humans: The Dark Shadow of Cannibalism.* Notre Dame, Ind.: Cross Cultural, 1994.

Scarry, Elaine. *The Body in Pain.* New York: Oxford Univ. Press, 1985.

Skidmore, Tomas E., and Peter H. Smith. *Modern Latin America.* 4th ed. New York: Oxford Univ. Press, 1997.

Sorokin, Pitirim A. *Hunger as a Factor in Human Affairs.* Gainesville: Univ. Press of Florida, 1975.

Souza, Raymond D. *Guillermo Cabrera Infante: Two Islands, Two Worlds.* Austin: Univ. of Texas Press, 1996.

Stallybrass, Peter, and Allon White. *The Politics and Poetics of Transgression.* Ithaca: Cornell Univ. Press, 1986.

Swift, Jonathan. *A Modest Proposal and Other Satirical Works.* New York: Dover, 1996.

Taber, C. R. "Soul, Spirit." In *The Perennial Dictionary of World Religions,* edited by Keith Crim, 699–702. New York: Harper and Row, 1989.

Thomas, Hugh. *Cuba: The Pursuit of Freedom.* New York: Harper and Row, 1971.

Thomte, Reidar and Albert B. Anderson, ed. and trans. Introduction to *The Concept of Anxiety,* by Søren Kierkegaard, 9–24. Princeton: Princeton Univ. Press, 1980.

Twigg, Julia. "Vegetarianism and the Meanings of Meat." In *The Sociology of Food and Eating,* edited by Anne Murcott, 18–30. Croft, England: Gower, 1983.

"Un saludo a voces." *Lunes de Revolución,* 4 January 1960, 2.

Updike, John. Foreword to *The Seducer's Diary*, by Søren Kierkegaard. Translated by Howard V. Hong and Edna H. Hong, vii–xv. Princeton: Princeton Univ. Press, 1997.

Uribe, Marcelo, ed. Introduction to *Orígenes: Revista de arte y literatura: Edición Facsimilar*, ix–lxx. Madrid: Ediciones Turner, 1989.

Vardy, Peter. *Kierkegaard*. Liguori, Mo.: Triumph, 1996.

Vargas Llosa, Mario et al. "Segunda carta de los intelectuales europeos y latinoamericanos a Fidel Castro." In *Fuera del juego: Edición conmeorativa, 1968–1998*, by Heberto Padilla, 123–24. Miami: Universal, 1998.

Vitier, Cintio, ed. *Diez poetas cubanos*. Havana: Orígenes, 1948.

———. "El PEN Club y *los Diez poetas cubanos*" *Orígenes* 5.19 (1948): 41–43.

———. "Jorge Mañach y nuestra poesía." *Diario de la Marina*, 26 and 30 October 1949, n. pag.

———. "La aventura de *Orígenes*." In *Para llegar a Orígenes*, by Vitier, 66–96. Havana: Letras cubanas, 1994.

———. "La poesía de Emilio Ballagas." In *Obra poética de Emilio Ballagas*, edited by Vitier, v–xli. Havana: Ucar, García y Cía, 1955.

———. *Lo cubano en la poesía*. Havana: Universidad Central de las Villas, 1958.

Woodall, James. *Borges: A Life*. New York: Basic Books, 1996.

Woods, Gregory. *Articulate Flesh*. New Haven: Yale University Press, 1987.

Yates, Wilson. "An Introduction to the Grotesque: Theoretical and Theological Considerations." In *The Grotesque in Art and Literature: Theological Reflections*, edited by James Luther Adams and Wilson Yates, 1–68. Grand Rapids, Mich.: Eerdmans, 1997.

———. "Francis Bacon: The Iconography of Crucifixion, Grotesque Imagery, and Religious Meaning." In *The Grotesque in Art and Literature*, edited by Adams and Yates, 143–92.

Young, Katherine, ed. "Still Life with Corpse: Management of the Grotesque Body in Medicine." In *Bodylore*, 111–33. Knoxville: Univ. of Tennessee Press, 1993.

Zambrano, María. "Carta a Virgilio Piñera (5 November 1941)." Reprinted in *Albur* 3.5 (1990): 160.

Index

Page numbers in italics refer to illustrations.

absurd, the, 84, 183, 199, 221; and contemporary Cuban reality, 13, 32, 34, 61, 130–31, 242; definition of, 122–23; in Piñera's short fiction, 12–13, 41, 121–23, 126–28, 130–31, 134, 135, 138, 140, 141, 144, 147, 151, 279 n. 5; and Piñera's worldview, 12–13, 130–31, 151, 279 n. 5; theater of, 83, 123, 151, 157, 226, 228, 231, 242, 244, 245, 280 n. 11, 288 n. 31
Acevedo, Leonor, 49, 76; crucial role in Borges's life of, 78–79
Aguirre, Mirta, 61
Aire frío, 11, 87, 97, 106–7
Albee, Edward, 244
"Álbum, El," 12, 43, 141–51, 281 n. 42, 282 n. 45; absurd elements in, 141, 143–44, 146; as aesthetic commentary, 144–49; and the grotesque, 141, 143; as sociopolitical commentary, 149–52
Albuquerque, Severino João, 250
Aleixandre, Vicente, 37, 66, 67, 70
Alfred A. Knopf, 263, 277 n. 68
"Algo pasa con los escritores," 93
Álvarez-García, Imeldo, 275 n. 27
Amado Blanco, Luis, 61–63
"Amores de vista," 286–87 n. 4
Anales de Buenos Aires, Los, 11, 49, 50
Anuario Cultural de Cuba, 36
Anuario Cultural del Ministerio de Estado, 35
Apollinaire, Guillaume, 24
Aramburu, Pedro, 81–82, 273 n. 109
Arche, Jorge, 24
Ardévol, José, 24
Ardura, Ernesto, 61
Arenas, Reinaldo, 8, 112; on Piñera and his works, 113, 115, 259. Work: *Antes que anochezca*, 113, 257
Argentina: dates of Piñera's stay in, 10, 44, 45, 61, 75, 84–85; literary culture and intelligentsia of, 9, 37, 47, 48–49, 51–60, 65, 75–78, 80, 81, 82, 155, 156, 270–71 n. 41; and Perón or politics, 46, 50, 81–82, 269–70 nn. 15 and 16, 273 n. 109; Piñera's literary activities in, 9–10, 46–55, 57–60, 65, 75–78, 80–82, 84–85, 155–56; Piñera's self-imposed exile in, 9–10, 12, 34, 44, 45–46, 49, 54, 61, 65, 75, 84–85, 155–56, 228, 267 n. 39, 271 n. 55. *See also* Buenos Aires
Arrufat, Antón: as collaborator in *Ciclón*, 70; condemnation of *Los siete contra tebas* by 110; on Piñera and his works, 89, 115, 163, 167, 188, 201, 229, 232, 235, 260, 272 n. 68, 278 nn. 86 and 87, 288 n. 6; revision and correction of Piñera's *La carne de René* by, 282 n. 3; and secret *tertulias* with Piñera, 113
Artaud, Antonín, 70
"Arte hecho revolución, la revolución hecha arte, El," 92
Asociación de Redactores Teatrales y Cinematógrafos, La (ARTYC), 62–63
Asturias, Miguel Ángel, 70
Aub, Max, 288 n. 29
"Aviso a los conformistas," 9, 41

Bacon, Francis (twentieth-century painter), 159, 166
"Balance cultural de seis meses," 90
Balderston, Daniel, 141, 213, 215, 216
Ballagas, Emilio, 21, 22, 34, 72–74, 196, 210, 266–67 n. 29; "Psalmo," 74
"Ballagas en persona," 9, 14, 72–74, 76, 210–11, 224–25, 285 n. 11
Banalizador, El, 14, 271 n. 54
"Baquerismo literario, El," 94
Baquero, Gastón, 24, 27, 28, 88, 266–67 n.

29; antagonistic relationship with Piñera of, 35–36, 94, 96, 156–57. Work: "Tendencias actuales de nuestra literatura," 36
Baraguá, 21
Baralt, Luis A., 21
Barreto, Teresa Cristófani, 41, 115, 116, 138–39
Batista y Zaldívar, Fulgencio, 11, 20, 70, 83, 86–88, 91, 102, 229, 280 n. 19
Baudelaire, Charles, 25
Baumeister, Roy F., 168, 170, 194
Bautista, María Luisa, 287 n. 18
Bay of Pigs invasion, 100–101
Beauvoir, Simone de: "Must We Burn Sade?," 70, 161, 176
Beckett, Samuel, 107, 244
Belgium, 64, 108, 263
Berlin, 288 n. 30
Bern: Piñera's desire to serve as cultural attaché in, 263
Bianco, José, 75–76, 79, 80, 273 n. 90, 279 n. 5; "Piñera narrador," 75
Biblioteca Nacional (Argentina), 49, 78, 80
Biblioteca Nacional José Martí (Cuba), 91, 116
Bioy Casares, Adolfo, 49, 75, 82
"Boda, La," 139–40; and Piñera's ridicule of matrimony, 140
Boda, La, 83–84, 225–31; absurd elements in, 226–27, 231; boycott and condemnation of, 84, 157, 229; as emblematic of Piñera's role as literary provocateur, 229; failed plans for staging in Vienna of, 107; and Piñera's repudiation of Cuban values and social conventions, 14, 84, 140, 223, 226–31, 255; as precursor to *El no*, 227; problem-ridden premiere of, 84; writing of, 83, 287 n. 6
body, 170, 173, 196; Christian concepts of, 13, 157, 160–64, 166–67, 171, 179–81; as driving force of human existence, 157, 160, 161, 164, 181; as locus of tragedy and comedy, 123–24, 126–28, 133
Bogotá: world premiere of *Dos viejos pánicos* in, 277 n. 76, 288 n. 30
Bohemia, 39
Borges, Jorge Luis, 11, 49–53, 55, 64, 82, 270 n. 16; collaboration in *Ciclón* of,
75–80; Piñera's criticism of writings of, 51–53; and relationship with members of *Sur*, 49–50, 57, 80. Works: *Cuentos breves y extraordinarios*, 49; *Ficciones*, 49, 76, 264; "Inferno I, 32," 77–78; "El inmortal," 53; "Insomnio," 50; "Nota de un mal lector," 78–80
Breton, André, 24
Broma colosal, Una, 116, 260–61
Brull, Mariano, 34
Brussels, 263
Bueno, Salvador, 88
Buenos Aires, 8, 9, 10, 11, 34, 41, 44, 45–47, 49, 51, 54, 63–65, 68, 72, 75–78, 81–82, 84, 87, 90–91, 93, 107, 108, 154–55, 157, 218, 262, 267 n. 39, 269 n. 2, 271 n. 57, 284 n. 48, 288 n. 30; breakdown of Piñera's exiles in, 45; comparisons to Havana of, 46, 93; Piñera's arrival in and initial impressions of, 46, 90–91; Piñera's depression and disillusionment in, 81–82, 154–56; Piñera's job at Cuban consulate in, 63–64, 82; success of *Ciclón* in, 75–76, 77. *See also* Argentina

Cabral, Manuel del, 32; *Por las tierras de Compadre Mon*, 32
Cabrera Infante, Guillermo, 8, 101, 285 n. 87; as collaborator in *Ciclón*, 69; as cultural attaché in Brussels, 108, 263; as director of *Carteles*, 274 n. 3; as director of *Lunes*, 89, 97; exile in London of, 110, 260; on Piñera and his works, 102, 115, 122, 157, 260, 262. Works: "The Death of Virgilio," 257–58; *Mea Cuba*, 277 n. 69; *Tres tristes tigres*, 110, 196–97, 263
Cabrera Infante, Sabá: *P.M.*, 101–2, 276 n. 44
"Cada cosa en su lugar," 9, 95–96, 275 n. 26
"Caída, La," 43, 128, 135–36
Caja de zapatos vacía, Una, 262
Calvo, César, 277 n. 77
Cantón, Wilberto, 94
Camagüey (city): colloquium on Piñera in, 262; and Piñera's formative years, 10, 20–22; as setting in Piñera's works, 63, 204

Camagüey (province): establishment of UMAP in, 108
"Cambio de frente político," 92
Camus, Albert, 37, 70, 127, 152, 198; *The Myth of Sisyphus*, 209–10
cannibalism, 124–31, 156, 176, 181, 280 n. 23, 280–81 n. 24
Canto, Estela, 50
Capdevila, Arturo, 55, 270 n. 27
Caracas, 288 n. 30
Cárdenas, 19, 152–53
"Carga," 43
"Carne, La," 12, 43, 123–32, 135, 136, 272 n. 71, 280 n. 15, 280–81 n. 24; and influence of Kafka, 127; paradoxical nature of, 12, 123–24, 127, 151; political undertones of, 125, 130, 152
Carne de René, La, 9, 13, 65–66, 71, 72, 107, 154–97, 219, 260, 262, 263, 271 n. 54, 280 n. 15, 283 nn. 26 and 38, 283–84 n. 36, 284 n. 70, 285 n. 4, 286 n. 18; clumsiness of, 199, 282 n. 3; homosexuality and sadomasochism in, 13, 74, 156, 158, 160–62, 167–72, 173–78, 181–83, 185, 192–96, 213; macho myth in, 13, 162, 183–88; parody/denunciation of Christian concepts in, 13, 71, 72, 156–58, 160–68, 170–73, 175–76, 178–85, 195–96, 206, 211, 213, 266 n. 24; reception of, 65–66, 156; subversion of image of submissive woman in, 185–92; writing and revision of, 66–67, 154–56, 271 n. 58, 282 n. 3, 285 n. 78
Carpentier, Alejo, 8, 76, 94
Carteles, 274 n. 3
Casa de las Américas, 98, 109, 243–44, 259
Casanova, 200
Castro, Fidel, 12, 34, 98, 99–104, 276 n. 49; address to First National Congress on Education and Culture by, 111–12; attitude toward homosexuality of, 240; march into Havana of, 11, 87, 90; and Marxist-Leninist ideology, 100, 104; and political prisoners in Cuba, 99, 100–101, 232, 236; Sierra Maestra campaign of, 83, 86, 99, 100. Work: "Palabras a los intelectuales," 88–89, 103, 258–59, 288 n. 34
Catherine of Siena, Saint, 171
Catholicism/Christianity, 10, 13–14, 26–27, 30–31, 42, 43, 59, 64, 71–72, 84, 94, 113, 134, 149, 156–58, 160–68, 170–73, 175–76, 178–85, 195–96, 199, 201–11, 213, 225, 227, 229, 266 nn. 18 and 24, 269 n. 67
"Cena, La," 43, 131–35, 151, 272 n. 71, 281 nn. 32 and 34; and dehumanizing power of hunger, 131, 134; grotesque humor in, 12, 123–24, 131, 133; irony in, 132–33, 135
Central Intelligence Agency, 100, 112
Cernuda, Luis, 66
Cervantes, Miguel de, 266–67 n. 29
Césaire, Aimé, 28, 32; *Cahier d'un retour au pays natal*, 32
Chacón y Calvo, José María, 28
Chanan, Michael, 101
choteo, 152, 282 n. 50
Ciclón, 66, 68–83, 87–89, 93, 178, 272 n. 71, 273 n. 100, 284 n. 48; Borges's collaboration in, 49, 76–80; diversity of contributors to, 69–70, 75, 273 n. 95; founding of, 68–69; Piñera's publications in, 11, 64, 70–74, 88, 196; polemical nature of, 68–69, 70–72, 80–81, 88, 93; post-Revolution issue of, 83, 87; reception in Buenos Aires of, 75–76, 78, 80–81; significance to Piñera's career of, 69, 81; suspension of publication of, 83, 273 n. 112
Cienfuegos, Camilo, 99
cinema. *See* Free Cinema
Clamor en el penal, 21, 265 n. 5 (chap. 1)
Clark, John R., 143
class, 101, 150, 228, 230, 255
Clavileño: Cuaderno Mensual de Poesía, 27–28, 30–31, 35, 266–67 n. 29
Cohen, J. M., 110, 277 nn. 77 and 78
Coldaroli, Carlos, 47
Colombia, 258, 277 n. 76, 288 n. 30
Columbia University: Piñera's desire to teach at, 271 n. 55
comedy, 13, 110, 123–24, 126–28, 131, 132, 135, 137–39, 143, 147, 151, 178
Comisión Nacional de Cultura de Buenos Aires, 46, 155
Comités para la Defensa de la Revolución (CDR), 233, 234, 236, 241, 244, 247
"Cómo viví y cómo morí," 269 n. 60
"Conflicto, El," 267 n. 36
Conteris, Hiber, 244, 288 n. 29

INDEX

Cortázar, Julio, 50, 75, 122, 279 n. 6; Paris meeting of Piñera and, 273 n. 89. Work: "Casa tomada," 50
Couffon, Claude, 107
Coward, David, 166, 272 n. 74
"¡Cuán gritan esos malditos!," 94
Cuba, 9–13, 38, 40, 43–44, 45–46, 54, 63, 65–66, 81–85, 86–11, 115–16, 125, 130, 148, 150, 152, 154–55, 184, 196, 198–99, 211, 220, 222, 224–25, 228–29, 231–47, 255–64, 273 n. 100, 276 n. 36, 280 n. 19, 282 nn. 45 and 3, 284 n. 63; and the Batista era, 11, 20, 70, 82–83, 86–88, 91, 102, 229, 280 n. 19; and the Castro era, 34, 88–89, 90–93, 99–106, 108–12, 236, 240, 258–59, 276 nn. 36 and 39; impact of Juan Ramón Jiménez's visit to, 23; literary/cultural establishment of, 29, 37–39, 58, 61, 63, 64, 68–69, 72–74, 77–78, 88–90, 96, 113, 141, 156, 210, 258–59, 268 n. 53, 275 n. 10; and the Machado era, 20, 30; poetic representations of, 33–34, 36, 156–57; poverty and hunger in, 125, 130, 150, 280 n. 19; rebirth of Piñera in, 260–62; and repression, 12, 14, 70, 73, 86–87, 89, 99–106, 108–12, 198, 229, 231–36, 240–47, 256, 258–59. *See also* Cuban Revolution; Havana
Cuban Revolution, 22, 45–46, 63, 83, 116, 198, 213, 274 n. 113, 284 n. 63; and cultural and social repression, 12, 34, 89, 99–106, 108, 110–12, 231–32, 235, 237, 240, 241, 244, 245, 255–56; foreign support of, 108, 111–12, 244, 263; Piñera's early support of, 11–12, 87–94, 96, 101–4, 232, 258; support by Cuban intellectuals of, 87, 101–2
"Cuba y la literatura," 64
Cuentos, 260
Cuentos completos, 278–79 n. 3
Cuentos fríos, 9, 122, 125, 138, 157, 269 nn. 60 and 15, 278–79 n. 3; publication and reception in Buenos Aires of, 75, 82; translation deals for, 108, 263
Cueva, La (Havana theater), 21
Cuza Malé, Belkis, 111

"De la contemplación," 28
Diario de la Marina, 36, 94
Díaz Mártinez, Manuel, 277 n. 77

Díaz Quiñones, Arcadio, 266 n. 18
Diego, Eliseo, 23, 266–67 n. 29, 272 n. 67
Diego, Gerardo, 66
Don Juan, 188–89, 219–20
Dorticós, Osvaldo, 102
Dos viejos pánicos, 14, 109, 223, 225, 242–56; death in, 242, 243, 245, 248, 251, 253; international praise and productions of, 243–44, 258, 259, 277 n. 76, 288 n. 30; and repression in Cuba, 14, 242–48, 256, 288 n. 34 242–46erata er 242–45pression in Cuba, 242–454

East Germany: trade delegation in Cuba from, 276 n. 36
Ediciones Alfaguara, 260
Ediciones Espuela de Plata, 267 n. 36
Ediciones R, 93, 97, 107, 232, 259
Edinburgh: Piñera's invitation to theater festival in, 107
Éditions du Seuil, 263
Éditions Gallimard, 107–8, 263
Editore Feltrinelli, 107
Editorial Argos, 47, 65, 271 n. 54
Editorial Losada, 75, 82, 84, 274 n. 117
Editorial Nacional, 106, 107, 276 n. 62
Editorial Seix Barral: Piñera's submission of *Presiones y diamentes* to, 274 n. 117
Electra Garrigó, 61–63, 84, 266 n. 24, 267 n. 36; negative reviews and reception of, 61–62, 66, 157, 274 n. !13; success after the Revolution of, 97–98, 274 n. 113
Eliot, T. S., 37
Encarne, El, 110
"En el insomnio," 50–51, 272 n. 71
En esa helada zona, 265 n. 5 (chap. 1)
Escuela Normal de Maestros de Camagüey, 20
"Espejismo de revistas," 93, 94
Espinosa-Domínguez, Carlos, 63, 275 n. 10
Espuela de Plata, 23–28, 30–31, 35, 270 n. 24; as important precursor to *Orígenes*, 24, 37; literary and artistic quality of, 24; Piñera's publications in, 10, 24; Piñera's rupture and continued tensions with, 10, 25–27, 28, 37, 96, 113, 140, 266 n. 20, 266 nn. 27 and 39
Estévez, Abilio, 113
"Exhortación a Rodríguez Feo," 93

existentialism, 41, 121–22, 125–26, 198–99, 208–10, 218

Falsa Alarma, 63, 83
fantastic: in Piñera's short fiction, 121, 122, 135
farce, 121, 126, 178
Feijoó, Samuel, 240
Fernández, Macedonio, 46, 49
Fernández, Pablo Armando, 108, 275 n. 10
Fernández Bonilla, Raimundo, 275 n. 27
Fernández de Avellaneda, Alonso, 29
Fernández-Ferrer, Antonio, 279 n. 6
Filántropo, El, 97, 98
First National Congress on Education and Culture, 111–12
Flaco y el gordo, El, 97
Florit, Euginio, 22, 271 n. 55
Fogonazo, Un, 116, 260
France/French literature, 47, 48, 64, 74, 108, 262–63, 272 n. 74, 273 n. 89; and *Ciclón*, 76; Victoria Ocampo's alleged obsession with, 56–58
Franqui, Carlos, 89, 100, 105, 108, 262, 275 n. 10
Free Cinema, 101
Freud, Sigmund, 70, 168–69, 185–86, 283 n. 34
Furias, Las, 32

Gaceta de Cuba, La, 23, 106, 125
Gaceta del Caribe, La, 61
Galich, Manuel, 288 n. 29
García Chichester, Ana, 162, 174, 194, 279 n. 4, 279 n. 6
García Marruz, Bella, 266–67 n. 29
García Marruz, Fina, 23, 72, 266–67 n. 29, 269 n. 67, 272 n. 67
García Vega, Lorenzo, 40, 272 n. 67, 278 n. 89
Gautier, Théophile, 25
Gaztelu, Ángel, 10, 24–28, 113, 266 nn. 20 and 21, 272 n. 67
Generation of 1936, 10, 23
Gianera, Pablo, 271 n. 57
Gide, André, 74
Gilgen, Read Grant, 140, 279 n. 4
Girondo, Oliverio, 49
Gombrowicz, Witold, 65, 69, 82, 139; and exile in Argentina, 46; influence on Piñera and his writings of, 11, 47, 51, 54, 57–60, 215–17, 285 n. 15; as kindred spirit with Piñera, 46–48, 57, 60, 81; as provocateur of Argentine intelligentsia, 47–49, 51, 54–57, 60, 81, 155, 269 n. 2. Works: "Aurora: Revista de la Resistencia," 54–58, 270 n. 26; "Contra los poetas," 81; *Ferdydurke*, 11, 47–49, 51, 54–55, 56, 59–60, 155–56, 215–17, 270 n. 27, 285 n. 15, 285–86 n. 16
"Gombrowicz por él mismo," 47
Gómez de Avellaneda, Gertrudis, 28
González, Odilio, 275 n. 27
González Puig, Ernesto, 266–67 n. 29
Goya, Francisco, 121, 279 n. 4
Goytisolo, Juan, 107–9, 243, 263; *Realms of Strife*, 108–9
"Gran Baro, El," 76
"Gran escalera del palacio legislativo, La," 84
Granma (newspaper), 115–16
Granma (yacht), 82–83
"Grito mudo, El," 22
grotesque: definition of, 123; ambivalent or paradoxical nature of, 12, 122, 123, 126, 143, 151; in Piñera's writing, 12, 41, 43, 121–23, 126, 133, 141, 143, 151, 193, 246
Guanabacoa, 19
Guanabo, 105
Guerra, Juan, 274 n. 113
Guevara, Alfredo, 101
Guevara, Ernesto "Che," 236
Guillén, Jorge, 66, 67
Guillén, Nicolás, 8, 22, 32, 34, 94, 107, 277 n. 66; *West Indies, Ltd.*, 32

"Hablemos de excesos," 94
Halperin, Maurice, 111
Havana, 10, 11, 20–22, 28–29, 35, 37, 64, 77, 82, 100, 105, 108, 115–16, 125; intellectual climate of, 46, 66–68, 93; Piñera's impressions of, 21, 46; Piñera's marginalized existence in, 8, 21–22; Piñera's visits during Argentinian exile to, 45, 82–84, 287 n. 6; reappearance of Piñera's works in, 260–62; as represented in film *P.M.*, 101; Revolution's impact on, 198, 245; as setting in Piñera's works, 198, 208, 281 n. 31; theater in, 61–63, 84, 99, 157

INDEX

Havana Lyceum, 28, 83, 267–68 n. 46
"Hay muertos que no hacen ruido," 284 n. 58
"Hechizado, El," 113–14
Heidegger, Martin, 273 n. 112
Heller, Ben, 26, 27
Hermandad de Jóvenes Cubanos, La, 20–21
Hernández, Felisberto, 50, 122, 279 n. 6
Hernández Busto, Ernesto, 237
homosexuality: and Ballagas, 73–74, 196, 210; as defining element of Piñera's identity, 8, 21, 39, 74, 105–6, 112, 218, 232–33, 240, 243; homophobia and repression in Cuba of, 70, 73–74, 104–6, 108–10, 112, 196, 210, 232–36, 238–40, 243, 275 n. 10; and Lezama Lima's *Paradiso*, 113, 236; and *Lunes*, 104, 232, 259, 275 n. 10; in Piñera's works, 13, 73–74, 109, 156, 158, 160, 168–70, 173–78, 181–82, 185, 192–94, 196, 201, 204, 210–13, 218–23, 232–36, 238–40, 285 n. 6, 287 n. 18
hunger: as central theme of Piñera's short fiction, 123–35, 143, 152, 280–81 n. 24, 281 n. 34; and Cuban food shortages, 22, 90, 125, 130–31, 152, 280 n. 19

Ichaso, Francisco, 37
Ionesco, Eugène, 107, 244
imperialism, 32, 111, 112; Castro's declared victory over, 100–101
Imprenta Nacional, 107, 232
Información, 35
Institución Hispanocubana, 22
Instituto Cubano de Arte e Industria Cinematográficos (ICAIC), 101
Instituto del Libro, 113
Instituto de Segunda Enseñaza de Camagüey, El, 20
Ínsula, 66
insularity, 33–34
"Inundación, La," 88, 92
Irby, James, 79
irony, 129–30, 132–35, 139, 151
Isla en peso, La, 32–36, 43; and Caribbean poetry, 32–33 criticism by Cintio Vitier of, 35–36, 42, 156–57, 267–68 n. 46; criticism by Gastón Baquero of, 35–36, 156–57; Lezama Lima's reaction to, 35; as representative of Piñera's role as literary provocateur, 10, 32–35, 96, 267 n. 40; shocking language and images in, 33–34, 157, 267 n. 40
Isla en peso, La: Obra poética, 262
Italy, 107, 277 n. 68

Jérez-Farrán, Carlos, 280 n. 11, 288 n. 31
Jesuits, 158, 165
Jesús, 63, 71, 157, 266 n. 24; negative reception of, 157
Jesus Christ, 63, 71, 149, 165, 171; parody of, 158, 160, 164, 166–68, 173, 179–80, 183, 195
Jiménez, Juan Ramón, 10, 272 n. 67; impact on Lezama Lima and other Cuban authors of, 22–23. Works: "Crítica paralela," 66–67, 271 n. 62; *La poesía cubana en 1936*, 22
Jiménez Leal, Orlando: *P.M.*, 101–2, 276 n. 44
July 26 Movement, 82–83

Kafka, Franz, 60, 71; influence on Piñera's works of, 41, 42, 122, 127, 279 n. 5. Work: *The Metamorphosis*, 269 n. 60
Kayser, Wolfgang, 123
Kennedy, John F., 100, 101
Kierkegaard, Søren, 13, 14, 164–65, 201, 222; *The Concept of Anxiety*, 201, 205; *The Gospel of Our Sufferings*, 164–65, 172–73, 182; *Purify Your Hearts*, 204; "The Rotation Method," 219–20, 221; *The Seducer's Diary*, 188–90, 220, 221
Klossowski, Pierre, 70
Koch, Dolores M., 279 n. 4

Laddaga, Reinaldo, 279 n. 6
Lam, Wilfredo, 37
language, 138, 145–46
Larreta, Enrique, 55; *La gloria de don Ramiro*, 270 n. 27
Leal, Rine, 63, 261
Leante, César, 263
Leiner, Marvin, 104, 105, 108, 245
Letras Cubanas, 261
Lezama Lima, José, 8, 10, 22–29, 36–43, 51, 52, 54, 59, 61–62, 64, 66–69, 71, 75, 88, 94–95, 113–14, 265 n. 10, 265–66 n. 13, 266 n. 26, 268 nn. 54 and 57, 270–71 n. 41, 271 n. 54, 271 n. 62, 272 nn. 67 and 71, 277 n. 77, 287 n. 18; clash with

Jorge Mañach of, 39; erudite style of, 31–32, 34, 39, 42; first literary endeavors of, 22–25; friendship and rupture with Piñera of, 10, 23–28, 37, 43, 113–14, 266 nn. 20, 21, and 27, 267 n. 39, 278 n. 87; influence on Piñera's verse of, 24–25, 32, 42–43, 95–96; as leading intellectual/literary figure, 10, 23, 28, 37, 94, 95, 113–14; Piñera's criticism of poetry by, 31–32, 35, 42, 54, 113; rupture with Rodríguez Feo of, 66–68; subversive tendencies of, 26, 113–14. Works: *Dador*, 88; *Enemigo rumor*, 31, 54, 95; *La fijeza*, 39; "La muerte de Narciso," 31, 32, 42; *Opiano Licario*, 278 n. 89; *Paradiso*, 113–14, 236, 278 n. 87, 278 n. 89; "Razón que sea," 270 n. 24 "Respuesta y nuevas interrogaciones," 39. See also *Espuela de Plata*; *Nadie Parecía: Cuaderno de lo Bello con Dios*; *Orígenes*; *Verbum*
Lida, Raimundo, 55
"Literatura y Revolución," 104
Lizaso, Félix, 37
"Llamamiento a los escritores," 92
Llera Quintana, María Cristina (Mrs. Juan Piñera), 19
Lockwood, Lee, 99, 240
Lonardi, Eduardo, 81–82, 273 n. 109
Lozano, Alfredo, 24, 268 n. 57
Luis, Adolfo de, 84
Luis, William, 274–75 n. 9
Lumsden, Ian, 184, 234, 238, 284 n. 63
Lunes de Revolución, 24, 34, 84, 100, 101–4, 274–75 nn. 9 and 10; and banning of *P.M.*, 101–2; circulation of, 89, 274–75 n. 9; Piñera's collaboration in, 12, 89, 91, 94–97, 104, 106, 259, 275 n. 10; reputation as haven for homosexuals of, 104, 232, 259, 275 n. 10

Machado, Gerardo, 20, 30
machismo: descriptions of, 184, 186, 212; and devaluation of women, 186–88, 220, 228, 239–41, 255; Piñera's criticism of *machista* society and, 13, 70, 73–74, 183–88, 196, 210, 212–13, 220, 224, 228, 237–41, 255; and the Revolution, 213, 237–38, 240–41, 284 n. 63
Madrid, 108, 260, 277 n. 76, 288 n. 30
Mallarmé, Stéphane, 28

Mallea, Eduardo, 49
Mañach, Jorge, 88; as detractor of *Orígenes*, 37–38; dispute with Piñera of, 29–30, 38, 39, 51; dispute with Lezama Lima of, 39, 268 n. 54. Works: "El arcano de cierta poesía nueva," 39; *Indagación al choteo*, 29
"Manifiesto de los intelectuales y artistas," 101–2
Marinello, Juan, 37, 38
Marlowe, Christopher, 185
marriage: criticism in Piñera's works of, 14, 140, 149–50, 218–43, 245–47, 255–56, 286–87 n. 4; traditional and revolutionary Cuban attitudes toward, 222–23, 224–25, 227–28, 231–34, 237, 240–41, 255–56
Martin, Eleanor Jean, 280 n. 11, 288 n. 31
Martínez, Luis, 20
Martínez Correa, José Celso, 288 n. 29
Martínez Estrada, Ezequiel, 49, 55
Marxism-Leninism, 92, 100, 104–5, 245. *See also* socialism
"Más Miscelánea," 94, 275 n. 22
Matanzas, 19
Matas, Julio, 83
Matos, Huber, 99
McQuade, Frank, 152, 279 nn. 4 and 5
Medellín, 288 n. 30
Méndez y Soto, E., 213, 286 n. 19
Menton, Seymour, 199
Merle, Robert, 76; *Oscar Wilde or the Destiny of Homosexuality*, 273 n. 95
Mes del teatro cubano, 229
Mexico, 38, 70, 82–83, 93, 277 n. 76
Meyer, Doris, 56
Miller, William, 174–75, 283 n. 34
Minorista generation, 37
Monal, Isabel, 91
Monde, Le, 111–12
Montes Huidobro, Matías, 276 n. 49, 288 n. 34
Morello-Frosch, Marta, 135
Morín, Francisco, 274 n. 113
Morris, David, 124, 128, 162, 163–64
"Muchas alabanzas," 43
Muecas para escribientes, 116, 260, 284 n. 58
Mundo, El, 61, 240
"Muñeco, El," 50, 269 n. 15
Murena, H. A., 76, 273 n. 95

Nación, La, 53, 65, 116
Nadie Parecía: Cuaderno de lo Bello con Dios, 27, 30–31
Narváez, Carlos, 279 n. 4
National Theater. *See* Teatro Nacional
neobaroque, 121
"New Man," 14, 104, 105, 238
Nietzsche, Friedrich, 70
Night of the Three P's, 105
Nin, Anaïs, 37
Niñita querida, La, 262
No, El, 196, 246, 247–49, 255–56, 261, 287 n. 15; and Cuban attitudes toward marriage, 14, 140, 222, 223, 225, 227–28, 231–43, 255–56; and homosexuality, 14, 232–36, 238–40, 287 n. 18; and *machista* devaluation of women, 239–41; Piñera's personal circumstances reflected in, 109, 232–33, 240, 242–43; and repression in Cuba, 14, 109, 231–36, 240–43, 247–49, 256
"Notas sobre la literatura argentina de hoy," 49, 51, 54
Novoa, Mario, 243
"Nubes amenazadoras," 89–90
Nueva Revista Cubana, La, 93

Obieta, Adolfo de, 46, 47, 49
Ocampo, Silvina, 75, 82, 84
Ocampo, Victoria, 11, 49, 54, 55–58, 80
Odysseus, 175, 235
O'Hara, Frank, 185
"¡Ojo con el crítico . . . !," 62, 63
Onetti, Juan Carlos, 198
Orbón, Julián, 272 n. 67
Oriente Province, 83
Orígenes (journal), 155–57, 278 n. 89; as Catholic journal, 43; demise of, 11, 66–69, 75, 271 n. 62, 272 n. 67; detractors of, 11, 37–39, 95; diversity of contributors to, 37, 46; Lezama Lima and Rodríguez Feo as co-directors of, 36–37, 41, 66–68, 268 n. 57, 271 n. 62, 272 n. 71; as major Latin American journal, 11, 37, 40; Piñera as detractor of, 11, 39–40, 43, 68–69; Piñera's publications in, 11, 40–42, 53, 58, 63
Orígenes group, 10, 11, 23, 24, 29, 32, 36–43, 54, 61, 64, 68, 72, 78, 95, 113, 266 n. 27, 269 n. 67; and marginalization by literary establishment, 29, 37–39, 268 n.

53; members of, 24, 272 n. 67; Piñera as problematic member of, 39–42; Vitier's anthology of writings by, 36, 38
Orlando, Felipe, 28
Ortega Sierra, Luis, 266–67 n. 29
Ortega y Gasset, José, 78–80

Padilla, Heberto, 94, 95, 108, 109–11, 115, 275 n. 22; arrest, detention, and forced confession of, 111; clash with Piñera of, 95. Works: *Fuera del juego*, 110–11, 253; "La poesía en su lugar," 95
"País del Arte, El," 9, 41, 49, 58–61, 141, 266 n. 24
Palls, Terry, 280 n. 11, 288 n. 31
Papeles de Buenos Aires, 46
Paris, 48; Piñera's 1964 visit to, 108, 262–63; Piñera meets Julio Cortazar in, 273 n. 89
"Parque, El," 136–39
"Partes, Las," 43, 128
Patafísica, 76
Pauvert, Jean-Jacques, 272 n. 74
Paz, Octavio, 70
Peláez, Amalia, 37
Penelope, 235
Pequeñas maniobras, 13–14, 107, 140, 196, 198–223, 225–26, 260, 263, 281 n. 42, 285 n. 15, 286 nn. 20 and 27, 286–87 n. 4; and Catholicism/confession, 13–14, 199, 201–11, 266 n. 24, 285 n. 6; compared to *La carne de René*, 13, 199–201, 211, 213, 219; and existentialism, 198–99, 208–10, 218; and Gombrowicz's *Ferdyduke*, 14, 215–17; and homosexuality, 13–14, 74, 200–201, 204, 210–13, 218–23, 226, 285 n. 6; and the picaresque, 199, 286 n. 19; and repression in Cuba, 198, 199; stylistics and flow of, 199; treatment of marriage in, 140, 219–23, 231, 286–87 n. 4; writing of, 83–84, 198, 218
Pérez, Louis A., Jr., 100, 276 n. 36, 280 n. 19, 281 n. 31
Pérez Cisneros, Guy, 24, 26, 37–38; "Presencia de 8 pintores," 37–38
Pérez León, Roberto, 265 n. 3 (chap. 1), 270 n. 26, 271 n. 62, 272 nn. 67 and 68
Perón, Juan Domingo, 46, 50, 269–70 nn. 15 and 16, 273 n. 109

Petronovich, Lewis, 280 n. 23, 281 n. 34
Peyrou, Graziella, 79, 218
Phillips, R. Hart, 125
Picasso, Pablo, 60
Piñera, Humberto, 20, 63, 88
Piñera, Juan Enrique, 116
Piñera, Juan Manuel (father), 19–20, 21, 108, 263
Piñera, Mrs. Juan Manuel. *See* Llera Quintana, María Cristina
Piñera, Luisa, 20, 21, 85, 87, 105, 108, 263
Piñera, Virgilio, *2, 18, 120*; aesthetics of, 8, 10, 12–13, 41–43, 52, 57–60, 122, 140–41, 144–45, 147–48; arrest and detention of, 105; and atheism/disdain of religion, 10, 13–14, 26–27, 30–31, 39, 42, 43, 59, 64, 71–73, 84, 94, 113, 134, 149, 156–58, 160–68, 170–73, 175–76, 178–85, 195–96, 199, 201–11, 266 n. 24, 269 n. 67; childhood and early education of, 10, 19–20; correspondence with Humberto Rodríguez Tomeu of, 12, 84, 97–98, 100, 105–7, 109, 114, 218–19, 258, 263, 274 nn. 117 and 3, 275 n. 29, 275–76 n. 31, 277 n. 74; critical assessments of works by, 121–22, 196–97, 279 nn. 4 and 5; death of, 115, 257–58; downfall and silencing of, 12, 34, 93, 97, 102–3, 115–16, 121, 232, 243–44, 258–60, 264, 277 n. 74; earliest literary work of, 20–21, 24; economic hardships of, 8, 19–22, 43–44, 65, 82, 86–87, 125, 131, 155–56, 274 n. 3; as "El Escriba," 89, 271 n. 51, 275 n. 10; exiles and marginality of, 8, 9, 10, 11, 12, 21, 39, 41, 43, 45–46, 49, 54, 61, 63–65, 74, 75, 81, 84–85, 108, 155–56, 228, 267 n. 39, 271 n. 55; final years of, 10, 14, 110–17, 258, 259, 264, 288 n. 6; generic diversity in works of, 8, 9, 12, 14, 40, 116, 121, 259, 261, 267 n. 36; growing influence and success in Cuba of, 89, 96, 97–99, 106–7, 258; homosexuality of, 8, 21, 39, 74, 105, 108–9, 112, 196, 224, 232–33, 243, 259, 275 n. 10; and polemics with Argentine intelligentsia, 9, 11, 51–54, 57, 60, 80–81, 270–71 n. 41; and polemics with Cuban authors and critics, 9, 10–11, 12, 24, 25, 27–30, 35–36, 40, 42, 51, 61–65, 68, 70–71, 74, 88–96, 266 n. 27, 272 n. 71; provincial origins of, 8, 19–22; rapprochement with Lezama Lima of, 113–14, 278 n. 87; rediscovery, publication, translation, and study of works by, 7–9, 11, 12, 14, 116–17, 121–22, 196, 260–62, 278–79 n. 3; shocking imagery and language of, 33–34, 42, 43, 122, 123, 126–27, 131–35, 138, 142–43, 146, 157, 177, 178, 197, 199, 267 n. 40; subversive personality of, 9–11, 20, 26, 28, 61, 157, 233; as supporter of the Revolution, 11–12, 87–94, 96, 101–4, 232, 258; and translation and promotion of *Ferdydurke*, 11, 47–49, 51, 54–55, 155, 285–86 n. 16; at University of Havana, 21–22, 29. *See also titles of individual works*
"Piñera teatral," 229
Pinter, Harold, 244
"Plumas respetuosas, Las," 9, 28, 94–95
Poesía y prosa, 36, 41–43, 141, 152, 157
Poeta: Cuaderno Trimestral de la Poesía, 10, 28–32, 96, 140
poetry: Caribbean, 32–33; Cuban, 22–23, 54, 92, 94, 95, 267–68 n. 46, 268 n. 53
Poland: German occupation and invasion of, 46, 276 n. 36
Polyphemus, 174–75
"¿Por dónde anda lo cubano en el teatro?," 229
Portocarrero, René, 24, 28, 37, 267 n. 36
Portuondo, José Antonio, 21, 272 n. 68
Prats Sariol, José, 266 n. 27
Presiones y diamantes, 84, 260, 274 n. 117; government objection to, 116, 243, 259
Prometeo, 62–63
"Puntos, comas, y paréntesis," 89

Quackenbush, L. Howard, 280 n. 11, 288 n. 31
Quasimodo, Salvatore, 70
Queneau, Raymond, 76; "Filósofos y vagos," 273 n. 95
Que vino a salvarme, El, 75

race, 32, 101
Radio del Estado, 51
Radio del Mundo, 48
Ramírez, Rafael, 162, 184, 190, 284 n. 63
"Rebelión de los enfermos," 109
"Reforma Literaria, La," 92
religion. *See* Catholicism/Christianity

Revista Cubana, La, 28
Revista de Avance, 29–30, 37–39, 64, 268 n. 53
Revista de Occidente, 37
Revolución, 100; circulation of, 89, 274–75 n. 9; Piñera's publications in, 12, 36, 62, 89–91, 94, 95, 97, 102, 104, 106, 271 n. 51, 275 n. 10
"Revolución se fortalece, La," 92
Revuelta, Vicente, 288 n. 29
Riccio, Alessandra, 28, 265–66 n. 13
Rodríguez, Álvaro, 273 n. 95
Rodríguez, Mariano, 24, 37, 88, 266 n. 21, 268 n. 57, 272 n. 68
Rodríguez Feo, José "Pepe," 11, 49, 61–62, 84, 85, 105, 113, 273 nn. 92 and 100; and *Ciclón*, 68–69, 72, 75–83, 273 n. 112; and clash with Lezama Lima over *Orígenes*, 66–69, 75, 266 n. 27, 271 n. 62; as cofounder and financial backer of *Orígenes*, 37, 41, 66–69, 268 n. 57. Works: "Una alegoría de la carne," 65–66; "Borrón y cuenta nueva," 68, 272 n. 71; "La neutralidad de los escritores," 83, 87–88
Rodríguez Monegal, Emir, 49, 57
Rodríguez Santos, Justo, 24, 266–67 n. 29
Rodríguez Tomeu, Humberto, 54; correspondence with Piñera of, 12, 84, 97–98, 100, 105–7, 109, 114, 218–19, 258, 263, 274 n. 117, 274 n. 3, 275 n. 29, 275–76 n. 31, 277 n. 74; friendship with Piñera of, 47, 63–64, 104–6, 284 n. 48; and translation of *Ferdydurke*, 47; and translation of *The 120 Days of Sodom*, 70, 284 n. 48
Rodríguez Tomeu, Julia, 115, 273 n. 95
Rogozinski, Jan, 99
Rojas, Rafael, 37, 38
Rússovich, Alejandro, 218, 271 n. 55

Sábato, Ernesto, 49, 55, 75, 198
Sade, Marquis de: influence on Piñera's worldview and writings of, 13–14, 71–72, 157–58, 161, 163–64, 166, 174, 176–78, 185, 206; legal debate over works of, 272 n. 74; Piñera's praise of, 70–71. Works: "Dialogue Between a Priest and a Dying Man," 162, 206–7; *Justine*, 163; *The 120 Days of Sodom*, 70–72, 176–78, 196, 272 n. 82, 284 n. 48

sadomasochism, 13, 156, 161, 162, 167–69, 171–72, 178, 181, 183–85, 194, 213
Saínz, Enrique, 266 n. 18
Sala Covarrubias, 98
Santí, Enrico Mario, 9, 49, 74, 266 n. 18, 269 n. 67, 278 n. 89
Santiago de Chile, 288 n. 30
Sarduy, Severo, 8, 69
Sartre, Jean-Paul, 98
Salinas, Pedro, 66, 67
Scarry, Elaine, 170
Schafer, Mark, 159
Sebastian, Saint, 171, 211; Piñera's parody of martyrdom of, 162, 168; as sadomasochistic/homoerotic icon, 162, 168, 179, 183, 185–86, 211, 213
"Secreto de Kafka, El," 41–42, 269 n. 60, 279 n. 5
Seguridad del Estado, 115, 257
"Señales de los tiempos," 92
sexuality, 13, 14, 31, 70–71, 73–74, 105, 113, 158, 184, 196, 200–201, 224, 245, 255. *See also* homosexuality; marriage
Sierra Maestra campaign, 83, 86, 99, 100
Siervos, Los, 84, 273 n. 100, 274 n. 113
Skidmore, Tomas E., 273 n. 109
Smith, Octavio, 272 n. 67
Smith, Peter H., 273 n. 109
socialism, 100, 104–5, 109, 111, 112, 238, 245. *See also* Marxism-Leninism
Sociedad Argentina de Escritores, 50
Sorokin, Pitrim A., 280–81 n. 24
"Sorpresa, La," 98
Souza, Raymond D., 89, 102
Soviet Union, 99, 276 n. 36
Spain, 37, 56, 66–67, 70, 108, 116, 121, 196, 260, 262, 277 n. 76, 282 n. 3, 288 n. 30
Stallybrass, Peter, 283 n. 26
Stevens, Wallace, 37
suffering, redemptive, 158, 162, 164–68, 171, 172, 182–83
Sur (journal), 75, 79, 80, 82, 156; Borges's attitude toward, 49–50, 57; compared to *Ciclón*, 76, 77; Piñera and Gombrowicz's criticism of, 54–58, 270–71 n. 41; Piñera's publications in, 75, 84
Sur group, 11, 80–81; Borges's attitude toward, 49–50, 57; Piñera and Gombrowicz's criticism of, 54–58, 269 n. 2, 270–71 n. 41

Swift, Jonathan, 41; "A Modest Proposal," 269 n. 61
Switzerland, 263

Tallet, José Zacarías, 277 n. 77
Tantalus, 51, 136
Teatro Atelier, 84
Teatro completo, 9, 86, 97–98, 106, 107, 122, 263; publication history of, 97, 275–76 n. 31
Teatro el Sótano, 274 n. 113
Teatro inconcluso, 116, 261
Teatro inédito, 116, 262
Teatro Nacional, 98
"Teatro Nacional funciona, El," 91
Teatro Prometeo, 97–98, 274 n. 113
Tel Quel, 70
"Terribilia Meditans," 30
"Terribilia Meditans . . . (II)," 31
theater, 21, 22, 61–63, 83–84, 91, 97–99, 106–7, 157, 229, 244, 261–62, 273 n. 113, 280 n. 11, 288 n. 31
Thomas, Dylan, 37
Thomas, Hugh, 99, 280 n. 19
Thomas, Saint (the apostle), 160
Torma, Julien, 76; "Euforismos," 273 n. 95
Torre, Guillermo de, 80
Torres-Robles, Carmen, 126–27, 135, 282 n. 50
tragedy, 121, 124, 126, 128, 135, 137, 152
Twigg, Julia, 189

Unamuno, Miguel de, 80
Unidades Militares para la Ayuda de Producción (UMAP), 108, 109, 236, 240
Unión, 106, 109, 261, 265 n. 6 (chap. 1)
Unión de Escritores y Artistas de Cuba (UNEAC), 107, 110–12, 261, 277 n. 66; condemnation of Antón Arrufat and Heberto Padilla by, 110; denial of membership to Piñera by, 261
United States, 38, 56, 70, 100–101, 125, 262, 264, 277 n. 68, 278–79 n. 3, 280 n. 19
University of Havana, 21–23, 29, 44, 236
"Unos cuantos niños," 269 n. 61
Uribe, Marcelo, 27, 41, 265–66 n. 13

Valdés, Vincentico, 101
Valerio Holguín, Fernando, 175, 213
Valero, Roberto, 113
Valéry, Paul, 28, 56–58
"Valores más jóvenes de la literatura cubana, Los," 53
Vardy, Peter, 219
Vega, Aníbal, 20
"Veinte años atrás," 94, 95, 275 n. 22
"26 de Julio," 92
Verbum, 23, 25, 37–38, 265–66 n. 13
Verde Olivo, 110
"Victrola: Revista de la Insistencia," 57–58
"Vida de Flora," 42–43
Vida entera, La, 110, 260
Vienna, 107
Villarnovo, René, 23
"Visita a la Biblioteca Nacional," 91
Vitier, Cintio, 23, 24, 26–28, 38, 40, 266–67 n. 29, 268 nn. 53 and 54, 272 n. 67, 278 n. 89; antagonistic relationship with Piñera of, 35–36, 41–42, 43, 51, 72–73, 93–94, 156–57, 267–68 n. 46, 275 n. 26; conversion to Catholicism of, 26, 72, 73, 266 n. 18, 269 n. 67. Works: *Lo cubano en la poesía*, 267–68 n. 46; *Diez poetas cubanos*, 36, 38; *Obra poética de Emilio Ballagas*, 73; "El PEN Club y *Los diez poetas cubanos*," 38; *Sedienta cita*, 35
Vitus, Saint, 171–72, 283 n. 38; legacy and martyrdom of, 172

Weizdörfer, Ewald, 279 n. 4, 279 n. 6
White, Allon, 283 n. 26
Wilde, Oscar, 74
Woodall, James, 50–51, 76, 270 n. 16
Woodyard, George W., 280 n. 11, 288 n. 31
Woods, Gregory, 185

Yates, Wilson, 123, 166

Zambrano, María, 28, 80, 267 n. 39